THE CALAIS GARRISON

War and Military Service in England, 1436–1558

For over two hundred years Calais and the English Pale were a military, commercial and cultural frontier. They were also home to the largest standing force under the command of the English crown. This book examines the nature of military service in Calais, the recruitment of soldiers, their weaponry, the financial problems that the defence of the Pale caused successive English regimes, and the role of chivalry and notions of professionalism in defining military identity. It also examines in detail the unsuccessful Burgundian siege of 1436 and the capture of Calais by the French in 1558. Based on extensive archival research, it places war and military service in England in the broader contexts of the development of the late medieval state and the European 'military revolution'.

Dr DAVID GRUMMITT is Senior Research Fellow, History of Parliament Trust.

Warfare in History
ISSN 1358–779X

Series editor
Matthew Bennett, Royal Military Academy, Sandhurst

This series aims to provide a wide-ranging and scholarly approach to military history, offering both individual studies of topics or wars, and volumes giving a selection of contemporary and later accounts of particular battles; its scope ranges from the early medieval to the early modern period.

New proposals for the series are welcomed; they should be sent to the publisher at the address below.

Boydell and Brewer Limited, PO Box 9, Woodbridge, Suffolk, IP12 3DF

THE CALAIS GARRISON

War and Military Service in England, 1436–1558

David Grummitt

THE BOYDELL PRESS

First published 2008
The Boydell Press, Woodbridge

ISBN 978–1–84383–398–7

The Boydell Press is an imprint of Boydell & Brewer Ltd
PO Box 9, Woodbridge, Suffolk IP12 3DF, UK
and of Boydell & Brewer Inc.
668 Mt Hope Avenue, Rochester, NY 14620, USA
website: www.boydellandbrewer.com

A CIP catalogue record for this book is available
from the British Library

Typeset by Pru Harrison, Hacheston, Suffolk

Contents

Illustrations

This book is produced with the generous assistance of a grant from Isobel Thornley's Bequest to the University of London

Acknowledgements

This book has been a long time in the making. During this time debts of gratitude have been incurred to many people. Jim Bolton, Andy Boyle, Anne Curry, Sean Cunningham, Michael Hicks, Malcolm Mercer, Tony Pollard, James Raymond, James Ross and John Watts have all given generously of their expertise at various stages. Hannes Kleineke, Tim Hochstrasser and Cath Nall have all read various chapters and the book is better for their comments. Steven Gunn and Michael K. Jones have shared references and ideas, as well as read and commented on almost the entire text. I am grateful for their encouragement, support and friendship for more than ten years. An enormous debt is due to Linda Clark, who carefully read the entire manuscript, saving me from many errors, both typographical and factual. Any that remain are entirely my own. Finally, thanks are due to Caroline Palmer of Boydell & Brewer for her patience and enthusiasm since we first discussed a book on the Calais garrison in the summer of 2000. The book is dedicated, however, to my parents who fostered and encouraged my love of history from a very early age.

Abbreviations

APC	*Acts of the Privy Council of England*, ed. J.R. Dasent (46 vols, 1890–1964)
BIHR	*Bulletin of the Institute of Historical Research*
BL	The British Library
The Brut	*The Brut, or the Chronicles of England*, ed. F.W.D. Brie (2 vols, Early English Text Society, original series, xxxi, xxxvi, 1906–8)
CCR	*Calendar of Close Rolls*
Chronicle of Calais	*A Chronicle of Calais in the Reigns of Henry VII and Henry VIII to the Year 1540*, ed. J.G. Nichols (Camden Society, old series xxxv, 1845)
Colvin, *The King's Works*	*The History of the King's Works*, ed. H.M. Colvin (6 vols, 1963–82)
CPR	*Calendar of Patent Rolls*
CS	Camden Society
CSP	*Calendar of State Papers*
DKR	*Deputy Keepers' Report*
EETS	Early English Text Society
EHR	*English Historical Review*
Grummitt, 'Calais 1485–1547'	David Grummitt, 'Calais 1485–1547: A Study in Early Tudor Politics and Government' (PhD thesis, University of London, 1997)
Lisle Letters	*The Lisle Letters*, ed. Muriel St Clare Byrne (6 vols, Chicago and London, 1981)
LP	*Letters and Papers, Foreign and Domestic, of the Reign of Henry VIII, 1509–1547*, ed. J. Brewer et al. (21 vols and addenda, 1862–1932)
Monstrelet	Enguerrand de Montstrelet, *La chronique de Monstrelet, 1400–1444*, ed. L. Douët d'Arcq (6 vols, Paris, 1857–62)
Morgan, 'Government of Calais'	P.T.J. Morgan, 'The Government of Calais, 1485–1558' (DPhil thesis, University of Oxford, 1966)
Oxford DNB	*Oxford Dictionary of National Biography: From the Earliest Times to the Year 2000*, ed. H.C.G. Matthew and B.H. Harrison (61 vols, Oxford, 2004)
POPC	*Proceedings and Ordinances of the Privy Council of England, 1386–1542*, ed. Sir N.H. Nicholas (7 vols, Record Commission, 1834–7)

PROME	*The Parliament Rolls of Medieval England 1275–1504*, ed. Chris Given-Wilson et al. (16 vols, Woodbridge, 2005)
Rainey, 'Defence of Calais'	John Riley Rainey Jr., 'The Defence of Calais, 1436–1477' (PhD thesis, Rutgers University, 1987)
Rymer	*Foedera, Conventiones etc.*, ed. T. Rymer (20 vols, 1704–35)
St. ta.	Sterling table (the money of account used at Calais)
Waurin	Jean de Waurin, *Recueil des croniques et anchiennes istories de la Grant Bretaigne, a present nomme Engleterre, par Jehan de Waurin, seigneur du Forestel*, ed. E.L.C.P. Hardy (5 vols, Rolls Series, 1864–91)

Place of publication is London unless otherwise stated. All dates are given in the new style, with the year beginning 1 January.

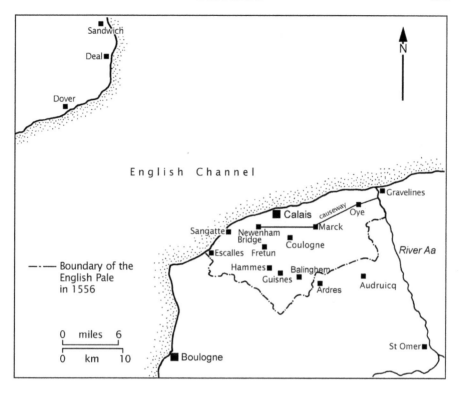

Fig. 1 Map of the Calais Pale

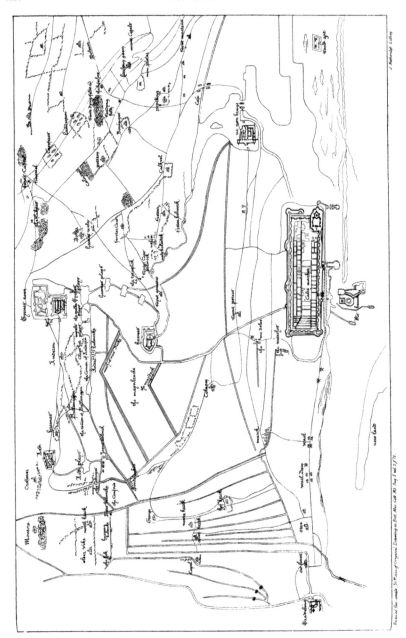

Fig. 2 Drawing of the Calais Pale, Temp. Hen VIII. Reproduced from *The Chronicle of Calais*, pp. xxviii–xxix. Facsimile based upon BL, Cotton MS Augustus I.II, f. 71, probably drawn in the early 1540s.

1

Introduction:
Calais in Context

On 24 June 1450 Caen, the last English stronghold in Normandy, fell to the French. Lancastrian Normandy was lost. Less than three years later English-held Gascony was also overrun, marking the end of the English presence on the continent and any pretensions to the throne of France. Symbolically at least, to some contemporaries and most subsequent observers, this was a symptom of the wider malaise that affected the dual-monarchy of Henry VI. Gascony, however, was not the last English possession on the continental mainland. Since 1347 English kings had held Calais in Picardy and a small area of land around it. Calais had been captured by Edward III in August of that year, the one tangible benefit of the Crécy campaign. By the third decade of the fifteenth century this area of English rule was known as the marches of Calais or, more rarely, the Pale. It remained in English hands until the successful French siege of January 1558. As the last foothold of English kings on the continental mainland, Calais became the focus of the crown's military and diplomatic efforts to assert its pretensions to the French throne. It served as the bridgehead for invasions of France by English kings in 1475, 1492, 1513 and 1544. Despite its importance in the English wool export trade, Calais was, as contemporaries recognised, above all a 'town of war'. It had the largest permanent establishment of military resources in late medieval and early Tudor England and served as the arena in which the English elite of the fifteenth and early sixteenth centuries could gain experience in war, diplomacy and politics. Because of its proximity to France and the Burgundian, later Habsburg Netherlands it was also the means by which European methods and theories of warfare were transmitted to England. It was also a centre of commercial and cultural exchange. In short, then, Calais, along with the northern border, was one of the twin *foci* of English politico-military culture. A study of military service and war in the Calais garrison between 1450 and 1558 provides a detailed picture of the larger experience of war in a period of social and political change which witnessed the end of the Middle Ages and the beginning of the early modern period.

A review of the present literature of war and military service in England in the fifteenth and early sixteenth centuries serves to underline the importance of a study of the Calais garrison. The military historian of late medieval England is poorly served if he or she wants to move beyond the history of specific battles or campaigns, in the mould of Colonel Burne, and to understand the nature and importance of the military experience in a wider context. Anthony Goodman's excellent studies of the military experience during the later fifteenth century come closest, but they are restricted by the paucity of archival material relating specifically to England in the mid-fifteenth century.[1] John Gillingham's account of the Wars of the Roses, despite its dustjacket's claim that it is 'an authoritative analysis of fifteenth-century warfare', concentrates on the pitched battles of the Wars, not the more common experiences of warfare and military service, characterised by regular musters, garrison duties and raiding. Gillingham's conclusion that the military experience in late medieval England was comprehensively different to that in Europe is based on the peculiar circumstances of the battles of Towton, Tewkesbury and Bosworth.[2] No detailed study of English armies and warfare akin to Michael Prestwich's work on the twelfth to fourteenth centuries has been attempted for the fifteenth century.[3] Recent work on the subject offers little more than a rehash of Goodman's conclusions with a few new examples.[4] For the early Tudor period the situation is even worse. Dominated by notions of an inexorable decline in the standard of English arms, exemplified by the decline of the yeoman-archer, hero of the victories of Crécy and Agincourt, the early Tudor period is set in contrast to the development of a national, militia-based army under Elizabeth I and the early Stuarts.[5] The most influential study of military service and war in the period 1509–1558 by Jeremy Goring remains an unpublished thesis, but his two articles in print serve only to reinforce the abject picture of the early Tudor military.[6] A recent, welcome note of revision has been sounded by Gervase Phillips. In his account of England's wars with Scotland in the early sixteenth century, Phillips has suggested that the early Tudor military may not have been so backward and different from its mainland European contemporaries after all. But, as the author himself has agreed, the work is that of a narrative history of the campaigns, 'a chronicle of one damn battle after another', firmly rooted in the Burnesian school of military history rather than a more general reappraisal of the capabilities of early Tudor armies.[7] Much work still remains to be done on the organisation, motivation, weaponry and tactics of English armies in the first half of the sixteenth century.[8]

---

1   Anthony Goodman, *The Wars of the Roses: Military Activity and English Society 1452–1497* (1981); *The Wars of the Roses: The Soldiers' Experience* (Stroud, 2005).
2   John Gillingham, *The Wars of the Roses: Peace and Conflict in Fifteenth-Century England* (1981), esp. pp. 254–7.
3   Michael Prestwich, *Armies and Warfare in the Middle Ages: The English Experience* (New Haven, CT, 1996).
4   Andrew W. Boardman, *The Medieval Soldier in the Wars of the Roses* (Stroud, 1998).
5   Mark Charles Fissel, *English Warfare 1511–1642* (2001); Paul Hammer, *Elizabeth's Wars* (2004).
6   Jeremy Goring, 'The Military Obligations of the English People, 1509–1558' (PhD thesis, University of London, 1955); Goring, 'The General Proscription of 1522', *EHR* lxxxvi (1971), 681–705; Goring, 'Social Change and Military Decline in Mid-Tudor England', *History* lx (1975), 185–97.
7   Gervase Phillips, *The Anglo-Scots Wars 1513–1550* (Woodbridge, 1999), and quote from 3.
8   James Raymond's recent work promises to place English armies in the early sixteenth century into a broader European context. His monograph, *Henry VIII's Military Revolution: The Armies of Sixteenth-Century Britain and Europe* (2007), appears to reinforce many of the points made in this study regarding the standing of English arms in the context of the six-

What, then, of the Calais garrison? Why then has there been little or no serious study of England's largest permanent military establishment in the late medieval and early modern periods? The first reason must be chauvinistic. Beginning in the early seventeenth century, English writers were keen to dismiss the importance of Calais to the English crown, thus belittling the significance of its loss, a tremendous blow to the national pride and morale of mid-Tudor England. Similarly, the French have shown little interest in writing the history of a small town on the margins of the French polity, that was for over two hundred years in English hands before, in the later sixteenth century, being captured by the Spanish. Both English and French writers have tended to concentrate more on the commercial and economic importance of Calais as the focus of the trade in English wool to the Low Countries. This, however, reflects historiographical fashions rather than the realities and concerns of the period between 1436 and 1558. The result of this is that the Calais garrison, one of the largest and best documented military establishments in late medieval Europe, receives only a passing notice in general military histories of the period.[9] Only one writer, the American John Riley Rainey Jr., has exclusively studied the Calais garrison.[10] His unpublished thesis, submitted in 1987, is, however, difficult to access and, being swamped by the mass of archival evidence, fails to address the question of the Calais garrison in the wider context of the nature of military service, the experience of war and the 'military revolution' in England. This present work represents an attempt to deploy a considerable, and in the main unknown, body of evidence to answer just those questions.

Because Calais was an English town and because its successive treasurers were accountable at the royal exchequer at Westminster we have an unparalleled collection of original, archival evidence which allows us to reconstruct military service in the Calais garrison in the sort of detail not available for any other English garrison or army in the late fifteenth or sixteenth centuries. These records fall into four main categories. First, there are the accounts and other records of the treasurer of Calais, preserved in the National Archives (formerly the Public Record Office) at Kew.[11] Into this category fall the muster rolls and inventories of military equipment which allow the reconstruction of who served in the garrison and the weapons with which they defended the town and marches. Second, there are the various other collections of official records, again mainly housed in the National Archives, which chart appointments to office in the garrison and the shifting attitude of the crown

---

teenth-century military revolutions. I am very grateful to Dr Raymond for permitting me to read a draft of his work before publication.

[9] See, for example, Philippe Contamine, *War in the Middle Ages*, trans. Michael Jones (Oxford, 1984), 165.

[10] Rainey, 'Defence of Calais'.

[11] The most important sources are the Exchequer, King's Remembrancer, Accounts Various (E101) under the sub-heading France, which contains the books of particulars of acount, as well as a mass of supporting receipts, vouchers and other documents. Until the 1490s audited copies of the treasurers' and victuallers' accounts were enrolled in Exchequer, Pipe Office, Foreign Account Rolls (E364).

towards Calais.[12] Thirdly, there are letters, both official and private. The historian of Calais is very fortunate in this regard as three of the great private letter collections of the fifteenth century, the Pastons, the Stonors and the Celys, all contain material relating to Calais and its garrison. For the sixteenth century the situation is even better. The Lisle letters, covering the period 1533 to 1540, give an unrivalled view of the life of the town, its deputy, Arthur Plantagenet, Viscount Lisle, its inhabitants and soldiers. Complementary to this collection is the 'official' correspondence of the state papers. The fourth category are the chronicles and literary accounts of the garrison in action. These are especially useful for the mid-fifteenth century and include sources from England, the Low Countries and France.

Armed with this unique array of evidence, we can begin to answer questions about the garrison that are not possible for other English military establishments in the same period. How many men served in the Calais garrison? Who were they and who were their leaders? How were they recruited and for how long did they serve? What were they armed with and how did they operate as a military force? How did the Calais garrison compare with other similar English and European bodies of fighting men in the same period? What was the role of the Calais garrison in civil war, rebellion and the king's wars in France? To what extent was the Calais garrison a professional force, a 'standing army' to employ a deliberate anachronism, comparable to the permanent military forces developing throughout contemporary western Europe? Was the fall of Calais in 1558 a symptom of the decline of England's military capabilities in the sixteenth century and evidence that it was falling hopelessly behind in the 'military revolution' which was then reshaping the nature of war in continental Europe? By reassessing war and military service in the Calais Pale with other areas under the dominion of the English king we can reassess the question of military resources and capability generally.[13] Moreover, the Calais garrison allows a comparison to be made with contemporary European armies and offers an important reconsideration of the role of England within the wider tactical, social and political changes to warfare in early modern Europe. Before answering these questions, however, it is first necessary to describe briefly the town and marches of Calais and their place within the English polity.

---

12 Principal among these are the Treaty or French Rolls (C76) which include enrolments of grants and orders relating to England's overseas, mainly French, possessions.
13 It is important to note that this study confines itself to the English military service and capabilities on land. While its members frequently served at sea (especially during the 1450s), the Calais garrison was a land force. Its principal function was the defence of the town and marches and English kings typically made separate arrangements for the defence of the English Channel and the Narrow Seas. That said, the institutions and military culture that defined the nature and experience of service at sea were little different from those which governed service on land. Moreover, it seems that the naval aspects of the defence of Calais diminished as the sixteenth century progressed: C.F. Richmond, 'The Keeping of the Seas during the Hundred Years War: 1422–1440', *History*, xlix (1964), 283–98; 'English Naval Power in the Fifteenth Century', *History*, lii (1967), 1–15; David Loades, *The Tudor Navy: Administrative, Political and Military History* (Aldershot, 1992).

The Calais Pale

In 1450 the English Pale stretched eighteen miles from near Wissant in Picardy to Gravelines in Flanders.[14] From the coastline it extended between eight and ten miles inland, a little less than the area secured by Edward III at the Treaty of Brétigny in 1360. The French, for example, had recaptured the town and castle of Ardres, near Guînes, in the late fourteenth century, while the Burgundians had made incursions in 1436. By 1485 the Pale contained twenty-five rural parishes as well as the parishes of Our Lady and St Nicholas within the town of Calais itself. The exact borders of the Pale were ill-defined, having been slowly encroached upon by French farmers.[15] The area of English government was known variously as 'Calais', 'Calais and the marches of the same' or 'the town and marches of Calais'. Although probably first employed in 1436, it was not until the 1490s that the term 'Pale' was commonly used to describe those lands around Calais held by the king of England.[16] In this book I have used the nouns 'Calais' and 'the Pale' interchangeably to refer to the town and marches. I have also used 'Calais' as an adjective to avoid the clumsy alternative 'Calaisien'.

The political, social and economic centre of the Pale was, of course, the town of Calais itself. The town had developed as a fishing port reclaimed from the sand dunes during the twelfth century.[17] By the middle of the fifteenth century it formed a large rectangle, enclosed by solid limestone walls, measuring some twelve hundred metres in length by five hundred metres in width.[18] On the harbour side the town was protected by Rysbank Tower, while on the west side the castle of Calais overlooked the estuary. The town's population was around four thousand, somewhat reduced from its early fifteenth-century heyday. Like most major medieval towns, access to Calais was controlled by a series of gates. Having passed through the Searcher's Tower, entry to the town was possible only through either the Lantern or Watergate. Exit from the town was either through the Milkgate or the Boulogne Gate. From the main entrance of the town itself, the Lanterngate, built by the merchants of the staple during the early 1480s, a street led to the main square of the town. The market square was the administrative and economic centre of the town. It was dominated by the Staple Inn, the

---

[14] See the early Tudor map of the Pale, reproduced as Figure 2, p. xiv.

[15] Viscount Dillon's description of the topography of the Pale, from the rental surveys compiled in the 1550s, remains the standard work ('Calais and the Pale', *Archaeologia* liii (1892), 289–388). This was largely based on his study of the two rental surveys of the 1550s: BL, Harl. MS 3880 a survey compiled in 1552 and E315/371–2, the much larger survey of 1556. Much of what follows is taken from this seminal work. See also Morgan, 'Government of Calais 1485–1558', 19–47.

[16] The *Oxford English Dictionary* cites Fabyan's Chronicle of 1494 as the first use of the term 'Pale' to describe the English lands around Calais but it was certainly in use from 1436: SC1/58/47.

[17] Alain Derville, 'Une Ville vers 1300: Calais', *Revue du Nord*, lxxii (1990), 737–56; F. Lennel, *Histoire de Calais* (3 vols, Calais, 1908–13), i. 1–45.

[18] See Figure 2. It is clear from modern maps that the eastern half of the street plan of the Tudor town of Calais remained in place until very recently (see, for example, BL, Maps, 14375, a plan of Calais produced for the USAF in 1943).

centre of the king's administration in Calais, which housed the exchequer, a
court room and the lodgings of the governor of the Pale. The other important
buildings in the town included the two churches – St Mary's and St Nicholas's –
which reflected the mercantile wealth of the town and of the staple company in
particular. The other major civic building in the town was Prince's Inn, built by
the French king as a royal residence but desolate by the mid-fifteenth century. In
1499 Henry VII granted the Inn to the staplers who rebuilt it as the centre of
their administration of the wool trade.[19] The remainder of the town, as can be
more clearly appreciated from Figure 2, was divided between the twelve streets
radiating from the Square, three long streets which ran east to west, and seventeen smaller streets running from north to south. From the 1556 survey it is clear
that there was little new building of private houses from the middle of the
fifteenth century, indeed some of the older houses may have become desolate.
However, the particulars of the treasurer's accounts – which include details of
the collector of rent's annual survey of the rent-paying properties in the town –
can be compared directly to the later surveys of royal property carried out in the
1550s. There were many areas of 'void ground', as well as many small tene-
ments with a much smaller number of more substantial houses. However, the
largest buildings in private hands were the wool-houses, in which the merchants
stored their wool, and the 'herring-hangs', for drying and storing the fish
brought to Calais during the annual herring fair.

Apart from Calais, the only significant centre of population in the Pale was
Guînes. The centre of the ancient county of that name, the town had been an
important administrative and commercial centre of the counts of Artois before
the Treaty of Brétigny. However, as most of the old administrative county of
Guînes was lost to the French, the town slowly declined in relation to Calais. It
was really only sustained by the military presence of the English. Before 1436
Guînes was one of a string of castles including Sandegate, Marke, Oye and
Hammes which formed a defensive cordon around the Pale. However, after the
Burgundian attack of that year only Guînes and Hammes remained, the others
having been razed to the ground by the attackers.[20] Guînes's strategic position –
it overlooked the road from Ardres to Boulogne and was visible from the other
English outpost at Hammes – ensured its continued importance and maintenance throughout the period of English occupation. In 1485 the town had some
seventy or eighty houses and was still dominated by the old medieval castle. The
houses themselves actually stood outside the fortifications and were protected
from attack by a mound and wooden rampart.[21]

The remainder of the Pale comprised arable land of varying quality. It was
divided by contemporaries into two distinct areas: the High Country on the
eastern side and the Low Country to the west. The boundary between them was
marked by the Hammes river which ran into the sea at Calais. At the time of
the Treaty of Brétigny, the High Country was heavily forested and largely

---

19 Colvin, *The King's Works*, iii(1). 339; C76/181, m 5.
20 Colvin, *The King's Works*, i. 423–6.
21 Dillon, 'Calais and the Pale', 300–1, 341–3; BL, Cotton MS Augustus I.II, f. 12.

uncultivated. However, by the end of the fifteenth century the forest had long since been encroached upon by both English and French farmers. The Anglo-French border along this stretch of the Pale was notoriously difficult to ascertain, bounded as it was by numerous copses, trees, stones and other locally recognised markers. The boundary of the High Country ran through the Forest of Guînes, through the small valleys overlooking the villages of Camp and Buckholt and between the villages of Ballingham and Brêmes. Towards the coast, the frontier ran between the English villages of Boninges, Calkwell and Pepeling and the Picard villages of Landerton, Fynes and Caffiers. The border here was indistinct and, despite the excellent network of roads and the opportunities for tolls that they offered, no attempt was made to limit intercourse between the French and English. The walls of Boulogne were clearly visible from the hills of the High Country in the early sixteenth century;[22] nevertheless, the wooded and difficult nature of the terrain was enough to convince successive English governments of the unlikelihood of French attack through the High Country.

The numerous tiny villages of the High Country were connected by myriad small lanes and tracks. The principal route running through the area was the Bullenway, which ran from Calais across the Scunage to Newembridge, crossing the Hammes river, to Sandingfield and eventually through Picardy on towards Paris. A smaller road led to Boulogne through Sandegate, Scales, Strones and Wissant. The main road to Guînes, known as the Buckway, crossed Newembridge and passed through the parishes of Froyton and Mellac. The High Country was a valuable asset to the Pale. The Forest of Guînes was the only native source of wood in the Pale and its privileges were closely guarded by the governor of Guînes castle. Nevertheless, it never proved sufficient to supply the Pale with all its timber needs and large supplies of wood were regularly imported from the English channel ports, particularly Rye.[23] There were also valuable sources of clay and chalk in the High Country, principally the six quarries at Fynes and others at Calkwell and Pepeling.

The western part of the English Pale consisted of a maze of streams, pools, water-meadows and marshes known to contemporaries as the 'Low Country'. Comprising about eighty square miles of the Pale, the Low Country stretched from Calais to Guînes and encompassed the lordship of Marke and Oye. As its name suggests, this area was only a few feet above sea-level and formed, when flooded, the principal natural defence of the Pale. During the fifteenth century an elaborate system of sluices and dikes controlled the flow of water into the Low Country. This allowed cultivation during times of peace but also enabled the English to flood the area if threatened by imminent attack. By the mid-fifteenth century these defences were controlled by sluices at Newembridge. From the early sixteenth century, despite the naming of commissions of the

---

[22] From Camp, just south of Guînes, at 150 feet above sea-level, the hills of the High Country rose to a height of some 300 feet.
[23] G. Mayhew, *Tudor Rye* (Falmer, 1987), 253. The loss of Calais meant a two-thirds reduction in the amount of traffic passing through the port of Rye.

sewers, the marshland of the Low Country had been increasingly drained for profit, both to locals and the king. This compromised the marsh as the natural defensive frontier of the Pale. Official concern at the dangers posed by the draining of the marshes reached a crisis in 1534 with the decision to flood the Meane Broke. This large area of marshland had been granted to Sir Robert Wingfield, the former deputy of Calais, in 1529 and he had duly settled it with his tenants. The antagonism generated by Wingfield and his network of friends and family towards the council of Calais was one of the main features of internal politics in Calais throughout the 1530s.[24]

The Low Country was sparsely populated with only a few centres of population. The oldest settlement was Marke, of more ancient origin than Calais; however, its role as a small market town had long since dwindled. Nevertheless, the lordship of Marke and Oye retained its own identity: the king's tenants there had their own chartered liberties and they represented a distinct community within the Pale.[25] The only other notable centres were Hammes, Wael and Colham. The remainder of the area was sprinkled with farms and tiny hamlets, dominated by large churches, which during the fifteenth century had been vital tools in the defence of the Pale. Communications in the Low Country were restricted to two main roads and a network of paths and canals. The main road ran from Calais to Marke and from there over the river Aa to Gravelines. The other main road led from Calais through the parish of St Peter's (known as the Scunage), around the Meane Brooke and Cowswade and on to Ardres.

The frontier between the Pale and Flanders, like that in the High Country, was ambiguous and contested. The main cause of tension, which came to a head in 1540–1, was the area known as the Cowswade. This area, claimed by the French, stood at the intersection between the English, French and Imperial territories. Also the Hapsburgs – as heirs of the dukes of Burgundy, who were in turn heirs to the counts of Artois, the ancient feudal lords of the area encompassing the English lands – claimed parts of the Pale. For example, in November 1505 Henry VII tried to force Archduke Philip of Austria to give up his family's old seigneurial claims to Calais.[26] Various other potential areas of tension existed along the border with Flanders: the Egmont and Moorbeck families claimed land near Fynes; and the governors of Gravelines contested the flats of the Aa estuary.[27]

From the treaty of Brétigny Calais had been recognised as being separate

---

24 The council of Calais informed Cromwell that the Pale was strengthened by the flooding of the marsh to the tune of ten thousand men: *LP* VII, 1511. The dispute over 'Wingfield's marsh' is covered by *LP* VII, 431, 1362, 1502, 1565. See also D.A. Waas, 'Arthur Plantagenet, Viscount Lisle and the Administration of Calais 1533–1540' (PhD thesis, University of Illinois, 1958), 114–23.

25 In 1509 the liberties of the lordship were confirmed by Henry VIII: C56/28, no 5. In 1521 those tenants who had farmed the rent of the lordship were brought before the treasurer of Calais for peculation and various other offences. They clearly represented an autonomous and well organised group outside the civilian jurisdiction of Calais or Guînes: E101/203/27.

26 *Calendar of State Papers, Venetian*, ed. R. Brown, C. Bentinck and H. Brown (9 vols, 1864–98), i. 860.

27 Morgan, 'Government of Calais', 26.

from the French crown claimed by successive English kings. In the fifteenth century it was accorded a similar constitutional status within the king's dominions as Ireland, Wales or Gascony. After the English defeats in the Hundred Years War, however, notions that Calais was a member of the English crown gained more popularity in both official and popular circles.[28] In 1436 Calais itself was a relatively homogeneous town. Edward III had vowed to populate the town with Englishmen; this he had, on the whole, succeeded in doing. Grants of land had been made to Englishmen willing to settle in the town; this was not restricted to soldiers, in fact the crown had tried to prevent soldiers and their families monopolising the new settlements. The population of the rural areas of the Pale were, however, a different matter. Although English and Latin were the official languages of the Pale, in the rural areas courts were still kept in the native French and Flemish tongues. Nevertheless, English rule had been established for nearly a hundred years and a system of royal administration had been superimposed upon the existing seigneurial jurisdictions. The bailiffs and beadles of the High and Low Countries ensured the relatively efficient taxation and security of a largely native rural population. Despite the problems of language and nationality there is no evidence that the Pale was in constant danger from disaffected French or Flemish peasants. Periodic restrictions placed on the passage and residence of aliens in the Pale were more likely to be responses to political crises elsewhere in England or Europe than to be directly due to events in the Pale. For example, in 1483 in response to the increasing diplomatic tensions between France and England the Council in Westminster sent orders to Lord Hastings, the mayor of the staple and the town corporation to expel all aliens from the Pale.[29] It was not until 1530, when the Reformation caused all foreigners in Calais to be regarded as potential fifth-columnists, that the crown began a systematic exploitation of the Pale's alien community, leading to their expulsion from the English territories in 1543.[30]

Between 1436 and 1558, then, Calais was an integral part of the English realm. Its defence and prosperity were a priority for all English governments. Calais was not one of the mere peripheries of the realm: in terms of contact and distance from the seat of political power in Westminster, it was as close as, say, the Midlands or home counties; it was certainly much closer than the other military frontiers of the English polity, such as Ireland or the Scottish marches. Because of its commercial importance, Calais was of far greater immediate consequence to the wealthy mercantile class of London than any of the other borderlands. Thus the experience of military service in Calais affected a far wider, and more influential, proportion of the English population than military service anywhere else in the realm.

---

[28] The changing constitutional status of Calais is discussed at length in David Grummitt, ' "One of the mooste Pryncipall Treasours Belongyng to his Realme of Englande": Calais and the Crown *c.* 1450–1558', in *The English Experience in France, c. 1450–1558: War, Diplomacy and Cultural Exchange*, ed. David Grummitt (Aldershot, 2002), 46–62.

[29] E28/92/57.

[30] Grummitt, 'Calais and the Crown', 56–7.

Calais at war

Calais was, as contemporaries frequently remarked, principally a 'towne of were'.[31] It may seem an obvious thing to say, but its garrison consisted principally of soldiers. In 1436 and 1558 Calais was besieged by opposing princes and, in between those dates, warfare was an ever-present feature of life in the Pale. At times (particularly during the 1430s, 1450s, 1520s and 1540s) it witnessed extensive fighting within its boundaries, while even years of relative calm (the 1440s, 1490s and 1530s) saw skirmishes and cross-border raids. Before analysing the military establishment in any detail, therefore, it would be useful to recite briefly the major campaigns and actions in which the Calais garrison was involved.

In July 1436 Philip the Good, duke of Burgundy laid siege to the Pale, capturing and destroying some of the outlying fortresses before being repulsed at the gates of Calais itself.[32] The garrison was involved in the punitive raids into Flanders led by its captain, Humphrey, duke of Gloucester, in the aftermath of the Burgundian defeat, but this was not the end of the threat to the Pale, nor of the involvement of the garrison in fighting with the Flemish. In the early months of 1437 Philip appears to have assembled an army and planned to launch a raid on the south coast of England, but this came to nothing and instead the Burgundians continued to launch raids into the Pale.[33] Indeed it was not until September 1439 that the English and Burgundians signed a truce, initially for three years but in the following year renewed for a further seven years.

The collapse of the English position in Normandy in 1449–50 brought renewed fears of an attack on the Pale. On this occasion it was both the resurgent French and, more especially, the Burgundians who threatened Calais. Towards the end of 1449 William Pirton, the lieutenant of Guînes, and Edward Grimston took a personal message to Duke Philip from Henry VI in an attempt to forestall the expected Burgundian assault. Further careful diplomacy in the following years, as well as prudent reinforcement of the Pale's defences, were necessary to ensure that the expected Burgundian attack never materialised. The French recapture of Gascony in 1452–3 also heightened fears for Calais and the Parliament of 1453 witnessed a concerted effort to improve the Pale's defences and its finances. Indeed, these measures probably succeeded in ensuring the safety of Calais from French attack for the remainder of the decade.[34]

The appointment of Richard Neville, earl of Warwick, as captain of Calais, in the wake of the first battle of St Albans in August 1455, transformed the Pale into an arena for the domestic struggle between the Lancastrian crown and its opponents. Warwick was unable to secure entry to the town until he had secured

---

31 See, for example, the appointment of Sir Thomas Kyriell as lieutenant of Calais in 1440: BL, Harl. Ch. 52 G12. The merchants of the staple made the same point and employed the same phrase in 1528: *Tudor Economic Documents*, ed. R.H. Tawney and E.E. Power (3 vols, Oxford, 1924), ii. 26.

32 See below ch. one.

33 James A. Doig, 'A New Source for the Siege of Calais in 1436', *EHR*, cx (1995), 410.

34 R.A. Griffiths, *The Reign of Henry VI* (1981), 522–9.

the garrison's finances through negotiations with the merchants of the staple, but by July 1456, with the garrison satisfied by the staplers of its arrears and current wages to the tune of over £20,000, the earl was able to take up his command.[35] During the period of Warwick's captaincy (1455–71), soldiers from the garrison were involved in three distinct forms of military activity. First, Warwick involved them in his campaign of piracy in the Channel; second, between 1459 and the early 1460s the garrison was involved in the civil wars both on the English mainland and in the Pale; and, finally, in 1470 it was involved in an abortive campaign against the Burgundians, the price of Louis XI's support for Warwick and the Lancastrian Readeption regime.

The earl of Warwick's privateering exploits from Calais in the late 1450s are well known. In November 1457, in response to the French raid on Sandwich the previous August, he was appointed keeper of the seas for three years and thereafter used his position to engage in piracy. Piracy was nothing new among the garrison, but it increased and gained 'official' recognition under Warwick's command. In March 1457 the earl had been commissioned to inquire into the activities of one of his lieutenants, Andrew Trollope, and again, in May the following year, he was ordered to investigate acts of piracy committed by members of the garrison. On 28 May 1458, however, Warwick himself led the garrison in twelve ships to attack a well-armed Spanish convoy of twenty-two ships off Calais. The battle raged for six hours, during which Warwick took six prizes and suffered eighty men killed and another two hundred captured. 'And as men sayne', remarked one participant, 'there was not so gret a batayle upon þe se this xl wyntyr'. Throughout the following summer Warwick led the garrison in capturing Hanseatic, Genoese and Spanish vessels. Clearly, the earl's exploits were popular among both the garrison and the seamen of the southern English ports.[36]

This popularity was undoubtedly a factor in ensuring Warwick's captaincy survived the crisis of 1459–61. Between the end of 1459 and the early 1460s the Pale played host to opposing Yorkist and Lancastrian forces. Moreover, elements of the Calais garrison played an important role in the some of the key engagements of the Wars of the Roses. In September 1459 Warwick crossed the Channel with some five hundred members of the garrison, led by the experienced war-captain, Andrew Trollope, and the earl's marshall of Calais, Walter Blount. While marching to rendezvous with the hosts of the other rebel lords, Warwick learned of the defeat of his father, the earl of Salisbury, at Blore Heath on 23 September. At Ludford Bridge on the River Teme, Warwick, joined by Salisbury and the duke of York from Ludlow, drew up his men in battle array to face the royal army. However, on the night of 12/13 October Trollope and the Calais contingent deserted their captain, perhaps wary of committing treason by

---

[35] G.L. Harriss, 'The Struggle for Calais: An Aspect of the Rivalry between Lancaster and York', *EHR*, lxxv (1960), 39–46.

[36] Michael Hicks, *Warwick the Kingmaker* (Oxford, 1998), 144–8; Rainey, 'Defence of Calais', 194–9; *Paston Letters and Papers of the Fifteenth Century*, ed. Norman Davis (EETS, special series, xx, 2004), ii. 340.

taking up arms against the king.[37] Thereafter Warwick, Salisbury and the earl of March fled to Calais, while York returned to Ireland. Shortly before Ludford Henry VI had appointed Henry Beaufort, duke of Somerset, as captain of Calais. Somerset set sail for the Pale at the end of month, arriving only hours after Warwick had returned. His men were repulsed at Calais and Somerset, now assisted by Trollope as his chief captain, headed for Guînes, where he was admitted without a fight. Hammes, under Sir John Marney, also declared for Somerset.[38] In January 1460 the Lancastrians attempted to send reinforcements from Sandwich, but a raid from Calais, led by John Dynham, captured the earl of Warwick's ships, impounded there the previous November, and the Lancastrian commander, Richard Wydeville, Lord Rivers, and his son.[39] Somerset remained in Guînes, another attempt to take Calais being defeated at Newembridge, and in June, when Warwick and the other Yorkist earls returned to England, he attempted to surrender the castle to the duke of Charolois. Only the timely intervention of Charolais's father, Duke Philip of Burgundy, prevented this. In the aftermath of the Yorkist victory at Northampton in July, Warwick returned to Calais where Somerset entered into negotiations. Convinced that no help was forthcoming from England, the duke agreed to surrender the town and castle and was allowed to return to England on the undertaking that he would not in future take up arms against Warwick.[40] The Lancastrian garrison at Hammes, however, remained and in March and again in September and October 1461 the Calais garrison mounted sieges. It is clear that a heavy bombardment took place on the latter occasion at least and three large guns were 'broken' by the attackers. On 24 October the castle surrendered and, led by their constable Thomas Huse, over a hundred of the defenders were received into Edward IV's allegiance.[41] However, some members of the former Lancastrian garrisons of Guînes and Hammes remained an annoyance to the garrison, mounting raids into the Pale from French-held territory. In 1461–2 an extra forty archers were despatched to Guînes to protect the town from a force of French and their English allies who had mounted raids into the county of Guînes and attempted to take the castle by force. Seventeen of the English 'thieves' were subsequently captured and hanged in Guînes castle.[42]

In contrast to 1459–61, the renewal of civil war in England between 1469 and 1471 saw little conflict in the Pale. It seems likely that members of the garrison saw action in Warwick's revival of privateering in the Channel in 1469, but their involvement was not as explicit as it had been in the late 1450s.[43] In the last months of 1470, with Edward IV in exile and Henry VI restored, principally due

---

37 Hicks, *Warwick*, 162–5; Waurin, v. 276; *The Historical Collections of a Citizen of London in the Fifteenth Century*, ed. James Gairdner (CS, new series, xvii, 1876), 205.
38 Waurin, v. 280–2; *The Brut*, ii. 528.
39 C.L. Scofield, 'The Capture of Lord Rivers and Sir Anthony Woodville on 19 January 1460', *EHR*, xxxviii (1908), 253–5.
40 Waurin, v. 291–2, 305–7.
41 E101/195/14, ff. 10–11; C81/1488/3.
42 E101/196/2, f. 34; 196/3.
43 Hicks, *Warwick*, 250–1.

to the 'Kingmaker's' actions, Warwick stood at the pinnacle of his power in Calais. Philippe de Commynes observed at the time that the garrison wore Warwick's badge of the Ragged Staff and were preparing for war against the duke of Burgundy, in fulfilment of the agreement made between the earl and Louis XI the previous summer.[44] In February 1471 Warwick wrote to the king informing him that formal hostilities had begun as promised and that members of the Calais garrison had already killed two members of the Burgundian garrison of Gravelines.[45] On Easter Sunday 1471 Warwick was killed at the battle of Barnet. It seems he was not accompanied by a contingent from Calais and it was not until May, after news of their captain's death, that three hundred men from the garrison left under the command of Sir George Brooke to serve with the Bastard of Fauconberg. They took part in the Bastard's abortive attempt to capture London and then returned to Calais via Sandwich.[46] In early August, on the back of a pardon offered to most of the earl's former servants, Warwick's lieutenants, Walter Wrottesley and Geoffrey Gate, allowed the new lieutenant, William, Lord Hastings, to enter the town and receive the submission of the garrison into Edward IV's allegiance.[47]

The restoration of stable government at home in the early 1470s allowed Edward IV to consider a reassertion of the English claim to the French throne. The plan had, in fact, been mooted in the late 1460s, but it was not until the Parliament of 1472 that the king's plans became clear. In the summer of 1475 Edward assembled thirteen thousand men, the largest English expeditionary army of the fifteenth century, for his invasion. The Calais establishment, particularly the victualler, William Rosse, and the chief smith, Giles van Rasingham, had played a pivotal role in assembling the weaponry, particularly large cannon, to make this army comparable to those assembled by the king's Burgundian ally, Charles the Bold, and his French adversary. The main body of the royal host was built around the contingents assembled by the royal household and by noblemen holding court office. Important among these was the lieutenant of Calais, William, Lord Hastings.[48] The soldiers of the Calais garrison fully expected to play a leading role in the forthcoming campaign, as demonstrated by the enthusiastic letters sent from Calais by Sir John Paston. Their sense of disappointment when Edward chose to make terms with Louis XI at Picquigny on 29 August

---

[44] Phillippe de Commynes, *Memoirs: The Reign of Louis XI, 1461–83*, trans. M. Jones (1972), 191–2.

[45] BL, Add. MS 48988, f. 40; A.R. Myers, 'The Outbreak of War between England and Burgundy in February 1471', *BIHR*, xxxiii (1960), 114–15.

[46] John Warkworth, *Chronicle of the First Thirteen Years of the Reign of King Edward IV*, ed. J.O. Halliwell (CS, 1st series, vi, 1839), 19–20; C.F. Richmond, 'Fauconberg's Rising of 1471', *EHR*, xxxv (1970), 673–92.

[47] *CPR, 1467–77*, 290–2; David Grummitt, 'William, Lord Hastings and the Defence of Calais, 1471–1483', in *Social Attitudes and Political Structures in the Fifteenth Century*, ed. T.J. Thornton (Stroud, 2000), 154–8.

[48] David Grummitt, 'The Court, War and Noble Power in England, *c.* 1475–1558', in *The Court as a Stage*, ed. Steven Gunn and Antheun Janse (Woodbridge, 2006), 45–8; 'The French Campaign of 1475 and What It Meant to Those Involved' at http://www.richardiii.net/tol.htm.

was palpable: Sir John's letter to his mother, telling her 'thys wyage off the Kyngys is fynysshyd', is matter of fact, but nevertheless revealing. Sir John finished his letter by explaining that 'I was in good heele whan I came hyddre [to Calais], and all hooll, and to my wetyng I hadde never a better stomake in my lyffe; and now wyth-in viij dayes [of the campaign being terminated] I am crasyd ageyn.'[49] Lord Hastings may have opposed the king's decision to make peace, and two years later events afforded an opportunity for the soldiers of the garrison to win the fame and honour that they had been cheated of in the summer of 1475. On 5 January 1477 Duke Charles the Bold had been killed at the siege of Nancy. The Burgundian dominions, now in the charge of his young daughter, the Duchess Mary, and the Dowager Duchess Margaret, Edward IV's sister, lay at the mercy of the French king, Louis XI. Hastings clearly wished to intervene on behalf of the dowager duchess and arms were sent from Calais to the Burgundians. In February Hastings arrived in Calais with reinforcements, and in April it seems that the garrison even left the Pale with the intention of lifting the French siege of Boulogne, an incident that provoked something of a diplomatic crisis. Nevertheless, denied support by the king, Hastings and the garrison could do nothing and it was left to Maximilian I, king of the Romans, to come to the Duchess Mary's rescue.[50]

The events of 1477 and the disappointment of the chivalric aspirations of Hastings and the garrison may have had an effect on Calais's disposition towards Richard, duke of Gloucester, and his seizure of the throne in the spring of 1483.[51] Certainly, many members of the garrison fought actively in the wars of both Charles the Bold and Maximilian during the 1470s and 1480s and this may reflect their desire to make real a chivalric conception of war and military service.[52] In May 1483 Gloucester made a pre-emptive strike against his Wydeville rivals for control of the government during Edward V's minority and then, on 13 June, seized the lieutenant of Calais, Lord Hastings, at a council meeting in London and had him summarily executed. The garrison did nothing and while Hastings's lieutenant, Sir John Dynham, remained in nominal charge, by the end of the reign several key castles had been placed in the custody of Richard III's servants. The threat to the stability of the Ricardian regime posed by Calais was heightened by the escape and flight to Henry Tudor of the Lancastrian prisoner, John de Vere, earl of Oxford, and his gaoler, James Blount, lieutenant of Hammes castle, in December 1484. Dynham began a siege of the recalcitrant castle of Hammes, but the Calais garrison appears to have taken no part in the campaign which saw Tudor win the throne at the battle of Bosworth in August 1485.[53]

[49] *Paston Letters*, i. 486–7.

[50] Michael K. Jones, '1477 – the Expedition that Never Was: Chivalric Expectation in Late-Yorkist England', *The Ricardian*, xii (2001), 275–92.

[51] David Grummitt, 'William, Lord Hastings, the Calais Garrison and the Politics of Yorkist England', *The Ricardian*, xii (2001), 268–71.

[52] See below, pp. 101–3, 107–8.

[53] Grummitt, 'Lord Hastings', 164–6; Grummitt, ' "For the Surety of the Towne and Marches": Early Tudor policy towards Calais 1485–1509', *Nottingham Medieval Studies*, xliv

Under the early Tudors the garrison was once again principally involved in campaigns against foreign, rather than domestic, rivals. In June 1489, led by its lieutenant, Giles, Lord Daubeney, and Henry, Lord Morley, the garrison played a significant role in aiding Maximilian's forces at Dixsmuide, besieged by the French and the Flemings (then in rebellion against their erstwhile protector). Fearing that the French, if they won Dixsmuide, would be in a position to move onto Gravelines and thus surround the Pale, Henry VII authorised Morley and Daubeney to lead two thousand Englishmen to relieve the siege. According to the Tudor chronicler Edward Hall, Daubeney, Sir James Tyrell, lieutenant of Guînes, and Sir Humphrey Talbot, the marshall of Calais, led several hundred of the garrision out of the Pale in secret to Dixsmuide. The English soldiers stormed the Flemish camp, banishing the Flemings and the German mercenaries, for the loss of only a hundred men (including Lord Morley). As Hall remarked: 'Thys felde was profitable to the Englishmen, for they that went forthe in clothe, came home in sylke, and they that went out on foote, came home on great horses, suche is the chaunce of victory.'[54] In October 1492 Henry set sail for Calais with an army of some twenty-five thousand, led by the duke of Bedford and the earl of Oxford, and prepared to besiege Boulogne. The campaign itself was of little military significance: within nine days peace proposals were accepted which resulted in the Treaty of Étaples on 3 November.[55] Although Calais was the starting point for the invasion of the Boullonais, the establishment there did not play an important part in the organisation of the campaign nor, unlike the 1475 campaign, did the garrison provide a large contingent of the royal army. The surviving indentures for service indicate that it was the royal household in England that provided the most important contingent of the army. Among the surviving indentures only Robert Bellingham, a king's esquire as well as a man-at-arms in the garrison who indented to provide a custrell and a page, fifteen demi-lances and five archers on horseback, can be linked to the Calais establishment.[56] Sir James Blount, lieutenant of Hammes castle, managed to excuse himself from service altogether.[57]

Calais, however, played a very different role in the French wars of Henry VIII. In 1513 the Pale was crucial, both as a base of operations and as a supplier of much of the manpower and administrative support. Between the middle of

---

(2000), 185–6. In the aftermath of Bosworth the Ricardian elements among the garrison, some two to four hundred men, apparently offered their services to Maximilian: C.S.L. Davies, 'Bishop John Morton, the Holy See and the Accession of Henry VII', *EHR*, cii (1987), 27.

[54] Edward Hall, *The Union of the Two Noble and Illustre Famelies of Lancastre & Yorke* (1548).

[55] John M. Currin, ' "To Traffic with War"? Henry VII and the French Campaign of Henry VII', in *The English Experience in France, c. 1450–1558: War, Diplomacy and Cultural Exchange*, ed. David Grummitt (Aldershot, 2002), 106–31.

[56] E101/72/3/1071; Grummitt, 'Court, War and Noble Power', 146–7.

[57] E101/72/4/1110. Blount's indentures are among a group where both parties' copies survive indicating that no agreement was reached. The blank spaces provided for the number of soldiers were not filled in and in some cases there is a note on of the dorse of the indenture explaining why the service could not be performed.

May and the end of June 1513 an army of some thirty or forty thousand men arrived in Calais with the intention of making good Henry VIII's claim to the French throne.[58] The preparations for this huge enterprise had been in train for over a year with the officials of the Pale crucial to their success. Moreover, the reserves kept in Calais accruing from the French pension were vital in providing ready cash to buy ships and supplies in the Low Countries. Sir Gilbert Talbot, the deputy, who supervised the payments from the French pension, and Sir Richard Wingfield, the marshall, were appointed joint commissary for supplies.[59] Sir John Wiltshire, the comptroller, also served in procuring ships and victuals for the forthcoming campaign.[60] When it finally got under way, Henry relied heavily on the military and administrative abilities of his servants in Calais. For example, Nicholas Marland, the under-marshall, was in charge of the ordnance in the Middle Ward of the army. John Tremayle, a man-at-arms and a groom of the king's chamber, was knighted at Lille in October 1513 for his services during the campaign.[61] The garrison provided the professional backbone of the Middle Ward, the main force of the army accompanied by the king himself: the spears and mounted archers formed the advance portion of the ward, while the artillery was commanded by Sir Richard Carew, lieutenant of Calais castle, with a thousand other soldiers.[62] The logistical support was also centred on Calais. The plan for 1513 envisaged a 'great staple of powder and shot' within the Pale and, as the army advanced towards Therouanne and Tournai, the supply line to Calais became increasingly stretched.[63] On 1 August the French commander of Boulogne attempted to cut the supply line by attacking the Pale at Newembridge. An English force of two hundred archers, led by Nicholas Marland, turned back this assault thus preserving the vital communications link to the front.[64] The importance of Calais as a logistical base was also demonstrated by the reinforcement of the garrison there. For example, in February 1513 Sir Nicholas Vaux, lieutenant of Guînes, received £142 2s. from Sir John Daunce, the treasurer of war, for the monthly wages of two hundred extra soldiers stationed at the castle of Guînes.[65]

In 1522 another English army, on this occasion commanded by Thomas Howard, earl of Surrey, crossed the Channel. By the terms of the secret Anglo-Imperial treaty of Bruges, made in August 1521, Henry VIII agreed to make war on Francis I, king of France, to assist the emperor, Charles V, in the ongoing struggle between the houses of Habsburg and Valois. Surrey, having escorted the emperor back from his visit to England in May, raided Brittany, sacking Morlaix and winning a considerable amount of plunder. In August the

58 Charles Cruickshank, *Henry VIII and the Invasion of France* (Gloucester, 1990), 1–19.
59 SP1/4, f. 71 (*LP* I ii, 1918).
60 BL, Add. MS 46454, ff. 15, 18.
61 SP1/229, f. 151 (*LP* I i, 1869); *LP* I ii, 2414 (Marland); SP1/5, f. 51 (*LP* I ii, 2049); *LP* I i, 1086; I ii, Appendix 26 (Tremayle).
62 Cruickshank, *Henry VIII and the Invasion of France*, 32–3.
63 E101/62/16.
64 Cruickshank, *Henry VIII and the Invasion of France*, 53–4.
65 BL, Stowe MS 146, f. 40.

earl landed in Calais and led a force of English and Netherlandish soldiers on a *chevauchée* throughout northern France. The campaign was abandoned in early October as the campaigning season came to an end, and most modern historians have condemned the exercise as wasteful in both resources and human terms.[66] Nevertheless, it provided an opportunity for displaying military prowess by members of the Calais garrison and was celebrated as such. Aware of the imminent coming of open war, the garrison had already been involved in cross-border skirmishing with the French throughout the early summer.[67] Surrey and the English captains with him clearly expected and wanted to engage the French in open battle, but they were to be disappointed. Frustrated by a perceived lack of imperial co-operation, Surrey decided to raid the Boullonais in early September.[68] It is clear that many captains and soldiers of the garrison accompanied the earl. Two of his leading captains were the treasurer of Calais, Sir William Sandes, and the marshall, Sir Edward Guildford, while Sir Richard Wingfield, a former deputy, was also present. Earlier, in June, Guildford had left Calais with twelve hundred men and challenged the captain of Boulogne to a duel, which was refused causing the marshall to set fire to the town instead. On 25 July Guildford and Sandes again marched out of the Pale with fourteen hundred men to offer the French battle. After Surrey had returned to Calais on 16 October, members of the garrison continued to take the fight to the French. Sandes, Sir Maurice Berekeley, the lieutenant of Calais castle, and Sir William Fitzwilliam, appointed to command at Guînes the following year, and three thousand men assaulted the French castle of Marguyson, razing it to the ground and carrying off many prisoners and livestock.[69] The following year saw a more ambitious expedition, an army of some eleven thousand commanded by Charles Brandon, duke of Suffolk, designed to march on Calais. Once again men of the Calais garrison were prominent and its captains included Sandes, Sir Richard and Robert Wingfield, Sir John Wallop (who would succeed Guildford as marshall the next year), Lord Leonard Grey, Thomas Palmer and Robert Seymour. The administration of Calais also played a vital role in organising Suffolk's army. In all 1,669 of the English force were drawn from the soldiers then in the Calais Pale. Although the expedition eventually petered out, the soldiers returning to Calais in miserable condition in November, the captains and men of the garrison again proved themselves capable soldiers.[70]

It was the years 1540–6 that witnessed the most intensive military activity in the Pale and by its garrison. From 1540, amid fears of a French attack, the garrisons of the Pale were increased massively and in 1544 Henry VIII once again crossed the Channel to wage war against France in concert with his Imperial allies. The performance of English soldiers in this period was mixed to say the least. The point needs to be stressed, however, that, especially in the crucial

---

[66] J.J. Scarisbrick, *Henry VIII* (1969), 95, 125; Michael A.R. Graves, 'Thomas Howard, third duke of Norfolk (1473–1554)' in *Oxford DNB*.

[67] *LP* III ii, 2308, 2352.

[68] *LP* III ii, 2517, 2549.

[69] Hall, *Chronicle*, 641, 644–8.

[70] S.J. Gunn, 'The Duke of Suffolk's March on Paris in 1523', *EHR*, ci (1986), 596–634.

years between 1544 and 1546, it is difficult to distinguish the activities of the regular garrison from the hundreds, and at times thousands, of foreign mercenaries and county levies then serving in the Pale. The sheer scale of Henry VIII's invasion of France in 1544 meant that the Calais garrison played a much reduced role to the one it had done in 1513.[71] In 1545 warfare moved inside the boundaries of the Pale itself. In September the French launched an assault, with twenty thousand men led by Oudart de Biez, governor of Montreuil, on the Low Country with the aim of surprising Guînes, destroying supplies in the Pale and preventing reinforcements from Calais reaching Boulogne.[72] The deputy of Calais, Lord Cobham, offered battle near Oye on 21 September. The action, involving eight thousand English soldiers – many, according to to the Welsh soldier-chronicler, Ellis Gruffudd, merely 'callow boys' – and as many foreign mercenaries ranged against a larger French force, was a display of remarkable military incompetence. Gruffudd relates how the foreign mercenary cavalry quickly deserted; how the French were too slow to take advantage of the poor tactics employed by Cobham that had left Calais and Guisnes unguarded; and how the officers of the Calais council were too timid to mount an effective counter-attack. The deputy and his council, it was claimed, had cowered inside the town of Calais and disaster was averted only by the timidity of the French. Furthermore, Cobham had only saved his own neck by procuring letters to be sent to the king persuading him that only 'a hundred Englishmen had been killed as against more than two hundred French'. Significantly, Gruffudd did not directly criticize the ordinary men of the garrison; this was backed up by Richard Blount, master of the ordnance, who complained to Sir William Paget that 'some of our captains do not attend upon their charge but remain nightly in the town, leaving the poor men [that is, the farmers of the Low Country] like sheep without a shepard'.[73] The French, however, proved just as ineffectual as the English and the campaign came to nothing. On 7 June 1546, at Camp between Guînes and Ardres, French and English delegates signed a treaty ending the war between the two exhausted combatants.

The renewal of war between England and France in 1549 saw little military activity in the Pale itself. Fighting came to an end in the following year by the treaty of Boulogne in March, the English agreeing to sell back the town which had been captured in 1544. While the period 1550–7 saw growing rumours of a French attack on the Pale and increased tension along the borders, there was very little actual fighting in which the garrison was involved. Cross-border incidents continued but there were few, if any, notable feats of arms performed in these years.[74] Indeed, the French attack on the Pale at new year 1558 marked the end of a decade of uncommon quiet among the Calais garrison.[75]

---

71 Fissel, *English Warfare*, 13–18; Grummitt, 'Court, War and Noble Power', 151–3.
72 The best account of this little-known campaign is in Gilbert John Millar, *Tudor Mercenaries and Auxiliaries, 1485–1547* (Charlottesville, VA, 1980), 151–8.
73 Ellis Gruffudd, 'Boulogne and Calais from 1545 to 1550', ed. M.B. Davies, *Fouad I University Bulletin of Faculty of Arts*, xii (1950), 29–36; *LP* XX ii, 787.
74 See Morgan, 'Government of Calais', 243–54 for the rumours and French plots of this period.
75 See below, ch. eight.

* * *

This book begins with the Burgundian siege of 1436. It introduces many of the themes recurrent throughout the book: the organisation and weaponry of the garrison and the centrality of war to the formation of the English polity. Most importantly, it illustrates the garrison at war at the beginning of our period and allows us to measure English military capability against that of its western European rivals. Chapter three looks at the organisation of the Calais garrison. How many men served in Calais at any one time? Did its size and composition change over time and was this related to military developments or merely financial and political constraints? The fourth chapter addresses the questions of who served in the Calais garrison. Who were its leaders and did they constitute the military elite of late medieval and early Tudor England? What sort of men served as the rank and file? How was the garrison recruited and how were reinforcements mobilised in time of emergency? Did this change over time, reflecting the changing distribution of military resources and obligations? The fifth chapter examines the motivations of those who served in Calais – notions of individual and princely honour, the role of chivalry and questions of professionalism and pecuniary interest are all examined in an attempt to determine what led men to adopt the military life. The sixth chapter looks at the weaponry and equipment of the garrison. In terms of its weaponry and the fortifications built in the Pale, does the defence of Calais challenge the notion that England somehow stood on the fringes of European developments in military technology? The seventh chapter examines the perennial problems of financing the garrison and logistics. How was the garrison supplied and maintained? The final chapter examines the fall of Calais in 1558 in the context of the alleged military decline of mid-Tudor England. Was the town's fall merely the product of bad luck and a rare display of French military prowess? This chapter also examines the English reaction to defeat: what does the fall of Calais reveal about the role of war and military service in the mid-Tudor polity?

2

The Burgundian Siege of 1436

With the probable exception of the battle of Agincourt, no English military action of the fifteenth century attracted so much contemporary comment as the siege of Calais by Philip the Good, duke of Burgundy, in the summer of 1436. At a time when Henry V's conquest of Normandy and the heady days of the treaty of Troyes were fast becoming a distant memory, the siege saw a national response unprecedented during the latter years of the Hundred Years War. Its aftermath witnessed the composition of a stream of popular and elite verse, the recording of the events by chroniclers and the appropriation of the siege and its significance by various groups within the English polity. The Burgundian siege of 1436 was an event of central significance to the military history of England in the later Middle Ages for a number of reasons. First, it reveals much about the practice of war: the mobilisation of the political community in a national war effort; the logistics of organising an expeditionary force at short notice; and the effectiveness of English armies on the continent. Second, it shows just how important Calais had become to the English, not only as a centre of trade, but also as a symbol of Edward III's conquests and of English military prowess in general. Finally, the response to the defeat of the Burgundians tells us much about the central role that war and military service played in the formation of national identity, the development of personal and political reputations, and the way in which war, like nothing else, captured the popular imagination at the end of the Middle Ages.

The siege of Calais in July 1436

On 6 September 1435, on the realisation that Philip the Good, duke of Burgundy, was determined to conclude a separate truce with Charles VII, king of France, the English delegates stormed out of the Congress of Arras. Fifteen days later the Burgundian and French princes signed the Treaty of Arras. Since, and even before, the Treaty of Troyes the English position in France had been assisted by the actions and armies of the Burgundian duke. In the early 1420s they had fought on the same side: the Burgundians continuing their war against the Armagnac faction who had murdered Philip's father, John the Fearless, in 1419, while the English sought to impose the terms of Troyes on the followers of the dauphin, Charles. In 1423 this partnership had resulted in the capture of the castles of Le Crotoy and Landrecies and victory at the battle of Cravant. In reality Anglo-Burgundian relations had been deteriorating steadily since Philip had concluded a general truce with Charles in December 1431, a situation further worsened by the marriage of the English king's uncle, John, duke of Bedford, to Jacquetta of Luxembourg in 1432. Now the English faced, at best, the withdrawal of a vital ally in the Hundred Years War and, at worst, a new enemy and a second front.[1] The situation was made even worse by the death, on 14 September 1435, of Bedford, regent of France and captain of Calais.

At the beginning of 1436 the military situation looked bleak for the English. In the autumn of the previous year the French had renewed their offensive in Normandy and in December Dieppe was captured in a surprise raid. This combined with a peasant revolt in the Pays de Caux and in January 1436 Harfleur, an important symbol of Henry V's conquests, fell. On 3 December 1435 Henry VI's council had informed the Norman estates of plans to send reinforcements to the duchy under the duke of York and the earls of Suffolk, Salisbury and Mortain. Nevertheless, more French successes followed in the early months of 1436 and not only in Normandy: on 17 April the English garrison in Paris, under Lord Willoughby, surrendered.[2] Furthermore, in January 1436 Duke Philip also began to consider offensive action against the English. In Ghent on 8 March he addressed the Four Members of Flanders regarding his intent to invest Calais and the marches. Ghent agreed to serve on the expedition with fifteen thousand men, with the other Members contributing a further fifteen thousand between them. With contributions from the other provinces of the Low Countries, Philip hoped to raise an army sixty thousand strong. In return the Flemings asked for concessions from the duke concerning local offices and fiscal policy and a ban on Englishmen selling cloth there, as well as a promise of the staplers' wool when Calais fell. Unfortunately for Duke Philip, the meeting was attended by an English spy and by 26 March letters asking for assistance in withstanding the proposed Burgundian siege (with a full report of the meeting in Ghent attached) had been dispatched throughout England.[3]

In fact military preparations were already well advanced by the time that news of Duke Philip's intentions arrived in England. Henry VI, still in his royal minority, attended his first council meeting on 1 October 1435 to appoint the experienced soldier Richard Wydeville as lieutenant of Calais. Indentures were also sealed with captains for men to be retained for two months 'upon the safeguard of our castle and town of Calais', expecting them to be ready to sail from Dover with their retinues six days later. The parliament which assembled at Westminster on the 10th of that month met principally to discuss military preparations against Burgundy and France.[4] On 29 October the indenture appointing

---

[1] For the congress of Arras see Joyceline Gledhill Dickinson, *The Congress of Arras, 1435: A Study in Medieval Diplomacy* (Oxford, 1955). For Philip's military role in the early 1420s see Richard Vaughan, *Philip the Bold: The Formation of the Burgundian State* (1962), 6–12. For the truce of 1431 and Bedford's marriage see R.A. Griffiths, *The Reign of Henry VI* (1981), 000–00.

[2] Michael K. Jones, 'The Beaufort Family and the War in France, 1421–1450' (PhD thesis, University of Bristol, 1982), 88–9.

[3] Vaughan, *Philip the Good*, 75–80; James A. Doig, 'A New Source for the Siege of Calais in 1436', *EHR*, cx (1995), 410–12.

[4] C81/1545/55; E404/52/11, 15, 17–20, 23–5, 28, 32–4; E101/71/3/883–90; *DKR*, xlviii. 306; B.P. Wolffe, *Henry VI* (1981), 80–1.

Humphrey, duke of Gloucester, as Bedford's successor as captain of Calais was read before the assembled lords. The indenture, like Bedford's two years previously, gave him command at the castles of Hammes, Ballingham, Marke, Oye, Sandegate and Rysbank Tower as well as Calais itself and the important fortress at Guînes. After discussion among the lords, it was agreed that Gloucester's tenure of these commands was to be reduced from twelve to nine years and the town's garrison was made the crown's financial priority. Concessions were also granted to the merchants of the staple in order to ensure their financial support if necessary. Moreover, the lords in parliament all agreed to serve at their own costs for six weeks if Calais were threatened. Gloucester's appointment to Calais was, in one sense, a personal victory. He had consistently argued, against Bedford, that the defence of Calais should be given priority over France and Normandy. On 1 November Gloucester's appointment was confirmed under the great seal and he was also named as the king's lieutenant in Artois, Flanders and Picardy.[5] In December members of the king's household, under Sir John Steward, were also despatched to bolster the Pale's defences, while obligations for a thousand marks were delivered to the treasurer of Calais, Richard Buckland, to pay those members of the garrison owed wages for Bedford's tenure as captain.[6]

As well as plans for the defence of Calais, preparations were also under way for the armies under York, Salisbury and Mortain bound for Normandy and France. On 20 February 1436 York indented to serve with nearly 2,700 men, while Salisbury agreed to serve with 1,300 men. These two armies alone would have probably satisfied the demands of the Norman estates that the English response be led by a great lord of the royal blood with a military reputation. The army led by Edmund Beaufort, earl of Mortain,[7] was retained for two years and originally destined for Anjou and Maine. It consisted of four hundred

---

5   E101/71/3/877, 879, 891; *PROME*, xi. 168–71; Griffiths, *Henry VI*, 194–6, 201; G.L. Harriss, *Cardinal Beaufort: A Study of Lancastrian Ascendancy and Decline* (Oxford, 1988), 253–5, 259; Rymer, x. 624. Gloucester was also to hold the captaincy of Guînes from 14 July 1436. Besides the regular garrison comprised in his indenture for the captaincy of Calais, Gloucester also agreed to serve with a crew of four mounted men-at-arms, 206 men-at-arms on foot and ninety-nine archers for a quarter of a year. In February 1436 the exchequer was ordered to allow the wages of these soldiers in the treasurer's account, by which time they had presumably returned to England. It appears that they were discharged before the Burgundian siege commenced: E159/212, *brevia directa baronibus*, Hilary 14 Hen VI, rot. 32d.

6   E403/721, mm. 9, 10; E404/52/187, 189.

7   Edmund Beaufort was the fourth son of John Beaufort, marquess of Somerset (d. 1410). His elder brother, John (d. 1444) inherited the comital, later ducal, title and was captured at the battle of Baugé in 1421. After his release in 1438, he emerged as one of the leading English commanders in Normandy until his disgrace following the failure of the 1443 campaign: M.K. Jones, 'John Beaufort, Duke of Somerset, and the French Expedition of 1443', in *Patronage, the Crown and the Provinces*, ed. R.A. Griffiths (Stroud, 1981), 79–102. Edmund held no English estates in his own right, such lands as he held in England came by virtue of his marriage to Eleanor, youngest daughter of Richard Beauchamp, earl of Warwick, probably at the end of 1434. Edmund had been active in the French wars since 1427 and in the summer of that year Bedford granted him the comté of Mortain in recognition of his deeds during the campaign. Thereafter, Edmund was afforded the courtesy title 'earl of Mortain': Jones, 'The Beaufort Family', 62–3.

men-at-arms and 1,600 archers. Beaufort sealed his indenture about a month before the other commanders and recruitment was well under way by the time that news of Duke Philip's plans to besiege Calais arrived in England.[8] On 2 April 1436 the earl of Mortain's army was ordered to muster at Winchelsea and soon after Easter it crossed the Channel. Its destination, however, was not France but Calais. According to the fullest English chronicle account of the siege, it was diverted there at Gloucester's behest, but it seems likely that the decision was taken by the king's whole council. It also appears to have been a last-minute one: Richard Wydeville, the former lieutenant, was sent to Mortain on the coast with instructions from the council.[9] While the decision to divert his army to Calais may have initially angered Beaufort, who may have wished to extend his own holdings in Maine, it made perfect military sense and ensured that the ordinary garrison of the town and marches was swollen to more than twice its normal size. It would also, as we will see, provide an opportunity for the earl to emerge as the *de facto* defender of Calais.

Following receipt of the news of Philip the Good's plans to besiege Calais, the domestic response in England was swift and impressive. Immediately the council despatched a force of twenty men-at-arms and two hundred archers. With the receipts of the taxation granted in the 1435 Parliament not yet collected, its cost, a thousand marks, was met by a loan from Cardinal Beaufort.[10] On 26 March, just eighteen days after Philip had addressed the Flemings, a letter was sent out to towns, religious houses and probably prominent individuals. Rehearsing the Burgundian plans and stating how, by Gloucester's advice, the town and marches of Calais had been reinforced with 'suffissaunce of nombre of men and ... stuff of vitaile, artillarie and al manere of habilmentes of werre', the king requested 'as many personys defensable and abilid for the were' to be put on standby to sail to the relief of Calais and the number of such men to be certified to the sheriffs. Enclosed with the letter was a copy of the spy's report of the meeting of Duke Philip with the Four Members of Flanders.[11] At the same time as efforts were being made to rouse the realm's military potential, commissioners were sent out to raise loans. On 24 February commissioners had been appointed in twenty-six counties to induce the leading men there to lend a 'considerable sum', repayable from the parliamentary subsidy due at Whitsun the following year. These employed the familiar machinery of the commission *de mutuo faciendo*, with noble and gentry commissioners assembling their neighbours, highlighting the emergency of the situation and demanding money according to their means repayable from future parliamentary taxation.[12] Unlike many previous and subsequent occasions, however, this request for loans for the defence of Calais was met with 'concern and enthusiasm'. Between 17 April and

[8]   E404/52/196; Jones, 'The Beaufort Family', 89–92; Harriss, *Beaufort*, 256.
[9]   E403/723, m. 1.
[10] E404/52/222, 394.
[11] Doig, 'New Source', 410–12; Historical Manuscripts Commission, Various Collections, iv. 197.
[12] *CPR, 1429–36*, 528–30; E28/57; *POPC*, iv. 352; Hannes Kleineke, 'The Commission de Mutuo Faciendo in the Reign of Henry VI', *EHR* ci (2001), 1–30.

11 July sixty-three individual lenders lent over £4,000 and by the end of the exchequer's Easter term in 1436 more than £48,000 had been received at the exchequer. While Cardinal Beaufort, the feoffees of those parts of the duchy of Lancaster set aside for the performance of Henry V's will, and London and other cities provided a sizeable proportion, the majority was raised by individuals in response to specific requests for the defence of the town and marches.[13] Between March and July a steady stream of proclamations and privy seal letters were issued in response to the Burgundian threat. In March the crown appealed for towns, religious houses and individuals to certify the number of armed men they could supply, although the final request for men was not made until Duke Philip had finally assembled his own army to lay siege to Calais. On 16 and 30 June further letters appealed for soldiers and on 3 July writs were despatched to the sheriffs of seventeen counties to the effect that all those willing to serve in the relief of Calais under Gloucester were to muster at Sandwich by 22 July. The response was widespread and immediate: the city of Salisbury despatched twelve men, for example, while forty were assembled at Norwich. At Canterbury the contingent was led by one of the jurats and a special banner was prepared, bearing the city's arms, to lead them into battle. Contingents were also forthcoming from the London livery companies (who also sent guns and other supplies) and various religious houses.[14]

Duke Philip's preparations, on the other hand, were beset with problems. Since plans were only finalised in March, the Burgundians had a very short space of time to assemble their army and all the necessary ordnance and supplies to conduct a siege. More than four hundred ships were assembled from Sluys, Beirvliet and Ardres, and Rotterdam, 'stuffed with the moste strange ordinaunce and other abillemens of were that evere ony man herd telle of', while carpenters, masons and waggoners were impressed from throughout the Low Countries. Most importantly, the duke assembled his largest artillery train to date. However, unlike the English, whose royally owned gunpowder weaponry was concentrated in Calais and at the Tower of London, Duke Philip was forced to rely on the private arsenals of the towns and his subjects in the counties of Flanders, Holland, Picardy and Artois. In all Philip's artillery train contained some 240 large guns, including seventeen bombards, and its size was commented upon by all contemporary observers. By 9 May the army was assembled. Despite their difficulties, it was an impressive force and ostensibly one to be contrasted, with characteristic hyperbole on the part of the English spy, to the force at Calais 'whiche is right feble arrayed and ordeyned'.[15] The logistical problems in

13 Harriss, *Beaufort*, 257–60; James A. Doig, 'Propaganda, Public Opinion and the Siege of Calais in 1436', in *Crown, Government and People in the Fifteenth Century*, ed. Rowena Archer (Stroud, 1995), 93–4.

14 Doig, 'A New Source', 412–13; Doig, 'Propaganda', 94–6; Canterbury Cathedral Archives, Canterbury chamberlains' accounts, 1393–1445, CC/FA 1, f. 243v.

15 Robert Douglas Smith and Kelly de Vries, *The Artillery of the Dukes of Burgundy 1363–1477* (Woodbridge, 2006), 110–12; Monique Sommé, 'L'Armée bourguignonne au siége de Calais de 1436', in *Guerre et société en France, en Angleterre et en Bourgogne XIVe–Xve siècle*, ed. P. Contamine et al. (Lille, 1991), 203; Doig, 'A New Source', 412.

assembling an army from the disparate parts of his realm were not the only ones facing Duke Philip. Edmund Beaufort, earl of Mortain, had crossed the Channel with his army soon after Easter, in early April 1436. By the end of the month news had reached Philip, as well as the towns of Ghent and Bruges, that Beaufort's army was in the field and carrying the war to the Burgundians. It first attacked Boulogne, burning the town's suburbs and shipping in the harbour. A second *chevauchée* into west Flanders burnt and plundered as far as Loos, stealing many head of cattle and defeating a Flemish attempt to intercept them. Henry VI was allegedly so delighted when he heard the news of Beaufort's exploits that he immediately despatched the Garter to him in Calais. A third raid, under the command of Beaufort's lieutenants, Roger, Lord Camoys and Sir Ralph Ashton, reached Ardres. On its return, however, it was surprised by Picard soldiers and only Camoys's bravery averted a rout. Nevertheless, Beaufort's pre-emptive strikes raised morale in Calais and undoubtedly disquieted the Burgundians. The coastal towns of Flanders, many denuded of their artillery to equip the princely siege train, appealed to Duke Philip for assistance and on 28 May a special force was raised to prevent further raids.[16]

By the end of June the Burgundian army stood on the borders of the Calais Pale. On the 30th of that month privy seal letters ordered those who had promised men for the relief of the town to assemble at Canterbury no later than the following 22 July. However, before they could be despatched news arrived of the capture of the outlying fortress at Oye two days previously. The postscript to the royal letter revealed the urgency of the situation: 'after the writyng of thees oure lettres come to us tydynges that the seid callyng himself duc [of Burgundy] hathe take oure fortalice of Oye and slayn al oure soudeours therynne'.[17] It continued that Philip planned to be outside the gates of Calais on 2 July.

Indeed, the outlying castles of the Pale had fallen quickly. At Oye a Burgundian herald had required Nicholas Horton, the captain, to surrender the castle. According to one account, the Flemings managed to exploit an open gate, surprising the garrison while they were considering their response. The earl of Mortain, now ad hoc commander of the defence of town and marches, suspected treason at Oye. William Bulleyn, the cousin of the castle's constable, was released from captivity without the payment of his ransom and, once he had returned to Calais, Mortain ordered him to be executed for allegedly spying for the enemy.[18] Mortain also ordered the castle at Marke to be reinforced and victuals and arms were sent to it from England. Its garrison repulsed numerous

---

[16] *The Brut*, ii. 575–6; Monstrelet, v. 231–8; Jones, 'Beaufort Family', 93–4.

[17] Doig, 'A New Source', 413–14.

[18] Monstrelet, v. 241–3; *The Brut*, ii. 576–7. Apparently 'much mone was made' in Calais on the death of Bulleyn 'for he was a gud Archer'. The castle at Oye may not have proved much of an obstacle to Philip. Its peacetime garrison was only four men-at-arms and twenty archers, although it had been increased to sixty or so by the time of the siege (fifty-six of whom were captured and hanged by the Flemings). It also appears to have been ill-stocked with weaponry. When the treasurer of Calais asked for allowance for ordnance and other equipment lost during the Burgundian attack, he only claimed for six longbows and an iron gun called a 'fowler' at Oye. Similarly, he only claimed for fourteen bows and a 'fowler' at Sandgate: E159/214, *brevia directa baronibus*, Trinity rot. 9; E101/71/3/891.

assaults by Flemish forces beginning on 2 July before coming to terms six days later. At Ballingham Richard Buckland's lieutenant, William Sellyng, surrendered the castle to the Picards 'shamefully, without eny stroke'. The defenders retreated to Guînes where Sellyng was immediately imprisoned. At Sandegate the lieutenant, Sir Thomas Knevet, hesitated before the Picard host and, 'by þe counsaile of one Sir Thomas Heneley, Preest, A traitour', surrendered the castle 'shamefully and cowardly'. The Picards then moved on to Guînes, where the English abandoned the town and retreated to the castle. By 9 July, a week later than planned, Philip's army stood outside the gates of Calais.[19]

Despite his quick victories at the small fortresses of Marke, Oye, Ballingham and Sandegate, the town of Calais itself would prove a much tougher proposition for Philip. The beginning of 1436 had seen a concerted effort to improve the town's defences. The financial administration was taken out of the hands of the corrupt and unpopular treasurer, Richard Buckland, and placed in the hands of Robert Whittingham, a London draper. On 12 January he received almost £1,500 in cash from the exchequer with which to pay wages and buy victuals, although he was not officially appointed treasurer until 10 February. In February and March he received further cash to ship reinforcements from England, while on 5 March more regular provision from the wool subsidy was earmarked for the garrison's wages. Eleven days later the council ordered the provision of twenty-eight new guns, crossbows 'of divers sortes', five hundred bows, five hundred gunstones, four hundred pavises, gunpowder and six ships 'full of tymbre for diuerses Abilmentez'. By the middle of March the experienced captain, Sir John Radcliffe, was installed as Gloucester's lieutenant in the town. With the mayor of Calais and lieutenant of the staple, Radcliffe oversaw the building of a wide ditch on the south side of the town and three earthen bulwarks. He also completed the brick bulwark at the Milkgate begun by Wydeville. Moreover, in April William Gloucester, master of the king's ordnance in Normandy, was ordered to make his way from Honfleur to join the earl of Mortain at Calais. In May a further £2,240, initially bound for Normandy, was diverted to Calais.[20] On 30 June Gloucester secured the appointment of his servant, the London mercer and merchant of the staple, William Cantelowe, to the office of victualler of Calais. Cantelowe was able to use his contacts within the merchant community to ensure a swift increase in the amount of victuals, ordnance and other weaponry, and building material sent to Calais.[21] If Calais's defences did not present enough of an obstacle to the attackers, the Burgundian naval blockade

---

[19] E28/58, 15 Nov.; *The Brut*, ii. 577–9; Monstrelet, v. 243, 257–8; Waurin, v. 163–70; M. Thielmans, *Bourgogne et Angleterre: Relations politiques et économiques entre les Pays-Bas Bourguignons et l'Angleterre, 1435–1467* (Brussels, 1966), 94–5.

[20] *DKR*, xlviii. 309–11; E403/721, m. 17; E404/52/194, 205, 215, 219, 225, 227, 347, 352, 356, 372, 383; *The Brut*, ii. 573; Griffiths, *Henry VI*, 202. For Radcliffe's career see below, p. 67.

[21] E101/192/10; E404/39/354; 52/373–4, 380–1; E403/669, m. 17. It is impossible to determine the precise amount of supplies received by Cantelowe and his predecessors in the weeks leading up to and during the siege as no particulars of account surive. Cantelowe's audited account merely lists the supplies received during the accounting period, from 30 June 1436 until 28 Nov. 1439.

was also a complete failure. The fleet was delayed by contrary winds and did not arrive outside the harbour until 25 July. It made some desultory attempts to block the harbour by sinking six ships laden with stone, doubtless harried by the defenders of Rysbank Tower which guarded its entrance. However, the obstacles were removed at low tide by the inhabitants of the town (who later presented the salvaged stone to St Mary's church in Calais) and the fleet sailed away just two days later. The Burgundian soldier and chronicler, Jean de Waurin, who was present at the siege, considered the failure to enforce the naval blockade the principal reason for Philip's failure.[22]

By land as well, the Burgundian siege did not proceed as the duke had planned. The defenders opened the sluices at Newenham Bridge and Oye and inundated the surrounding countryside. Moreover, they were able to keep the gates open and every day led their cattle to graze in the pastures just outside the town. In one attack mounted to capture the defenders' cattle the Flemings lost twenty-two men killed and thirty-two captured. Indeed, the English defence was an aggressive one: they sallied out of the town 'très souvent dehors, de pied et de cheval', constantly disrupting the Burgundian efforts to construct field fortifications. Monstrelet and Waurin also both draw attention to the squabbles and tensions between the Picards and the Flemings and within the Flemish contingent itself. While this partly reflects the chroniclers' own bias, it also reveals some of the problems inherent in the Burgundian state's war machine.[23] Neither, it seems, did Philip's much-vaunted artillery train have much effect. The Ghentenaars erected a bulwark on a hill overlooking the east side of the town and from there 'many tymes þai shot al ouer þe toun; but al þeire gunshot neuer did harm'. The failure of the Burgundian artillery was not, as the townsmen thought, due to the intervention of the patron saint of gunners, St Barbara, but rather to the effectiveness of the English counter-gunnery which clearly unsettled the besiegers. Philip had even been forced to move his camp from the west end of the town when the English artillery sent a shot through his own tent.[24] On 26 July the Brugeois contingent moved against the Boulogne Gate. The defenders sent out some footmen to skirmish with them, while a larger force of men-at-arms lay concealed in the bulwark there under the command of Lord Camoys. The men-at-arms ambushed the Brugeois, forcing them to flee. Their retreat was met by jeers from the Ghentenaars and resulted in 'a great debate amonges hem' as the Burgundian host descended into inter-city rivalry.[25] Two days later, however, it was the turn of the Ghentenaars to feel the force of English arms. A wooden artillery tower had been constructed at the west end of

---

[22] Vaughan, *Philip the Good*, 77–9; *The Brut*, ii. 579; Monstrelet, v. 254; Waurin, v. 170–1, 176–7, 193. According to *The Brut* the Flemish and Dutch ships abandoned the blocakde upon news that the earl of Devon had set sail with a fleet from the western ports of England: *The Brut*, ii. 469.

[23] Monstrelet, v. 244–9; Waurin, v. 166–7, 172; *The Brut*, ii. 579; *Historical Poems of the XIVth and XVth Centuries*, ed. R.H. Robbins (New York, 1959), 80.

[24] *The Brut*, ii. 578; *Historical Poems*, 81.

[25] *The Brut*, ii. 580. Monstrelet and Waurin both appear not to recognise the subtlety of the rivalries within the Flemish camp: Monstrelet, v. 252–6; Waurin, v. 175–81.

the town and had resisted several earlier attempts to take it. On the morning of
the 28th the defenders, probably led by Sir John Radcliffe, assaulted the tower
again. It was guarded by three or four hundred Flemings and it appears that
Duke Philip himself was present. On this occasion, their commitment to the
siege waning after the failure to blockade the harbour, the Brugeois put up little
resistance. Eighty Flemings were killed and the majority of the rest captured.
According to one source, a captured Fleming 'seyde that the duke of Burgoyn
was nought thre men from hym in the same bastill that tyme that he was taken'.
All sources agree, however, that the majority of the Flemish prisoners were put
to death on the orders of the earl of Mortain because an English man-at-arms,
taken prisoner by the Flemings earlier, had been killed.[26] The fall of the tower
broke the spirit of the Burgundian besiegers. That night the advance force of
Gloucester's relief army, led by Lionel, Lord Welles, arrived in Calais. Their
arrival was greeted with so much noise that the Ghentenaars believed it to be
Gloucester himself and abandoned their positions on the east side of the town. In
the morning of Sunday, 29 July the Brugeois contingent, upon seeing that the
Ghentenaars had left, did likewise. The defenders wanted to give chase to the
fleeing Flemings, but Lord Welles produced the king's letters of privy seal that
none were to move beyond gunshot of the town until Gloucester's arrival: 'And
ne had þat ben, there had ben gret good geton þat tyme'.[27]

While Mortain and the defenders of Calais were breaking the siege, the
English relief army was assembling under the duke of Gloucester. The king's
letter of 30 June had ordered those in receipt of royal fees and others who had
promised men back in March to assemble at Canterbury on 22 July; on news of
the fall of Oye they were ordered to make their way directly to Sandwich for
embarkation on the same day.[28] The assembling of the relief army under Gloucester had, in fact, progressed slowly. Clearly Duke Philip's intentions were
known by the middle of March at the latest and the Burgundian army was
assembled by 9 June. The letter sent to the abbot of Bury St Edmunds a week
later had asked him to 'to redy as many men as ye may goodly sende us to the
helpe and socoure of the saide rescuese', certifying the crown of the number of
soldiers he could send, exactly what had been asked at the end of March.

---

26 *The Brut*, ii. 580; Monstrelet, v. 252–4; Waurin, v. 180–1; Doig, 'A New Source', 415–16;
A Chronicle of London from 1089 to 1483, ed. Edward Tyrell and N.H. Nicolas (1827), 120–1.
Different sources give different dates for the assault on the tower. 'Gregory's Chronicle' is
certainly too early in ascribing the action to 12 July. Monstrelet and Waurin give 27 July,
while the account contained in a version of *The Brut* and 'John Benet's Chronicle' give 28
July. Similarly, the English sources differ in giving credit for the victory. The main version of
The Brut and 'Gregory's Chronicle' credit Mortain and Camoys with the assault on the tower,
while *An English Chronicle* and the Bury St Edmunds abbey account both assign the victory
to Radcliffe: *The Brut*, ii. 469; 'John Benet's Chronicle', ed. G.L. and M.A. Harriss, *Camden
Miscellany* XXIV (CS, 4th series, ix, 1972), 185; *The Historical Collections of a Citizen of
London in the Fifteenth Century*, ed. James Gairdner (CS, new series, xvii, 1876), 178–9; *An
English Chronicle 1377–1461*, ed. William Marx (Woodbridge, 2003), 60.
27 *The Brut*, ii. 581. For the recriminations on the Burgundian side following the Flemings'
retreat see Vaughan, *Philip the Good*, 79–82.
28 Doig, 'A New Source', 413–14; SC1/58/47; E28/57/7, 43–4.

Perhaps, with the English military priority still Normandy, the council had hoped that the earl of Mortain's raids into Flanders in April would have dissuaded Duke Philip from his enterprise against Calais. Gloucester and the king were in Canterbury by 21 July, but it was not until four days later that indentures were sealed with the captains of Gloucester's army. They agreed to serve for a month in what was one of the largest English armies assembled during the fifteenth century. Gloucester's own retinue was some five thousand strong and included the duke of Norfolk's contingent and those of the earls of Huntingdon and Ormond. The earls of Warwick, Stafford and Devon and lords Hungerford, Welles, Beaumont and Cromwell also agreed to serve, bringing the total number of men up to 7,765.[29] Part of the reason for the delay may have been financial. The relief army was an expensive proposition, costing £6,084 in wages alone, and with the exchequer's many other commitments there may simply not have been the cash to pay the soldiers' wages before this date.[30] Another, altogether more intriguing, reason is that there were political considerations at play. Gloucester, while the obvious choice to lead the army, may have faced opposition on the king's council from Cardinal Beaufort and the other councillors, notably Archbishop Kemp and Lord Cromwell. In the middle of June it seems that plans were afoot to place the young Henry VI at the head of the army: in the letter sent to the abbot of Bury St Edmunds on 16 June the king had written that 'we dispose us with goddis mercy to yeve rescours therto in oure persone'. This plan appears to have been abandoned almost immediately. Two days later proclamation was made in London that those intending to join the relief army should make their way to Sandwich and Dover. On this occasion command was to be assumed by the admiral of England, the earl of Huntingdon. By 30 June, as we have seen, Gloucester had been named as the army's commander. It seems unlikely that the duke was unwilling to lead the army himself, but he may have delayed his departure over fears about the governance of England with the impending end of the king's minority and there may have been opposition among the other councillors to his appointment with such wide powers. Indeed, as soon as the duke left Canterbury for Calais his arch rival Cardinal Beaufort set about establishing his own authority about the king.[31] Gloucester's possible fears for his own position are revealed by the king's instruction on 24 July to John Fray, chief baron of the exchequer, and two other exchequer judges to make their report to the keeper of the privy seal on certain

[29] E101/71/3/893–8; Wolffe, *Henry VI*, 81; Griffiths, *Henry VI*, 203–4.

[30] E403/723, mm. 13–14.

[31] *Calendar of Letter-Books Preserved among the Archives of the Corporation of London at the Guildhall: K, Henry VI*, ed. R.R. Sharpe (1911), 205–7; Doig, 'A New Source', 413; Griffiths, *Henry VI*, 44–5, 231–2; Harriss, *Beaufort*, 264–7, 273–5; John Watts, *Henry VI and the Politics of Kingship* (Cambridge, 1996), 129–31. Another alternative, of course, is that there was simply no money to pay the relief army. It was not until 23 July that it was agreed that Cardinal Beaufort should receive all the customs in Southampton (largely unaffected by Duke Philip's interruption of the staplers' wool exports) until he was satisfied of a loan of 9,000 marks. A loan of £6,000 from Beaufort was entered on the receipt roll on 17 July and the payments of wages to the commanders of the relief army entered on the issue roll the following day: Rymer, x. 649–50; E28/57/93; E401/747, m. 29; E403/723, m. 13.

'matters' concerning the duke which they had been ordered to investigate by the chancellor and treasurer of England. The keeper of the privy seal was then to issue a writ ordering the exchequer to do 'þat of right aught to be doon and suche also as by reson and conscience aught to be doon'. The exact circumstances of the investigation are unclear, but it is possible that Gloucester secured an indemnity from actions then in progress against him before agreeing to lead the army in person. The formal appointment of the duke as lieutenant-general of the army did not occur until 27 July, two days after indentures had been sealed with its captains, and, furthermore, the king's grant of the county of Flanders to Gloucester on 30 July may have been another part of the deal by which he agreed to sail to Calais.[32]

As we have seen, as events transpired the relief army was not necessary to break the siege of Calais. Gloucester arrived in Calais on 2 August, accompanied by the duke of Norfolk and the earls of Warwick, Stafford, Huntingdon, Oxford, Ormond and Devon. On hearing this news and that of the Flemish retreat, Jean le Croy abandoned the siege of Guînes.[33] Duke Philip, brooding over the disaster which had overtaken his army, learnt of Gloucester's arrival from his spies in the town on the following day. Four days after his arrival, cheated of the glory of relieving the siege, Duke Humphrey launched a *chevauchée* through Picardy and into Flanders, leaving the earl of Mortain in command at Calais. The villages of Poperinge and Belle were burnt during eleven days of raiding. Simultaneously the English fleet, presumably the ships that had transported the army from Sandwich, raided along the Flemish coast as far as the Zwin estuary and the island of Cadzand. On 24 August Gloucester returned to England.[34] The siege had ended in total victory for the English. Although the Burgundians had taken and subsequently destroyed the castles of Marke, Oye, Ballingham and Sandegate, the defences of both Guînes and Calais had proved sufficiently strong to withstand their assault. Large amounts of booty were captured from the retreating Burgundians. At Guînes the defenders captured 'a gret brasen gune of Dogeon' and two other iron bombards.[35] In return the treasurer of Calais claimed allowance for sixty bows, eighty sheaves of arrows, one hundred gunstones and three barrels of powder expended by the

---

32 E28/57/97; *DKR*, xlviii. 314; Rymer, V, i. 33–4. The process in the exchequer against Gloucester may have been related to enfeoffments he and his wife had made previously without royal licence for which he had been fined and received a royal pardon on 30 November 1435: *CPR, 1429–36*, 503–6; Griffiths, *Henry VI*, 44–5.

33 *The Brut*, ii. 581–2. Both Monstrelet (v. 257) and Waurin (v. 189) state that Philip ordered le Croy to abandon the siege of Guînes and join him at Gravelines.

34 Thielmans, *Bourgogne et Angleterre*, 100–4; Vaughan, *Philip the Good*, 82–4; Jones, 'Beaufort Family', 96; Griffiths, *Henry VI*, 204–5.

35 *The Brut*, ii. 582. The 'brasen gune' was almost certainly the copper alloy Dijon which was incorporated into the Calais arsenal where it remained until 1464 when it was employed by Edward IV to batter the Lancastrian stronghold at Bamburgh. It is probable that it was the same great bombard 'de Dijon' that first appeared in the Burgundian artillery inventories in 1414: David Grummitt, 'The Defence of Calais and the Development of Gunpowder Weaponry in England in the Late Fifteenth Century', *War in History*, vii (2000), 260; Smith and De Vries, *Artillery*, appendix one.

defenders.[36] All the chronicle sources agree that the Flemings left behind a large proportion of their artillery on 28–29 July. The precise amount is difficult to gauge, but on 20 January 1437 the treasurer of Calais delivered to the victualler twelve 'long guns of iron' and four iron fowlers, as well as the bombard *Dijon* taken from the Burgundians. Material, including gunstones, was also recovered from the ruins of the castles destroyed during the siege. The victualler also accounted for over a thousand gunstones of various sizes as well as other material captured from the Burgundian artillery train.[37] Contemporary and subsequent commentators on the siege from the Burgundian side blamed Philip's failure on the collapse of the attempted sea blockade and the rivalry between the Flemish contingents, and English historians have tended to follow their lead. Nevertheless, the siege had demonstrated the ability of the English, when pressed and united in a national war effort, to provide for the defence of Calais against a large and well-equipped foe. Moreover, in combat the English had proved more than a match for their Burgundian adversaries; their gunpowder weaponry was comparable and the fighting abilities of the Calais garrison proved beyond doubt.

War, political culture and national identity in Lancastrian England

The siege of Calais in 1436 illustrates many of the recurrent themes of this book. It serves to show how war tested and determined political relationships between the king and his subjects and within the wider political community. It also demonstrates the cultural and social significance of war. The siege of Calais provided the opportunity for political and military reputations to be made and developed; it also allowed Englishmen of all social groups to consider and assert their own identities, whether they be personal, local or national. The aftermath of the siege, in which a rhetorical battle was waged to identify Burgundian failures and contrast them with the heroic deeds of English individuals and communities, also proved significant in defining the political culture of Lancastrian England and particularly the reputation of Humphrey, duke of Gloucester.

The raising of the army to relieve the siege highlights above all the reciprocity that underpinned the relationship between the crown and its subjects in the late Middle Ages. For a national military effort on the scale of the one made in the early summer of 1436 the crown relied on the goodwill of its greatest subjects, the nobility and other lay and ecclesiastical landowners, and these in turn relied on their own tenants, servants and friends to fulfil their military obligations. The negotiations which lay behind Gloucester's appointments, first, as captain of Calais in November 1435 and, second, as lieutenant-general of the relief army in July the following year, have already been discussed. It was not so much the private resources that the duke could deploy in his public duty that

---

[36] E159/214, *brevia directa baronibus*, Trin. rot. 9. This probably does not include all the munitions used in the defence of Guînes as more may have been covered in the victualler's account, the particulars of which are no longer extant.
[37] E101/192/10.

were at stake here, but rather the political impact that his appointment would have. Nevertheless, in the opening session of the parliament of February 1437 it was the question of the payment of the garrison's wages that led Gloucester to enter once again into negotiations concerning his tenure as captain. Two parliamentary petitions later and amidst unrest among the garrison, Gloucester resigned his captaincy in January 1438.[38] The process of negotiation and the concept of 'good lordship' which was central to military service in fifteenth-century England permeated throughout political society. The abbot of Bury St Edmunds, for example, had put his company at the disposal of the earl of Stafford. On his return from Calais, on 30 August 1436, Stafford wrote to the abbot 'thankyng you entierly and youre towne ... of the grete tendernesse and right good hert you have schweyd un to the kynge owre soveraigne lorde and to me in sendyng an honest and convenable company of men'. They had acquitted themselves honourably and the earl ended by promising 'I on my partye in tyme to come schal be right gladde as feithfully as I can to doo for you, for your saide towne and for hem that may be to youre plesirs'.[39]

What perhaps made the process of negotiation less problematic for the raising of the relief army than for other military expeditions of the early and mid-fifteenth century is the way in which the situation was portrayed as one of national emergency. In a letter to the duke of Burgundy in September 1435, Hugh de Lannoy, governor of Holland, had written that 'the common people of England are so tired of war that they are more or less desperate' and blamed the government for not making peace at the Congress of Arras.[40] While many may have been indifferent to war waged to defend English lands in France, an attack on part of the English realm was something quite different. As James Doig has demonstrated, the propaganda campaign waged against the Burgundians in 1435 and 1436 had two prongs. First, it attacked Duke Philip's perfidy in reneging upon the oath he had taken to Henry V as king of France in 1420 and argued that Henry VI was now forced to defend his French crown against the rebellion of Duke Philip. Second, and more importantly, it concentrated support for the defence of Calais by underlining the town's very Englishness. The Burgundian threat to Calais was directed not against Henry's kingdom of France, but against England.[41] In February commissioners had been appointed to gather a loan for the defence of the town and marches. Their instructions were unusually detailed and highlighted the Englishness of Calais. They were to remember 'what a preciouse Jeuell the saide towne of Calais is to *this Reame*'. The economic importance of the town was highlighted. Moreover, they were to point out 'what

---

38 *PROME*, xi. 168–71, 204.
39 Doig, 'A New Source', 414–15.
40 Vaughan, *Philip the Good*, 104–5.
41 Doig, 'Propaganda', 89–93. For the Englishness of Calais and its constitutional position from 1360 as being held in full sovereignty as part of the realm of England, see David Grummitt, ' "One of the Mooste Pryncipall Treasours Belongyng to his Realme of Englande": Calais and the Crown, *c.* 1450–1558', in *The English Experience in France, c. 1450–1558: War, Diplomacy and Cultural Exchange*, ed. David Grummitt (Aldershot, 2002), 46–62.

a bolewark and defence it is to this lande and Inhabitauntes therof'. The efforts of Edward III in conquering the town were recalled and, if it were lost, it would be 'the greatist dishonor rebuke sclandre and shame that myght gader to *this Reame*'.[42]

This sense of patriotism, a jingoistic identification with a sense of Englishness defined primarily through martial prowess, was also apparent in the popular verses composed to celebrate the raising of the siege. In this they reflected the wider corpus of early fifteenth-century verse in which 'expressions of nationalistic feeling' were the most recurrent theme. War, particularly set-pieces like Agincourt or the siege of Rouen in 1419, provided the perfect occasion for poets to express more widely views on the nature of Englishness.[43] The siege of Calais similarly produced a number of popular, patriotic verses which enjoyed a wide circulation. The author of the account of the siege contained in Lambeth Palace MS 6 copied one such poem after his account of the siege with the note that 'Wherefore amonges Englisshmen were made many rymes of þe Flemmynges'.[44] The poem, known as 'Mockery of the Flemings', draws heavily from the chronicle account which immediately precedes it, but also employs jingoistic metaphors to contrast the cowardice of the Flemings with the virtues of the English. The Flemings' attempts to stop the earl of Mortain's raid in April are first lampooned and contrasted with the English who returned to Calais without losing a man:

> Remembres on þat wurship ye wann the first day,
> When the Erle of Mortain come passing with his pray
> Before youre toune of Grauenyng, wher ye, as men bold,
> Come rennyng on hym fersli, as lyons of Cotteswold …
> Ye laid vpon þenglisshmen so myghtily with your handes,
> Til of you iij. Hundrid lay strecthid on the sandes.[45]

This, of course, drew upon familiar images of foreigners, especially Flemings, as cowards, men who made their living through guile and dishonesty, but was given particular focus by the events of 1436. The poems' authors also drew specifically on the language of royal proclamations and other texts that had vilified the duke of Burgundy for making war on Henry VI. From the chancellor's opening address to the parliament of 1435 through the proclamations and royal letters of the spring and early summer of 1436, the perfidy of Duke Philip and his breaking of his oath were constantly stressed. The two poems known as 'In Despite of the Flemings' and 'Scorn of the Duke of Burgundy' mirror this official rhetoric and portray the English victory as a consequence of Philip's falseness. The latter concludes by asking the duke:

> What hast thou wonne with al thy bysinesse
> And alle thy tentys to Caleys caryed doun,

---

[42] *POPC*, iv. 352; E28/57 (my italics). The same language and sentiments were repeated in the appeal for men sent out in March: Doig, 'A New Source', 410–11.
[43] V.J. Scattergood, *Politics and Poetry in the Fifteenth Century* (1971), 41–4, 55–68.
[44] *The Brut*, ii. 582; *Historical Poems*, 83.
[45] *The Brut*, ii. 582; Doig, 'Propaganda', 98–9.

> Thyn ordynauncys, which cost gret rychesse,
> Bastyle, and cartys of fagot gret foysoun,
> Of thy gounnys the dredeful noyse and soun?
> Peyse al to-gedyr, with many anothyr sygne,
> Thy cowardly flyght, cokeney of a chaumpyon,
> Whyche darst not fyght, and canst so wel malygne.[46]

Appealing to a more popular audience, the poetry generated by the end of the siege provided an opportunity to celebrate English prowess in general and that of certain individuals in particular. This is most apparent in the text known as 'The Siege of Calais', which survives in two manuscripts. The first copy follows immediately from a version of 'Scorn of the Duke of Burgundy', while the second is written on a flyleaf of a manuscript containing poems by the fourteenth-century poet, Laurence Minot.[47] In this text the focus is not primarily the treachery of the duke of Burgundy or the cowardice of the Flemings, but the deeds of Englishmen present at the siege. The first individual to be introduced is the earl of Mortain. Assuming the traditional stance of a commander addressing his soldiers on the eve of battle, Mortain hosts a dinner, assembling the garrison, and talking to them with a familiarity reminiscent of Henry V at Agincourt:

> The Erle of Morteyne made a dyner
> And said, 'felowes, be of gode chere!
>   And nothing we haue we doute
> I trust to god to see that day,
> That for al thaire proude aray
>   Fful low that they shul lowte.'

Each of the other captains is then praised for his efforts in ensuring that the defences were well-appointed: Sir John Radcliffe, 'That loued worshipp and dred repref, / Kept full gode gouernance'; John, Lord Dudley, in command at Calais castle, 'Made full gode ordenance'; Lord Camoys guarded the Boulogne Gate, while Sir William Ashton and Sir Geffrey Warburton guarded the Milkgate and set the watch. All sections of Calais society are identified as playing a role in the town's defence, reflecting the sense of national involvement the siege appears to have engendered. The poet draws attention in turn to 'þe trew soudeours', 'the maire and burgeis', 'worthy merchantes', 'gode comon' and even

---

46 *The Brut*, ii. 601; Doig, 'Propaganda', 89–92, 99. It has been suggested that both of these poems were written by John Lydgate and were officially sponsored in an attempt to deflect attention away from the Flemings in general and towards Philip in particular: H.N. MacCraken, 'A New Poem by Lydgate', *Anglia*, xxxiii (1910), 283–6; Ralph Klinefelter, 'A Newly-Discovered Fifteenth-Century English Manuscript', *Modern Language Quarterly*, xiv (1953), 3–6.
47 English College Rome MS 1306 (printed in Ralph Klinefelter, ' "The Siege of Calais": A New Text', *Proceedings of the Modern Language Association of America*, lxvii (1952), 888–95 and *Historical Poems*, 78–83) and BL, Cotton Galba EIX (printed in *A Collection of Political Poems and Songs Relating to English History, from the Accession of Edward III to the Reign of Henry VIII*, ed. Thomas Wright (2 vols, Rolls Series, 1859–61), ii. 151–6). All references will be to the text in the Rome MS.

> The women, both yonge and olde,
> With stones stuffed euery scaffolde –
>   They spared no swete nor swynk;
> With boiled cauldrons, grete and smale,
> Yif thay wolde haue sawted the wall
>   Al hote to gif hem drynke.

The failure of the duke's artillery is noted, as are the efforts of the English archers, before the attack on the Brugeois 'At Saint Peters on the pleyn' is described. Here the success for this attack appears to be credited to the earl of Mortain, while the report contained in *The Brut* manuscript gives the victory to Lord Camoys. The failure of the naval blockade is noted ('Than began the dukes sorow, / His shippes whan he saw brent'), before the crucial attack on the artillery tower is described. Here the poet avoids identifying an individual, instead drawing attention to the efforts of the whole garrison in resisting the Burgundian attack:

> And soon after, within a while,
> Drawen dovn his bastyle,
>   With many an hardy man;
> His men of armes were leide to grovnde
> And som ascaped with dethes wounde;
>   But there were fewe taan.

This text, as well as the various chronicles and other accounts of the siege, also illustrate the central importance of war in the making of political reputations in the fifteenth century. 'The Siege of Calais' records the flight of Duke Philip and the men of Flanders from the walls of the town and explains it thus:

> Ffor thay had verray knowyng
> Of the duc of Gloucester commyng
>   Calais to rescowe;
> And because they bode not there,
> In flandres he sought hem fer and nere,
>   That thay may ever rewe.

In other words, it was the imminent arrival of Duke Humphrey, and the martial reputation he brought with him, that ultimately broke the Burgundian siege rather than the actions of the defenders, stalwart as they were. Other poems written in the immediate aftermath of the siege have the same rhetorical force. 'Mockery of the Flemings' remembers the earl of Mortain's raids in April 1436, contrasts the inherent 'reputacioun' of the English and their 'gentill blode of olde antiquite', and the bravery of the defenders of Calais with the cowardice of the Flemings, but still attributes the flight of the Ghentenaars 'for dred and for fere / Of the duyk of Gloucester – & yette was he not þer!'[48] Similarly, 'Scorn of the Duke of Burgundy', after recounting Duke Philip's treachery and the events leading up to the siege, noted:

---

48 *Historical Poems*, 85.

Phelippe, thrugh thy prudence and reule politik
    To let Calais of rescow and vitaille,
þou didest abolge shippes with walles of bryke;
    But whan thou knew thy purpos myght not availe,
    And duc humfray at Sandwich redy to saille
        To rescow Calais and doo his ligeance,
    Thou flygh away for drede of bataille:
    Neuer prince brak sege with gretter myschance.

The poem then moves from a celebration of the end of the siege to a contrast of
Gloucester and Burgundy's virtues:

Beholde duc humfray with knyghtly desire
    To meve thy courage the felde forto take;
He soght the in flandres with swerd and with fyre,
    Nyne daies brennyng, no pees did he make.
    Where art thou, Phelippe, whan wiltow þy swerd shake?
        Where is thy strong power and grete alliance?
    Thy land is distroied, and thou dar not awake.
        Thus endith thy purpos with sorow and myschance.[49]

The longest English prose account of the siege also stressed Gloucester's agency
and may have been circulated, along with the poetry, in an attempt to advance
the duke's political reputation. The account of the siege in Lambeth Palace MS 6
is remarkable for the congruency it shows with other prose accounts, principally
Monstrelet, and the various English verse accounts of the siege. It seems certain
that it was compiled shortly after the conclusion of the siege, perhaps from a
combination of oral reports and official newsletters.[50] Nevertheless, it consistently stresses Gloucester's importance in the political and military context of
the siege. The first item noted under Henry VI's fourteenth regnal year was not
the assembly of the parliament at Westminster in October 1435, but that
'Humfrey, Duke of Gloucester, Protectour and Deffendour of Englond, was
made Capteyn of Caleis'. Gloucester's lieutenant, Sir John Radcliffe, is credited
with improving the defences of the town (even ringing the alarm bell and
standing to the garrison 'for a sport, because it was Saint George day; And for
þat he wolde se howe saudioures wold bokkell and dresse hem to þeire
harneys'), and the duke himself with the decision to divert the earl of Mortain's
army to Calais:

And sone afterward, Edmond, Erle of Morteyn, and the Lord Camys, Sir
William of Asshton, knyghte, And Sir Geffrey Werburton, knyghte, shuld

---

49 Ibid., 86–9. 'Scorn' survives in the same English College, Rome MS, as a version of the
'Siege of Calais'. This is an important Lydgate anthology probably compiled in the late 1440s
or early 1450s. At the time of the siege of Calais Lydgate was writing The Fall of Princes at
the request of Duke Humphrey. Lydgate's involvement in the rhetorical campaign waged
against the duke of Burgundy is further alluded to by his reference to the siege in *The Debate
between the Horse, Goose and Sheep*: J. Lydgate, *Minor Poems*, ed. H.N. MacCracken
(EETS, extra series, cxcii, 2 vols, 1910–34), ii. 539; Douglas Gray, 'John Lydgate (*c.*
1370–1449/50?)' in *Oxford DNB*.
50 *The Brut*, ii. 571–82.

haue shippit att Wynchilsey to haue gon into Fraunce with the number of iij M[l] men of speres and Archers; but because there was so gret a noys of þe seege comynge to Caleis, þei were contirmaundit be þe Kyng and þe Duyke of Gloucestre to go thider, and strenghe þe toun till rescous myght be had.[51]

Once the siege had begun the author stresses the Burgundian fear of Gloucester's arrival and he recounts how a spy agrees to 'give hem warnyng of þe comyng of þe Duyk'. Similarly, as in the verse accounts, the Flemings at Calais and Picards at Guînes flee on the news that Gloucester 'wes commyng to rescowe' the town and marches. The version of the duke's role that the account conveys is confirmed by the manuscript's compiler when, after copying the verse known as 'Mockery of the Flemings', he notes that 'the Flemmynges were thus shamefully fled frome Caleis, & þe Picardis from Guisnes fledd, & gon þeire way, for drede and fere of þe commyng of the Duyk of Gloucestre'.[52]

There is evidence to suggest that Gloucester looked upon the campaign as an opportunity to enhance his own martial and political reputation and may have felt cheated by the earl of Mortain and the garrison's success in breaking the siege. Monstrelet reports how Gloucester despatched Pembroke herald to Calais to offer battle formally to Duke Philip. Philip consulted his council and agreed to his request.[53] When his advance force, under Lord Welles, finally arrived to find the Burgundians in retreat, orders were issued that no pursuit was to be made until the duke himself arrived. His raid into Flanders, then, might be seen as a means of venting his own and his soldiers' frustration at missing the siege itself. Duke Humphrey may also have been keen to avenge the events of 1425, when he had attempted to assert the rights of his wife, Countess Jacqueline of Hainault, in the Low Countries. The previous year Philip had prevented Gloucester's army bound for Holland (which had reverted to Jacqueline after the death of the childless John of Bavaria) from marching through Flanders. It crossed Artois from Calais under Burgundian escort and remained in Hainault. In March 1425 Philip crossed into the county and successfully besieged the English-held castle of Braine-le-Comte. Philip then challenged Gloucester to single combat. The challenge was accepted and a date set for 23 April. However, shortly before it was due to take place Gloucester returned to England – with one of Jacqueline's ladies-in-waiting, Eleanor Cobham, as his mistress – leaving his wife to Philip's mercies. In December an English army was defeated at Brouwershaven in Zealand, putting an end to Gloucester's adventures in the Low Countries.[54]

A rhetorical campaign to enhance the reputation of Duke Humphrey as the rescuer of Calais suited the duke's political purpose in the wake of the Burgundian siege. That Gloucester had not lifted the siege, particularly in the context of the negotiations and grants which seem to have been the preliminary to his accepting command of the relief army, weakened his position in the king's

---

[51] Ibid., ii. 574.
[52] Ibid., ii. 583–4.
[53] Monstrelet, v. 249–50; Waurin, iv. 173–4.
[54] Vaughan, *Philip the Good*, 34–44; Marc Boone, 'Jacqueline of Bavaria in September 1425: A Lonely Princess in Ghent?', *The Ricardian* 13 (2003), 75–85.

council and reduced his ability to press his preferred policy of giving fiscal and military priority to the defence of Calais over that of Normandy and the other English possessions in France. On 29 October 1436 the council discussed the need to reinforce Guînes with a crew of thirty mounted men-at-arms. Gloucester was asked to accept payment in the form of victuals recently purveyed for the royal household rather than money and accepted only 'undre this protestacion' that it should not form a precedent nor be prejudicial to any indentures he had made. As George Holmes has pointed out, this was done amidst Gloucester's failure to secure adequate funding for the garrison generally. In the year up to 10 February 1437 the treasurer had received only £4,989 18*s*. 6½*d*. from the exchequer to meet a wage bill amounting to £10,335 14*s*. 7¼*d*. for the regular garrison. Moreover, the ban on English wool exports entering the Low Countries meant that the staplers were unable to offer the credit that usually offset shortfalls in the payments coming from England.[55] In the parliament that assembled at Westminster on 21 January 1437 Gloucester made a theatrical attempt to impose his pro-Calais policies on the council by playing on popular enthusiasm for the recent defeat of the Burgundian siege. On 25 February he knelt before the king and claimed that 'qe pur ceo qe bon et due purveiance n'ad pas estee fait, ne unquore est fait, pur paiement fair as ditz souldeours de lour gages, mesmes les souldeours soy retrahent, et departent de jour en jour hors de les ville et marchez avauntditz'. Furthermore,

> Pur qoy l'avauntdit duk, humblement supplia au roi, qe tout ceo soit qe autrement qe bien aveigne as ditz ville et marches, qe Dieu defende; qe null defaute ne negligence soit mys ne rette au dit duk, ne a les souldeours avauntditz pur icell; qar il disoit, q'il est celluy persone qe tout ditz ad desirez, et tout ditz desirera tant come il vivra, l'onur et profit du roi, et la salvation de les ville et marches avauntditz; entaunt q'il serra tout temps prest pur emploier sa persone a viveret morir, pur la defense d'icelles; et supplia au roi, qe iceste sa supplication fuisse enactez, pur sa excuse envers le roi en temps avenir.[56]

The measures put in place by this parliament for the funding of Calais reveal Gloucester's political weakness at this time. It was agreed that 20*s*. of the 34*s*. 4*d*. paid by denizen merchants as customs on each sack of wool should be reserved for the payment of the garrison's wages, although in a second petition of 25 March Gloucester succeeded in securing an agreement that any shortfall in this amount should be made up by the treasurer of England from other sources.

One text in particular appears to point to the way in which Gloucester hoped to use the siege to make a claim to his greater political importance. Titus Livius Frulovisi's *Humfroidos*, a rather tortuous Latin poem of 1,140 hexameters, survives in a single copy in Biblioteca Colombina, Seville, MS 7.2.23. It was composed about 1437 and is a companion to the author's *Vita Henrici Quinti*, developing the portrait of Gloucester in that text and making explicit comparisons between the duke's demeanour in 1436 and his brother's before Agincourt.

55 E28/58/40; E364/72, rot. M; G.A. Holmes, 'The "Libel of English Policy" ', *EHR*, lxxvi (1961), 207–9.
56 *PROME*, xi. 204.

It is dedicated to Duke Humphrey and describes the Congress of Arras and Philip the Good's abandonment of the English cause. Roughly one half of it is dedicated to an elaborate account of Gloucester's role in the siege of Calais and his subsequent *chevauchée* into Flanders. While much of the text relies on familiar *topoi*, its account of the siege and subsequent raid reveal the author to have been well-informed. Although dedicated to Duke Humphrey, the poem is, as Alessandro Petrina has pointed out, addressed to the king and, while it may not have circulated widely in England, it was intended as a political statement. It claims that Philip the Good had deliberately avoided Gloucester's challenge to meet in battle and that when Gloucester arrived back in England he was met by Henry VI who declared: 'you most brave hero will now hold the heart of our house with great glory'. By its explicit analogies to Henry V, drawing attention to Gloucester's status as heir presumptive to the thrones of England and France, and by claiming that Gloucester was accompanied by an eagle 'high in the sky' during his raid into Flanders, Frulovisi signalled the duke's claim to be the true guardian of Henry V's wishes. As executor of his late brother's will, he had been entrusted with the defence of Henry VI's patrimony, particularly, in the context of 1436, against the perfidy of the duke of Burgundy. The campaign gave him the opportunity to establish his role as the king's principal councillor and Frulovisi celebrated this and made a rhetorical case for it. It almost certainly reflected Duke Humphrey's belief in his right to be *primus inter pares* among the king's councillors and probably reflected sentiments current in Gloucester's household and circle at that time.[57]

Gloucester certainly succeeded in establishing his popular reputation as the saviour of Calais. A political programme that favoured Calais and the defence of the Narrow Seas over Normandy and France and which advocated the continuing restrictive trading practices of the merchants of the staple was synonymous with Duke Humphrey and found its fullest expression in *The Libelle of Englyshe Polycye*, a poem written at some point between the autumn of 1436 and the early months of 1438. Its passages on the siege of Calais and Gloucester's part in it bear a marked resemblance to the other English accounts of the siege and, like them, it has been linked to Lydgate and the duke's circle. Its widespread circulation (evident by the eighteen extant manuscripts) is testimony to the popularity of the sentiments it expressed.[58] The same sentiments were also expressed in the preamble to the Commons' grant of a subsidy at the end of the parliament. According to the preamble the Commons, through their speaker William Burley, had towards the end of the parliament made

---

[57] Susanne Saygin, *Humphrey, Duke of Gloucester (1390–1447) and the Italian Humanists* (Leiden, 2002), 69–77; Alessandro Petrina, *Cultural Politics in Fifteenth-Century England: The Case of Humphrey, Duke of Gloucester* (Leiden, 2004), R. Weiss, 'Humphrey Duke of Gloucester and Tito Livio Frulovisi', in *Fritz Saxl 1890–1948, A Volume of Memorial Essays*, ed. D.J. Gordon (Oxford, 1957), 218–27. I am grateful to David Rundle for pointing out that the surviving copy of the poem was clearly intended for an Italian audience.

[58] *The Libelle of Englyshe Polycye*, ed. Sir George Warner (Oxford, 1926); Holmes, ' "Libel of English Policy" ', 211–16; Scattergood, *Politics and Poetry*, 90–5.

diversis commendationibus, tam de strenuitate et nobili gestu, per carissimum avunculum regis Humfridum ducem Gloucestrie, aliosque dominos temporales, anno ultimo preterito, in et pro rescussu ville Cales', ac resistentia ipsius se ducem Burgundie dicentis, inimici et rebellis ipsius domini regis, multipliciter exhibitis et illatis, eorum personis, bonis seu rebus minime parcentes.[59]

Despite the popular perception of Gloucester's importance in breaking the siege, the events of 1436 had, in fact, done nothing to strengthen his position in the king's council. This was evident in the council meeting in April 1437 where parliament's decision to exempt cloth exported by denizens from the payment of poundage, a tax frequently employed for the safeguard of the Narrow Seas, was discussed. Most councillors were probably against this and in May they issued a prohibition on denizen exports of cloth, making Italians and the merchants of the Hanse (both condemned by the author of *The Libelle*) the only legal exporters, although denizens could purchase licences. Gloucester had failed to secure the funds necessary to guard Calais and the Narrow Seas. He had been sidelined in the council and apparently remarked 'Som parlement hath be that the King hath no graunte'.[60] On 8 January 1438, amidst further discontent among the garrison, Gloucester resigned his command. Indeed, it seems the king and other councillors were clear to whom the credit for breaking the siege should go. On 28 August 1442 Edmund Beaufort was created earl of Dorset. His grant remembered his faithful service 'in the rescue of the town of Calais against attack by the self-styled duke of Burgundy and the rebels his partisans'.[61]

Nevertheless, the siege of Calais played an important role in the development of the later image of 'Good Duke Humphrey'. This is particularly evident in the London chronicles and those *Brut* continuations probably written in the third quarter of the fifteenth century. Elsewhere I have argued that, in their depiction of Cade's rebellion in 1450 and the events leading up to it, these chronicles present a broadly pro-Yorkist narrative in which Humphrey, duke of Gloucester is presented as a national and chivalric hero juxtaposed against the evil counsellors (including Edmund Beaufort, later duke of Somerset and lieutenant-general of Normandy when it fell in 1450) responsible for the civil discord of the 1450s.[62] In the London-based chronicles of the mid-fifteenth century credit for lifting the siege is almost universally given to Gloucester. Probably one of the earliest to be compiled, British Library, Cotton MS Julius B.1 recounts the action on 29 July that led to the flight of the Flemings and then notes

59 *PROME*, xi. 216. Burley, a man with close connections to Gloucester, had replaced Sir John Tyrell, one of the duke's longest standing servants, as speaker on 19 March 1437: J.S. Roskell, Linda Clark and Carole Rawcliffe (eds), *The House of Commons 1386–1421* (4 vols, Stroud, 1992), ii. 432–5.

60 *POPC*, v. 77–9; Holmes, ' "Libel of English Policy" ', 206–7.

61 *Calendar of Charter Rolls*, vi. 34; Jones, 'Beaufort Family', 96–7.

62 David Grummitt, 'Deconstructing Cade's Rebellion: Discourse and Politics in the Mid-Fifteenth Century', in *The Fifteenth Century* VI: *Identity and Insurgency in the Late Middle Ages*, ed. Linda Clark (Woodbridge, 2006), 107–22.

Gloucester's arrival on 2 August. In this text the earl of Mortain comes over to Calais as part of Duke Humphrey's relief army. The account ends with a description of Gloucester's raid into Flanders. This scribe's interest in Gloucester can be gauged by the fact the narrative from his arrival in Calais until his return to England comprises fourteen lines of the printed text, while that from the duke of Burgundy's arrival before Calais until the Flemings' retreat is just thirteen lines.[63] Gloucester's agency is even more explicit in the London chronicle contained in Lambeth MS 306, a commonplace book probably compiled in the early 1460s. In this text, although the author recognised that 'the peple of Calleys had broke the sege', the earl of Mortain is not mentioned and the narrative concentrates on the whereabouts and deeds of 'my Lord of Glowseter'. His raid into Flanders is described ('And ther he made dyverse knyghtis') and the account for Henry VI's fourteenth regnal year ends with the duke's triumphant return to England.[64] There are exceptions to this London tradition. One is 'Gregory's Chronicle' (British Library, Egerton MS 1995). This narrative, while confused in its chronology of the siege, recognises Mortain's role, giving an equal amount of space to the description of the attack on the Flemings' artillery tower as to Gloucester's August *chevauchée*.[65] Greater divergences from the pro-Gloucester narrative are apparent in Trinity College, Cambridge, MS 0.9.1. The author notes that Mortain was sent to Calais 'with a grete peple of men of armes and archers … in the defence of oure Kyng, and to destroye oure enemys'. The assembling of the relief army under Gloucester is noted, but it was Mortain and Lord Camoys that 'with a certeyn of theire peple, issued oute of Caleys, and brake the sege'. The comment that 'this was doon ere the Duke of Gloucestre come ouer þe see to Caleys with his Navye and people' hints at the contested nature of the narrative.[66]

The construction of a narrative that stressed Gloucester's agency in lifting the siege is most apparent in the pro-Yorkist continuation of *The Brut* generally known as 'An English Chronicle'. According to this account, Gloucester was sent to Calais 'forto breke the seide sege … with other mony lordes, and a grete novmber of peple'. Before that the author mentions that Mortain and Camoys were sent to the town (but only with five hundred men); nevertheless, the siege was broken by the 'counsell and manhode of Ser Iohn Radcliffe, lieutenaunte of Caleis'. The real reason the besiegers fled, however, was that 'þe Duke of Burgoyne herde of þe commynge of þe Duke of Gloucestre with so grete power'.[67] The stress on Radcliffe's part in breaking the siege is important. The brief account contained in the Bury St Edmund's register and the 'Waltham

[63] *Chronicle of London*, 120–1. For the popularity of Duke Humphrey among Londoners generally see Frank D. Millard, 'An Analysis of the Epitaphium Eiusdem Ducis Gloucestrie', in *The Fifteenth Century* III: *Authority and Subversion*, ed. Linda Clark (Woodbridge, 2003), 117–36.

[64] 'A Short English Chronicle', in *Three Fifteenth-Century Chronicles*, ed. James Gairdner (CS, new series, xxviii, 1880), 61–2.

[65] *Historical Collections*, 178–9.

[66] *The Brut*, ii. 469–70.

[67] *An English Chronicle*, 60–1.

Annals' are the only other prose narratives to mention Radcliffe's role. As James Doig has pointed out, the abbey of Bury St Edmunds had connections with both Gloucester and Lydgate and it may have suited the duke's purpose to lay stress on the part played by his lieutenant in breaking the siege.[68]

That the narratives of the siege, and particularly the role played by the duke of Gloucester, were contested during the mid-fifteenth century is evident from the fact that there are texts which explicitly deny the duke's agency in lifting the siege. The most important of these is the Latin chronicle edited by J.A. Giles. Broadly Lancastrian in its sympathies, it states that the siege was broken by the earl of Mortain, although the specifics are not mentioned. More significantly, it is disparaging of Gloucester's military abilities and his raid into Flanders. The author claims that the duke lost three companies of his men and failed to repulse a Flemish counter-attack.[69] Similarly, John Hardyng, probably writing in the 1450s, credited Mortain with the lifting of the siege and says of Gloucester that 'he rode into Flanders a little waye and little did to count a manly man'.[70]

*   *   *

The siege of Calais by Philip the Good, duke of Burgundy, in the summer of 1436 was an event of considerable importance in the military, political and cultural history of late medieval England. At a time when the ability of the Lancastrian dual monarchy to maintain its war effort was coming under considerable strain, it demonstrated the ability of the English to raise and put in the field a well-equipped and substantial army. It also demonstrated the fighting prowess of the English soldier. In terms of individual feats of arms, the organisation of the town's defences and their ability to adapt to the new challenges presented by gunpowder weaponry, the English showed themselves able not only to defeat the Burgundians but to take the offensive to them. The effectiveness of the domestic military response to the Burgundian attack was doubtless facilitated by the place that Calais held in the popular imagination of fifteenth-century Englishmen. The town was considered English and its strategic, symbolic and economic importance is evident in the emotive language with which the crown appealed for money and men, and in the verse and prose which the siege generated among contemporaries. The siege also reveals the importance of war to the political culture of late medieval England. Success in war depended upon the reciprocal relationships that underpinned the English polity. In turn, these relationships were in part articulated by war. My study of the way in which Humphrey, duke of Gloucester, attempted to use his role in the crisis of 1435–6 to bolster his political position at home reveals the central importance of war in determining domestic politics in the fifteenth century. Reputations were made and broken by war and the rhetorical campaign waged by Duke Humphrey in the aftermath of the siege was an attempt to mitigate the unfortunate fact that

---

[68] Doig, 'A New Source', 408, 415–16; C.L. Kingsford, *English Historical Literature in the Fifteenth Century* (Oxford, 1913), 55.

[69] *Incerti Scriptoris Chronicon Angliae de Regnis Trium Regum Lancastrensium: Henrici IV, Henrici V, et Henrici VI*, ed. J.A. Giles (1848), 15–16.

[70] J. Hardyng, *Chronicle*, ed. H. Ellis (1812), 396.

it was others who were, in reality, principally responsible for the Burgundian defeat. Gloucester was largely unsuccessful in using the siege to advance his political influence at the time, but by the 1450s the relief of Calais had become an important component in the development of the myth of 'Good Duke Humphrey'. The power of this rhetoric, and the continued interest that the siege of Calais generated, is evident from its survival in the texts of later fifteenth-century and mid-Tudor chroniclers.

3

The Organisation of the Garrison

How many men served in the defence of Calais at any one time? To answer this question the composition and different status of those bodies of men that formed the Calais garrison must first be understood The soldiers involved in the defence of the Pale were not all recruited and paid for in the same way, nor did they all serve under the one commander. The defence of Calais, certainly at the beginning of our period, was undertaken by a series of separate retinues, each under the command of one of the captains of the town or the various fortresses in the Pale. Those in regular wages, that is limited in number by the terms of the captains' indentures and paid for by the treasurer of Calais, comprised the regular garrison. To these should be added the temporary reinforcements or 'crews' which augmented the defences in times of crisis and those in 'petty wages', in other words, men in private wages who did not form part of the regular establishment. The aim of this chapter is to identify the numbers involved in the defence of Calais and the way in which they were organised as a military force. Did the numbers involved and the way in which they were deployed change over time? To what extent did the organisation of the Calais garrison serve as a model for English military establishments elsewhere? Finally, what does the Calais garrison reveal about the wider organisation of English arms in the late fifteenth and early sixteenth centuries?

The regular garrison or 'ordinary'

Two sources can be used to gauge the composition of the regular garrison or 'ordinary' in the fifteenth century. First, there are the 'indentures for war'. This is an artificially created series of documents, housed in the National Archives, which contains the agreements between the crown and captains defining the terms of military service in the Pale and elsewhere. They defined the nature of the military contract, and each party to the agreement retained one half of the indenture, so-called because of the indented border of the top half of the document which, when joined with its counterpart, verified its authenticity. The terms of the indenture limited both the numbers of men that the captain agreed to provide and the wages they were to receive from the crown. The administrative purpose of these records, vital to a clear understanding of their meaning, was to serve as a precursor to the royal command to the necessary financial authority, in this case the treasurer of Calais, to pay the wages specified in the indenture.[1]

---

[1] Indentures for war relating to Calais are in E101/68–74.

The second source for the numbers involved in the regular garrison are the particulars of account of the treasurer of Calais. These record the amounts paid out to various captains, the numbers in their retinues and any deductions because of absences. They survive in an incomplete series, in a largely unaltered format, from 1347 until the mid-1530s. Like the indentures for war, the administrative purpose of these records must be understood in order to appreciate the information they contain and, as with many other 'official' records relating to Calais, their usefulness to the historian declines as the sixteenth century progressed. During the reign of Henry VIII the sources for the garrison's composition multiply to include muster rolls, surveys and censuses of military manpower, the ordinances of 1535 and the resulting Calais act, yet they do little to clarify its composition, as official and private records contradict each other as to the numbers serving in the defence of the Pale. During the reigns of Edward VI and Mary the confusion in military organisation, as the ancient establishment was merged with and augmented by a massive influx of troops during the 1540s, is mirrored in the records and an accurate picture of the composition of the regular garrison is almost impossible to achieve.

The 'official' composition of the garrison in the fifteenth century was clearly stated in the indentures signed between the king and each new captain. On 14 September 1451, for example, Edmund Beaufort, duke of Somerset, indented for the custody of the town and castle of Calais and the office of king's lieutenant in the marches. A week later this agreement was confirmed when he was granted the captainship of the town and castle of Calais by letters patent.[2] His indenture bound him to serve with a retinue comprising thirty (increased from six hitherto) mounted men-at-arms at 12*d.* a day, including himself at 6*s.* 8*d.* and his deputy at 2*s.*, 30 mounted archers and two hundred men-at-arms on foot (reduced from three hundred), all at 8*d.* a day, and two hundred foot archers at 6*d.* He also received wages for forty crossbowmen, eighteen of whom received 10*d.* a day and the rest 8*d.*, twenty carpenters and fifteen masons.[3] In the treasurer's accounts, however, the precise details of the captain's retinue were somewhat obscured: the description in the indenture of mounted men-at-arms and archers and men-at-arms on foot were listed as the captain, his lieutenant, the marshall of Calais and 257 men-at-arms on foot. This was the long-established size of the captain's retinue: it was the same as in the 'nombre of Soldiours in the Retinue of the capiteyne of Cales', a document dating from the captaincy of Richard Neville, earl of Warwick (1455–1471), while Humphrey, duke of Gloucester had been paid for the same number of men during the 1430s.[4]

---

[2] The indenture is E101/71/4/929. For the grant see *DKR* xlviii. 389.
[3] This is also the same size retinue as appears in BL, Add. MS 51020, ff. 54–5 (*Excerpta Historica*, ed. Samuel Bentley (1833), 26–8), where the captain is identified as Richard Beauchamp, earl of Warwick. This document is, however, wrongly ascribed to 1415–17 by Bentley. The range of offices to which the earl is assigned can only relate to the indentures Richard Neville, earl of Warwick, made with Edward IV in 1462: E101/71/5/941–2, 944, 946.
[4] There are no extant particulars of account during Somerset's captainship. The Warwick document is BL, Add. MS 46455, f. 66, while the numbers for Gloucester's retinue are taken from E101/192/13, f. 14.

In the outlying fortresses of the Calais Pale similar indentures limited the
retinues of the captains. At Calais castle there was the captain or lieutenant paid
2*s*., twenty-nine men-at-arms at 8*d*. and twenty foot-archers at 6*d*. At Rysbank
Tower the captain or his lieutenant served alongside a man at arms at 12*d*. and
sixteen men-at-arms or crossbowmen (*balistarii*) at 8*d*. At Guînes the ordinary
consisted of the captain or his lieutenant at 2*s*. a day, forty-nine men-at-arms at
8*d*. and fifty foot archers, while at Hammes the captain or his deputy served
alongside a single archer on horseback at 8*d*., seventeen men-at-arms on foot
and twenty-two foot archers.[5] In reality the garrisons were not always maintained at full strength. Absences were caused by the soldiers' illnesses and their
tending to other interests in England and Europe, as well as the inevitable delay
in filling vacancies in the retinues. The 1466 muster lists 527 men serving in
Calais, Calais castle and Rysbank Tower.[6] The 1502 muster lists the garrisons of
the town and castle of Calais at almost full strength: 551 men, compared to 553
specified in Giles, Lord Daubeney's indentures for their custody.[7] When the
garrisons at Hammes, Rysbank and Guînes are added, the size of the ordinary of
the late fifteenth-century garrison of the Pale was 712 men. Royal policy,
however, sometimes served to reduce the garrisons of the Pale. In 1502, Henry
VII, eager to maximise revenue from the Pale, ordered that, during times of
peace with France, the new lieutenant of Guînes, Sir Nicholas Vaux, should only
retain sixty rather than the usual hundred men in the garrison; the 500 marks per
annum that were saved on the wage bill were to be applied to repair of the
castle.[8] As the repair of the castle of Guînes was one of the Calais treasurer's
responsibilities anyway, it is clear that this was actually a ploy to increase the
cash coming to the king's coffers. Moreover, it may be that the ordinary garrison
of Calais was kept under strength, despite the evidence of the 1502 muster, and
it was this that allowed Lord Daubeney to allegedly siphon off £7,000 in wages
for vacant posts. This cost him the lieutenancy of Calais in 1505.[9]

The discrepancy between the description of the retinue in the treasurer's
accounts and that in the indentures for war highlight a factor that has led to
confusion in many discussions of the composition of English armies during the
late Middle Ages. During the fourteenth century the description of the ordinary
retinues of the captains of the Calais garrison had been more precise and gave a
more accurate impression of the military composition and likely tactical roles of
the soldiers. The treasurer's account for the year from November 1375, for
example, lists among the captain of Calais's retinue sixty-three *scutiferii*,
sixty-four *hobelarii* and 244 foot archers. Elsewhere in the Pale the retinue at
Calais castle had fifteen men-at-arms, eight *hobilarii* and twelve foot archers; at
Guînes there were nineteen mounted *scutiferi* and twenty on foot, as well as

5   See BL, Add. MS 51,020, printed in *Excerpta Historica*, 27–8, as well as the treasurers'
accounts and indentures for war.
6   BL, Add. MS ff. 58–65v.
7   E101/55/23.
8   *CCR, 1500–9*, 99.
9   David Grummitt, ' "For the Surety of the Towne and Marches": Early Tudor Policy
towards Calais 1485–1509', *Nottingham Medieval Studies*, xliv (2000), 200–1.

twenty 'mounted archers' and forty foot archers.[10] These different descriptions had a more direct relevance to the actual tactical role the soldiers were expected to perform: thus at the outlying castle of Guînes the high number of mounted men probably reflects the importance of scouting and intelligence gathering by members of the garrison there; meanwhile in the town of Calais itself probably only the sixty-four hobilars were regularly mounted, the rest being employed to guard the walls. By the mid-fifteenth century, however, the treasurer's accounts list the soldiers in only three categories: mounted men-at-arms at 12s., men-at-arms on foot at 8d. and archers at 6d. This categorisation was an accounting fiction, designed to simplify the exceedingly complex task of mustering, paying and recording the garrison's wages. It is clear from the indenture that the duke of Somerset concluded in September 1451 that his retinue included mounted archers (light horsemen probably used for scouting and reconnaissance), but in the treasurer's accounts these had been subsumed into the mass of dismounted men-at-arms who received the same daily rate of pay of 8d.[11]

This appreciation of the significance of the terms used to describe the men of the garrison has important ramifications for the way in which we analyse the composition and tactics of fifteenth-century English armies generally. During the fifteenth century the same descriptions – mounted and dismounted men-at-arms and archers – were used in all documents relating to armies. These descriptions, found in muster rolls, indentures for war, warrants for payment and accounts, were used because they were the standard descriptions employed by garrison treasurers and the various exchequers in England, Calais, Ireland and Normandy that paid soldiers their wages. Thus the term 'archer' equated to a soldier who received a daily wage of 6d., a 'man at arms on foot' or 'mounted archer' that soldier in receipt of 8d., and a 'man at arms on horseback' that soldier who received 12d. These descriptions, therefore, unlike the more elaborate ones of the fourteenth or sixteenth centuries, or indeed those found in other types of records, bore no direct resemblance to the actual military role the men performed in the garrison or on the battlefield. Thus the mass of archers at 6d. may have been lightly armoured men carrying bills. Similarly, skilled archers, sometimes called mounted archers and paid 8d., could be found among those listed in musters and accounts as the identically paid dismounted men-at-arms. The mounted men-at-arms at 12d. represented the archetypal fully armoured knight, who, in English armies at least, in the fifteenth century fought more frequently on foot than on horseback. Thus, it is a mistake to assume, as Michael Powicke and others have done, that the English armies which fought in the later Hundred Years War, with their preponderance of men listed as archers, paid at 6d. a day, were somehow 'second best' and represented a withdrawal from military society by the aristocracy, the mounted men-at-arms.[12] Rather, as Anne

---

[10] E101/180/4, ff. 4v–7v.

[11] E101/71/4/929.

[12] M. Powicke, 'Lancastrian Captains', in *Essays in Medieval History Presented to Bertie Wilkinson*, ed. T.A. Sandquist and M. Powicke (Toronto, 1969), 371–82. During Edward III's campaigns the ratio of men-at-arms to archers was usually 1:1; at Agincourt and throughout Henry V's conquest of Normandy a ratio of 1:3 was the norm. During Henry VI's reign,

Curry has suggested, the changing ratio represented military experimentation and the growing importance of pole-armed, non-armigerous soldiers in English armies. In 1449 Sir Walter Strickland recruited sixty-nine archers and seventy-four billmen with mounts and seventy-one archers and seventy-six billmen on foot to serve in Normandy with the earl of Salisbury.[13] The precise composition of this force, however, was masked by the official records of the English financial authorities. By 1475, for Edward IV's invasion of France, the ratio of those described as men-at-arms in the accounts to archers was almost 1:8. Lander remarked on this 'astonishingly high' ratio, stating that 'nowhere was the highly desirable figure of three to one attained', that is the ratio of archers to men-at-arms that had proved so successful at Agincourt sixty years earlier.[14] This, however, is to misunderstand the nature of the exchequer documents from which Lander drew his conclusions; the ratio of 1:8 did not represent a weakening of English military resources, but rather a continuing process of evolution concerning the organisation of English armies. In fact, the Burgundian ordinance companies organised by Charles the Bold in 1472 had a ratio of men-at-arms to other soldiers of about 1:7,[15] and, as we shall see, the inventories of military equipment maintained by the Calais authorities suggest that in the late fifteenth century the Calais garrison, and English armies operating in Europe more generally, were employing similar organisation, weaponry and tactics to their European counterparts.

Within the ordinary garrison the indentures regulating military service resulted in a pyramidal structure. Just as the king indented with the captain, so the captain, free by the terms of his indenture and grant of office to recruit his own retinue to fulfil his obligation to the crown, could indent with lesser captains and they, in turn, could indent with the men who would serve as soldiers The importance of this system is something I shall examine in detail in the next chapter, but as no private indentures survive specifically for service in the Calais garrison the extent to which it governed military service there remains unclear. Two muster rolls, one from 1466 and the other from 1502, do, however, give some idea of the extent of private retaining within the regular garrison. In 1466, and again in 1502, the clerk who compiled the muster rolls recorded which soldiers were dependent for their wages – that is, were retained by – one

---

however, as the financial pressures of the war effort continued, the ratio rose to an average of about 1:5.5. For the 1440 expedition it reached as high as 1:20: Anne Curry, 'English Armies in the Fifteenth Century' in *Arms, Armies and Fortifications in the Hundred Years War*, ed. Anne Curry and Michael Hughes (Woodbridge, 1994), 44–5.

[13] Curry, 'English Armies', 44; Andrew W. Boardman, *The Medieval Soldier in the Wars of the Roses* (Stroud, 1998), 82.

[14] J.R. Lander, 'The Hundred Years War and Edward IV's 1475 Campaign in France', in *Tudor Men and Institutions: Studies in English Law and Government*, ed. A.J. Slavin (Baton Rouge, LA, 1972), 96.

[15] R. Vaughan, *Charles the Bold: The Last Valois Duke of Burgundy* (1973), 207. William, Lord Hastings's indenture for the reinforcements he took to Calais in 1477 make this situation explicit. He was allowed to 'convert the saide men of armes vnto Archers on fote or the saide Archers into men of Armes so that the wages excede not the wages and rewardes afore lymyted': BL, Add. Ch. 19808.

of the garrison's office holders or mounted men-at-arms. In 1466, 193 (36.6 per cent) of the 527 soldiers listed were part of a personal retinue.[16] The greatest personal retinue, comprising two mounted men-at-arms, six dismounted men-at-arms, two mounted archers and thirty foot archers, belonged to John, Lord Wenlock, lieutenant of the captain, Richard Neville, earl of Warwick. The next two largest retinues were those of the Gascon marshall of Calais, Gaillard Durefort, Lord Duras, and the porter, Sir John Courtenay, with thirty-three and eighteen men respectively. The smallest retinues consisted of the nine individuals who retained one foot archer each. The 1502 roll shows a similar pattern, although the number of those retained had halved to 104 out of 551 (18 per cent), probably because of the crown's policy of restricting personal retaining among the officers of the garrison.[17] The sixteenth-century muster rolls show that this system of personal retinues had been standardised to a degree: the porter, for example, received the wages of six soldiers at 8*d.* and seven at 6*d.*, while the marshall had five soldiers at 8*d.* and eleven at 6*d.* The spears in the garrisons also received the wages of between three and one foot archers.[18] By Henry VIII's reign, however, this no longer represented private retaining by indenture as it had in the fifteenth century, but it did perhaps correspond more closely to the military organisation of the garrison than it had done earlier. Each of the senior military office-holders was assigned a stretch of wall to watch, and in 1558, during the French siege, Sir Antony Aucher, the marshall, 'with his soldiers', probably those in wages with him, repulsed the first French attack from the castle into the town.[19]

During the reign of Henry VIII the sources for the composition of the ordinary garrison multiply and its actual military organisation is made explicit for the first time. The treasurers' accounts continued to follow the form, with small alterations, that had been established in the first half of the fifteenth century. Thus in 1508–9 Sir Gilbert Talbot, the deputy, received wages for his retinue in the town of Calais itself consisting of himself and the marshall, each of knightly rank and receiving 2*s.* a day, twenty-one mounted men-at-arms at 12*d.*, eighteen archers on horseback at 8*d.*, two hundred men-at-arms on foot at 8*d.*, and two hundred foot archers at 6*d.* There was also the treasurer's retinue, as there had been in the fifteenth century, comprising five mounted men-at-arms, five mounted archers, five dismounted men-at-arms and five archers on foot. The forty crossbowmen, carpenters and masons were also listed under the treasurer's retinue.[20] Even during the 1540s, when the number of soldiers in Calais was vastly augmented, the treasurers' accounts continued to record an ordinary

---

[16] BL, Add. MS 46455, ff. 58–65.

[17] E101/55/23. For a discussion of the document's significance see Grummitt, 'Early Tudor Policy towards Calais', 189–90.

[18] BL, Cotton MS Faustina E. VII, f. 85 (*LP*, XV, 609 (1)). For the payment of the spears' men continuing into the late 1530s see E101/206/1.

[19] See below, p. 000.

[20] E36/269, 364–5 (*LP*, I i, 193). To this should be added five men-at-arms on horseback at 12*d.*, and 12 archers on horseback at 8*d.* This was a special retinue that had been allowed to William, Lord Hastings in the 1470s as a honour guard to attend upon him during his absences from Calais. However, in 1508–9 the money due to be paid for this retinue was kept

garrison defined more by the bureaucratic procedures of the Calais exchequer than the reality of military life. In 1543 the deputy, Lord Cobham, was paid £5,046 for three knights, twenty-six men-at-arms, thirty mounted archers, two hundred men-at-arms on foot and two hundred archers on foot, despite the Calais Act of 1536 which had reduced his personal retinue to forty-one men.[21] Elsewhere, at the castles of Calais, Hammes, Guînes, and Rysbank Tower, the numbers in the ordinary garrisons corresponded to those of the fifteenth century. The only early Tudor innovation that occurs in the treasurers' accounts was the new fortress at Newembridge, built in 1525–6, which was garrisoned by its lieutenant at 2*s.* per day, a constable at 8*d.* and eleven soldiers at 6*d.*[22] However, the two surviving muster rolls from the 1530s allow us to gain a more accurate impression of the way in which the garrison of the town of Calais was organised. The first probably dates from April 1530 and is among the State Papers of Henry VIII's reign in the National Archives.[23] The second is from 1539–40 and is now among the Cotton manuscripts at the British Library.[24] Both show that the ordinary garrison was divided into 'le Vynteyne' and 'le Constablerie', as well as groups of 'spears', a banner-watch, 'skewrers', sergeants, day-watches and porters. Each pair of vintners, receiving 8*d.* each a day, had between fourteen and eight men under them, all at 6*d.* a day. Each constable, at 8*d.* a day, had four men at 6*d.* under them. The 'spears', corresponding to the mounted men-at-arms of the fifteenth century, were paid 18*d.* or 12*d.* a day, and each had between three and one men serving under them. The language of military organisation, if not the actual organisation itself, was reminiscent of the organisation of infantry in English armies in the Middle Ages and may reflect an older organisation of the Calais garrison into small, tactical units, partly independent of the system of personal retinues.[25]

The muster rolls reflect the numbers in each category that were confirmed in 1535 by the commissioners, led by Sir William Fitzwilliam, a courtier and soldier with Calais experience,[26] sent to Calais to investigate the state of the town. The following year, as a result of the commission, the number of the ordinary garrison was defined by statute with the passing of the Calais Act by the

---

by the king as the office of lieutenant of Calais was vacant: E159/259, *brevia directa baronibus*, Hilary, rots 4–5.

[21] E351/530, m. 3.

[22] For Newembridge see *LP*, XV, 609 (1). By 1543 three of the archers at 6*d.* had been restyled *vibrellator* or 'gunners' in the accounts, while the remainder were called 'soldyers': E351/530, m. 3.

[23] SP1/51, ff. 213–22 (*LP*, IV, 5102 (2)). For its dating and a full transcript see *Lisle Letters*, i. 684–7.

[24] BL, Cotton MS Faustina E. VII, ff. 74–83 (*LP*, XV, 609 (1)). It is also summarised in *Chronicle of Calais*, 136–40, where it wrongly dated to 1533. For the correct dating of this document and a full printed version of it see *Lisle Letters*, i. 680–4.

[25] For vintenars and constables in the thirteenth and fourteenth centuries see Michael Prestwich, Prestwich, *Armies and Warfare in the Middle Ages: The English Experience* (New Haven, CT, 1996), 127–8.

[26] Fitzwilliam had been lieutenant of Guînes from May 1523 until October 1526 and lieutenant of Calais castle from 1526 until the end of 1529: *LP*, III ii, 3037; E36/272.

Reformation Parliament. There were to be twenty-four spears, nineteen archers on horseback, four scourers, six tipstaffs, twelve vintenars, eighteen constables, 125 soldiers at 8*d*. and 226 at 6*d*., as well as an extra four men at 8*d*. a day and twenty-seven men who received an annual payment of 10 marks, besides those in the retinues of the office-holders, now institutionalised into the council of Calais. The twelve vintenars were to have twenty archers each under them, while the eighteen constables were each to have ten men-at-arms at 8*d*. The reality, however, as the 1539–40 muster shows, was slightly different. In total the ordinary of the garrisons within the Pale, as established by the 1535 commissioners, was 493 with a further 281 in personal retinues, giving a total of 774 men. In reality the garrison was maintained a little under strength: 382 individuals were named as being in receipt of wages in 1539 with a further 308 unnamed men serving under those individuals, but receiving their wages from the treasurer of Calais.[27] Nevertheless, the Calais Act of 1536 did represent an attempt to reform the situation that had arisen in the late 1520s when the garrison appears to have been consistently under strength. In 1528 the number of the ordinary appears to have been four hundred and in the survey of householders among the garrison in 1534 490 men were listed.[28] The most important aspect of the reforms of the mid-1530s, however, was the reduction in size of the deputy's retinue from its medieval strength of some 450 to a mere forty-one men. Those who had been part of the retinue received their wages direct from the treasurer and had only one immediate lord, the king. This, as we shall see, had important consequences for the identity of the Calais garrison and the Tudor military as a whole.

A document entitled 'Ordenances for Watch and Ward of Calais', dating from the commissioners' report on the Pale's security in August 1535, shows how the organisation set down by the act was used for the daily defence of the town of Calais.[29] It is unlikely that the ordinances of 1535 were entirely new, indeed they may have been part of the 'good, olde, and holsome lawes, ordenances and constitutiones' which Fitzwilliam and the others had found neglected. One of most important duties of the garrison was the opening and shutting of the gates. Here the porters played the principal role: on the striking of the morning watch bell, ten porters, accompanied by the master porter, a fife and drum and members of the watch, marched to the deputy's lodgings in the market square to receive the keys to the town's four gates. The porters had custody of the town's keys until the nightly locking of the gates, at which point they were returned to the deputy. The tipstaffs' duties of watch and ward revolved mainly around keeping a check on the bills containing the names of strangers abiding within the town and charging those responsible for keeping the various watches. The vintenars and their companies were charged with keeping the 'scout watch' and 'stand watch', that is, the nightly watches upon the town walls, while the

---

[27] See the discussion of the size of the ordinary in the mid-1530s in *Lisle Letters*, iii. 564–9 and Rainey 'Defence of Calais', 113–14.

[28] For 1528 see SP1/51, ff. 196–223 (*LP*, IV ii, 5102(2)). For 1534 see E101/62/18.

[29] BL, Cotton MS Faustina E. VIII, ff. 89–102v, printed in full in *Chronicle of Calais*, 140–62, and summarised in *LP*, XV, 609 (2).

constables and their companies maintained the 'search watch' in the town itself. The tipstaffs were to give the watchword to the vintenars and constables who, in turn, passed it to their men. The banner-watch was the most honourable and most important of the watches. They were charged to watch the town nightly during the 'herring time', when foreigners were invited to Calais to trade in herrings, and during the Christmas period. The vintenars and their companies were also, in rotation, to maintain a daily watch in the marketplace, while the chief officers of Calais, the spears, mounted archers, six tipstaffs and four of the vintner companies were to be ready at all times to assemble in the marketplace with harness and weapons should the alarm be raised. Gunners were also given specific instructions on firing guns to warn strangers when they could enter and should leave the town.

Henry VIII's French campaigns of the mid-1540s and the consequent build-up of military manpower had its impact on the ordinary garrisons of the Pale. The numbers established in 1535 were modified and 'extraordinary' soldiers added to the garrisons at Calais and Guînes. Moreover, by 1545 six bulwarks had been built (Hookes, Crabbars, Harraways, Bootes, Ballingham and Andren) in the Low Country to strengthen the defensive ring around Calais itself.[30] These soldiers should be distinguished from the crews which served for short periods of times, particularly at Guînes, as they were envisaged as permanent additions to the garrison, paid for by the treasurer of Calais. The declared account of Sir Thomas Cornewallis, treasurer of Calais for one year from 6 April 1554, provides an insight into the size of the Calais garrison at the end of the period of English occupation. It records pay for thirty-one men-at-arms (at 12*d.* or 18*d.* a day), 286 men-at-arms (most at 8*d.*), forty-one mounted archers, 316 archers (or 'soldiers' mainly at 6*d.*) and forty crossbowmen. Including the officers of the Calais garrison and outlying fortresses, this meant the ordinary or 'ancient' establishment was reckoned to be 730 men, with 303 in 'their own wages' and the remainder serving in the retinues or *familia* of the office-holders or spears. Added to these were the 'extraordinary', appointed by Henry VIII in the mid-1540s: twenty gunners at Calais, forty-four at Guînes, eight at Newembridge, and the garrisons of the bulwarks of Hookes (a chief gunner and fifteen soldiers), Harraways (a captain, petty captain, porter, gunner and fifteen soldiers), Bootes (a captain, petty captain, porter, gunner and eighteen soldiers), and Ballingham (a captain, petty captain, porter, gunner and seventeen soldiers). This made a total regular garrison for Calais and the marches of 879 men.[31] The Calais garrison, therefore, was not a static and monolithic organisation; rather it evolved over time to meet the changing military and political circumstances of the age.

To what extent was the organisation of the ordinary at Calais reflected in other English garrisons in the fifteenth and sixteenth centuries? The first point to make is that the regular garrison at Calais was much larger than other garrisons throughout the dominions of the English king. In Lancastrian Normandy,

30 Colvin, *The King's Works*, iii. 373–5.
31 E 351/535.

for example, most of the garrisons were small. In the mid-1430s, when the number of the garrison troops was at its highest, there were some five or six thousand soldiers distributed among almost fifty regular garrisons and a number of temporary establishments.[32] In September 1441, when Henry, Lord Bourgchier, indented for the castle of Neufchatel, he agreed to serve with three mounted men-at-arms, seventeen men-at-arms on foot and sixty archers, making it one of the largest garrisons in Lancastrian France.[33] Similarly, the garrisons of Tudor England were much smaller than that of Calais. In 1488 Sir Richard Salkeld was retained as constable of Carlisle castle with a retinue of twenty archers.[34] In Berwick, the largest regular garrison on the British mainland, there were usually fewer than a hundred men. In 1544 Sir Cuthbert Radcliffe was appointed captain of Berwick castle with forty soldiers, including a constable, two porters, three watchmen, a priest and a cook, and ten gunners.[35] There was also a permanent establishment of fifty gunners serving in the town itself.[36] The new system of coastal forts erected by Henry VIII after 1539 were also manned by small garrisons, which relied on their commanders to use their local power and influence to augment the defences in times of emergency. By the end of 1540 there was a total of 170 soldiers and gunners in the twenty-six castles and bulwarks between Gravesend and Portland.[37] Typical of these was Camber castle near Winchelsea, Sussex: in July 1544 Philip Chute was appointed its captain with a garrison of eight soldiers and six gunners.[38] The largest of the new Henrician fortifications of the early 1540s was the fortress and two bulwarks built at Hull. In October 1543 the garrison of the castle, under Sir Michael Stanhope, comprised a lieutenant, a constable, a sergeant, a yeoman porter, an under-porter, a master gunner and eight gunners, six horsemen and twenty-nine soldiers. In each of the two bulwarks were a captain, two soldiers, a deputy, a porter, an under-porter and eight gunners. As at Calais, the garrison was divided between the retinues of the officers who had the power to appoint soldiers under them. Thus Stanhope had the nomination of four of the gunners, the horsemen and twenty-six of the soldiers, while the other three soldiers were to be appointed by the lieutenant and constable. The remaining places were to be filled at first by Stanhope but thereafter were in the king's gift.[39] The elaborate ordinances compiled for the regulation of the Hull garrison were, however, based upon those used at Calais. When outside their lodgings the soldiers were to carry their halberds 'as is accustumed and used at Calays'.[40]

---

[32] Curry, 'English Armies', 51–9.
[33] L.S. Woodger, 'Henry Bourgchier, Earl of Essex and his Family (1408–83)' (DPhil thesis, University of Oxford, 1974), 18.
[34] E404/80/267.
[35] *LP*, XIX i, 141/51.
[36] *LP*, III, 511, 813.
[37] *LP*, XVI, 372.
[38] *LP*, XIX i, 1035/142.
[39] E101/60/14.
[40] SP1/169, f. 72 (*LP*, XVII, 140). The ordinances failed, however, to prevent a protracted dispute between the townsmen and the garrison: David Grummitt, 'War and Society in the North of England, *c.* 1477–1559: The Cases of York, Hull and Beverley', *Northern History* (2008), 1–16.

Calais provided a more likely model for the English garrisons installed in the French conquests of Henry VIII: Tournai between 1513 and 1519 and Boulogne between 1544 and 1551. In Tournai, however, the Henrician government never managed to organise its garrison along the lines of Calais, despite some evidence of plans to do so. Shortly after its capture, five thousand men were still being retained to garrison the town, over a thousand of whom were foreign mercenaries being retained in the hope that they could be used in a renewed campaign the following summer.[41] Without an adequate means of paying for this size of establishment, however, a drastic reduction of the garrison was clearly necessary. In 1514 instructions to the new governor of Tournai, Sir William Blount, Lord Mountjoy, stated that 'all the garrison keeping watch and ward should be divided into constables and vintenars', in other words the organisation of the Calais garrison was to be adopted in Tournai.[42] The heavy involvement of men who had previously served in Calais, such as Mountjoy, must have ensured that the pattern of Calais was an obvious model around which to base the defence of Tournai. Unlike Calais, however, the citizens of Tournai could not be entrusted with maintaining their own duties of watch and ward nor would they agree to bear any of the cost of the garrison themselves. In March 1517 another Calais veteran, Sir Richard Whetehill, urged the king against reducing the garrison to a thousand men, arguing that the population of the city was closer to twenty thousand than the ten or eleven thousand estimated by the English government, and that the hostility of the population necessitated a strong English presence.[43] In terms of its organisation, the Tournai garrison retained its original system of companies more akin to those employed in the field army of 1513 than those to be found at Calais. By the time of its return to the French in 1519 the garrison of Tournai, in so far the fragmentary accounts allow us to reconstruct it, appears to have been moving closer to the organisation and size of the regular Calais garrison. Each of the principal officers had a personal retinue of varying sizes, from the 1515 establishment of 330 men under the captain of the guard to the two under-porters, twelve porters and twenty-nine soldiers serving under the porter of Tournai. Nevertheless, as almost all military service in early Tudor England at this time was still organised by personal retinues, it would be wrong to read too much into this. Unlike early Tudor Calais, the garrison of Tournai was constantly undermined by problems over pay, resulting in mutinies and letters of complaint from the garrison. As Cruickshank observed, these problems of pay only illustrate the wider conclusion that 'conditions in Tournai are quite different from those of Calais'.[44]

The pattern of the Calais garrison was, however, used as a model for the defence of Boulogne, the second Henrician conquest in France, captured in September 1544. At the beginning of the English occupation the scale of the

---

41 See C.G. Cruickshank, *The English Occupation of Tournai 1513–1519* (Oxford, 1971), ch. 3 for a discussion of the garrison and defence of Tournai, on which this paragraph is largely based.

42 *LP*, II, 148.

43 SP1/13, f. 53 (*LP*, II, 1664); Cruickshank, *Tournai*, 85.

44 Cruickshank, *Tournai*, 102.

garrison was similar to, and as untenable as, Tournai. An account of the garrison at Boulogne made towards the end of 1544 lists 2,918 men in the 'high town' and castle of Boulogne, 1,867 in 'Base Boulogne', the lower part of the town, and 701 men in 'the Old Man', a fortress based around the old Roman beacon tower and lighthouse. This force comprised fifty-four men-at-arms, 160 light-horsemen, twenty-four demi-lances (northern English horsemen under the command of the marshall, Sir Ralph Ellerker), 185 yeomen of the guard, 3,449 footmen, 1,353 'hacbutteres' or handgunners (of whom 945 were English), and 146 gunners, as well as 166 brewers and bakers. The garrison was organised into personal retinues, much the same as those for the field army with which Henry VIII had taken the town, ranging in size from the four hundred footmen and a hundred handgunners of Sir Thomas Poynings in 'Base Boulogne', to the three footmen serving under William Eliot, the clerk of the market.[45] By the middle of 1545 the garrison of Boulogne and its fortresses had risen to 8,065, of which 737 were foreign mercenaries.[46] It is clear that, from the beginning of the English occupation, the long-term defence of Boulogne was to be modelled upon the Calais garrison. To this end, towards the end of 1544, a copy was made of the 'Ordinaunces of Calleis for Bullen', that is to say, the ordinances for watch and ward formalised in 1535 were to be applied to the new English town of Boulogne. The oaths of the office-holders and soldiers of Calais were also copied and sent to the town, as well as proclamations for the government of Calais made by successive governors since the 1470s.[47] The Treaty of Camp, signed on 7 June 1546, which brought peace to the Boullonais and ceded the town to the English for eight years, allowed these ordinances to be employed and the garrison of Boulogne to be reduced to its peacetime complement. In August of that year the garrison of Boulogne was set at seven hundred men, divided, as in Calais, between the personal retinues of the office holders. The largest retinue was the 150 men of marshall, while the smallest was the one man appointed to serve under the keeper of the council chamber.[48] As at Calais, this system of personal retinues ran alongside an institutional organisation designed to facilitate the duties of watch and ward within the town. All but fifty-three members of the garrison were included in this organisation, including the house-holds of the major office holders. The main burden of watch and ward, again as in Calais, fell on the constables, the twenty vintenars and their companies of twenty men.[49] There are no figures for the size of the Boulogne garrison after the resumption of hostilities in the late summer of 1549. It is clear, however, that the size of the garrison, as well as the various bands of troops serving in and around Boulogne and Guînes, were substantially increased. The account of the treasurer, Sir Robert Cotton, shows that he spent the massive sum of £94,760 on payments for soldiers in Boulogne between 21 April 1548 and 2 May 1550.[50] By

---

[45] SP1/196, ff. 43–6 (*LP,* XIX ii, 799(2)).

[46] *LP,* XX ii, 200(3).

[47] *LP,* XIX ii, 801.

[48] SP1/223, ff. 23–3v (*LP,* XXI i, 1414(2)).

[49] SP1/223, ff. 141–2 (*LP,* XXI i, 1488).

[50] E101/540/7 (now EXT 7/20).

the terms of the Treaty of Boulogne in late March 1550 it was agreed that the town was to be returned to the French.[51]

'Crews' and 'petty wages': the extraordinary defence of Calais

As well as the ordinary garrison there were two other groups of soldiers employed in the defence of Calais. The first of these consisted of those in 'petty wages', that is, men who did not receive their pay from the treasurer of Calais, but who were the private servants of existing members of the ordinary garrison. The second group were the 'crews' or bands of reinforcements periodically brought over to augment the defences of the Pale. At times, as in the 1460s and 1540s, these emerged as a semi-permanent addition to the Calais garrison. The history of their recruitment and organisation, in particular, serves to highlight the wider picture of military recruitment and service in England as a whole.

During the fifteenth century the evidence for men serving in 'petty wages' is scant. Nevertheless, in the fifteenth century it was the assumption of all office-holding, including membership of the Calais garrison, that the duties of that position could be exercised by deputy. Thus men charged with duties of watch and ward and those soldiers taking advantage of the forty days' annual leave were required to find sufficient replacements to ensure that their responsibilities were met. The Paston letters provide evidence that men who had positions in the regular garrison were attended by men who they paid from their own pockets. On his way to Calais in June 1473 Sir John Paston wrote to his brother asking him 'iff ye knowe any lykly men and fayre condycioned and good archerys, sende hem to me, thowe it be iiij, and I wyll have them and they shall iiij marke by yere and my levere'.[52] In Calais these men would have served as his household servants (hence the grant of Paston livery) and fulfilled an unspecified military role (hence the need for 'good archers'). Their pay, less than 2*d.* a day, compared unfavourably with the 6*d.* a day of the archers in the ordinary garrison, but service in 'petty wages' was clearly seen as a means of finding a permanent position in the king's wages. By November 1474 Sir John Paston's patron, the lieutenant of Calais, William, Lord Hastings, had found a position 'in hys owne wages' for one 'Bernaye', possibly one of the men whom Paston had recruited the previous year.[53] At 6*d.* a day, or almost £10 a year, a position in the Calais garrison was a valuable commodity, creating, as we shall see, its own problems of patronage and influence.[54] In the sixteenth century the numbers of those in 'petty wages' are revealed by the survey of the garrison compiled in 1534. This document divides the garrison between those who kept a household in Calais, which presumably means that they rented a lodging with their family

---

51 Jennifer Loach, *Edward VI* (New Haven, CT, 2000), 107–8.
52 *Paston Letters and Papers of the Fifteenth Century*, ed. N.B. Davis (EETS, special series, xx, 2004), i. 463.
53 Ibid., 479. Possibly one of the Berneys of Reedham, kinsmen to the Pastons, and their long-time supporters.
54 In the 1470s Sir John Fortescue considered £5 per annum to be a good living for a yeoman: Sir John Fortescue, *The Governance of England*, ed. C. Plummer (Oxford, 1885), 151.

and servants, and those who did not, that is those who lived alone, or lodged in the household of their master. The survey lists 137 men in petty wages, of whom only fifty-eight kept a household.[55] By the time of the 1539–40 muster, however, most of those in petty wages had progressed to their own wages, finding positions within the system of constableries and vinteynes.

The 'crew', on the other hand, was a short-term expedient designed to boost the defences of the Pale during emergencies or, in the mid-fifteenth century, to assist new captains to establish their authority. The term 'crew' has both a general and a specific meaning. Its specific meaning related to the practice evolved in the late 1420s of basing a specified number of men in a fortress to dominate a hostile hinterland through *chevauchée* tactics. It was derived from the French 'crue' which was current in both the French army and that of the dukes of Burgundy. Newhall argued that its adoption by the English was a direct result of the siege of Orléans in 1429 which forced the Lancastrian government to adopt a more flexible approach to the war.[56] Rainey states that 'crews' (a force of three hundred men at Calais and thirty at Guînes) first appeared at Calais in 1451 under the duke of Somerset.[57] But this rather misses the general meaning of the term: 'An augmentation or reinforcement of a military force; hence a body of soldiers organised for a particular purpose, as to garrison a fortress, for an expedition, campaign etc.; a band or company of soldiers.'[58] Thus the fifteenth- and sixteenth-century 'crew' at Calais comprised any temporary number of soldiers above those specified in the indentures and patents of the officers. Only under the earl of Warwick, and in the rather different circumstances of the 1540s, did the crews gain any measure of permanency in Calais. In August 1462 Edward IV allowed Warwick to retain the crew of twenty men-at-arms on horseback at 12*d.* per day, twenty archers on horseback at 8*d.* and 260 foot archers at 6*d.* payable by the hands of the treasurer of Calais, which he had employed since March the previous year and had its origins in the crew brought to Calais by the duke of Somerset in 1451. In all other respects the crew's conditions of service were identical to those of the regular garrison.[59] In July 1466 Edward IV ordered it to be disbanded as a precursor to the merchants of the staple taking financial responsibility for the garrison. That the king was able to do is, perhaps, a telling statement of the balance of power between Edward and Warwick by 1466.[60]

Warwick's crew of the 1460s was the exception rather than the rule. Most crews sent to Calais in the fifteenth century were of the order of the forty men-at-arms and 104 archers that Gervase Clifton crossed the channel with in August 1450;[61] the twenty men-at-arms and eighty archers that William Fiennes,

---

[55] E101/62/18.

[56] R.A. Newhall, *Muster and Review* (Cambridge, MA, 1940), 128.

[57] Rainey, 'Defence of Calais', 115–16.

[58] *Oxford English Dictionary.*

[59] BL, Add. MS 25459, f. 308. In terms of winnings of war and the forty days' annual leave the conditions of service mirrored those of Warwick's own retinue.

[60] C76/150, m. 6.

[61] E159/231, *brevia directa baronibus*, Easter, rot. 2.

Lord Saye, took to Guînes; or the 120 men-at-arms and 530 archers that Richard Wydeville, Lord Rivers, took to Calais in December 1451 amidst fears of another imminent Burgundian assault. These latter crews were to embark from Dover and remain in Calais for six weeks, receiving their wages direct from the exchequer in Westminster.[62] Like the regular garrison, the description of the crews' composition and the ratio between men-at-arms and archers owe more to the accounting procedures of the exchequer than the reality of their military organisation. That this was the case is confirmed by the extraordinary allowance made to William, Lord Hastings, to alter the composition of the crew of sixteen men-at-arms, thirty-seven mounted archers and 478 foot archers that he took to Calais in the wake of the death of Duke Charles the Bold in February 1477. Hastings entered into a separate indenture with the king for this force, distinct from his existing indenture as lieutenant of Calais, which stated that Hastings could 'convert the saide men of armes vnto Archers on fote or the saide Archers into men of Armes so that the wages excede not the wages and rewardes afore lymyted'.[63]

Below the level of the royal indenture and warrant, private indentures were concluded that defined the terms of military service in greater detail. A rare example of this survives for some of the men who served in the crew sent to Calais under Richard Seyntbarbe in July 1451. It concerns Richard Halle and Reginald and Arnold More, who agreed to serve as archers for a quarter of a year under one Thomas Crafford. Each agreed to bring to the muster and serve with a jack or quilted jacket, a sallet, a bow and twenty-four arrows, a dagger, a bill and that indispensable piece of an archer's equipment, a leaden mall. As usual they also agreed to give Crafford a third of any winnings or ransoms they took during the period of service.[64] This suggests that during the middle of the fifteenth century the recruitment and organisation of such forces was very much delegated by the crown to private individuals. As long as the broad terms of the crown's indenture were met, and no more money than originally budgeted for was spent, the exact nature of military organisation was something that the captains and the soldiers themselves could determine. Perhaps the most important difference between the fifteenth-century crews and the ordinary garrison was in terms of pay. While the wages of the garrison proper were guaranteed by the crown and amounts owing to individual soldiers entered into the treasurer's book of accounts, the crown made no such undertaking to those men recruited to serve in extraordinary forces. Captains were paid for their retinues and individuals soldiers struggled to find redress when wages were not forthcoming.[65]

62 E404/68/57–9.

63 BL, Add. Ch. 19808.

64 BL, Royal MS 17 B.xlvii, ff. 24–4v. That this was common practice for the organisation of such forces in the fifteenth century is shown by the fact that it was copied, along with a similar document for a man-at-arms and his retinue of twenty archers, into the commonplace book of a Londoner.

65 An example of the problems this caused can be found in a petition submitted to the chancellor of England in the 1440s. John Buxsell claimed he had been recruited by Sir William Oldhall, the former lieutenant of Calais and chamberlain to the duke of York, to serve in the Oldhall's retinue during the duke's 1441 expedition to Normandy. Despite mustering, cross-

The organisation and nature of the reinforcements sent to the Pale under the early Tudors demonstrate the changing nature of military forces under Henry VII and Henry VIII. As we shall see in the next chapter, during the sixteenth century the way in which the reinforcements for the Pale were recruited and commanded changed, reflecting wider changes in early Tudor government. Similarly, changes in the organisation and weaponry of 'crews' in the sixteenth century represented the Tudors' continuing efforts to ensure that the English military continued to compete with its French and Scottish enemies. The first sign of these changes in the reign of Henry VII was the specialisation of crews sent to the Pale, fulfilling military roles not usually carried out by the regular garrison. This is evident in the numbers of crews comprised solely of gunners sent to the Pale by Henry VII. Table 1 lists the reinforcements sent to Calais between 1485 and 1509.

Table 1: Reinforcements sent to Calais, 1485–1509

Date	Composition	Commander
Easter 1487	24 gunners	Oliver Bardisley
5 June 1488	24 gunners	Lord Daubeney
Easter 1489	99 soldiers	Sir John Fortescue
Easter 1489	39 archers	James Isaak
Easter 1489	30 gunners	William Alford
Easter 1489	100 soldiers	Lord Daubeney
Easter 1489	4 men-at-arms and 194 archers	Sir Thomas Bourchier and John Neville
Easter 1490	24 gunners	Oliver Bardisley
4 December 1490	100 soldiers?	Lord Daubeney
July 1491	300 soldiers	Lord Daubeney
Michaelmas 1491	168 archers	Lord Daubeney
July 1491–1 Nov. 1492	24 gunners	Lord Daubeney

Source: E405/75–8; E404/79

Whereas the crews sent to Calais in the last year of Edward IV's reign had been traditionally comprised of men-at-arms and archers and large in number (in the spring of 1483 there were almost nine hundred extra soldiers in the Pale),[66] those of Henry VII's reign were generally smaller and included five crews comprised entirely of gunners. In part this may reflect Henry VII's policy of

---

ing to Normandy and being captured by the French, Oldhall, it was claimed, refused to pay Buxsell his wages of £13 13s. 4d., leaving him in 'grete poverte': C1/26/275. Claims over the appropriation of wages for expeditionary forces were also levelled at York himself and another of his captains, Sir Thomas Kyriell: *CPR, 1446–52*, 6–7; P.A. Johnson, *Duke Richard of York 1411–1460* (Oxford, 1988), 52–4.

[66] 'Financial Memoranda of the Reign of Edward V: Longleat Miscellaneous Manuscript Book II', ed. Rosemary Horrox, *Camden Miscellany* (CS, 4th series, xxxiv, 1987), 223–5.

central control over the crown's gunpowder weaponry, but it also demonstrates a flexibility regarding the tactical situation and the composition of royal forces.[67]

This flexibility was continued into the reign of Henry VIII and is most evident in the Pale during the massive reinforcement of its defences during the early 1540s. This began in earnest in 1542 as tension between England and France mounted over the disputed land between Guînes and Ardres, known as 'the Cowswade'.[68] By July 1542, for instance, there were a hundred horsemen and seven hundred footmen serving in the crew at Guînes.[69] The following month three hundred men were mustered in Calais itself, serving under the deputy, Lord Maltravers, the treasurer, Sir Edward Wooton, and the lieutenant of Calais castle, Sir Edward Bray.[70] The feature of the English military build-up in and around the Calais Pale and Boulogne during the 1540s which was most frequently remarked upon is the number of foreign mercenaries employed. This was due, it is argued, to the ineffectiveness of Tudor armies when compared with their French and Imperial counterparts: as Dr Millar writes 'to assure themselves of at least a chance of victory the early Tudors were obliged … to retain in their service foreign mercenaries and auxiliaries, dedicated professionals who, it was hoped, could combat the stratagems of an equally professional adversary'.[71] Prys Morgan estimates the number of mercenaries resident in the Pale was around ten thousand at the end of Henry VIII's reign; Dr Millar goes further, 'at least 15,000'.[72] Nevertheless, the majority of reinforcements sent to Calais during the 1540s were English. For example, in December 1545 a note in the privy council register noted the origin and number of the reinforcements: 'For the Pale at Calays: Bucks' CCCC; Cambridge CCC; Northampton CCC; Beds' CCC; Huntingdon C; Warwyk CC; Hertford CC; Middlesex CC.'[73] Moreover, during the 1540s English armies generally showed themselves able to use the latest weaponry and tactics. Handguns, for example, were not the preserve of Italian mercenaries. In December 1548 the council of the north asked the citizens of York to provide fifty 'haquebutters' or handgunners to be sent to the Haddington fort in Scotland. Similarly, of the bands of handgunners in Boulogne in 1544 the majority were Englishmen.[74] It may be that the crown favoured recruitment of foreign mercenaries as it lessened the burden on local

---

[67] For Henry VII's policy towards gunpowder weaponry see David Grummitt, 'The Defence of Calais and the Development of Gunpowder Weaponry in England in the Late Fifteenth Century', *War in History*, vii (2000), 267–9.

[68] For this dispute see David Grummitt, 'Calais and Henry VIII: "un petit morceau d'Angleterre outremere" ', in *Le Detroit: Zone de recontres ou zone de conflits*, ed. Stéphane Curveiller et al., *Bulletin Historique et Artistique du Calaisis*, clxxiii (2001), 127–38.

[69] *LP*, XVII, 552.

[70] *LP*, XVII, 683.

[71] Gilbert John Millar, *Tudor Mercenaries and Auxiliaries, 1485–1547* (Charlottesville, VA, 1980), 23–5.

[72] Morgan, 'Government of Calais', 139–40; Millar, *Tudor Mercenaries*, 146.

[73] *APC*, i. 572.

[74] *York Civic Records*, v., ed. Angelo Raine (Yorkshire Archaeological Society Record Series, cx, 1946), 4; SP1/196, ff. 43–6 (*LP*, XIX ii, 799(2)).

communities in England, particularly at a time of generally high taxation and, in the late 1540s, economic hardship. Mercenaries were also part of the composition of all European armies at this time and their employment may have been designed to show that England was part of the mainstream of European military culture.

The size of the crews defending the Calais Pale in the 1540s and 1550s are difficult to gauge. The books of particulars of account of the Calais treasurer do not survive for this period and the extant declared accounts only record the total amount delivered to the crews for wages. It is clear, though, that by the early 1550s the crews at Calais, Guînes and the new bulwarks built in the Low Country were an established part of the Pale's defences Between July 1552 and April 1554 the treasurer of Calais, Sir Maurice Denys, delivered £13,053 for the wages of the crews, compared to £14,130 for the regular garrison.[75] The reduction in numbers of the extraordinary garrisons of the Pale began in 1552, two years after the Treaty of Boulogne had made them surplus to requirement. The reduction of forces in the Pale became a priority for the Marian regime eager to reduce royal expenditure across the board.[76] The treasurer's account shows evidence that the size of the crews was indeed reduced: for the year ending at April 1555 there were only three bands of a hundred footmen, as well as eighty-six gunners returned from the English garrison at Boulogne, in Guînes, and a further ten Boulogne gunners at Calais.[77] Reinforcements continued to be sent over to Calais throughout Mary's reign, such as the three hundred men mustered and despatched amidst rumours of a French attack in November 1556,[78] but when the crisis did finally come in January 1558 the crown was fatally slow to respond. Despite general appeals to mobilise military resources, reminiscent of the response to the Burgundian siege a century earlier, few reinforcements actually crossed the Channel. Most, like the thirty men mustered in Norwich who spent three idle days at Ipswich waiting to embark for Calais, were sent home again once news was received of the town's fall.[79]

* * *

During the period 1436 to 1558, then, the Calais Pale was home to the largest concentration of military manpower within the dominions of the English crown. The regular garrison of some seven hundred was augmented by soldiers in petty wages, eager for a position or 'room' within the regular garrison and 'crews' of men, serving for a specified period of time. During times of acute crisis, such as 1436 or during the 1540s, the number of soldiers in Calais was in the thousands. Particularly after the end of the Hundred Years War in 1453, Calais provided the most frequent arena of military service in late medieval and early Tudor

---

[75] E351/533.
[76] *APC*, iv. 102; *Calendar of State Papers, Domestic Series, Mary I, 1553–1558*, ed C.S Knighton (1998), 4, 16, 234.
[77] E351/535, rots 6–6d. The total cost of the extraordinary crews in 1554–5 was £6,042 13*s.* ½*d. st. ta.*
[78] *CSP, Domestic, Mary I*, 511.
[79] See below, p. 173.

England; military life in the Pale thus defined the experience of soldiering for several generations of Englishmen, reflecting changes brought about by both military and political pressures. The next chapter will look at who served in the Pale and the factors which determined service in the defence of the town and marches.

4

The Nature of Military Service in the Pale

Who served in the Calais garrison and how and where were they recruited? Military service before the advent of the professional army and the emergence of an ethos of service to the nation state is usually discussed in terms of the balancing of obligations and rewards. Indeed, in the Middle Ages the relationship between the king and his subjects was defined by reciprocity.[1] First, in England every able-bodied man had the obligation to serve the king in the defence of the realm, an obligation set down in the terms of the Statute of Winchester in 1285. Second, the feudal system, whereby land was held either by explicit military service or by the implicit assumption that tenants would attend upon their lord in war, created a set of relationships that could be adapted to serve the demands of war. Military service also led to reward: either directly through the payment of wages or by the capture of prisoners for ransom or booty, or indirectly by allowing access to patronage networks which could result in the granting of fees, lands and offices by grateful kings or lords. In return the prince promised to defend the realm and ensure the provision of justice to his subjects. This reciprocal system of obligation and reward was apparent in determining who served in the Calais garrison as elsewhere across the spectrum of military service. In this chapter I want, first, to explore the terms by which men served in Calais and, second, how the captains and soldiers were recruited. How did the nature of military service in Calais reflect the changing balance between reward and obligation, between recruiter and recruited, in the military relationship between the crown and its subjects?

The captains

Several factors determined who served as a captain in the Calais garrison; the balance of these various factors changed over time, reflecting different political and military circumstances. The most important captain of the Calais garrison was the governor of the Pale: until 1471 he was usually styled as the captain of Calais, from 1471 until 1505 the king's lieutenant, and from then until 1558 the king's deputy. Regardless of the style, the governor was the leading military and political figure in the Pale. The ordinances of Richard Neville, earl of Warwick,

---

[1] See, for example, Philippe Contamine, *War in the Middle Ages*, trans. Michael Jones (Oxford, 1984), 77–101, where the weakness of medieval princes in forcing their subjects to fight for them is stressed, and Michael Prestwich, *Armies and Warfare in the Middle Ages: The English Experience* (New Haven, CT, 1996), chs. 3 and 4.

in 1465 made the responsibilities and power of the governor explicit. Warwick was frequently absent from Calais during the 1460s and appointed a lieutenant to run the daily government of the Pale. His ordinances stated that all

> capitaignes counsillours and officers of the seid towne be of gode due & diligent oubeissaunce & attendance to the lieutenant of the seid towne by the seid capitaine deputed ... shewyng hem of true and lovyng & faithfull affeccion to him bi their advise counsell and assistence.[2]

Warwick's ordinances show the power of the captain of Calais during the fifteenth century: he could appoint men to the garrison and the subordinate commands; he enjoyed the right to hear criminal and civilian pleas in the marches and adjudicate between the different jurisdictions in the Pale;[3] and he had the authority to grant safe conducts to those crossing the Channel. In effect, during the fifteenth century, the crown handed over responsibility for the government and defence of Calais to the captain. The office was usually granted to a leading magnate or prince of the royal blood, highlighting the way in which fifteenth-century kings were dependent upon their nobility to guarantee the defence of the realm and public authority.[4] This arrangement was reciprocal and the individual responsibilities of the captain and the crown were defined by his indenture. While the captain agreed to serve with a certain number of men, the crown granted him the right to appoint all soldiers and officers in the garrison. Although the captain agreed to hold the town and marches for the king, not delivering them to anybody but by the king's express commandment, he was allowed to surrender the town if it was beseiged and if no help was forthcoming from England within two months. Similarly, in the earl of Warwick's indenture for the keeping of Hammes castle made with Edward IV in 1462, it was to be lawful for Warwick and his retinue to depart from the castle if they were not paid for two months.[5] The terms of these fifteenth-century indentures, while differing in their specifics between the various commands in the Pale, showed a remarkable consistency. Thus, Warwick's indenture for Hammes castle made in 1462 was an almost verbatim copy of the indentures entered into by Robert Whittingham in August 1440 and Fulk Vernon seven years later, while his indenture for Guînes mirrored those of Sir Thomas Fynderne in 1452 and Sir William Pirton in 1447.[6] Similarly, the indenture which Edmund, duke of Somerset, sealed for his custody of Calais castle in December 1451 copied the

---

2   C76/149, m. 14.
3   See, for example, the dispute over precedence between the mayor of Calais and the mayor of the staple that Warwick settled in 1467: C76/151, m. 15.
4   For the relationship between crown and nobility during the fifteenth century see Christine Carpenter, *The Wars of the Roses: Politics and the Constitution in England, c. 1437–1509* (Cambridge, 1997), 27–46.
5   For the governor of Calais's indenture see, for example, the one between Henry VII and Giles, Lord Daubeney, made in 1486: E101/72/3/1061. Warwick's indenture for Hammes castle is E101/71/5/3.
6   Hammes: E101/71/4/906 (Whittingham), 919 (Vernon); Guînes: E101/71/4/930 (Fynderne).

terms of that sealed the previous year by Ralph, Lord Sudeley.[7] Indeed, the terms and conditions that the captain of Calais served under remained almost unchanged from the early 1420s to the early sixteenth century.[8]

Certain qualities were necessary for prospective captains in the Calais Pale. Before 1466 and the act of retainer, the financial means to guarantee the payment of the soldiers' wages and the defence of Calais when the subventions from the crown fell short was an important factor. In January 1437 Humphrey, duke of Gloucester, made an impassioned plea before parliament for the wages of the Calais garrison. He asked that 'null defaute ne negligence soit mys ne rette au dit duk, ne a les souldeours avauntditz pur icell' if some disaster befell the town because of lack of wages.[9] His inability to prevent soldiers leaving the Pale because of lack of pay may have been behind his resignation from the post early the following year. Similarly, in 1450 Humphrey Stafford, duke of Buckingham, was owed £19,395 in wages for his retinue for almost eight years as captain. Buckingham was granted the reservation of the wool customs from the port of Sandwich until the debts was cleared.[10] This was despite the proviso, made on his appointment, that the duke could take gold, jewels and plate to the value of £5,000 to Calais every time he crossed the Channel, in spite of the laws forbidding the export of bullion.[11] Six years later, when the arrears due to the retinue of Edmund Beaufort, duke of Somerset, were finally paid, £22,985 was delivered in cash forwarded by the merchants of the staple.[12] Clearly, captains did not meet wage bills of this magnitude out of their own pocket, but they could use their position and contacts to arrange and guarantee the credit arrangements that could ensure that the garrison did not mutiny or desert. Private finance was also necessary for maintaining a household in Calais that reflected the honour of the governor and of the town and marches itself. Sir John Radcliffe, Gloucester's lieutenant in 1436, was 'welbelovet [by] the sawdiours ... for he kept and helde a gud and open housold to who that come and welcome'.[13] The necessity for the governor of Calais to keep an honourable household was a constant one throughout the period and one which was not eased by the act of retainer in 1466. Even during the 1530s the cost of maintaining their households and of entertaining the constant stream of diplomatic visitors to Calais left successive deputies, John, Lord Berners, and Arthur Plantagenet, Viscount Lisle, heavily in debt.[14]

The need for the governor of Calais to maintain an honourable estate underlines the fact that the office was more than just a military command. The Pale was a showcase of English royal power to foreign visitors and the splendour of

---

7 E101/71/4/928 (Sudeley), 932 (Somerset).
8 Compare E101/69/7/510, Richard Beauchamp, earl of Warwick's indenture of 1425, with that of Lord Daubeney in 1486 discussed below.
9 *PROME*, xi. 204.
10 *RP*, v. 206–7.
11 *POPC*, v. 214.
12 E101/195/1.
13 *The Brut*, ii. 573.
14 *Lisle Letters*, i. 22–4, 240–1.

its buildings, the garrison and its captains needed to reflect this. When Cardinal Beaufort visited the town in 1439 for the conference at Oye he was so alarmed at its dilapidated appearance that he ordered an extensive rebuilding programme which was, in Colvin's view, the most ambitious royal building programme since Edward I's castle building in Wales.[15] During the 1460s the earl of Warwick pursued from Calais a pro-French foreign policy at increasing odds with the pro-Burgundian one sponsored by Edward IV from England, but as Lord Hastings's letter book from the late 1470s and the Lisle correspondence of the 1530s show, the governor of Calais was more usually an important diplomatic representative of the king, whose own staff, organised from and based in Calais, carried out a constant formal and informal diplomatic exchange with England's neighbours. The captain was also responsible for maintaining a spy network.[16] In the sixteenth century the symbolic importance of Calais as the English foothold in continental Europe was demonstrated in 1500 when Henry VII met the Archduke Philip of Austria there, in 1520 at the Field of the Cloth of Gold, in 1532 when Henry VIII met Francis I, and in 1539 when Anne of Cleves was received by the deputy and garrison on her way to England.[17] The governor of Calais, therefore, was expected to fulfil a diplomatic role and represent his master; his bearing, character and status, therefore, would hopefully reflect honourably upon the king.[18] A mid-sixteenth-century text concerning royal protocol states that the deputy of Calais 'was to have all thinges as if the kyng were there in parson'.[19] As the Venetian ambassador observed as late as 1558, Calais was still 'the key and principal entrance' to the dominions of the English king and thus fulfilled a symbolic and diplomatic role almost as important as its military role.

Most importantly, however, the captains of the garrison, and particularly the chief governor, had to be experienced military figures who could provide adequately for the defence of Calais and who, by virtue of their martial abilities and achievements, could command the respect of the other captains and soldiers. During the mid-fifteenth century the dukes of Gloucester, Somerset and York and the earl of Warwick were all military figures, combining service on the

---

[15] Colvin, *The King's Works*, i. 432.

[16] The Hastings letter book is Huntington Library, Hastings MS 13886. For Warwick's Calais-based diplomacy of the 1460s see Edward Meek, 'The Practice of English Diplomacy in France 1461–1471' and for Lisle during the 1530s, David Potter, 'Cross Cultural Friendship in the Sixteenth Century: The Lisles and their French Friends', both in *The English Experience in France, c. 1450–1558: War, Diplomacy and Cultural Exchange*, ed. David Grummitt (Aldershot, 2002), 63–84, 200–22.

[17] Grummitt, 'Calais 1485–1547', 92–5.

[18] For the importance of diplomats as representatives of the king during Henry VIII's reign see David Starkey, 'Representation through Intimacy: A Study in the Symbolism of Monarchy and Court Office in Early Modern England', in *The Tudor Monarchy*, ed. John Guy (1997), 42–77. This argument, however, could be extended beyond the narrow focus of Henry's gentlemen of the privy chamber between 1519 and 1547 to include those men throughout the fifteenth and sixteenth centuries who, by virtue of their military and chivalric achievements, could represent the king honourably to other princes sharing the same set of cultural values.

[19] BL, Add. MS 71,009, f. 29.

battlefield and in the administration of military commands, like Normandy, with service at court and in the localities. Each could command substantial private resources from their own lands, as well as attracting men to their service as military and chivalric figures in their own right. Whatever Warwick's shortcomings as a field commander, his reputation was one of a chivalric and successful knight: it attracted men to his service, which, in turn, provided him with the resources to take on more military responsibilities.[20] Similarly, in the 1470s Lord Hastings's military and chivalric reputation among the garrison was in sharp contrast to that of his rival, Anthony Wydeville, Earl Rivers.[21] Nevertheless, not all noblemen enjoyed a reputation like Warwick or Gloucester, and occasionally the crown looked to non-noble captains, whose military expertise was their principal qualification, to take command at Calais.

The importance of military credentials to appointment at Calais is shown by the career of Sir John Radcliffe, Gloucester's lieutenant in Calais during the Burgundian siege of 1436. Radcliffe, 'one of the most important military captains of his day', had served in France since 1413 and perhaps at Agincourt, and was successively bailli of Evreux in Normandy, constable of Bordeaux, captain of Fronsac castle, seneschal of Aquitaine and lieutenant of Calais. During his service in Guienne during the 1420s it was said that 'by hys labour in knyghthood', he brought 'to hys sovereign lord's obeysance ... many dyverse cytes, townes and fortresses'. When the stronghold of Bazez capitulated it was because the defenders feared 'to fyght with Radeclyff and hys power'. In 1426 he was unsuccessfully nominated for the Order of the Garter, beaten by his friend Sir John Fastolf, but was finally elected three years later. His appointment to Calais by Gloucester was primarily a recognition of his military credentials. His own resources were slender: he had retired from the post of seneschal of Aquitaine over the non-payment of his retinue's wages. As we have seen, he distinguished himself in command of the town during the siege of 1436.[22] Similarly, on Gloucester's retirement as captain, his two successors, Sir Thomas Rempston and Sir Thomas Kyriell, were men of knightly rank appointed because of their military credentials. Rempston, lieutenant of Calais between November 1437 and February 1439, had first served in Henry V's first French campaign in 1415. He held several captaincies of castles in Normandy during the 1420s and 1430s, and was seneschal of Aquitaine between April 1440 and July 1442, although he had been taken prisoner at the English defeat at Patay in June 1429. Coming amidst rumours of a Burgundian attack on Guînes, Rempston's appointment was further evidence of the military necessity of appointing experienced captains to command in Calais. Despite having been taken prisoner again in 1442 at St Sever in Gascony, Rempston was named as

[20] For Warwick's military reputation see Michael Hicks, *Warwick the Kingmaker* (Oxford, 1998), 308–10.
[21] David Grummitt, 'William, Lord Hastings, the Calais Garrison and the Politics of Yorkist England', *The Ricardian*, xii (2001), 262–74.
[22] J.S. Roskell, L. Clark and C. Rawcliffe (eds), *The House of Commons, 1386–1421* (4 vols, Stroud, 1993), iv. 159–60.

one of the four guardians of the Calais Pale in March 1450.[23] Kyriell, who served between December 1439 and August 1442, had fought in Normandy under both Henry V and Henry VI, where he had emerged as a skilled and pugnacious field commander with a reputation for ruthlessness. He had also commanded fortresses there as well as, notably, Le Crotoy on the Somme estuary in 1436. He would command the English army at the disastrous battle of Formigny in 1450, but would later redeem himself leading the counter-attack against the French raid on Sandwich in 1457. Kyriell did not fall in battle; rather he was executed after the Yorkist defeat at the second battle of St Albans in February 1461.[24] Despite their military credentials, men like Rempston and Kyriell could only be stop-gaps as governors of Calais when the political and financial pressures, as well as contemporary opinion, demanded that the nobility were the natural holders of such positions. The appointment of Kyriell's successor, the duke of Buckingham, was done amidst great secrecy and growing concern that the credit agreements that underpinned the garrison's wage payments had broken down. Indeed, the mutiny that occurred among the garrison in August 1442 may have been staged to gain Buckingham's admittance on favourable financial terms.[25]

Gloucester's appointment of Radcliffe in 1436 is also indicative of the freedom of fifteenth-century governors of Calais to appoint their own captains to the subordinate commands in the Pale. For example, Edmund Beaufort, duke of Somerset, captain of Calais from 1451 until 1454, appointed Osbert Mountefort, his former treasurer general of Normandy, as his deputy at Rysbank Tower. Similarly, Sir Richard Wydeville, Lord Rivers, another of Somerset's companions in arms from Normandy, served as his deputy in the town of Calais itself. In the 1460s the earl of Warwick, having indented for all the major commands in the Pale, appointed all his own deputies. This patronage allowed him to attract to his own service royal servants such as Sir John Wenlock, Lord Wenlock, who served as his lieutenant of Calais from at least 1466, as well as local men, vital to the efficient government of the town, such as Richard Whetehill, lieutenant of Guînes from January 1461. In an effort to counter Warwick's private authority in the Pale, reinforced by his freedom to appoint deputies, Edward IV confirmed all of Warwick's deputies by letters patent in April 1470, thus transforming them at a stroke into his own officers.[26]

After 1471 there is, however, evidence that the changed political circumstances and the shifting nature of the relationship between the crown and the nobility had an impact on who served as captains in Calais. The securing of adequate and guaranteed finance for the Calais garrison and Edward IV's desire to assert royal authority in the Pale altered the balance between the crown and its captains. The relationship had moved from the reciprocity of the first half of the fifteenth century to one where the terms of service were increasingly dominated

23 Ibid., iv. 192–4.

24 Anne Curry, 'Sir Thomas Kyriell' in *Oxford DNB*.

25 R.A. Griffiths, *The Reign of Henry VI* (1981), 454, 470–1, 506, 519–21, 815, 872.

26 Grants to Richard Whetehill at Guînes, John Blount at Hammes, Wenlock in Calais and Otwell Worsley at Calais castle and Rysbank Tower: C76/154, m. 6.

by the crown. On 18 July 1471 William, Lord Hastings, the king's chamberlain and his companion in exile the previous year, indented as lieutenant of Calais for ten years, an appointment confirmed by the issue of letters patent. Soon afterwards Hastings concluded a private indenture with John, Lord Howard, one of the king's knights of the body, to serve as his deputy there, and on 25 July this agreement was also ratified by letters patent.[27] These events were highly symbolic of Hastings's relationship with the king and the new royal policy towards the town and marches. Hastings was not a great regional magnate in his own right; his lands and the resulting *manraed* he commanded came from royal stewardships and other grants dependent upon his proximity to the crown. Moreover, Hastings served as lieutenant not captain of Calais. Although Hastings's patent gave him the privileges enjoyed by previous captains (the same fees and wages, the same size of retinue and the power to appoint men to the garrison) the title *locum tenens* demonstrated clearly that his authority descended from the king.[28] In some ways the title of lieutenant was the more honourable of the two, recognising that the governors of Calais were not merely military commanders – as, say, the captain of the Lancastrian garrisons in Normandy had been – but the representative of the king, responsible for the government of part of his realm, the equal, for example, of the king's lieutenant in Ireland.

The trend for the king to appoint captains who already had existing ties to him, mainly as members of his household, was repeated throughout the Pale during the 1470s. Edward IV appointed Sir Ralph Hastings as lieutenant of Guînes in 1479, while Sir John Blount, Lord Mountjoy, served as lieutenant of Hammes castle between 1470 and 1477 (when he was replaced by his brother, James). Similarly, Sir John Donne, lieutenant of Rysbank Tower 1481–4, Sir John Scott, marshall of Calais 1471–8, and Thomas Radcliffe, porter of Calais during the 1470s, were all closely linked to Edward IV, having fought alongside him during the Wars of the Roses and/or served in his household. While Hastings retained the right, in theory, to make appointments as previous governors had, it is clear that, in practice, appointment to office in the Pale was almost always at the crown's instigation.[29] These policies were continued by Henry VII. His appointment of his chamberlain, Lord Daubeney, as lieutenant in March 1486 mirrored Edward IV's appointment of Hastings, and as the reign progressed vacancies among the captains of the Calais garrison were increasingly filled by members of the king's own household.[30] On Daubeney's

---

[27] C76/155, m. 18; C81/834/3232, 3240, 3248. For Hastings as lieutenant of Calais see David Grummitt, 'William, Lord Hastings and the Defence of Calais', in *Social Attitudes and Political Structures in the Fifteenth Century*, ed. T.J Thornton (Stroud, 2000), 150–67.

[28] Howard had served as one of the king's carvers since the beginning of the reign and was one of Edward's most trusted military captains. He had been treasurer of the royal household between 1467 and 1471: Charles Ross, (2nd edn, New Haven, CT, 1998), 324–5: E403/824, m. 3.

[29] Grummitt, 'Hastings and the Defence of Calais', 166.

[30] For Henry VII's policies towards Calais see Grummitt, ' "For the Surety of the Towne and Marches": Early Tudor Policy towards Calais 1485–1509', *Nottingham Medieval Studies*, xliv (2000), 184–203.

dismissal in 1505, amidst accusations of peculation, the office of governor of Calais was again changed. The lieutenancy remained vacant and Sir Gilbert Talbot, a household knight, took possession of the town as the king's deputy in Calais.[31]

The clearest indication of the changing nature of military service for the captains of the Pale comes in the decline of the indenture system as a means of defining the terms of that service. In 1486 Giles, Lord Daubeney, was the last governor of Calais to indent for the custody of the Pale (for seven years) as medieval governors had. Letters patent granting the office to Daubeney, in recognition of his services to Henry Tudor in exile and during the capture of the throne during the previous summer, had been issued two days earlier.[32] Lord Daubeney did not enter into a second indenture for the safe keeping of Calais after 1493; rather he continued to hold the office at the king's pleasure. As Daubeney's other offices in Calais – lieutenant of Calais castle, of Rysbank Tower, and of Guînes castle – were regranted to others after 1501, the system of indentures slowly gave way to a system whereby military commands in the Calais garrison were granted solely by the king's letters patent or by word of mouth (as was the case with Sir Gilbert Talbot in 1505) with no indenture being sealed between the king and new captain. The relationship between the crown and its captains had moved decisively in the crown's favour. Office was now held by the king's grace and granted for life, or during the king's pleasure, in the same way as non-military offices. A further way in which the changed balance of reward and obligation was manifested was in the excessively large recognizances that Henry VII's captains entered into. For example, in August 1508 Edmund Dudley, Henry's chief debt recorder and collector, noted in his account book, 'Item, delivered a Recognizance of Sir Richard Carew & others for the sauf keping of the castell of Caleis, of himself MMiiij^{c}li and of other sureties Mvj^{c}li'.[33]

Significantly, only in the outlying castles of the Pale, at Guînes and Hammes, did the crown continue to indent with its captains. In 1502 and 1503 Sir Nicholas Vaux and William Blount, Lord Mountjoy, indented for the custody of Guînes and Hammes respectively. Both were also bound in recognisances to ensure their safe keeping of the castles; their sureties were constantly renewed until the end of the reign.[34] That indentures were continued at Guînes and Hammes reflected the more militarised conditions of service in the garrisons at the borders of the Pale. Here the agreement had more of the reciprocity of the early fifteenth-century agreements. In 1503 Mountjoy, for example, was granted

---

31 Ibid., 201. In March 1485, however, Richard III had appointed his bastard son, John, as captain of Calais, despatching him to the Pale with two of his household knights. Whether this was a long-term strategy or merely designed to overawe the deputy of Calais, Lord Dynham, into obedience is unclear: Rosemary Horrox, *Richard III: A Study in Service* (Cambridge, 1989), 206, 292.

32 E101/72/3/1061; E101/55/16, printed in *Materials for a History of the Reign of Henry VII*, ed. W. Campbell (2 vols, 1873), i. 361–3.

33 BL, Landsdowne MS 127, f. 46v.

34 C76/183, m. 8; C76/185, m. 7; *CCR, 1500–9*, 99, 131 2, 226, 767, 836, 903, 979; C54/376, mm. 34d, 39d, 40d.

the farm of the castle's rural hinterland but in return was to meet the costs of any crew sent from England during time of war. The indenture also reflected the control over military commands in the Pale that Henry VII now exercised. Mountjoy was bound in the sum of ten thousand marks and required to find sureties for the same sum. Moreover, he was to pay for the maintenance of the castle, which was 'very ruinous and greatly decayed', for which obligation he entered into further bonds.[35] In another echo of fifteenth-century conditions of service, the lieutenants of Guînes and Hammes were also allowed to appoint their own deputies. There is no evidence that these were royal appointments, although the deputies chosen had close links with the crown and would later receive office in the Pale in their own right. On 1 November 1504, for example, Robert Wooton went to Guînes as Vaux's deputy with £40 *st. ta.* per annum and the right to nominate two men in the garrison there; in April 1508 he was appointed high porter of Calais.[36] Similarly, John Gage served as deputy at Guînes before his appointment as comptroller in August 1522.[37] Furthermore, into the sixteenth century lieutenants of Guînes and Hammes and their deputies continued to pursue their own commercial interests to ensure the victualling of the castles and they continued to be sworn as members of the staple company. Both Mountjoy and Vaux were significant shippers of wool to Calais in the early years of Henry VIII's reign.[38]

Vaux's new indenture with Henry VIII, made in October 1509 for twenty years, was also reminiscent of the fifteenth-century terms of service. It still stipulated that it was lawful for Vaux to vacate the castle if the garrison's wages had not been paid for two months. In effect, as the garrison's wages were now guaranteed by the staplers, this clause was an obsolete remnant of earlier indentures. On the same day he entered into an agreement to farm the lordships of Guînes, Sandegate and Ballingham. There were subtle changes, however, which shifted the balance further in the king's favour: the peace-time garrison was to remain at the sixty established by Henry VII, of which only forty were to be appointed by Vaux and the remainder by the king; rather than being required to furnish a crew of one hundred men in time of war, as required by the terms of the 1502 indenture, Vaux was to furnish as many men 'as schalbe thought gode and resonable by oure said soveraigne lord'. Henry VIII also bound Vaux to keep the castle secure, as he did for Mountjoy's new grant at Hammes.[39] It is unclear when the conditions of service for the lieutenants of Hammes and Guînes ceased to be regulated by indenture. Certainly, the grant in May 1523 to Sir William Fitzwilliam of the lieutenancy of Guînes referred to an indenture, and the grant

[35] *CCR, 1500–9*, 226.

[36] BL, Add. MS 38092, f. 52; *CPR, 1495–1509*, 564.

[37] SP70/147, f. 24; *LP,* III ii. 2444.

[38] E122/204/3; 83/3; 82/5. These accounts probably do not reflect the full extent of their trading in wool, but are all that are revealed by the patchy survival of the customs accounts. The practice of granting trading licences to captains of Guînes and Hammes persisted into the 1530s. For instance, in 1531 Lord Sandes and Lord Grey were licensed to purvey livestock and grain to Guînes and Hammes for victualling: C76/206, mm. 1, 2.

[39] *CCR, 1500–9*, 99; C54/377, mm. 1d, 3d, 5d; *LP,* I i. 194–5, 214, 216, 218/4, 225, 231; 257/39; *Chronicle of Calais*, 203.

of Hammes to William, Lord Grey de Wilton, in June 1531 recited an indenture of the previous April, although that may have related to the financial conditions of Grey's tenure as much as the military.[40] There is no evidence that Sir William Sandes indented for Guînes in 1526, although as late as September 1546 George Browne's grant of Hammes does refer to an indenture.[41] But by the 1540s indentures, as meaningful documents for regulating the service of English captains in the Pale, were a thing of the past; the power of the crown was such that the reciprocity of the fifteenth century (the sense in which the military contract was agreed between the king and his subject, recognising their respective powers and limits and bestowing benefits on both parties) had been replaced by a system in which the crown largely dictated who served and under what terms.

The decline of the indenture as the basis for military service in early Tudor Calais illustrates a point of wider significance for the way in which Henry VII and Henry VIII sought to mobilise their subjects for war. As Jeremy Goring noted, from about 1512 indentures for war ceased to be concluded between the king and his subjects for military service in foreign wars and to put down domestic rebellions.[42] In 1511 the Statute of Winchester of 1285 had been reissued, reinforcing the general obligation of men between the ages of sixteen and sixty to possess weapons and armour commensurate with their wealth and social standing. This, in turn, was followed by a new emphasis on the commission of array as the main instrument for the crown's enforcement of 'the military obligations of the English people in peace and war'. As in the Middle Ages, however, this was only one half of the way in which the early Tudors mobilised their subjects for war. They also relied on what Goring termed 'the quasi feudal' method of recruitment: that is, they commanded their leading subjects to raise men from their own tenantry or, more importantly, from the tenantry and *manraed* they commanded as stewards of crown lands and from other offices in the crown's gift.[43] During the 1490s the crown's military resources were increasingly placed in the hands of stewards of the royal lands and members of the extended royal affinity and regulated by the licensing of certain individuals to recruit large retinues from the crown lands, which could then be mobilised when

---

40 *LP* III ii. 3027; v. 318/41. It was stated that Grey purchased the office in 1531: indenture 6 April 22 Hen VIII, privy seal 16 May 22 Hen VIII: C82/643, no. 22.
41 No grant for Sandes's lieutenancy of Guînes survives. He appears as lieutenant in the treasurer's accounts from 6 April 1526, after Fitzwilliam had been moved to the treasurership of the king's household by Wolsey: E36/272, 297; Grummitt, 'Calais 1485–1547', 127. For Browne see *LP*, XXI ii. 200/42. His indenture was sealed five months before his grant and, like Lord Grey's, may have recorded a financial rather than a military obligation.
42 Jeremy Goring, 'The Military Obligations of the English People, 1509–1558' (PhD thesis, University of London, 1955), 17. One of the last military indentures was that between the king and Lord Thomas Howard in April 1512, Howard agreeing to serve at sea with three thousand men. It is interesting to note that this reflected the reciprocity of medieval indentures for war in such things as the division of spoil taken on the seas: C54/379, mm. 6d, 13.
43 *Tudor Royal Proclamations*, ed. L. Hughes and J.F. Larkin (3 vols, New Haven, CT, 1964), i. 85 93; Goring, 'Military Obligations', 14–15; Jeremy Goring, 'Social Change and Military Decline in Mid-Tudor England', *History*, lx (1975), 185–97.

required without the need for specific indentures for war.[44] Thus, while soldiers for Henry VII's invasion of France in 1492 were raised and commanded by captains indenting in the medieval manner, in 1513 Henry VIII sent letters to individuals ordering them to prepare a certain number of men for the forthcoming invasion.[45]

The importance, then, of crown office and royal and other stewardships became increasingly apparent for the captains of the Calais garrison. This trend was already apparent in the fifteenth century and the particularly close link between captains in Calais and stewardships in the duchy of Lancaster was already well established by the 1440s. Humphrey Stafford, duke of Buckingham, William, Lord Hastings, and the various members of the Blount family all held important office in the duchy.[46] The extent to which this allowed them to contribute men to the regular defence of Calais is unclear, but the evidence for duchy office contributing to the captains' ability to reinforce the Pale in times of crisis is well documented.[47] In the sixteenth century, however, the link between military command in Calais and an important position within the military nexus of the royal affinity became increasingly apparent. A good example of this is Sir William Sandes, a knight of the body since Henry VII's reign and treasurer of Calais between 1517 and 1526, when he was elevated to the peerage and became chamberlain of the king's household and lieutenant of Guînes. In 1503 Sandes was named in a case before the Hampshire bench concerning the conduct of men retained by him as steward of several royal manors in the county. One of the defendants claimed that he had received a red rose badge, royal livery, from Sandes so that he might 'doo the kings service when he shuld be commandid and to no nother entent'.[48] It is clear that this system, which depended upon the military resources of the growing royal affinity, circumvented the previous personal arrangements that had governed the relationship between captains and their deputies. For example, Giles, Lord Daubeney's deputies as lieutenant of Calais in the last decade or so of the fifteenth century were men not recruited personally by him, but rather were members of the royal affinity chosen by the king and commanding royal, not personal, military resources.[49]

To some extent this close relationship between military command in Calais

---

[44] Dominic Luckett, 'Crown Office and Licensed Retinues in the Reign of Henry VII', in *Rulers and Ruled in Late Medieval England*, ed. Rowena E. Archer and Simon Walker (London 1995), 223–38; S.J. Gunn, 'Sir Thomas Lovell (*c.* 1449–1524): A New Man in a New Monarchy?', in *The End of the Middle Ages?*, ed. John L. Watts (Stroud, 1998), 117–54.

[45] For 1492 see E101/72/3 and 4. For 1513 see, for example, the letter to Sir David Owen ordering him to provide a hundred men: *LP*, I i. 1640.

[46] R. Somerville, *History of the Duchy of Lancaster, i. 1265–1603* (1953), 492–586.

[47] See below, p. 000.

[48] Luckett, 'Crown Office and Licensed Retinues', 231–2.

[49] For example, Thomas Fiennes, esquire of the body and Daubeney's deputy at Calais castle between 1486 and 1494 and again in the early 1500s, was steward of duchy of Lancaster lands in Sussex, where he was expected to find a hundred men for the king's service when called upon to do so. He was also a member of the king's household: E101/198/13, f. 42; Grummitt, 'Early Tudor Policy towards Calais', 187; Luckett, 'Crown Office and Licensed Retinues', 227, 235.

and the royal household and wider royal affinity had a detrimental effect on the purely military nature of commands in the Pale. The trend for non-military offices in the Pale – the collectors of rent, customers and receivers and bailiffs of the outlying lordships – to be used as patronage for rewarding royal servants had gained pace by the end of the fifteenth century. Frequently these officers were absentees for whom royal office in Calais was just one part of a wider *cursus honorum* of royal service at court and in the localities. Men such as James Worsley, one of the collectors of customs in Calais in the early part of Henry VIII's reign, for example, combined titular office in Calais with office in the royal wardrobe, the customs at Poole, Dorset, in the Isle of Wight and with the custody of the royal menagerie in the Tower of London, and were, in the main, also absentees. The bulk of administrative tasks in the Pale were carried out by less than half a dozen permanent residents.[50] By the beginning of the sixteenth century this trend was also being felt in relation to the Pale's military commands. In 1486 six of the nine major offices in the Pale were held by members of the royal household; by 1515 all the major offices were held exclusively by members of the household. Thus during the first part of Henry VIII's reign military command in the Pale was sometimes subordinated to the demands of politics and patronage at the Henrician court. While positions were sometimes held by absentee courtiers, appointment to office in Calais could also be used as a weapon in court politics. David Starkey has likened Calais to a 'Tudor India', where potential rivals could be sent to languish away from court. One of the best examples of this manipulation of office occurred in 1519. Cardinal Wolsey, afraid of the influence of the francophile 'minions' in the Privy Chamber, succeeded in persuading Henry to expel four of them (Sir Edward Neville, Nicholas Carew, Francis Bryan and Francis Poyntz) from court. Carew was sent to take up his new position as lieutenant of Rysbank Tower in May. Although he and the others were back at court by October it was long enough for Wolsey to appoint 'four sad and ancient knights' to counterbalance them in the Privy Chamber.[51] At the same time Sir John Pecche was translated to Calais to take over as deputy. Another casualty of Wolsey's purge of Henry's court in May 1519 was Sir Edward Guildford, who was moved to Calais to become high marshall. This freed Sir Richard Wingfield to come to court as the one of the new knights of the body in the Privy Chamber.[52] Similarly, the changes in military command in 1526 can be interpreted as owing more to court politics than military necessity.[53]

---

50 Grummitt, 'Calais 1485–1547', ch. 3. For Worsley see *LP*, III i. 102/7, 854/14; LC 9/50, f. 206v. He was, however, also chief steward of Petersfield (*LP*, III i. 2016/8) and captain of the Isle of Wight from May 1520, suggesting some military responsibilities.

51 *LP*, III i. 247; David Starkey, 'Intimacy and Innovation: The Rise of the Privy Chamber 1485–1547', in D. Starkey et al., *The English Court from the Wars of the Roses to the English Civil War* (1990), 102–4.

52 *LP*, III i. 152, 230. See, however, the alternative view of this incident put forward by Greg Walker, 'The "Expulsion of the Minions" of 1519 Reconsidered', *Historical Journal*, xxxii (1989), 1–16.

53 Grummitt, 'Calais 1485–1547', 120.

By the mid-1530s there were growing concerns that the absenteeism of office holders, captains and soldiers was compromising the military effectiveness of the Pale's garrisons. In 1535 Sir William Fitzwilliam's commission to the Pale reported on the state of the defences which, the following year, resulted in the Calais Act. This was primarily a set of military ordinances, firmly in the tradition of those issued for other military establishments such as Berwick and the Channel Islands, which were enshrined in statute.[54] The act insisted upon the permanent residence of all office holders and soldiers in the Pale and, as we have seen, confirmed and extended the military responsibilities of the captains. Moreover, the events of the period 1539–40 further clarified the military roles of the Pale's captains. First, the Franco-Imperial rapprochement of 1539 heightened tension in the Pale and reinforced the strategic importance of Calais and Guînes. Second, the fall of Thomas Cromwell in May 1540 and the restructuring of the privy council the following August allowed the Calais council, institutionalised in 1536, to emerge as a permanent governing body for the Pale supervised directly from Westminster. As John Dasent observed, the 'English Pale in France', including Calais and, from 1544, Boulogne, was one of the 'five great categories' that made up the bulk of the council's business.[55] Between April 1542 and July 1543, for instance, the reinforcement of the Pale's defences, the payment of the garrisons and the arrangements for victualling were constant themes for discussion in the council. It is evident that the direction of these affairs was in the hands of the king and privy council, however, although their daily implementation was left largely to the Calais council.[56]

Nevertheless, the extent to which the captains of the Pale were 'demilitarised' during the early sixteenth century should not be overestimated. While other pressures such as court politics and patronage did have an impact, the main qualification for serving as one of the captains remained military. This continued to be the most important factor in determining who served as a captain throughout the period 1436 to 1558. Either through proved prowess on the field of battle or through military reputation gained through lineage or chivalric achievement, the captains of the Pale consistently reinforced Calais' reputation as a town of war. Lord Lisle, for example, participated in feats of arms at court in 1510 and 1511 along with such intimates of the king as Charles Brandon, Edmund Howard and Thomas Knyvet. In 1513 he took part in the naval campaign against France, nearly losing his life in the shipwreck of the *Nicholas of Hampton* and was dubbed a knight outside Tournai on 14 October 1513.[57] As a group the Tudor captains of the Pale, men like Sir John Wallop, Sir William Fitzwilliam, the Wingfields, or even Arthur Plantagenet, Viscount

---

[54] 27 Hen VIII. c. 63 (*Statutes of the Realm*, ed. A. Luders et al. (11 vols, 1810–28), iii. 632 50).

[55] *APC*, i. xviii.

[56] *APC*, i. 22, 123, 127, 132, 133, 146, 153. No register survives between 22 July 1543 and 10 May 1545. After this date it becomes increasingly difficult to disentangle orders which specifically refer to Calais from those concerning Boulogne and the administration of the huge field army maintained in the Pale.

[57] David Grummitt, 'Arthur Plantagenet, Viscount Lisle' in *Oxford DNB*.

Lisle, were experienced soldiers and in this respect were not fundamentally different from their fifteenth-century predecessors.[58] Sir Thomas Rempston, for instance, like Sir William Fitzwilliam, had combined service in war in Calais, Normandy and Guienne with service as a royal official, local justice, knight of the shire and county gentleman.

Despite changes in the political, social, economic and, from the 1530s, religious conditions of the sixteenth century, it is clear that military service among the captains of the Calais garrison continued to be determined principally by military ability and reputation. Indeed, the growing power of the crown, in terms of its ability to finance the defence of the Pale and provide sufficient manpower from its own estates and from county militias, made the private resources of the captains less important and allowed the crown to dictate the conditions of service more forcefully than it had been able to in the fifteenth century. This did not mean that the nobility were excluded from command to be replaced by captains from lower social origins. Rather, as I will argue in a later chapter, it led to the redefinition of notions of nobility. Mid-Tudor England had an elite, including nobility and gentry, whose virtues and claims to nobility were defined by their military and chivalric achievements.

The soldiers

Any attempt to analyse who served as soldiers in the Calais garrison and the means by which they were recruited is hampered by archival problems. The loss of the archives of the English exchequer in Calais in 1558 (only those documents returned to Westminster are now extant) means that the muster book and rolls that recorded the names of the garrison are, for the most part, lost. Thus it is impossible to reconstruct lengths of service and for the most part even to know the names of those who served as soldiers. The kind of prosopographical analysis undertaken by Anne Curry of the garrisons of Lancastrian Normandy is simply not possible for the Calais garrison between 1436 and 1558. Moreover, there are no private indentures for service by soldiers of the ordinary garrison in Calais and precious few other instances where the relationship between men and their captains is made explicit. The interpretation of an alternative source of evidence, letters of protection for men crossing the Channel to enter the retinues of one of the captains of Calais, is also fraught with difficulties. These royal letters, which gave immunity from legal process in England during the duration of the period in retinue (usually one year, renewed annually), were frequently obtained as a ploy to escape creditors in England as the numerous revocations, because the recipient 'tarried in England', demonstrate.[59] Nevertheless, from what evidence remains it is possible to suggest some tentative conclusions for the fifteenth century and, as the amount and nature of the evidence changes, to

---

[58] For the careers of three Tudor captains of the garrison, highlighting the continued importance of military skill as a qualification for service in the Pale see below, pp. 108–11.

[59] J.S. Critchley, 'The Early History of the Writ of Judicial Protection', *BIHR*, lv (1972), 196–213.

reach more firm conclusions on the nature of service in the garrison for the sixteenth century.

The fifteenth-century protections and two surviving musters suggest that very few soldiers in the Calais garrison had permanent links with their captains. This reinforces the conclusion reached by those who have studied the military retinues of those English captains serving in the latter stages of the Hundred Years War. In all of the retinues assembled by John Talbot, earl of Shrewsbury, that served in France between 1428 and 1448 only eleven permanent followers, that is indentured retainers or tenants, can be identified. Similarly, in Henry Bourgchier's retinue in 1441 only five of forty-nine had permanent ties with him.[60] That the Calais garrison attracted a cosmopolitan group of men, for most of whom military service was just one part of a wide and varied career, is shown by the protections. One example of a well-travelled Englishman serving in the garrison in the fifteenth century is John Colt. In January 1468 Colt received a protection to enter Warwick's retinue and is described as a merchant and gentleman of Newcastle-upon-Tyne and London. In 1471 he was pardoned as a soldier of Calais, yeoman of Northumberland, merchant of Newcastle and gentleman of London and Essex. The following year he received another protection as soldier and merchant of Calais, London and Essex.[61] The relationship between Colt and Warwick is nowhere made explicit, although his attachment to Warwick in 1470–1 ensured that he sued out a royal pardon following Edward IV's return.[62]

There were various reasons that attracted men to a military career in Calais. Not least of these was the desire to escape legal or family problems back in England. The protection granted to Thomas Walton, late of Preston, mercer, and soldier of Guînes in May 1467 contained a clause that his service with Warwick in the Pale was to be accompanied by a pardon of all processes against him in the king's courts.[63] One of the best documented soldiers of Calais who first came to the Pale to escape problems in England is Richard Lovelace. Lovelace was a Kentish gentleman who had fled to Calais in 1468–9 to escape justice over a family land dispute and entered, first, into the duke of Clarence's retinue and then that of the earl of Warwick. By 1477 he had entered the service of Lord Hastings, serving in his expedition to reinforce the Pale that year. The following November he received a protection to enter Hastings's retinue at Calais. In 1484 he was retained for life by Richard III and the following year pledged his

---

[60] A.J. Pollard, *John Talbot and the War in France, 1427–1453* (1983), 70–1, 83, 95; L.S. Woodger, 'Henry Bourgchier, Earl of Essex and his Family (1408–83)' (DPhil thesis, University of Oxford, 1974), 29.

[61] C76/151, m. 10; *CPR, 1467–77*, 290 (part of a list of pardons to 'all and evereche of the persones of oure said Towne' where the geographical and occupational spread of the garrison is clear: C81/835/3251); C76/156, m. 20.

[62] John's kinsman, possibly his older brother, Thomas, was one of Warwick's most intimate servants, serving as his deputy in the exchequer and as the king's councillor during the time of the earl's ascendancy between 1462 and his death in 1467: J.C. Wedgwood and A.D. Holt, *Register and Biographies of the Members of the House of Commons, 1439–1509* (2 vols, London, 1936–8), ii. 208–9.

[63] C76/151, m. 16.

allegiance to the new king, Henry VII, receiving an annuity of fifty marks. In 1497 he was knighted for his service against the Cornish rebels at Blackheath and served as undermarshall of Calais until at least 1502.[64]

Lovelace was clearly a skilled soldier and probably a natural troublemaker: service in Calais, then, provided a legitimate outlet for his particular qualities. Service in Calais was also attractive to what we might justifiably call 'professional soldiers', such as Andrew Trollope.[65] Men like Lovelace and Trollope formed the military backbone of the garrison, serving as men-at-arms and commanding their personal retinues. In Somerset's retinue of 1451 Trollope was listed with a retinue of twenty-four men, twelve among the ordinary and twelve in the 'crew' and in 1502 Lovelace had six men in his retinue.[66] Many also served in Calais for long periods, regardless of political circumstances and changes of dynasty. Lovelace, for instance, served in Calais for at least thirty-five years. Another interesting name with long service in Calais that transcended dynastic change was Hugh Conwey. A Hugh Conwey appears as a man-at-arms on foot under Giles Seyntlow, the comptroller, in Somerset's retinue in 1451. By 1461 he had transferred to the Yorkist household, probably via Warwick, and was made bedell of Marke and Oye; in 1464 he participated in Warwick's campaign to reduce the northern Lancastrian strongholds, serving in the defence of Newcastle-upon-Tyne. In 1483, perhaps because of his north Wales origins and links to the Stanleys, he joined the conspiracy to place Henry Tudor on the throne. Serving in Henry VII's household, he was made treasurer of Calais in 1504 and died in 1517.[67]

The 1466 act of retainer with the merchants of the staple (by which the staplers accepted formal responsibility for paying the garrison) allowed the crown new opportunities to dictate more firmly the conditions of service in the Pale. This had an effect on who served in the garrison. The last quarter of the fifteenth century saw the increasing importance of crown office as a means of recruiting men to serve in the Pale. This is evident from a list of men serving in the garrison at Guînes with Sir James Tyrell who received the king's pardon in July 1486.[68] Tyrell had accumulated a number of offices under Richard III which allowed him to construct a powerful affinity for the use of his royal master. Tyrell's main power base was in Wales and the marcher lordships. This influence survived Richard's defeat at Bosworth: on 19 February 1486 Tyrell was confirmed as sheriff of Glamorgan and Morgonnak and 'steward of all the king's castles and lands in that county'.[69] That Tyrell used these offices to

[64] *English Historical Documents* iv. 1327–1485, ed. A.R. Myers (Oxford, 1969), 1101–16; *British Library Harleian Manuscript 433*, ed. R. Horrox and P.W. Hammond (4 vols, Gloucester, 1979–83), i. 272; E101/201/3, f. 41v; P.W. Fleming, 'The Lovelace Dispute: Concepts of Property and Inheritance in Fifteenth-Century Kent', *Southern History*, xiii (1990), 1–18.
[65] For Trollope's career see below, pp. 106–7.
[66] E101/54/16; E101/55/23.
[67] E101/54/16, 4; C76/145, m. 23; E 404/72/4/76; Ralph A. Griffiths and Roger S. Thomas, *The Making of the Tudor Dynasty* (Stroud, 1985), 93–6; C66/594, m. 10; *LP* II ii. 3257.
[68] PSO2/2 Signet warrant, 12 July 1486.
[69] *CPR, 1485–94*, 114; Charles Ross, *Richard III* (1981), 157.

supply part of the garrison at Guînes is evident from the list of those pardoned in July 1486. The document lists twenty-eight men, including Tyrell himself, with their aliases and former places of residence – just over a quarter of the nominal establishment at Guînes. They probably represent those soldiers who were in a direct relationship with Tyrell and elected to remain in the Pale after Bosworth. They, no doubt, considered it prudent to seek royal approval. Twelve men came from areas where Tyrell had close links: six came from Cheshire, Wales or the marches; one was from Cornwall;[70] three were from East Anglia, Tyrell's home region; one was from Shropshire;[71] while two were from North Yorkshire.[72] The nature of the networks of patronage which helped build the garrisons of the Pale in the late fifteenth century is shown by the case of Richard Lloyd of Assheton, Essex: in 1485 he owed his grant of the office of bailiff of the hundreds of East and West Budleigh (Devon) to the good offices of Tyrell.[73] Of the remaining seventeen men named in the pardon, seven came from the north Midlands, an area associated with the previous lieutenants, William, Lord Hastings, his brother, Ralph, and John, Lord Mountjoy. John Bonnington, a Derbyshire gentleman, had been retained by indenture with Hastings in April 1475. On 30 January 1485 Richard III granted him the constableship of Guînes castle.[74] That these men were able to transfer between captains demonstrates how, by the end of the fifteenth century, the growing strength of the crown and the use of the crown lands to increase the power and influence of the royal affinity had lessened the direct ties between captains and their soldiers and reinforced the crown's role, directly or indirectly through royal office, as the principal source of appointment to the garrison.

There is increasing evidence that, as the crown increased its control over appointments to the Calais garrison, these were used as a means of patronage to reward the king's servants. The prospect of regular wages and of gaining honour and 'worship' through military service made a position within the garrison an attractive and much sought-after commodity. This was nothing new in the early sixteenth century: the Pastons, for example, had been constant suitors of Lord Hastings in the 1470s to gain positions in the garrison for themselves and their servants. Places in the garrison were usually solicited by the prospective soldier, eager to come to the Pale for his own reasons or attracted by the prospect of

[70] On 9 August 1484 Tyrell replaced Lord Dynham as chief steward of the duchy of Cornwall lands: *CPR, 1476–85*, 474.

[71] In September 1484 Richard III appointed Tyrell as sheriff of Wenlock, steward of Maghen and constable of Newport castle: Wedgwood and Holt, *House of Commons, 1439–1509*, ii. 889–90.

[72] Tyrell's links with Yorkshire are more tenuous. On 10 March 1478 Edward IV granted him an annuity of £20 out of the manor of Rosse in Holdernesse: *CPR, 1476–85*, 88. Presumably Tyrell would have had some contacts with the area in order to realise his annuity. John Thirlewall is described as 'late of Thirlewall, Yorks ... late of Yalding, Kent'. Tyrell also received a large portion of Kent lands from Richard III: Wedgwood and Holt, *House of Commons, 1439–1509*, ii. 890.

[73] Horrox, *Richard III*, 189.

[74] *CPR, 1476–85*, 534; W.H. Dunham, 'Lord Hastings' Indentured Retainers 1461–1483', *Transactions of the Connecticut Academy of Arts and Sciences*, xxxix (1955), 119.

entering the service of a great lord. In June 1475 Sir John Paston wrote to his brother, Edmund, from Calais: 'I heer telle þat ye be in hope to come hyddre and to be in such wagys as ye schall can lyve lyke a jentlyman' and advising of a position in the garrison that had just become vacant.[75] From about the middle of Henry VII's reign the demand for positions in the garrison increased, however, and the crown often usurped the captains' right of appointment to their garrisons. As early as November 1492 the king ordered the treasurer, Sir John Turberville, to pay £12 3s. 4d., the wages of 'John Gythyns, yoman huisher of oure Chambre'. By 1502 Gythyns was listed as a foot archer in the garrison receiving the same rate of pay – 6d. a day – as a yeoman of the crown, while his fee at the Westminster exchequer had been taken by Richard Davy.[76]

Further evidence of the use of positions in the garrison as a means of retaining royal servants comes from the letters missive warranting extraordinary payments addressed to the treasurer of Calais. For example, in February 1504 the king ordered the wages of John Tremayle, a man-at-arms on horseback at 12d., to be paid notwithstanding his absence from Calais 'attending upon us' from Halloween the previous year. The same year the marshal, Sir Thomas Bourchier, was absent for most of the year attending the king. The treasurer was ordered to meet his wages and those of two other soldiers who accompanied him, the gunner, Hans Calkyn, and Thomas Shyppey.[77] This trend was also apparent in the increasing number of royal annuitants whose fees were payable by the treasurer of Calais. By the 1500 all those members of the garrison who still received pay for personal retinues were either royal office holders or annuitants.[78] During the first years of Henry VIII's reign pressure to fill vacant positions in the garrison increased. For example, at some time before 1513 Henry VIII wrote to Sir Gilbert Talbot, the deputy, ordering him to admit John Russell, a gentleman usher of the chamber, to the room of a spear (man-at-arms on horseback) with two men under him.[79] Similarly, in October 1515 the king ordered the then deputy, Sir Richard Wingfield, in a clear breach of the terms of his appointment, to admit 'our welbiloved servaunte John Rawlyns (to) the Rowme of oon of our fyve speres within that our said towne and marches of Calais whiche the said Lord Dawbeney decessed late had of the gift and graunt of the late king our fader'. In theory the deputy had the freedom to appoint all soldiers in the garrison, but the reality was very different.[80]

The correspondence of Arthur Plantagenet, Viscount Lisle, deputy of Calais between 1533 and 1540, shows the scramble for patronage in the garrison that greeted every new deputy. Within days of his appointment Lisle was barraged

[75] *Paston Letters and Papers of the Fifteenth Century*, ed. N.B. Davis (EETS, special series, xx, 2004), i. 486.

[76] E101/200/20; 55/23, f. 7. I am grateful to Anita Hewerdine for information regarding Gythyn's fee at the exchequer.

[77] DL28/2/6, f. 49v; DL28/2/10, f. 37v.

[78] Grummitt, 'Early Tudor Policy towards Calais', 189–90.

[79] BL, Add. MS 46454, f. 14; Diane Willen, *John Russell, First Earl of Bedford: One of the King's Men* (1981) 5–6.

[80] E314/33/55; C82/340 (*LP* I i. 190/39).

with requests from influential people hoping to find positions for their clients. For example, on 30 March 1533 the duchess of Suffolk requested that Lisle 'be so good Lord unto John Williams, this bearer, as to admit him into the room of a soldier in Calais, with the wages of viij d by the day'. Similar requests were forthcoming from the marquis of Exeter, Sir Francis Bryan, Sir William Kingston and Thomas Cromwell, as well as a host of lesser people.[81] Although, according to his patent, most positions or 'rooms' in the garrison were in Lisle's gift, the deputy knew the political realties affecting such grants. Aware that the king had granted the next vacant spear's room to Richard Blount, a client of Sir William Kingston, Lisle assured Cromwell that 'Notwithstanding I have the gift of all the spears in my patent and all other of the Retinue, yet the King's Grace's pleasure and your desire shall be ever fulfilled in me'.[82] However, even when Lisle tried to follow the king and Cromwell's direction he found himself in trouble. Between 1533 and 1536 Lisle became embroiled in a bitter dispute with Sir Richard Whetehill, himself a soldier and one of the leading Calais burgesses, over a spear's room for Robert, Sir Richard's son. This arose not through Lisle's bias against Whetehill, but simply because the king had granted the same room to more than one man. Lisle had the impossible task of attempting to disentangle the mess without incurring royal censure.[83] In 1535 Lisle was forced to defend himself to the royal commissioners against accusations of taking bribes and of selling rooms to men unfit to furnish them.[84] As early as August 1533 Sir Richard Whetehill had protested to Kingston that Richard Blount was not of sufficient wealth to occupy a spear's room (presumably he could not afford to keep servants or buy his own horse and armour) and that George Browne was set to sell his room to the highest bidder.[85] Lisle was not alone in feeling the pressure of patronage. During the 1530s Sir John Wallop, lieutenant of Calais castle, also tried unsuccessfully to secure the appointment of his own men to 'rooms' in the castle's garrison.[86]

The reformation of the conditions of military service in the Calais garrison was one of the principal aims of the commission, led by Sir William Fitzwilliam, in August 1535. They were charged to inquire whether the garrison was at full strength; if the soldiers were fit enough to carry out their martial duties; if they were properly equipped; whether the watch and ward was 'kept at howres and tymes accustomed'; and how many of the soldiers were employed in civilian trades.[87] Fitzwilliam reported: 'We have found this town and marches far out of order, and so far that it would grieve and pity the heart of any good and true

---

[81] See, for example, *Lisle Letters*, i. 5, 5b, 5c, 7, 11.

[82] *Lisle Letters*, i. 38.

[83] The broad details of this long dispute are outlined in W.G. Davis, 'Whetehill of Calais', *The New England Historical and Genealogical Register*, cix (1949), 7–10. The principal letters of the affair, that ultimately involved such luminaries at Henry's court as Norris, Bryan, and the earl of Sussex, are *Lisle Letters*, ii. 152, 252, 259, 260, 296; iii. 633, 669, 680, 742 and 747.

[84] SP1/92, f. 265 (*LP*, VIII, 795); *Lisle Letters*, ii. 553 8.

[85] SP1/78, f. 125 (*LP*, VI, 983).

[86] *LP*, XI, 323.

[87] BL, Cotton MS Caligula E. II, ff. 160–6 (*Chronicle of Calais*, 133–5).

Englishman to hear the same.' The result of the enquiry, the 'act declaryng certeyn Ordenances to be observyd in the Towne of Calais and Marches of the same' of the following year, was principally a thorough scheme for the remilitarisation of the garrison.[88] The act sought to reverse the abuses that had characterised its management since the mid-1490s. The deputy and other officers were forbidden to take payment for admitting people into the garrison. 'Rooms' in Calais could only be sold with a licence from the king. No burgess or artificer could serve in the garrison and no soldier in Calais, Guînes, Hammes or the fortresses of Rysbank and Newembridge was to keep shop or act as a victualler. Only trades directly linked to military needs, for example, smith and armourer, and a few exceptions for partnerships were allowed. The act sent shock waves through that part of the garrison that was not fulfilling its military obligations. In October 1535 Ralph Broke wrote to Lord Lisle of his dismay that 'every man of arms shall be furnished with horses and harness; and further, that every man should be there resident by Candelmas day next coming or else lose their rooms, notwithstanding the king's placard or signed bill'. The trouble, Broke explained, was that as a servant of the duke of Norfolk he was expected to attend upon his lord at Holt castle that Christmas and could not be in Calais. Two months later Lisle's agent in London, John Hussey, also a member of the garrison, was alarmed to discover his wages had been checked by the treasurer for absence.[89]

The increasing regulation of the nature of service in the garrison and the return of open warfare to the Pale in the early 1540s only served to increase the prestige of serving in Calais. Positions in the garrison continued to be sold under the king's licence, with guidance from the Calais council and as long as the military obligations of the position were maintained, and the sums for which they changed hands reflect their value. In May 1549, for example, Richard Tary agreed to sell his position of a man-at-arms in the garrison, worth 18*d.* a day with the nomination of one man at 6*d.*, to John Tamworth for £85, once Tamworth had obtained the king's licence to enter the garrison. The sum of £85 was more than three times Tamworth's prospective annual wage, demonstrating the prestige of serving at Calais and the prospects it offered for the advancement of a military career.[90] Nevertheless, the importance of honour and the prestige of serving in the garrison should not overshadow the pecuniary benefits of serving. The prospect of regular pay after the act of retainer in 1466 and the crown's increasing control over appointments to the garrison at all levels meant that the average length of service probably increased from the end of the fifteenth century. As soldiers were no longer personally tied to their captains, the change-over of retinues that had characterised service in the first part of our period was no longer so apparent. That the military obligations of individuals soldiers – watch and ward, for example – did not have to be performed in person and the fact that there was an ever-present pool of those in petty wages ready to meet

---

[88] See above, pp. 50–1.
[89] *Lisle Letters*, ii. 461, 501.
[90] BL, Harl. Ch. 76 E 39.

such obligations enabled men to serve in the Calais garrison for many decades, often into old age.

As no register of admissions to the garrison survives, lengths of service can only be reconstructed from anecdotal evidence. Reginald Clifton, for example, was a man-at-arms under Lord Hastings during the 1470s: in 1477 he was sent to Boulogne to prepare a possible defence of the town against Louis XI of France by the soldiers of Calais. Twenty-one years, and three kings, later he was still serving when he made a transfer of land to John Broke, merchant of the staple, before the mayor of Calais. Similarly, John Cokeson, the water bailiff of Calais between 1497 and 1539, served in the garrison for over forty years.[91] That these individuals were not exceptional is evident from a set of depositions taken in December 1551 to determine the boundaries of the county of Guînes. The enquiry followed the normal practice of gathering together and taking statements from the oldest inhabitants of the county. They included one Robert Chamberlayne, aged eighty-two, 'havyng served as Soldiour in the kinges maiesties Castell of Guysnes the space of xlix yeres and yet remayneth Soldiour in the saide Castell'; one Thomas Fayre, aged sixty-five, then serving as a gunner in Guînes castle having previously served as a soldier for more than thirty years; and Anthony Hutchynson, who had been a soldier at Guînes since 1531 and possibly since as long ago as 1526.[92] What these examples show is that the Calais garrison contained a sizeable proportion of men who had years of experience as soldiers and whose years at Calais helped define the military identity of the town and marches. The identification of the Calais garrison as a purely military force, as we shall see, was further reinforced by the terms of the 1536 act, which heightened the distinction between the military and civilian populations of the town, and the decade of almost continuous warfare from 1541.

The crews

The command and recruitment of the extraordinary forces sent over to boost the defences of the Calais mirror the command and recruitment of armies for foreign service generally in late medieval and early Tudor England. The way in which, say, a hundred men were recruited for a crew for Guînes was similar to how the multiple contingents were gathered to form an army to wage war against continental enemies on a grander scale. Thus, the developments for the defence of the Calais serve to illustrate developments in the political and military culture of England more generally. The recruitment of crews between 1451 and 1558 will serve to show how political change affected the ways in which English armies were recruited. Five will be examined in detail. First, there is the crew that Edmund Beaufort, duke of Somerset, took to Calais in 1451. Second, the force of some five hundred men that served under William, Lord Hastings, between 1477 and 1480 in the aftermath of the death of Charles the Bold, duke

---

[91] E101/55/23, f. 3v; SP 1/5, f. 51; E101/62/18, f. 3; C76/178, m. 1.
[92] SP70/147, ff. 18–25.

of Burgundy, and the threat to the Pale posed by the French attack on Picardy and Artois. Third, there are the crews that Sir Nicholas Vaux commanded at Guînes between 1512 and 1514 and his contingent for the king's army which invaded France in 1513. Finally, there are the forces raised in 1558 for the abortive attempt to relieve the siege of Calais by the Duc de Guise.

The men who served in Somerset's crew of 1451 reflect the duke's career as a military commander in Lancastrian France and the fact that there was a pool of experienced soldiers available in the early 1450s for service in Calais. His captains included such Lancastrian stalwarts as Osbert Mountefort, Andrew Tyrell and Sir Richard Wydeville, Lord Rivers. These men had long careers of service in Lancastrian Normandy, at times serving under the Beauforts. For the remainder of the men-at-arms and archers definite links between Somerset, the captains and the soldiers are more difficult to establish. It is clear from the database of men who served in Lancastrian Normandy, compiled by Anne Curry from the surviving muster lists, that soldiers served for long periods in many different retinues and under many different captains.[93] Some of the men who served in Calais in 1451 had years of experience as soldiers in the Norman garrisons. Thomas Lilborne, for example, may be the Thomas Lilborne who had served under John Beaufort, earl of Somerset, in Avranches between 1428 and 1444; similarly, Dycon Baron may be the soldier of that name who served under Sir John Fastolf and Sir Richard Wydeville at Fresnay between 1427 and 1442. Of the 260 men of the crew, fifty-four had the same name as men who are known to have served in Normandy, suggesting a significant minority who had previous military experience.[94] More surprising perhaps is that there is little evidence that captains were able to bring their old Norman retinues directly for service in Calais. The largest personal retinue within Somerset's crew in 1451 was the eighty-one men serving under Rivers. Of these, however, only one can be identified as previously serving under him: James of Orell who was among the garrison at Alençon in 1446. This lends weight to the suggestion that members of mid-fifteenth-century retinues for overseas service had few if any permanent ties to their captain. We know, however, that there were large number of redundant soldiers from Lancastrian Normandy in the south of England in 1450 and 1451 and this would doubtless have provided a ready pool of men for Somerset to lead to Calais.[95]

[93] I am grateful to Dr Curry for allowing me access to this important source. For a discussion of the preliminary findings revealed by the database see Anne Curry, 'English Armies in the Fifteenth Century' in *Arms, Armies and Fortifications in the Hundred Years War*, ed. Anne Curry and Michael Hughes (Woodbridge, 1994), 66–8.

[94] This is only a very rough estimate of course: the problems of identifying men with the same name as the same individual are compounded by the erratic survival of Norman muster lists from which the database is primarily compiled.

[95] For the some of the problems caused by the returning soldiers see R.L. Storey, *The End of the House of Lancaster* (2nd edn Stroud, 1999), 61–2; Anne Curry, 'The Loss of Lancastrian Normandy: An Administrative Nightmare?', in *The English Experience in France, c. 1450–1558: War, Diplomacy and Culture Exchange*, ed. David Grummitt (Aldershot, 2002), 44–5.

The composition of the forces that Lord Hastings led to Calais between 1477 and 1480 can be more accurately reconstructed by the survival of three separate muster rolls, resulting from a dispute in the exchequer over the army's wages. They demonstrate how Hastings was able to use his position in the royal household and the *manraed* of crown stewardships, as well as his own private resources and contacts, to fulfil the terms of the indenture he concluded with the king to muster the force. The Hastings retinue is evidence of the changes in political structure and landholding which allowed Edward IV to exert greater control over the recruitment and composition of military forces after 1471. An analysis of the men-at-arms and mounted archers illustrates this. The three crews which accompanied Hastings to Calais between 1478 and 1480 contained a total of twenty-six mounted men-at-arms and forty-one mounted archers. These were usually filled by men of gentry or wealthy yeoman status. They included Hastings's indentured retainer, Humphrey Stanley, and such well-wishers as Sir John Paston and his associates, Tyrrey Robsert, John Nesfeld and Thomas Oxenbrigge.[96] Hastings's associates from the north Midlands, John Coke and Sir John Ferrers, Hastings's nephew, were present as well as the professional soldier, Robert Lovelace. In total fifteen of the twenty-six men-at-arms had identifiable links to Hastings or came from areas in which he was the dominant magnate. An interesting name among the mounted men-at-arms is Sir Philip Chesnall. Chesnall does not seem to appear in English records until Easter term 1482 when, as master of the king's henchmen, he was sent on embassy to Archduke Maximilian of Austria.[97] Perhaps, like Sir Thomas Everingham who would serve as Hastings's deputy in Calais in the early 1480s,[98] Chesnall had spent the period prior to 1477 in Burgundian service. Alternatively, his inclusion may be indicative of the inextricable links between Hastings's affinity and the king's.

In the cases of twenty-three of the forty-one mounted archers a likely association with Hastings can be suggested. The largest identifiable group was from the royal household. Ten can be identified from other sources as being of the king's chamber or yeomen of the crown. Some were linked both to the household and personally to Hastings: for example, John Shirley, one of his indentured retainers since April 1474, received robes from the royal wardrobe in 1478–9.[99] The link with the household was also reinforced by the manner in which the

---

[96] The date of Stanley's indenture is not known; his retention is only known from the seventeenth-century list in BL, Add. MS 5,948, f. 249v. For the links between Hastings, the Pastons and their associates, Nesfield, Robsert and Oxenbrigge see Grummitt, 'Hastings and the Defence of Calais', 161–2.

[97] E405/70, rot. 8. Chesnall does not appear in the printed patent or close rolls, nor was he among those retained to serve in Edward's 1475 campaign. There are no records of payments to him by the exchequer before 1482 when he appears as master of the king's henchmen in the royal household.

[98] For Everingham in Burgundian service see below, p. 102. Albeit a Yorkshireman, his family had links with Hastings and the Midlands; Royal Commission on Historical Manuscripts, *Report on the Manuscripts of the late Reginald Rawdon Hastings, Esq., of the Manor House, Ashby de la Zouche* (4 vols, London, 1928–47), i. 1; *Harleian Manuscript 433*, i. 126.

[99] Dunham, 'Indentured Retainers', 119; E101/412/10, f. 36v.

expedition's wages were paid. Of the £3,600 charged to Hastings between February and July 1477 all but £409 was received directly from Peter Curteys, one of the king's chamber servants, or one of his assistants, in effect delivering money directly from the king.[100] The importance of the duchy of Lancaster estates in the north Midlands is also evident. Hastings's power base in the north Midlands rested on his duchy stewardships of Tutbury in Staffordshire, Leicester and High Peak in Derbyshire.[101] Three mounted archers held minor office in those duchy lands under the stewardship of Hastings. William Marshall, of North Muskham, Nottinghamshire, along with William Norton, was appointed feodary of Pontefract honour in November 1477. Thomas Clerke succeeded Hastings as deputy feodary of Kenilworth castle and honour in July 1475. The same year he was also deputy to Richard Hastings as constable, porter and collector of rents at Melborne in the honour of Tutbury, while George Gage was receiver of duchy lands in Northamptonshire.[102] At least two men – both members of the Franke family[103] – had existing links to both Calais and the north Midlands, while in another seven cases a geographical affinity to the lieutenant can be identified. Moreover, as Dunham pointed out, four indentured retainers – William Palmer, Henry Columbell, Richard Eyre and Rauf Pole – served as foot archers, an odd role considering their social rank, yet explicable by the particular terms of Hastings's indenture to raise the force, which stated that he could 'convert the saide men of armes vnto Archers on fote or the saide Archers into men of Armes so that the wages excede not the wages and rewardes afore lymyted' and the fact that descriptions on muster rolls corresponded more closely to levels of pay than the military reality of the soldiers' service.[104]

The importance of stewardships of crown lands in the recruitment of soldiers is evident in the crews which Sir Nicholas Vaux assembled around Guînes during Henry VIII's first French war and which contributed to his contingent for the royal army in 1513. The move towards exploiting the *manraed* of the expanding crown estate rather than the resources of private lords in the last decades of the fifteenth century has already been noted, but the way in which this system could be mobilised for the defence of the Pale can be demonstrated by the case of Vaux. He had been lieutenant of Guînes since 1502 and this appointment was confirmed by Henry VIII on his accession. Between November 1509 and January 1510 a series of grants made Vaux the chief commander of the crown's military resources in Northamptonshire. On 8

---

100 E364/112, rot. E dorse.
101 Ian Rowney, 'Resources and Retaining in Yorkist England: William, Lord Hastings and the Honour of Tutbury', in *Property and Politics: Essays in Later Medieval English History*, ed. A.J. Pollard (Gloucester, 1984), 139–55; Rowney, 'The Hastings Affinity in Staffordshire and the Honour of Tutbury', *BIHR*, lvii (1984), 35–45.
102 Somerville, Duchy of Lancaster, i. 519, 562, 588; *CCR, 1461–8*, 311; DL29/372/6201.
103 John Franke was brother of Thomas, Guînes pursuivant in 1484. His other brother Geoffrey was an esquire of the body to Richard III. William Franke, presumably another brother, received a protection to cross to Calais in the retinue of the mayor of the staple in 1481: *Harleian Manuscript 433*, i. 104, 278; ii. 11, 16, 164; *CPR, 1477–81*, 272.
104 BL, Add. Ch. 19808.

November he received a grant of the stewardships in that county and Bucking-hamshire lately held by Henry VII's fallen minister, Sir Richard Empson. At the same time he received the stewardship of the lands of Margaret, countess of Richmond, the king's grandmother, who had died the previous June.[105] On 30 January 1510 Vaux received a further grant of stewardships in Northampton-shire and Buckinghamshire.[106] It is clear that he mobilised these resources for the defence of Guînes between 1512 and 1514 and that they provided his retinue for the king's invasion of France in 1513. Between February and August 1514 Vaux maintained large crews in and around Guînes, but the main evidence that soldiers were recruited from the Northamptonshire manors in his stewardship comes from his bill for the payment of conduct money for return of his 1513 retinue to England. Vaux received £18 18*s.* for the conduct of his retinue of one petty captain and seventy-two footmen from France back to their muster point in Northampton.[107] Vaux, unusually, appended a list of the men in his retinue to his petition for pay. Several of the surnames in that list can be found in the bailiffs' accounts for the manors under Vaux's stewardship and three men can be identi-fied as royal tenants: John Colyn and John Freemen were tenants at the Rich-mond manor of Collyweston, while John Taylor held land in Maxey, another Richmond manor.[108] Many more have surnames that suggest a link with the estates in Vaux's charge.[109]

Such methods, dubbed 'quasi feudal' by Jeremy Goring, remained important throughout the early Tudor period: in 1528 Henry VIII again looked to indi-vidual gentlemen to raise a crew for Guînes from their tenants, friends, and those under their 'rule'. As a result of renewed warfare on the borders between the French and Imperial armies, that had resulted in numerous incursions into English territory, Henry decided to 'send a certaine crewe of men, well elect and chosen, unto our said towne ... there to remaigne for a season upon the tuicion and defense of the same' under the command of the lieutenant of Guînes, William, Lord Sandes. One signet letter survives commanding Sir Adrian Fortescue to muster at Guildford on 4 May with ten archers.[110] In fact, as Sandes informed Wolsey, similar summonses had been sent to forty-one men to provide soldiers.[111] Men like Sandes also took care to ensure that their own, as well as the king's, tenants would attend them in war. Sandes is one of the few

---

[105] *LP*, I i. 257/32. Vaux was perfectly placed to take over the Richmond estates having been brought up in the countess's household: Michael K. Jones and Malcolm G. Underwood, *The King's Mother: Lady Margaret Beaufort, Countess of Richmond and Derby* (Cambridge, 1992), 121–2.

[106] *LP*, I i. 357/45.

[107] E36/2, pp. 311–17 (*LP*, I ii. 3135); E101/56/25/58–9.

[108] SC6/Hen VIII/2728, 2691. The lack of contemporary court rolls, rentals or surveys for this period makes the task of tracing tenants very difficult.

[109] In the court roll for Great Harrowden for 1545 7 five tenants shared surnames with men listed in the 1513 retinue: Northamptonshire Record Office, YO 529. I owe this reference to the kindness of Dr Steven Gunn.

[110] BL, Cotton MS Faustina, E. VII, f. 113 (*LP*, IV ii. 4127). Others like it must have been despatched as the original clerk left a blank for the appropriate number of men to be filled in.

[111] *LP*, IV ii. 4199.

sixteenth-century landowners in southern England who we know issued leases containing clauses that bound the tenant to perform military service.[112] In 1526, the year in which Sandes was appointed to Guînes, the Northamptonshire manors of Steane and Hinton were leased to one Fulk Barker on condition that he was 'to fynde to ... Lord Sandes thre Able men in harnes and to paye foure poinde to horse them with to serve the kyng in warre'.[113] Perhaps as a result of leasing land with incumbent military obligations, Sandes was able to meet his responsibilities to defend Guînes. In March 1528 he reported to Wolsey that he could provide sixty horsemen, whereas in May 1522 the crown's demand for two hundred men from Sandes had been met by a claim he could not levy more than ten men, besides his household servants.[114] The other connection that continued to be exploited during the early Tudor period to raise soldiers was friendship: in 1523 when Sir Edward Guildford, marshall of Calais, was asked to furnish five hundred men to serve in France in the army led by the duke of Suffolk he sent his agent, one 'Copuldyke' – possibly John Copuldyke, customer at the Lantergate in Calais – to Kent to 'speke with Thomas Aldy and my cousyn Crayford and other my frendes to appoint me the tallest men that be in that parties' and to approach Lady Ringley, 'sure I shall have her tenauntes and the best that she can do'.[115]

During the 1540s, however, the scale and duration of the warfare with France and the constant maintenance of hundreds of extra troops in and around Calais and Guînes may have revealed the shortcomings of the 'quasi feudal' system. Nevertheless, this way of raising troops was not abandoned. In August 1542, for example, John Scudamore, steward of several duchy of Lancaster manors in Herefordshire and the Welsh marches, was ordered to muster 124 men 'of your tenauntes and others within your offices and Romes' for the defence of Calais and Guînes.[116] During the 1540s, however, there is evidence that the crown increasingly relied on the system of commissions of array, Goring's 'national' system of recruitment, to meet its need for soldiers. The number of foreign mercenaries in the Pale during the 1540s also highlights the pressures that traditional Tudor ways of raising armies were coming under. A general summons of the nation's military resources to assist in the defence of Calais had only happened once in the fifteenth century, in 1436, when religious houses and towns, as well as royal servants, had been required to furnish contingents for Gloucester's relief effort. But during the 1540s the use of commissions of array to raise men for the defence of the Pale and the presence of county militiamen in and around Calais were more common. In December 1545, for example, hundreds of reinforcements for the Pale were identified not by their aristocratic

112 Goring, 'Military Obligation, 93–4. Military clauses in leases in the north of England were, of course, still relatively common.
113 C1/892/6.
114 SP1/24, f. 130 (*LP*, III, 2238, where the number is incorrectly given as twenty men); *LP*, IV ii. 4058. Part of the problem in May 1522 was that Sandes was in Calais, serving as treasurer, and 'thesse CC men must be levied in Ingland'.
115 BL, Egerton MS 2093, f. 57v.
116 C115/110/7418.

captains but as the men of Gloucestershire, Warwickshire and other counties that had raised contingents.[117] In particular, the 1540s and 1550s are notable for the crown's attempt to increase the contribution of towns as providers for royal armies. A programme of incorporation of boroughs from the 1540s increased the direct links between the crown and the governors of English towns. In part this was driven, as Robert Tittler has noted, by the need of 'the emergent Tudor state' to depend 'more heavily than ever on small groups of reliable men at grass roots level to carry out its expanding role of governance', but it also enabled the crown to enforce the military obligations of urban communities.[118] This trend did not confine itself to towns: the move towards a militia based system of national defence, albeit one still commanded by aristocratic lord lieutenants, was confirmed by the Militia Act of 1558. In part, its passage was hastened by the poor response to the calls for the defence of Calais earlier that year, but the Militia Act only confirmed long-term trends in the development of the Tudor military. The act superseded the medieval requirements of the Statute of Winchester and provided the basis for the armies of Elizabeth I and those which would, in the next century, fight the British Civil Wars.[119]

The attempt to raise soldiers for the defence and relief of Calais and Guînes in 1557–8, then, highlights this period of transition. On 2 January 1558 Queen Mary wrote under her signet to various lords and gentlemen, explaining that the French had approached the Pale and 'mean some exploit towards that or some other of our pieces that side' and commanding each of them to levy from their servants, tenants, friends and others, exploiting the *manraed* of any royal offices they held, fifty able footmen to be sent immediately to muster at Dover.[120] This was an attempt to levy a quasi feudal force in the same way as Henry VI had done in 1436 or Henry VIII had done in 1528. Soon afterwards, however, the queen asked for a more general mobilisation for the defence of the Pale.[121] The response of some towns to this second request is indicative of the changing nature of military service. In Norwich, the city sent thirty men. After holding a civic breakfast they marched to their embarkation point at Ipswich; after waiting there for two or three days, however, news was received of Calais's fall and the footsore soldiers returned home.[122] Norwich raised, clothed and paid for its men out of civic funds; they were commanded by the city's own captains. This was in stark contrast to Henry VIII's reign, when Norwich's contingents for royal

---

[117] *APC*, i. 572. This is discussed further in David Grummitt, 'The Court, War and Noble Power in England, *c.* 1475–1558', in *The Court as a Stage*, ed. S.J. Gunn and A. Janse (Woodbridge, 2006), 150–5.

[118] Robert Tittler, *The Reformation and the Towns in England: Politics and Political Culture, c. 1540–1640* (Oxford, 1998), 20.

[119] 'An Acte for the having of Horse, Armour and Weapon', 4 & 5 Philip and Mary, c. 3 (*Statutes of the Realm*, iv. 316). On the militia based system of defence see C.G. Cruickshank, *Elizabeth's Army* (Oxford, 1966); Lindsay Boynton, *The Elizabethan Militia, 1558–1638* (1971).

[120] SP11/13, no. 3 (*Calendar of State Papers, Domestic Series, Mary I, 1553–1558*, ed. C.S. Knighton (1998), 678).

[121] SP11/12, no. 6 (*CSP, Domestic Mary*, i. 681).

[122] Goring, 'Military Obligations', 210–12.

armies had been raised by the Howards, dukes of Norfolk, and commanded by Howard servants. The fall of the Howards in 1546 had strengthened the direct links between Norwich and the crown, links which had not been broken by the Howards' restoration in 1553, and which were manifested in the city's response to the royal military demands. Similarly, Canterbury furnished three contingents of thirty, sixty-three and eighty-seven men to serve with the lord warden of the Cinque Ports, Sir Thomas Cheyne. This contribution far outnumbered any of those the city had contributed to the wars of the fifteenth century or Henry VIII.[123] Local elites found themselves in new roles raising men: in July 1558 John Scudamore was ordered, with others, to raise 1,500 men from the county of Herefordshire as well as from his own tenants.[124] The scale of the reinforcements for Calais in the 1540s and 1550s demonstrates the changing military needs of the Pale and the increasing size of armies needed to wage war on an early modern European scale. But it also reveals the success of the Tudors in tapping the military resources of their subjects and further shifting the balance between the crown and its subjects in determining the nature and terms of military service.

* * *

The changing nature of the forces which served in the Calais garrison, both the captains and soldiers, the ways in which they were recruited and the terms of that service, reveal much about the way in which the crown attempted to harness the military resources of its subjects in the fifteenth and early sixteenth century. In part, the growing size of armies and the different skills required were part of a wider European transformation of warfare and military service. In England, as we shall see, the Calais garrison was in the vanguard of this wider European 'military revolution'. But they also reveal more about the relationship between English monarchs and their subjects. From about the 1470s the crown was able to be more forceful in dictating the terms of service to the captains of the Calais garrison and felt less constrained in its choice of who fulfilled positions of military responsibility. The defence of Calais was no longer the private endeavour of the great lord who had agreed to serve as captain. This was due to the expansion of the royal affinity, tying men at all levels of society into a nexus of service centred around the king's person, and the simultaneous expansion of the royal demesne, through feudal accidents, forfeiture and attainder during the civil wars of the mid-fifteenth century, as well as dynastic consolidation. This was not achieved, as was once thought, through a parallel decline in the role of the nobility in the government of England. Rather, as we can see in the Calais garrison, the nobility continued to be employed as soldiers and governors, but their authority and the means to carry out their duties derived increasingly from the crown.[125] This trend continued to be evident in the reigns of Henry VIII and

---

123 Canterbury Cathedral Archives, FA 16, f. 33v.
124 C115/100/7424; 101/7603.
125 The developments in government at the end of the fifteenth century are usefully summarised in Rosemary Horrox, 'Yorkist and Early Tudor England', in *The New Cambridge Medieval History*, vii. c. *1415–1500*, ed. Christopher Allmand (Cambridge, 1998), 477–95.

his children: the aristocracy continued to serve as captains in the Calais garrison, leading their own tenants and the king's in the defence of the Pale. By the 1540s the links between the crown and the landowning, and thus militarily important, classes, and the mutual benefits derived from that relationship,[126] were such that the crown was able to demand and achieve ever greater military assistance from its subjects, allowing Henry VIII, Edward VI and Mary I to wage war on a scale comparable with their European contemporaries.

---

[126] The partnership between royal government and various elites, including landowners, is explored in S.J. Gunn, *Early Tudor Government, 1485–1558* (Basingstoke, 1995), 23–71.

5

Chivalry and Professionalism in the Calais Garrison

The various reasons that drew men to military service in the Calais garrison have been explored in the previous chapter. But to what degree was the garrison a community, bound together by chivalric ties of military brotherhood, with an institutional identity that transcended the various retinues of which it was comprised? To what extent was it a 'professional' force, composed of men who exclusively or mainly followed the profession of arms, and was this professionalism incompatible with the chivalric ethos? To talk of a 'professional' army in the fifteenth and early sixteenth centuries may appear to be anachronistic. Nevertheless, there was a distinct group of men, from various social backgrounds, who made their living through war and military service. These men comprised a 'professional' military force.[1] For the late medieval aristocracy war was, of course, part of their *raison d'être*; they were defined as much by their service in war as by the political power that they derived from their ownership of land. Indeed, the two were inextricably linked. However, there was also a class of men who shared the martial and chivalric ideals of the aristocracy, but who were not notable landowners. Instead their claims to gentility and political importance rested almost exclusively on their military service and the prowess they had displayed in war. Further down the social scale there were men who made their living from war, becoming skilled in its arts, and who travelled from campaign to campaign and from retinue to retinue in return for wages. This

---

[1] Despite the conceptual and historiographical problems of the term 'professional' in relation to the practice of arms in the fifteenth and sixteenth centuries, it will be used here to denote those men whose principal identity and livelihood were war and military service. Certainly contemporaries identified men as soldiers, alongside merchants, lawyers, gentlemen and a whole host of lesser trades. J.S. Nolan, writing of the later Elizabethan military, preferred the concept of 'institutional memory' to denote a degree of permanence among the Elizabethan forces deployed in Ireland and the Low Countries. By this criterion the Calais garrison was certainly a professional force with an 'institutional memory' of over two hundred years and one which had an impact upon most parts of the late medieval and early Tudor military establishment: J.S. Nolan, 'The Militarisation of the Elizabethan State', *Journal of Military History*, lviii (1994), 381–420, esp. pp. 96–8. The most recent discussion of the concept of 'professionalisation' is by David Trim in his excellent introduction to a collection of essays: *The Chivalric Ethos and the Development of Military Professionalism*, ed. David J.B. Trim (Leiden, 2006), 1–38. Trim suggests seven 'markers' of military professionalism in early modern Europe, including a discrete occupational identity, permanence, regular pay, a formal hierarchy, training, efficiency and a distinctive self-conceptualisation, all features of the Calais garrison in this period.

chapter will examine the ways in which the Calais garrison was defined by the outlook and beliefs of these groups of men, and how their notions of professionalism and service were transformed over the course of the fifteenth and early sixteenth centuries by developments both in the art of war and in the political culture of which they were a part.

Chivalry and war in the fifteenth century

'There can be no doubt', observes Malcolm Vale, 'that the ideal qualities of chivalry – honour, loyalty, courage, generosity – have fulfilled a fundamental human need, felt especially among warrior élites, whose social function has been to fight. Chivalry was often no more, and no less, than the sentiment of honour in its medieval guise.'[2] In the later Middle Ages notions of chivalry were the defining set of values for the military classes of Europe. For the aristocracy honour and virtue were most readily to be found on the battlefield. The qualities this set of beliefs encouraged continued to be tested, vindicated or rejected in war throughout our period. The knightly class, which continued to command armies and control the conduct of war, viewed battle and military service as a means of expressing their chivalric beliefs. War was often fought according to chivalric principles, and the chivalric outlook of the protagonists often governed why and when battles occurred and who lived and who died once combat had been joined.[3] At its most basic level war provided the opportunity for the performance of chivalric or honourable deeds, as well as the display of chivalric virtues, such as mercy and discipline. On a wider level war and military service allowed the pursuit of honour which was increasingly tied to the 'common weal' and formed an important component of late medieval political culture. By the middle of the fifteenth century it was clearly established in chivalric advice manuals throughout western Europe that the most honourable form of military service was that which strove for the good of the whole body politic; war in the service of the prince, then, was the ultimate expression of fifteenth- and sixteenth-century chivalry in both a military and a political context. During the course of the fifteenth and early sixteenth centuries the medieval language of chivalry was slowly transformed into a Renaissance vocabulary of honour, although the principles remained essentially the same.[4]

The nature and organisation of war at the end of the Middle Ages served to reinforce the central role of chivalry and notions of virtue and honour. In the later Middle Ages lords' retinues were still conceived as primarily military

---

[2] Malcolm Vale, *War and Chivalry: Warfare and Aristocratic Culture in England, France and Burgundy at the End of the Middle Ages* (1981), 1.
[3] M.K. Jones, 'The Battle of Verneuil (17 August 1424): Towards a History of Courage', *War in History*, ix (2002), 375–411; S.J. Gunn, 'Chivalry and Politics at the Early Tudor Court', in *Chivalry in the Renaissance*, ed. S. Anglo (Woodbridge, 1990), 116–18.
[4] Vale, *War and Chivalry*, 14–32; M.H. Keen, *Chivalry* (1984), 240–3; C.T. Allmand and M.H. Keen, 'The Boke of Noblesse of William of Worcester', in *War, Government and Power in Late Medieval France*, ed. C.T. Allmand (Liverpool, 2000), 291–302; Richard Barber, *The Knight and Chivalry* (2nd edn, Woodbridge, 1994), 291–302.

institutions: the Hundred Years War and the frequency of military service for the English aristocracy ensured that war often defined the nature of the lord/servant relationship. Some retinues, most notably perhaps that of John of Gaunt in the second half of the fourteenth century, were first and foremost a brotherhood-in-arms: as Simon Walker has shown, 'it was the ideals of knighthood and knightly conduct drawn from the chivalric code that governed the conduct of the Lancastrian affinity'. The indenture for war, the formal mechanism by which lords assembled their war retinues, also created a 'more potent bond between lord and man implicit in the compact of brotherhood-in-arms', by suggesting a chivalric association based upon loyalty and mutual support. The indenture formalised these chivalric associations in terms of pay, length of service and the arrangements for the ransoming of prisoners. In Gaunt's case the bonds created in war also found their expression in the duke's conduct in domestic politics and local government.[5] In this respect Gaunt's retinue was probably unusual. By the early fifteenth century it was more common for a war retinue to be comprised mainly of men whose relationship with their lord was more casual and based solely upon military service.[6] Nevertheless, this does not mean that the nature of those bonds was any less strong. In Normandy in the late 1440s the circle of men around the lieutenant-general, Edmund Beaufort, duke of Somerset, was motivated by a sense that the duke was the leader of a chivalric brotherhood-in-arms. These men were drawn from the professional military community of Lancastrian Normandy, as well as from Beaufort's own following in England, and had frequently served with the duke's brothers in earlier campaigns. When Somerset served as captain of Calais in the early 1450s many of his companions from Normandy, men like Andrew Trollope and Osbert Mountefort, followed him to serve in the Pale.[7]

Given the permanence of military institutions in Calais, it is no surprise that in the fifteenth century the Pale fulfilled a role as a chivalric theatre, where men could perform feats of arms, win honour and engage in the fellowship of arms. One of the clearest expressions of the importance of Calais in this regard survives in *The Beauchamp Pageant*. This pictorial account of the life of Richard Beauchamp, earl of Warwick, contains the best known representation of the siege of Calais in 1436. It shows the duke of Gloucester and the earls of Warwick and Stafford mounted in battle array, leading an English army and driving the Burgundians from the gates of Calais. Duke Philip's artillery is left stranded before the walls, while the defenders look from the ramparts upon the deeds of their rescuers. The accompanying text reads:

> Here shewes howe Philip, Duc of Burgoyne, beseged Caleys and Humfrey, Duc of Gloucestr', Richard, Erle of Warrewik, and Humfrey, Erle of Stafford, with a greet multidude went over the see and folowed the duc of Burgoyn he

---

5 Simon Walker, *The Lancastrian Affinity 1361–1399* (Oxford, 1990), 55–7; Barber, *Knight and Chivalry*, 208–10.

6 A.J. Pollard, *John Talbot and the War in France, 1427–1453* (1983), 86–8.

7 Michael K. Jones, 'The Beaufort Family and the War in France, 1421–1450' (PhD thesis, University of Bristol, 1982), esp. pp. 208–79; E101/54/16.

euer fleying before them. And there they sore noied the countrey with fire and swerde.

Crucially, of course, this was a misrepresentation of the actual events of the siege; nevertheless, the account contained in *The Pageant* would have been entirely plausible to its readers and drew attention to the symbolic significance of the events of July 1436. An earlier drawing in *The Pageant* showed Warwick receiving the letters patent appointing him captain of Calais from Henry V, underlining the fact that these deeds were done in the service of the prince. The text notes that while captain 'he ful notably gwided al thynges undre his governaunce'. Similarly, the function of the Pale as an arena for chivalric deeds in peacetime was highlighted by drawings of the tournament held near Guînes just before Christmas 1414. *The Pageant* was probably compiled during the 1480s under the patronage of Beauchamp's granddaughter, Anne Beauchamp, widow of Warwick the Kingmaker, and was a self-conscious celebration of the late earl's chivalric and military reputation. The drawing of Beauchamp at the siege of Calais forcefully conveyed this and he was indeed one of the leading military commanders of the Lancastrian period, having served as captain of Calais from 1414 until 1429 and dying in 1439 while the king's lieutenant-general in Normandy. His own dismissal from Calais and his replacement by the duke of Bedford had taken place amidst the earl's exasperation with the failure of Bedford's servants there to make adequate provision for the town's defence and *The Pageant* doubtless served to underline the family's commitment to Calais, English interests in France and a chivalric view of war and politics.[8]

Set-piece battle provided the best arena for displays of prowess and this partly explains the prominence afforded by contemporaries to the events of 1436. During the siege a group of soldiers from the garrison sallied out to destroy a huge siege engine, the 'Bastyle', constructed by the Flemings. The chronicler of the abbey of Bury St Edmunds drew attention to the feats of arms performed by Sir John Radcliffe, the duke of Gloucester's lieutenant of Calais, in language heavy with chivalric meaning and significance: 'Sicque prefati domini Johannis Radclef indicante industria cordeque virili predicatam turris cum omnibus eadem invente est capta et destructa per omnia. Idea laudes.'[9]

Battle was thus presented as a chivalric episode in which the individual knight was able to win honour. The importance of the siege as a stage upon which reputations were made and honour won persisted long after the event. By the end of the fifteenth century the contested narratives that had revolved around the duke of Gloucester's role in lifting the siege had given way to an account that saw 1436 as an integral part of the wider image of a chivalric knight enjoyed by 'Good Duke Humphrey'. The accounts accepted Gloucester as the saviour of Calais. Polydore Vergil, writing in the reign of Henry VII, observed:

---

[8] *The Beauchamp Pageant*, ed. Alexandra Sinclair (Donington, 2003), esp. plates 25–31, 48. For the controversy and recriminations surrounding Warwick's dismissal in 1429, which saw the earl angrily blame Bedford's servants Richard Wydeville, Lewis John and Richard Buckland, see *Letters of Queen Margaret of Anjou and Bishop Beckington and Others*, ed. C. Munro (CS, old series, lxxvi, 1863), 34–43.

[9] James A. Doig, 'A New Source for the Siege of Calais in 1436', *EHR*, cx (1995), 412.

While as the Burgoignion continued the siege in this sort, the duke of Glocester, with an armie furnished in all poyntes, made haste oute of Englande to succour his people. When the duke of Burgoigne hearde of his terrible approche, and that he lay upon thother shore awayting the winde to transport, he was past hope of gayning the towne: and so in the dead of night, forsaking the siege, drewe homeward.

In Vergil's narrative of Henry VI's reign, Gloucester was portrayed as a noble knight and protector of the realm; his subsequent murder 'by these pernicious practises of his enemies' was the occasion of the collapse of Lancastrian rule. The siege of Calais thus became an exemplar of Duke Humphrey's chivalry, patriotism and nobility.[10] Later Tudor chroniclers appear also to have accepted a pro-Gloucester narrative of events. Edward Hall, drawing heavily on Monstrelet and other Flemish sources as well as English ones, credited Gloucester with lifting the siege. It was the imminent approach of Gloucester's army which, in the final analysis, was responsible for the Flemings' flight. 'Seyng his enemies reculed', the duke then launched his punitive raid into Flanders. Having 'sufficiently plagued and wasted the countreys of the duke of Burgoyne', Gloucester returned to Calais 'settyng there all thynges in good ordre' before leaving for England.[11] 'Fabyan's Chronicle', however, drawing on a tradition within the London chronicles, was more circumspect and remembered that the siege 'endured upon iii. weeks, in which season many knightly acts were done and exercised upon bothe parties'.[12]

In a wider sense service in Calais was portrayed in a chivalric context. Richard Neville, earl of Warwick's reputation among contemporaries derived in part from his role of captain of Calais. Indeed, the feats of arms performed by the Calais garrison under his command established his reputation in London and the south-east of England to a greater extent than his efforts in reducing Lancastrian strongholds in the north of England. After his attack on the Spanish merchant fleet in the spring of 1459 he was portrayed as the only man willing and able to defend the

> honour and profit of the king and the land … for which manhood and his great policy and deeds and worship in fortifying Calais and other feats of arms all the commonalty of this land had him in great laud … and so repute and take him for as famous a knight as was living.[13]

Professor Ferguson was surely mistaken to suppose that 'Warwick's knighthood is here placed … in a context of national interest rather than of chivalric values'. In fact, the two were inextricably linked. What the chronicler was celebrating was not Warwick's attack on a foreign source of competition to English trade,

---

10 *Three Books of Polydore Vergil's English History*, ed. Sir Henry Ellis (CS, old series, xxix, 1844), 60–1, 72–3.

11 Edward Hall, *The Union of the Two Noble and Illustre Famelies of Lancastre & Yorke* (1548), ff. 51–51v.

12 Robert Fabyan, *The New Chronicles of England and France*, ed. H. Ellis (1811), 610.

13 *Six Town Chronicles of England*, ed. R. Flenley (Oxford, 1911), 41.

but his feats of arms in the chivalric arena of the Calais garrison performed for the good of the commonweal.[14]

Coupled with this sense of the Pale as an arena for the performance of chivalric deeds was the notion that the garrison was a brotherhood-in-arms, whose members were drawn together by a sense of martial honour. Notions of honour clearly influenced the garrison's action both in Calais and in national politics during the fifteenth century. The evidence for this sense of fellowship is elusive, but William, Lord Hastings, appealed to a sense of collective martial and chivalric identity when, in a letter written to Sir John Paston and Sir John Middleton in September 1473, he asked to be remembered to '*my felawes* the souldeours'.[15] The ideal of a fellowship-in-arms was also perpetuated by remembering the past deeds of the garrison, creating an 'institutional memory' which persisted throughout our period. In this the battle of Agincourt in 1415 played a special part. The presence of members of the Calais garrison at the battle has not been stressed by previous historians of the battle. In fact, as shown by the list of obligations delivered to the king after the battle for the payment of the king's third due for the ransoms of prisoners, members of the garrison had played an important role in the victory. Early in Henry VI's reign the money from these obligations was distributed among the soldiers of the garrison in settlement of the arrears of their pay.[16] As late as the 1530s Agincourt was still remembered annually in Calais as

> a solempne tryumphe, goyng in procession, laudyng God, shotyng gonnes with the noyse and melodye of trumpettes and other instruments, to the great reioysng of your subjects beyng aged, the comforte of them that be able men, [and] the encouragyng of yong children.[17]

Other military events were celebrated, particularly those in which the town had been directly or indirectly involved, such as the capture of Berwick by Richard, duke of Gloucester, in 1482. Lord Hastings, at this time Gloucester's political ally, commanded a general procession, bonfires and volleys of gunfire from the bulwarks and the walls.[18]

The sense of community within the garrison itself and the way in which it was perceived by the wider political nation was also strengthened, paradoxically perhaps, by the occasional mutinies which marked the fifteenth century. These appear to have been highly symbolic events, organised with the support of their

---

[14] Arthur B. Ferguson, *The Indian Summer of English Chivalry* (Durham, NC, 1960), 41.

[15] *Paston Letters,* ii. 410. The italics are my own.

[16] E159/199, *brevia directa baronibus*, Hilary, rot. 19; 211, recorda, Michaelmas, rot. 27. The Calais soldiers who served at Agincourt must have been distinct from the soldiers sent by the lieutenant of Calais, Sir William Bardolf, to relieve Henry V's beleaguered force on its way back to Calais. These may have been part of the crew sent to reinforce the town in preparation for the campaign and who suffered 'great slaughter' when they were intercepted by the French en route to their rendezvous with the king: *Excerpta Historica*, ed. Samuel Bentley (1833), 25.

[17] S. Anglo, 'An Early Tudor Programme for Plays and Other Demonstrations against the Pope', *Journal of the Warburg and Courtauld Institutes*, xx (1957), 178.

[18] *The Cely Letters 1472–1488*, ed. A. Hanham (EETS, cclxxiii, 1975), 169.

captains and designed to reinforce the identity and loyalty of the garrison, rather than to challenge the authority of the crown and its representatives. In 1406, 1423, 1433, 1442 and 1454 the garrison exercised this collective identity and seized the wool stocks belonging to the merchants of the staple, hoping to sell them and realize their arrears of pay. In December 1406, faced with arrears amounting to some £30,000, the soldiers seized the staplers' wool. This was designed to demonstrate the inextricable link between the soldiers, who guaranteed the safety of the English staple, and the merchants, who provided the wealth for the crown to meet its military obligations. Indeed the soldiers may have seized the wool with the merchants' tacit agreement; certainly, it seems their captains knew of the plan. On 17 January 1407 the soldiers petitioned the king under the seal of Sir Richard Aston, the deputy of the captain of Calais, John Beaufort, earl of Somerset. They drew attention to the 'outrage pouverte and wrychidnes that we ben in', and subscribed their petition, 'Your humble, obeissantes and trewe ligemen alle youre poure soudiours that taken youre wages in youre towne of Caleys'. In return they were pardoned and effective measures put in place to tackle the problem of their arrears.[19] In the summer of 1442 the mutiny may have been engineered by servants of the new captain, Humphrey Stafford, earl of Stafford, and designed to ensure favourable terms for the duke's entry into the town that August. Certainly, Stafford appealed to the king's council to be allowed to go to Calais to restore order, while in the negotiations that followed representatives of the garrison submitted the soldiers' grievances to the king's council and the soldiers appointed attorneys at the exchequer who continued to represent them for the remainder of the decade. Similarly, when the members of the garrison later petitioned the duke to intercede on their behalf for their arrears, their request was presented by Stafford's late lieutenant, Sir John Marney, and his marshall, Richard Witherton.[20] In May 1454 the garrison again resorted to mutiny. Once again their action demonstrated that they were capable of collective action in co-operation with their captains (on this occasion Lords Rivers and Welles). The garrison's mutiny, as well as being about their arrears, was politically motivated, designed to resist the authority of Richard, duke of York, who had, the previous year, as protector of the realm during the insanity of Henry VI, ordered the captain, the duke of Somerset, to surrender all the Pale's castles into his hands. A letter from the king's council to the garrison in December reveals the way in which the soldiers organised their collective response to York's demands. They appointed attorneys and negotiated with royal commissioners over their pay and the terms on which they would admit the new captain, the earl of Warwick, into the town the following year.[21]

---

[19] *Royal and Historical Letters during the Reign of Henry IV*, ed. F.C. Hingeston (2 vols, 1965 reprint), ii. 145–7; David Grummitt, 'The Financial Administration of Calais during the Reign of Henry IV', *EHR*, cxiii (1998), 277–99; G.L. Harriss, 'Financial Policy', in *The Reign of Henry V*, ed. G.L. Harriss (Oxford, 1985), 167.

[20] *POPC*, v. 200–1, 203–4; E159/227, *recorda*, Michaelmas, rot. 3; E207/16/5/29.

[21] *POPC*, vi. 278; G.L. Harriss, 'The Struggle for Calais: An Aspect of the Rivalry between Lancaster and York', *EHR*, lxxv (1960), 34–44.

Indeed, the unity of the garrison, captains and soldiers, was vital to the successful outcome of these collective actions. In the spring of 1433 the soldiers had seized the staplers' wool in protest over their lack of pay. Moreover, they had refused admission to Sir William Oldhall, the duke of Bedford's lieutenant at Calais. Oldhall, outraged at this apparent defiance of the captain's authority, rode directly to Rouen to complain to Bedford. The mutiny elicited a sharp response. Bedford was en route to the Low Countries for his marriage to Jacquetta of Luxembourg and stopped in Calais to quell the unrest. Despite receiving assurances of good will from the treasurer of Calais, Richard Buckland, the soldiers, having agreed to allow Bedford to enter the town, found certain of their number arrested and hanged for mutiny. Customs obligations promised to the soldiers were also withdrawn and, on his return journey to Rouen, Bedford stopped again in the town to mete out further punishment to the garrison, banishing eighty of them who, as a result, 'lost al that hem was owyng'. Oldhall's actions undermined the collective identity that underpinned the effectiveness of the garrison. The account of the mutiny in a version of *The Brut* makes this explicit. The soldiers, after the seizing the wool, made their fellowship formal by the swearing of oaths. They welcomed Bedford 'riȝt wurchiply' expecting him to redress their grievances; instead he made the mayor of the town pass judgement on four of the ringleaders who were quickly executed 'the whiche was made great mone amonges the pepill'. Oldhall clearly lost the soldiers' support as a result of his actions and was soon replaced by the former lieutenant, Richard Wydeville. Bedford, moreover, the author of *The Brut* account stated, 'had neuer after bodily hele till he dyet'.[22]

The sense of the garrison as a community-in-arms was reinforced by ties of kinship and marriage among its members. Unsurprisingly, several members of the garrison married their daughters to their fellow soldiers, while families from outside the Pale frequently married into established local families. In July 1429, for example, the lieutenant of Calais, Richard Wydeville, married his daughter, Joan, to William Haute, a Kentishman and soldier in the garrison. The match may have been arranged by Sir John Steward, another Kentishman and captain of Rysbank castle, who had served alongside Wydeville in Normandy and whose retinue Haute had recently joined. This match reinforced the two men's companionship-in-arms and in 1436 they served together in the army assembled to lift the Burgundian siege.[23] Later in the fifteenth and early sixteenth centuries the Whetehills, originally a mercantile family who became soldiers and administrators in the garrison, used their connections to marry into aristocratic families who had seen service in Calais.[24]

Further evidence of the interest in the chivalric context of war and military service comes from a number of literary manuscripts associated with Calais in the fifteenth century. The town operated as a point of cultural exchange between

---

[22] *The Brut*, ii. 570–1.

[23] *Excerpta Historica*, 249–50; E403/723, m. 13.

[24] W.G. Davis, 'Whetehill of Calais', *The New England Historical and Genealogical Register*, cii (1948), 241–53; ciii (1949), 5–19.

the Low Countries and England as merchants and diplomats brought back manuscripts, works of art and ideas from the Burgundian Low Countries. Anne Sutton and Livia Visser-Fuchs have identified an influential group of book owners among the captains of the garrison in the late fifteenth century whose interests centred upon chivalric and historical texts.[25] Merchants connected with Calais served as an important conduit of this material from the Low Countries and their importance in this regard was exemplified by William Sonnyng, an inhabitant of Calais who in the 1470s owned, among other manuscripts, a copy of Honoré Bouvet's *Arbres des batailles*. This interest in chivalric texts, however, predated the Yorkist period. Most significantly, in 1458–9 Vegetius's *De re militari* was translated into English verse by a member of the Calais clergy. A copy of this was acquired in the 1460s by the Hastings family, while English prose translations of Vegetius were owned by the Seyntlow and Paston families, both of whom had connections with the garrison. An English translation of Chartier's *Quadrilogue invectif* was owned by the Whetehill family, while towards the end of the fifteenth century the Haute family owned a manuscript of Christine de Pizan's *Livre du corps de policie*. The cluster of military texts that are known to have been owned by men with Calais connections is significant. The ownership of these texts was an important statement about the wider outlook and commitment to chivalric behaviour among the members of the garrison. As Cath Nall has argued, their translation into the vernacular was not a politically neutral process but one which engaged their readers in a wider political discourse over the nature of military service, the cause of English defeat in the Hundred Years War and the importance of chivalric modes of behaviour.[26]

Moreover, these individuals were not only soldiers. The captains of the Calais garrison throughout the fifteenth century frequently combined military service with political responsibility back in England. In the Lancastrian period men like Richard Buckland, Richard Wydeville, William Haute, Sir Gervase Clifton, Sir William Oldhall, Sir John Radcliffe and Sir Thomas Kyriell combined service in Calais, as well as in Normandy and Gascony, with responsibilities in England.[27] All served as knights of the shire, sheriffs and justices of the peace. Their status as career soldiers did not preclude their active involvement in domestic politics. In the Yorkist and early Tudor period too the captains combined service in the garrison with careers in local affairs and at court. The chivalric ethos and identity they developed in the course of their military service must have, to a large degree, shaped political culture in England.

25 A.F. Sutton and L. Visser-Fuchs, *Richard III's Books: Ideals and Reality in the Life and Library of a Medieval Prince* (Stroud, 1997), 282.
26 Julia Boffey, 'Books and Readers in Calais: Some Notes', *The Ricardian*, xiii (2003), 67–74; D.L. Wakelin, 'The Occasion, Author and Readers of Knyghthode and Bataile', *Medium Aevum*, lxxiii (2004), 260–72; C.R. Nall, 'The Production and Reception of Military Texts in the Aftermath of the Hundred Years War' (DPhil thesis, University of York, 2004).
27 The forthcoming volumes of the 1422–1460 section of the *History of Parliament* will shed more light on the domestic careers of these important individuals.

In the late Middle Ages chivalry was an international concept. By the middle of the fifteenth century the centre of chivalric theory and practice was Valois Burgundy. During the 1460s, as England developed closer links with Burgundy, the way was eased for soldiers in the Calais garrison to realize their chivalric ambitions in the service of the duke of Burgundy. As early as 1464, for example, at least thirty or forty of the Calais garrison accompanied Anthony, Bastard of Burgundy, on his abortive crusade against the Turks.[28] This may have been an especially attractive proposition to those soldiers who saw their military service in chivalric terms. The piety of individual members of the garrison in the fifteenth and early sixteenth century should not be underestimated. In the muster taken in 1466 during Warwick's captaincy four archers were recorded as absent on pilgrimage, while in 1502 Reginald Clifton, a mounted archer, received leave to undertake a pilgrimage to Santiago de Compostela.[29] Nevertheless, personal piety and ideas of crusade were only one part of a wider European martial culture. From the mid-1460s onwards English soldiers, and especially those who had connections with the Calais garrison, were prominent in Burgundian service. Although these men were not recruited or paid for by the English crown, their presence in Burgundian armies was a result, in part, of the marriage of Edward IV's sister, Margaret, to Charles the Bold in 1468.[30] In the 1470s Sir John Middleton, who served in Calais from at least 1473, commanded the English contingent in the Burgundian army at the siege of Neuss in 1475. Middleton also served at the disastrous siege of Nancy, returning to Calais with a small company of survivors.[31]

Not every Englishman who served with the Burgundians won honour, however, and members of the garrison were equally aware of the less auspicious deeds performed by their fellow countrymen in Burgundian service. Anthony Wydeville, Earl Rivers, whose reputation among the garrison was already compromised by his capture, along with his father, by the earl of Warwick at Sandwich in 1460, further tarnished his image in 1476 by his actions at the Burgundian camp before the battle of Morat. According to the Milanese ambassador, when Rivers, having offered his services to Charles the Bold, was told of the approach of the enemy he made his excuses and quickly left the camp. This was a serious breach of chivalric honour: as the duke told the ambassador, Rivers left 'because he is afraid'.[32] This may go some way to explaining why the Calais garrison, which had already rejected Rivers as lieutenant of Calais in

---

[28] Jehan de Waurin, *Cronicques*, ed. L.M.E. Dupont (3 vols, Paris 1858–63), iii. 184.

[29] BL, Add. MS 46455, ff. 62–2v; E101/55/23, f. 3.

[30] Mark Ballard, 'An Expedition of English Archers to Liège in 1467 and the Anglo-Burgundian Marriage Alliance', *Nottingham Medieval Studies*, xxxiv (1990), 152–74; Anthony Goodman, *The Wars of the Roses: The Soldiers' Experience* (Stroud, 2005), 100–7.

[31] Richard Vaughan, *Charles the Bold: The Last Valois King of Burgundy* (1973), 229. Middleton had been appointed as an ambassador to treat with the Burgundians regarding trade matters in 1469, and appeared on the commission of sewers at Calais four years later: C76/153, mm. 17–18; 157, m. 9.

[32] *Calendar of State Papers and Manuscripts Existing in the Archives and Collections of Milan*, ed. Allen B. Hinds, i. 1385–1616 (1912), i. 227.

1470, supported Hastings and Gloucester against him and the queen's party in the succession crisis of 1483.[33] After 1477 the military links between the garrison and Burgundy became even more pronounced. The death of Charles the Bold at the siege of Nancy that year, leaving as his heir his young daughter, Mary, transformed the political situation in north-western Europe. The Burgundian disaster at Nancy was soon followed by an attack on Picardy and Artois by the French king, Louis XI. This was seen as directly threatening Calais, leading to the despatch of reinforcements under the lieutenant of the town and marches, Lord Hastings. Some prominent Englishmen with links to Calais fought for the Dowager Duchess Margaret and Archduke Maximilian, who had married Mary, to defend the Burgundian territories against Louis XI.[34]

Just as service in Calais meant an easy transition into Burgundian service, so those Englishmen who had served the Burgundian cause were also attracted to service in the garrison. Sir Thomas Everingham, for example, was an experienced soldier who may have first served in Burgundy with a force of archers paid for by Edward IV in 1472. In 1474 he appeared in the service of the duke of Burgundy, also leading an English contingent at Nancy. Soon afterwards he passed into Hastings's service in Calais. Five years later he was knighted before the battle of Guinegate by Maximilian and in 1480–1 he returned to the Netherlands, leading a band of 120 English soldiers in the capture of the town of Dordrecht. Perhaps because of his chivalric outlook, Everingham was drawn into the service of Richard, duke of Gloucester, and rose to national prominence in England as a knight of the body when Gloucester became king. A northerner, Everingham chose the chivalric allure of the Calais garrison and service in north-west Europe over a more obvious (but less glamorous perhaps) career on the northern borders. On 26 February 1484 he was appointed lieutenant of Rysbank Tower, not only, as has previously been stressed, as a northern partisan of Richard III, but as a fellow soldier who could command the respect of the Calais garrison at a difficult time for his royal master.[35]

In the fifteenth century, then, chivalric values exerted a great influence on the attitudes and actions of the Calais garrison. Notions of chivalry and questions of honour were apparent in many of the military and political events in which the garrison played an important role. The Burgundian siege in 1436 and the resulting punitive expedition into the Low Countries led by the captain of Calais, Humphrey, duke of Gloucester, can be explained in chivalric terms. As we have seen, the siege generated a large corpus of contemporary English literature, much of it nationalistic and xenophobic in tone.[36] The siege also, however, involved questions of personal honour among the main protagonists, Henry VI, Duke Philip the Good and Gloucester, and the conduct of operations followed

---

33 David Grummitt, 'William, Lord Hastings, The Calais Garrison, and the Politics of Yorkist England', *The Ricardian*, xii (2001), 262–74.

34 See above, p. 14.

35 Edward L. Meek, 'The Career of Sir Thomas Everingham, "Knight of the North" in the Service of Maximilian, Duke of Austria 1477–1481', *Historical Research*, lxxiv (2001), 238–48; *CPR, 1477–85*, 460.

36 See above, pp. 33–6.

established chivalric formulae. First, it is clear that Henry VI and the English regime saw the actions of the duke of Burgundy as those of a treacherous and rebellious subject: by attacking Calais Philip had reneged on his written agreements and sworn oaths and acted dishonourably.[37] Second, by making Gloucester lieutenant-general of the forces assembled to resist the duke and by granting him the county of Flanders, the king transformed the campaign into one that would revolve around issues of personal honour.[38] The personal emnity between Gloucester and Burgundy can be traced back to 1424 when Gloucester had invaded Hainault to press the claims of his wife, Jacqueline of Bavaria, to the counties of Holland, Zeeland and Hainault. Gloucester's campaign, which ended in failure, had been mounted from his own private resources, without the backing of the council in England. In the words of an early twentieth-century biographer, the campaign represented the actions of a 'foolish knight errant'.[39] Gloucester continued this feud in 1436. Philip had promised to meet Gloucester in battle outside Calais; Humphrey expressed his wish to honour the agreement, excusing himself from setting a time because of the wind and weather that had delayed his departure from England.[40] According to Jean de Monstrelet, when Gloucester heard that Philip had reneged on the agreement and retreated to Lille, he determined to follow him. Gloucester's raid into Picardy following the raising of the siege was designed to bring Philip to battle in an attempt to force him to honour a chivalric agreement.[41] The raid, if viewed in these terms, was not quite the damp squib presented by some contemporaries. Gloucester's men were only retained for a month to relieve Calais and therefore the duke was forced to retire after demonstrating his willingness to engage Duke Philip in battle. He returned to London in triumph on 24 August, having fulfilled his chivalric duty once it was evident that Philip would not honour the agreement to meet him in battle.[42]

The chivalric ethos was also evident in Calais during the Wars of the Roses. Historians have pointed to the lack of chivalry evident in the conduct of the civil wars of the mid-fifteenth century. The habitual killing of noble prisoners, the high casualty rates and frequency of pitched battle all point to the waging of *guerre mortale*, in which chivalric conventions and limitations were not observed. This is explicable by the fact that the engagements were not seen as clashes of equal knightly opponents, but as war waged against traitors and rebels.[43] Nevertheless, chivalric factors determined to a degree the nature of the campaigns fought in the Pale. Such considerations were present, for example, in the interaction between Richard Neville, earl of Warwick and captain of Calais,

[37] See, for example, the language of the proclamations printed in Rymer, x. 646–7.
[38] Rymer, x. 651–3.
[39] Kenneth H. Vickers, *Humphrey, Duke of Gloucester* (1907), 125–61; R.A. Griffiths, *The Reign of Henry VI* (1981), 179.
[40] Waurin, iv. 173–4.
[41] Monstrelet, iv. 263–4.
[42] Vickers, Gloucester, 250.
[43] Andrew W. Boardman, *The Medieval Soldier in the Wars of the Roses* (Stroud, 1998), 53–60.

and his Lancastrian rival for the captaincy, Henry Beaufort, duke of Somerset. In 1459 Warwick captured the fleet which had transported Somerset to the Pale. Those sailors who had not previously served the earl were allowed to go free, but those who had, and who had reneged on their allegiance to him, were beheaded.[44] The struggle in the Pale, principally the siege of Somerset's stronghold at Guînes, revolved around the honour of the duke and Warwick. Somerset enlisted the help of the count of Charolais (the future Charles the Bold) to obtain a safe conduct from Warwick. It was eventually granted on Somerset's promise never to take up arms against the earl and the duke returned to England in October 1460.[45] Somerset, of course, reneged upon this agreement, commanding the Lancastrian army, alongside Andrew Trollope, at Wakefield, the second battle of St Albans and Towton. In the wake of the Lancastrian defeat, Somerset travelled to France and then to the Low Countries, but by September 1462 he was in negotiations with Warwick to enter the grace of the new king, Edward IV. Although he joined the Lancastrian forces in Northumberland, he quickly came to terms with Edward and he was restored to favour in January 1463, even joining Warwick's army besieging Alnwick castle. In November, however, he once again joined the Lancastrian forces in the north. The earl of Warwick's ruthless and vigorous campaign in the north of England in 1464 to reduce the Lancastrian strongholds, resulting in the duke's defeat and execution at Hexham in April, should be viewed not only as a campaign fought on behalf of the king against a rebellious subject, but also as a personal struggle against a knight who had more than once broken a solemn, chivalric agreement.[46]

Professionals and mercenaries

Changes in the art of warfare, it is often argued, reduced the influence of chivalry on its conduct in the late fifteenth and early sixteenth centuries. The increasing size of armies, the adoption of uniforms, changes in weaponry and armour, discipline and drill, and the increasing amount of control exercised by the prince over his armed forces restricted the potential of war and military service to serve as the expression of medieval notions of chivalric behaviour. Classical generals, rather than chivalric heroes, became the models for aspiring military commanders. Symptomatic of these changes was the rise of the professional soldier: war was taken out of the hands of noble amateurs and increasingly the mercenary captain or centrally funded standing force came to dominate the military art.[47] Calais, as the largest permanent military establishment

---

[44] Waurin, v. 280; *The Brut*, ii. 528.
[45] Waurin, v. 290–1, 307.
[46] M.K. Jones, 'Henry Beaufort, 2nd Duke of Somerset (1436–64)', in *Oxford DNB*.
[47] For a discussion of these general trends, which would not reach their fruition until the end of the seventeenth century, see Thomas Arnold, *The Renaissance at War* (2001), 86–105; Barber, *Knight and Chivalry*, 328–35; Trim, 'Introduction', 23–30.

controlled by the king of England, provides an important opportunity to assess the meaning of 'professionalism' in this period. To what extent did the pressure to conform to patterns of military service and trends in warfare elsewhere in Europe lead to the 'professionalisation' of military service in Calais and displace the dominant medieval ethos of chivalry in the garrison?

Professionals – that is, men recruited into the garrison for their specialist military skills – were not an innovation of the age of the 'military revolution'. Military specialists, usually foreign nationals, had been a feature of the garrison since the town had been conquered by Edward III in 1347. In the 1370s, for example, the garrison contained forty Genoese crossbowmen, captained by John Maryns and Louis Daven, who received wages of ten francs per calendar month.[48] Military professionalism must also account for many more of the non-English members of the Calais garrison in the fifteenth century. The English garrisons in Normandy and Gascony had contained large numbers of the king's French subjects and the loss of these territories between 1450 and 1453 meant that many of them followed their English captains to England and service in Calais. One such soldier was the Gascon, Gaillard de Durefort, Lord of Duras and Blanquefort. Following the loss of Gascony Duras fled to Calais. He was initially compensated for his losses in his native land with an annuity payable at the English exchequer, but in 1457, when he entered Warwick's service, the payment of his annuity was reassigned at Calais. In November 1461 he received the Garter for his efforts in reducing the Lancastrian garrison at Hammes. He served on several commissions in the Pale and as Warwick's marshall from 1465 until 1470, when he transferred his allegiance to Edward IV. In 1475 he led a force of two thousand archers to Brittany before being reconciled with Louis XI and returning to France.[49] Moreover, Duras brought a large number of Gascons with him to serve in the Calais garrison. In 1466 he had thirty-three men serving in his personal retinue, the second largest after Warwick's own, most of whom were Gascons.[50]

Service in Calais, however, was not only attractive to former subjects of the English king. Perhaps the most unusual soldier to have served in the garrison in the fifteenth century was Georgios Bissipates, knight, 'formerly of Constantinople'. Bissipates was one of those pardoned by Edward IV in 1471 for his allegiance to the earl of Warwick. He was the son of a Byzantine nobleman, who had fled Constantinople at a young age and initially sought service with the king of France. After leaving Calais, he returned to France and served as captain of Lisieux in 1474 and in 1487 he married into the French aristocracy.[51] Another foreign professional soldier pardoned in 1471 was Antonio

[48] E101/180/4, f. 6. Each franc was worth 2*s*. 3*d*.

[49] E101/195/17, f. 38v; 196/15, f. 25; C.L. Scofield, *The Life and Reign of Edward the Fourth* (2 vols, 1923), i. 259; E405/61, rot. 4d.

[50] BL, Add. MS 46455. Only eight of the thirty-three have English names.

[51] *CPR, 1467–77*, 291. In the pardon he was styled 'George Bissipate, knight, soldier of the town of Calais, alias late of Constantinople, alias George Bissipatte, "Greke" '. For his career see Rainey, 'Defence of Calais', 133.

della Turre of Milan. Turre had become associated with Warwick through the papal legate, Francesco Coppini, and secured a place in the garrison as early as 1460. In 1466 he mustered as a man-at-arms in Warwick's retinue and apparently held the recordership of the town.[52] It seems likely that these two individuals were professional soldiers, attracted to Calais by the opportunities it provided for lucrative and honourable employment. Other foreigners were recruited into the Calais garrison to fulfil specific military roles, particularly as gunners. In the mid-1440s, for example, the 'king's gunner' in Calais was one Herman Donker.[53] In the 1460s and 1470s, as the gunpowder weaponry of the Pale was modernised and expanded, more gunners were brought from the Low Countries, chief among them Giles Van Ransingham and his fellows, Robert Potte and Giles Gonner.[54] In this respect practice in Calais mirrored that in Yorkist England generally: the gunners in charge of the royal ordnance in the 1460s appear to have been exclusively from the Low Countries and Germany.[55] Foreign gunners continued to be employed in Calais into Henry VII's reign: the muster roll of 1502 names Hans van Cache, Conrad Backenstors, Harman Coone, Pieter van Iper and Guylbert van Aulste as gunners, suggesting that over half of those members of the garrison called gunners were of foreign extraction.[56] As late as 1509, Sir Nicholas Vaux's indenture for Guînes required him to admit only Englishmen into the garrison except for 'Gonners, crossebowe makers, spyes, Beerbruers, Armourers and smythes'.[57]

Professionalism, however, was not restricted to foreign military specialists. The Hundred Years War led to the development in England of a class of men whose social position, wealth and political importance were not dependent upon their social rank but on their military skill. War gave an opportunity to younger sons: for example, Richard Wydeville was the younger son of a Northampton-shire landowner, whose career in the garrisons of Lancastrian Normandy qualified him to serve as lieutenant of Calais in the 1420s and 1430s. While Wydeville's connections also brought him land and political influence in England, other men appear to have followed the profession of arms without taking on domestic responsibilities at home.[58] In the mid-fifteenth century this class was exemplified by Andrew Trollope. Trollope had served his apprenticeship in Lancastrian Normandy, coming to Calais with Edmund Beaufort, duke of Somerset and Osbert Mountefort, whose lieutenant he had been at Fresnay castle, in 1451.[59] He temporarily transferred to the service of the earl of Warwick, but his desertion at Ludford Bridge in October 1459 was instrumental

---

52 BL, Add. MS 46455, f. 59; *CPR, 1467–77*, 290; Rainey, 'Defence of Calais', 132.
53 E101/194/16, f. 31.
54 E101/197/14, f. 23; E101/197/20, f. 23.
55 See, for example, the names in E403/823, m. 3; 827a, mm. 5, 8.
56 E101/55/23, ff. 5, 8v.
57 C54/377, m. 5d.
58 Michael Hicks, 'The Changing Role of the Wydevilles in Yorkist Politics to 1483', in *Patronage, Pedigree and Power in Late Medieval England*, ed. C.D. Ross (Gloucester, 1979), 60–86.
59 E101/54/16, 3.

to the Lancastrian victory.[60] He then returned to the Pale, enabling Henry Beaufort, duke of Somerset, to capture Guînes castle. Trollope's qualities were acknowledged by both English and European contemporaries. The Burgundian chronicler, Jean de Waurin, called him 'ung tres soubtil homme de guerre', and during the period 1459–61 Trollope acted as Somerset's principal military adviser and captain, devising the plan, for instance, that led to the capture and death of Richard, duke of York, and Richard Neville, earl of Salisbury, at Wakefield in December 1460. Trollope, however, was no mere strategist; his professionalism and the esteem he was held in were also built on personal prowess. At the second battle of St Albans in February 1461 he was knighted by the Prince of Wales. According to the author of 'Gregory's Chronicle', having received the honour, he responded: 'My lorde, I have not deservyd hit for I slowe but xv men, for I stode stylle [having impaled his foot upon a caltrap] in oo place and they come unto me, but they bode stylle with me.' He was killed fighting for the Lancastrians at Towton the following month.[61] Trollope, like his aristocratic contemporaries, was doubtless influenced by notions of chivalry, but it was principally his skill and experience that identified him as a military professional.[62]

Some English professionals, however, clearly operated as mercenaries, hiring themselves out to serve in whatever wars were currently in progress. One such example is John Turnbull. In 1451–2 he served in the duke of Somerset's crew in Calais as a mounted man-at-arms. Turnbull made his living by violence: in 1454 he was among those accused of an act of piracy involving the robbery of a Dutch ship. By the 1470s he had entered Burgundian service, commanding a company of ninety-six Englishmen at the siege of Nancy. Turnbull and his colleagues paid a heavy price for following the profession of arms: after the debâcle at Nancy

---

[60] The reasons for Trollope's desertion have never been explained. However, in the controlment of the Calais treasurer's account ending in June 1458 the payment of 40s. 1d. due from the £20 annuity granted to Trollope from the lordship of Sandegate the previous May was noted as 'disallowed by the earl of Warwick'. Two months earlier Trollope had been granted the farm of the castle and lordship for an annual rent of £10 st. ta. The background to these grants is not clear, but they may have been made by the king at Somerset's rather than Warwick's instigation. It thus may have been an attempt to woo Trollope away from Yorkist service. Warwick's refusal to pay the annuity may have been the cause of the former's desertion, or rather his return to Beaufort and Lancastrian allegiance. Indeed, Trollope's insistence that he had returned to England in Warwick's company to defend the king only to find himself arrayed against his royal master may have had an element of truth to it: E101/195/7, f. 38v; PSO1/20/1020; John Watts, *Henry VI and the Politics of Kingship* (Cambridge, 1996), 345, 352.

[61] *Letters and Papers Illustrative of the Wars of the English in France during the Reign of Henry the Sixth, King of England*, ed. J. Stevenson (Rolls Series, 2 vols in 3, 1861–4), ii. 264, 330; Waurin, v. 325; *The Historical Collections of a London Citizen in the Fifteenth Century*, ed. J. Gairdner (CS, new series, xvii, 1876), 214; Philip A. Haigh, *The Military Campaigns of the Wars of the Roses* (Stroud, 1995), 31–7, 63.

[62] Chivalry and professionalism were not mutually exclusive, but practical experience and competency, rather than prowess and social rank, differentiated the military professional from the professional warrior: M. Warner, 'Chivalry in Action: Thomas Montague and the war in France, 1417–1428', *Nottingham Medieval Studies*, xliii (1998), 146–73.

only thirty-four of them returned to England.[63] The career of Turnbull and those like him was part of a wider European transfer of military skills. However, not all of the English soldiers were as highly regarded as Trollope or Turnbull. According to Commynes, the three hundred English soldiers at the siege of Nancy were mainly comprised of men from the garrison of Guînes and many were inexperienced in siege warfare. Their commander, a man named Colpin, was 'a valiant man although from humble stock', but when he was killed by a gunshot many of his compatriots' stomach for the fight disappeared.[64] Nevertheless, despite tensions between civilians and soldiers and a growing rhetoric against mercenaries of all descriptions, the professional captain or military specialist was a valued servant of all the princes of later medieval Europe.[65]

While for some, service in the Calais garrison or with the duke of Burgundy may have had a chivalric rationale, for others war was simply their means of making a living. The Low Countries in the 1480s, for example, saw several bands of English mercenaries in action. Indeed, war may have merely legitimated some men's inherently violent conduct. Those who had seen service in Calais frequently appear to have been involved in crime in fifteenth-century England. Even in the Pale, the boundaries between legitimate violence carried out in the service of the prince and criminality were, at times, blurred. Long before the earl of Warwick's privateering exploits, the garrison had resorted to piracy to supplement their wages. In 1448–50, for example, the treasurer of Calais took a third of the profits of the garrison of Hammes castle's capture of Breton and Spanish ships, although no money was forthcoming from ransoms elsewhere among the garrison because 'of the abstinence of war'.[66] In 1461–2 a reward was paid to certain soldiers for apprehending seventeen 'thieves' who had been terrorising the county of Guînes. Possibly they were part of the former Lancastrian garrison of the castle, some of whom had evidently allied themselves with the French and resorted to a career of brigandage.[67]

The military professional continued to be a feature of the Calais garrison into the sixteenth century. Sir John Wallop, marshall of Calais between 1524 and 1530, lieutenant of Calais castle from 1529 until 1541, and then lieutenant of Guînes until his death there in July 1551, was perhaps the closest the Tudor military establishment came to men like Sir Thomas Rempston or Sir John Radcliffe.[68] Wallop came from a minor gentry family and enjoyed little landed wealth himself until the death of his uncle, Sir Robert, in 1535 enabled him to enter into a large inheritance.[69] His first taste of action was probably with the

[63] E101/54/16, 7; *CPR 1452–61*, 173; Vaughan, *Charles the Bold*, 220.

[64] Philippe de Commynes, *Memoirs: The Reign of Louis XI, 1461–83*, trans. M. Jones (1972), 294–6; Vaughan, *Charles the Bold*, 385.

[65] For contemporary views on soldiers and mercenaries in particular in England and the Low Countries see Steven Gunn, David Grummitt and Hans Cools, *War, State and Society in England and the Netherlands, 1477–1559* (Oxford, 2007), 273–7.

[66] E101/194/8, f. 21.

[67] E101/196/2, ff. 24, 34.

[68] For Radcliffe and Rempston see above, p. 000.

[69] Alan Bryson, 'Sir John Wallop' in *Oxford DNB*.

former deputy of Calais, Sir Edward Poynings, at the siege of Venlo in 1511, where he may have been knighted. As a knight he served on the seas during the campaign of 1513 and his contribution to the French campaigns of 1522 and 1523 led to his appointment as marshall of Calais in March 1524.[70] In large part, though, his military experience was gained fighting the Moors under Emmanuel, king of Portugal, between 1516 and 1518, and serving in Ireland under the earl of Surrey from 1518 until 1521. Wallop's military credentials clearly gained him a reputation and political importance beyond that conferred by his ownership of land. He became a gentleman of Henry VIII's privy chamber, and between 1526 and 1540 he was used frequently as an ambassador to both the French and Imperial courts, where he took a particular interest in military matters.[71] On the death of Lord Sandes, lieutenant of Guînes, in December 1540, he and Sir Thomas Poynings took charge of the castle and, despite his brief disgrace in early 1541 for unknown causes, he received the lieutenancy of Guînes in March that year.[72] In 1543 Wallop was made provost marshall of the army that cooperated with Imperial forces against the French, earning him the personal praise of the emperor, Charles V.[73] Confirmation of Wallop's position in the military elite of early Tudor England came on Christmas Eve 1543 when he was elected to the Order of the Garter. From 1544 until his death from the sweating sickness seven years later, he was constantly involved in the defence of Guînes. On more than one occasion his feats of arms were noted by the privy council: in June 1545 the councillors wrote to both him and Lord Grey de Wilton 'wyth thankes for theyre lusty courages in the defense of theyre peces', promising further reinforcements.[74] Wallop had none of the land, wealth and personal following that had characterised many previous captains of Guînes, but his skills as a soldier and his military reputation were common traits held with many of his predecessors. Indeed, it was as a soldier, still defined in chivalric terms, that he was remembered by his contemporaries. The London diarist, Henry Machyn, recorded his death in July 1551 in language heavy with chivalric significance:

---

[70] *LP*, IV i, 208.

[71] In 1536 Henry VIII even ordered Wallop to act as a spy and to 'devise to reasort to the Frenche king's campe and suche principal fortresses as ye may have recourse unto without danger and diligently to vue and peruse the force and strengthe of the same, conveyyng such lykelihoods therupon as ye wold gather if ye shuld be an actor in the same playe yourself': BL, Add. MS 25114, f. 201 (*LP*, XI, 445). Wallop continued to report intelligence from Guînes in the 1540s with the eye of a sixteenth-century military attaché: *Calendar of State Papers, Domestic, Edward VI 1547–1553*, ed. C.S. Knighton (revised edn, 1992), 317, 319.

[72] *LP*, XVI, 678, 694. The circumstances of the charges of treason levelled against Wallop in January 1541 are unclear but involved letters to Richard Pate, the archdeacon of Lincoln and ambassador to Charles V, who fled to Rome in December 1540. His pardon, after a full submission, was procured at the intercession of Queen Katherine Howard, underlining the close ties between Wallop and the Howards.

[73] *Calendar of Letters, Despatches, and State Papers, relating to the Negotiations between England and Spain, Preserved in the Archives at Simancas and Elsewhere* (13 vols, 1862–1954), vi(2), 504.

[74] *APC*, i. 198.

The xiij day of Juyle ded the old knyght and gentyll sir John [Wallop] and knyght of the castyll [of Gynes], for he was a nobull captayne as ever was, the wyche I [pray] Jhesu have mercy on ys solle; and he was bered with standard and [banners] of ys armes, cote armur, elmet, target of the garter, sw[ord] and viij dosen of skochyons; and a marmed was ys crest ...[75]

Wallop was the exemplar of the mid-sixteenth-century professional captain. His feats of arms were performed in the service of the prince, but it was as much his expertise in the technicalities of war that attracted the praise of contemporaries. Moreover, he combined war with a career at court and in diplomacy.

The career of Sir Thomas Poynings, marshall of Calais from October 1540 until the summer of 1542, was similar to that of Wallop and demonstrates the way in which the Pale could provide a military apprenticeship for Tudor captains in wider service to the crown, as well as the importance of family traditions of service in fashioning a career in arms. Poynings was one of the three illegitimate sons of Sir Edward Poynings, himself one of the leading military figures of the reigns of Henry VII and Henry VIII, whose fame spread not only throughout England and Ireland but also to the Low Countries. Sir Edward himself had served briefly as Daubeney's deputy in Calais in the early 1490s. Another of Sir Edward's sons, also Edward, served as a spear in the garrison from at least 1539 and later at Boulogne, while a third son, Adrian, served in Boulogne as captain of the citadel there and the 'Old Man' bulwark. He later commanded the garrison at Portsmouth.[76] Thomas himself first served in 1536, leading a hundred men from among his Kentish tenantry against the Pilgrimage of Grace. Despite the grant of extensive lands in the West Country at the beginning of 1540, in October he was moved to Calais where he took joint custody of Guînes castle.[77] There, Poynings took part in several border raids, burning French villages and attracting the praise of the other captains.[78] In 1544 he further distinguished himself. In June he and Wallop led an attack to the gates of the French castle at Ardres and in July Sir John Russell singled out Poynings's exploits at Montreuil in a letter to the king.[79] From there Poynings went to the defence of the newly captured Boulogne; in October he led an attack that was repulsed by the French Dauphin. In January 1545 he was chosen by the king as the commander of Boulogne. His appointment reflected the altered conditions of military service in mid-Tudor England and the concept of professionalism then developing. He did not owe his appointment to his landed wealth or prowess, but to his skill, experience and reputation at court. The king considered him the

---

[75] *The Diary of Henry Machyn, Citizen and Merchant-Taylor of London, from A.D. 1550 to A.D. 1563*, ed. J.G. Nichol (CS, 1st series, xlii, 1848), 8.

[76] For Sir Edward Poynings see Steven Gunn, 'Sir Edward Poynings: An Anglo-Burgundian Hero', *Publications du Centre Européen des Etudes Bourguignonnes*, xli (2001), 168. For Edward see *Lisle Letters*, i. 683. Edward, while captain of the guard at Boulogne, was killed in January 1546 leading his company at the disastrous skirmish at St Etienne: *LP*, XXI i, 33. For Adrian see *LP*, XXI i, 248, 425, 1092.

[77] *LP*, XI, 580; XVI, 317, 599.

[78] *LP*, XVIII i, 960; XVIII ii, 17.

[79] *LP*, XIX i, 654, 994 (SP1/190, f. 166).

'most experienced in wars with the Frenchmen upon the frontiers and as speaking their language'.[80] Poynings, however, continued to lead from the front: in July the Imperial ambassador, Chapuys, reported that he had had his horse shot from under him during one encounter.[81] His career was cut short when he died of plague in August 1545, but his military credentials had been recognised by his nomination, albeit unsuccessful, to the Order of the Garter earlier that year.[82] Service at Calais, then, served as an important part of the *cursus honorum* of the early Tudor military elite and provided practical training in the field for those destined for higher things.

The careers of these men reveal the changing nature of war and military service. While individuals like Poynings were doubtless aware of the chivalric and military reputations of their forebears, their own service took place in an altered political and cultural context. Increasingly in the early sixteenth century the captains of the Calais garrison were judged by their political and administrative competence, rather than their prowess in arms and chivalric reputation. As one recent commentator has observed, sixteenth-century armies were led by men whose understanding of war was defined by 'an underlying sense of generalship, of field management as an art form', and this trend is apparent in the Calais garrison.[83] While military professionals, like Wallop and Lord Grey de Wilton,[84] continued to hold the subordinate commands in the Pale, the post of governor (by Henry VIII's reign styled the 'king's deputy' of Calais) was usually given to a man more noted for his diplomatic and political attributes. The active leadership of the garrison in war, the most important function of late medieval governors and the defining feature of the captaincies of men such as the duke of Gloucester or the earl of Warwick, had given way to the demands of a court-based Tudor polity and the new type of warfare practised in early sixteenth-century Europe.

Perhaps the most successful deputy of Calais in Henry VIII's reign was Henry Fitzalan, Lord Maltravers. His career exemplifies the altered circumstances of early Tudor captains. Heir to the earldom of Arundel, Maltravers was sent to Calais, his first position of responsibility, at the relatively young age of twenty-nine. An anonymous eulogy remembered his time at Calais. Recalling how the king had increased the funding available to the garrison, it noted how Maltravers had:

> used the matter so, as in the place of artificer, or lame and decrepid person, then possessing the roome of soldiers, he furnished the places with strong and valiant personages. And where the speres and men-at-arms of Callis were then nakedly furnished, he furnished them of horse and supplye, for exersice of feates of armes; he replennished the same full amply, partly with liberall

[80] *LP,* XIX ii, 79; XX i, 121, 125/30.

[81] *LP,* XX i, 1197.

[82] *LP,* XX i, 566; XX ii, 162.

[83] Arnold, *Renaissance at War,* 105.

[84] For the career of Lord Grey de Wilton see Julian Lock, 'William, Thirteenth Baron Grey de Wilton (1508/9–1562)' in *Oxford DNB* and for his defence of Guînes castle in January 1558 see below, pp. 173–6.

bestowing necessaries amonge them, partly with incouraging them by his owne example to looke to the matter, and not to the bravery [i.e. handsome equipment] till tyme for that should serve; and so he contented himselfe to accompanye them to theare exercises with watering headstales, in stede of riche showe, which noe doubte allured them more to use that exercise then otherwise they easely might have borne, for so nether had they excuse for theare deputees curious expectation, nor of any want of habilitye; and thearby in reason might not omit theare service theare. He did not spare to make them banquets, to provoke them to exercise. He was glad when they amonge themsleves would (unlooked for) breake down his garden walls, thearby to enter and set up and use the tilt, and fighte at the turney, as a thinge they thought best contented him. Then was his horse and furniture liberally by guifte bestowed amonge them.[85]

Here the medieval virtues of chivalry – personal examples of prowess, largesse and the fellowship-of-arms – are juxtaposed with a stress on military exercises reminiscent of Vegetius and the logistical concerns of a Renaissance general. However, for all the language of chivalry, the successes for which Maltravers was remembered were administrative, logistical and diplomatic. His reputation as a good captain among the soldiery was mainly based upon his success in solving the problems of supply and discipline that had plagued his predecessor, Lord Lisle's, administration. These, then, were the concerns of a sixteenth-century professional soldier, albeit cloaked in the language of honour. The elegy also drew attention to his diplomatic efforts in 'soundry waighty matters pertaining to his realme and the kinge his maister'. In 1540–1 Maltravers successfully negotiated the dangers presented by the French incursion into the English-held 'Cowswade' near Guînes. His success and reputation therefore did not depend on his feats of arms, despite the chivalric rhetoric, but were built upon his careful diplomacy and administrative skill.[86]

Culturally too the mid-sixteenth century captains of the Calais garrison may have thought of their service in different terms from their late medieval prede-cessors. By the 1540s the individuals characterised here as military profes-sionals may have looked to the new Renaissance traditions of generalship, rather than the chivalric culture of north-western Europe, for their models of soldierly conduct. James Raymond has recently argued that the surge in English interest in texts designed to instruct men in the new forms of warfare which character-ised the European 'military revolution' was characteristic of mid-Tudor rather than Elizabethan England.[87] A number of men associated with the garrison were in the vanguard of this trend. Most important among them was Thomas Audley,

---

85 *Chronicle of Calais*, 190–1.

86 The Cowswade dispute is described in David Grummitt, 'Calais and Henry VIII: "un petit morceau d'Angleterre outremere" ', in *Le Detroit: Zone de recontres ou zone de conflits*, ed. Stéphane Curveiller et al., *Bulletin Historique et Artistique du Calaisis*, clxxiii (2001), 127–38.

87 James Raymond, *Henry VIII's Military Revolution:The Armies of Sixteenth-Century Britain and Europe* (2007). I am very grateful to Dr Raymond for allowing me to read a draft of his book before its publication.

who, towards the end of Henry VIII's reign, composed the *Booke of Orders for the Warre both by Land and Sea* for the instruction of the future Edward VI.[88] Audley's text advocated the integration of pike and shot formations with traditional English bow- and bill-armed soldiers, the regular training of men in the latest military techniques, and the use of field gunpowder artillery. Moreover, he stressed the importance of regular wages and the provision of victuals, and he urged the young prince to seek 'diverse mens opinions, as well strangers as Englishmen'.[89] In short, the *Booke of Orders* sought to remodel the English practice of war on that which had developed in northern Italy in the first decades of the sixteenth century and now characterised European warfare more generally. In August 1544 Audley was recommended by Sir John Wallop for the post of provost-marshall at Guînes. Wallop's letters to the privy council revealed that it was precisely the qualities of a Renaissance military professional that recommended Audley. He described Audley as

> an honest man and as mete to serue ... in the warres for his good understanding and knowledge therin as any do know of his diligence and can very well sett a nombre of men in ordre from one thowsand unto ten thowsand and upwards.[90]

Audley, like Wallop, Poynings, Lords Grey de Wilton and Maltravers, were typical of what C.S.L. Davies described as 'that characteristic Elizabethan figure, the professional captain'.[91] Their professionalism was not measured principally by their individual prowess, although this remained important and to some extent defined their public image, but by their ability to order their men in formation, to provide adequately for their supply, to liase effectively with their various allies and mercenary partners, and to ensure their service was performed honourably and according to the demands of their royal master.

It is more difficult to trace the emergence of this new concept of professionalism among the soldiers. Nevertheless, certain distinctive characteristics existed among the ordinary soldiers. The long-term nature of service in the Pale, regularised pay after 1466, the hierarchy of spears, constables, tipstaffs and vintenars, the training and opportunities for promotion were all features of military life in Calais and correspond to David Trim's suggested criteria for military professionalism. More importantly, perhaps, the garrison was possessed of a 'distinctive self-conceptualisation'.[92] Certainly, notions of a fellowship-in-arms persisted among the ordinary soldiers into the early sixteenth century, drawing upon an 'institutional memory' dating back to the fourteenth century. An example of the sense of fellowship among the soldiers can be found in 1504. In

---

[88] Several manuscripts of this important text survive: W.St.P. Bunbury, 'A Treatise on the Art of War by Thomas Audley', *Journal of the Society for Army Historical Research*, vi (1927), 65–78, 129–33.
[89] BL, Add. MS 23971, f. 1.
[90] SP1/172, f. 109v (*LP*, XVII, 632).
[91] C.S.L. Davies, 'The English People and War in the Early Sixteenth Century', in *Britain and the Netherlands*, ed. A.C. Duke and C.A. Tamse, vi. (The Hague, 1977), 9.
[92] Trim, 'Introduction', 6–11.

that year, a disturbance among members of the garrison occurred in the market-place. A group of soldiers attacked Bartholomew and John Flamank, two soldiers who had made themselves unpopular in the town. Their unpopularity arose partly because of a dispute over the wardenship of St Mary's church, but, more significantly, over a report made by John to Henry VII concerning poten-tially treasonable talk among the captains. In reporting the conversation, over-heard while he was in the household of his master, the deputy, Sir Richard Nanfan, Flamank had broken the bond between soldier and captain, servant and master, and undermined the sense of trust vital to the garrison's *esprit du corps*.[93] Similar sentiments were evident in the early 1520s. In January 1523 the deputy, Lord Berners, wrote to Wolsey about the conduct of a man whom the Cardinal had recommended for a position in the garrison. In an incident in the Channel soldiers from the garrison captured a French ship from Dieppe. Berners reported that there were

> serten sowdeours of thys town who dyd quytt them selff ryght well. And a [...] odyr ther was a seruaunt off your grasses ffir whom yt hath plessyd your grase to wrytt ffir hym to me to admytt hym into a vyntenars roume the wych was lattly Yays. And so at the bordynge of thys ffrench shype as yt ys reportyde by them that were ther he ranne vnder the haches & durst neuer loke vp tyll all was done. Wher ffir all the towne hier wonderyth on hym & sayth he is nott mete to serve your grase her in thys towne.[94]

Wolsey's attempt to give positions in the garrison to those evidently not of a martial persuasion threatened to undermine the sense of fellowship.

As we have seen, this latter episode was indicative of a more general trend in the 1520s and early 1530s to see positions in the garrison as part and parcel of a wider system of patronage and office-holding in early Tudor England. That is not to say, however, that this was necessarily detrimental to the effectiveness or professionalism of the garrison. The clauses in the 1536 Calais act that sought to sharpen the distinction between the military and civilian communities in the town were more a response to the inevitable problems caused by the irregulari-ties in the soldiers' pay and more than a decade of peace that had prevailed since 1523 than any demilitarisation of the garrison as a whole. Similarly, the religious turmoil that engulfed Calais in the late 1530s and led to the dismissal of Lord Lisle as deputy in 1540 involved many members of the garrison, but it did not lead to mutiny nor the dismissal of evangelicals among the soldiery.[95] Never-

93 The so-called 'Flamank Information' is SC1/58/57–8, printed in *Letters and Papers Illus-trative of the Reigns of Richard III and Henry VII*, ed. J. Gairdner (2 vols, Rolls Series, 1861–3) i. 231–40. The dating of this document is discussed in David Grummitt, '"For the Surety of the Towne and Marches": Early Tudor Policy towards Calais 1485–1509', *Nottingham Medieval Studies*, xliv (2000), 184–203. Both brothers were eventually dismissed from the garrison: BL, Add. MS 46455, ff. 123–8.

94 SP1/18, ff. 18–18v (*LP*, III ii, 2803).

95 For the religious problems in 1538–40, which played an instrumental role in the fall of the king's chief minister, Thomas Cromwell, see Grummitt, 'Calais 1485–1547', 70–87; A.J. Slavin, 'Cromwell, Cranmer and Lord Lisle: A Study in the Politics of Reform', *Albion*, ix (1977), 316–36; Philip Ward, 'The Politics of Religion: Thomas Cromwell and the Reforma-

theless, there is only anecdotal evidence of the effectiveness of the regular garrison (as opposed to the mass of reinforcements sent to the Pale) during the last years of English rule. Much of the evidence for the 'unprofessionalism' of the garrison in the mid-sixteenth century comes from the soldier-chronicler, Ellis Gruffudd. His disparaging comments on the standard of English soldiers should not, however, be taken as representative of all Englishmen serving in Calais and Boulogne in the mid-1540s. Gruffudd's comments on the 'callow boys' who served alongside Lord Cobham at the battle of Oye Sluice in May 1545, for example, were made by a man who was himself a professional soldier, having served in the garrison since the early 1520s, and who was presumably used to the higher standard of military skill he had observed among his fellow members of the garrison.[96] Indeed, Gruffudd himself provides evidence that members of the garrison were aware of and competent in the new skills demanded of the professional soldier of the mid-sixteenth century. In 1544 there were members of the garrison among the 'gentlemen and common soldiers' who used this expertise to organise the supply train for the royal army.[97]

While the mid-sixteenth century garrison still exhibited at times the same professionalism and *esprit de corps* as their predecessors, there can be no doubt that the ethos of service and concept of professionalism was undergoing a change. Just as the independence of the captains to recruit their own retinues, the reciprocity of their relationship with the crown, and the extent to which service in the garrison as a means of achieving personal honour in war were all curtailed under the early Tudors, so the ideals that underpinned service among the soldiers were also changed. Direct connections between the crown and individual soldiers, through the payment of annuities or membership of the royal household, was one way of achieving this, but a wider, and less tangible, redefinition of the nature of military service in the Pale was also effected, particularly during the reign of Henry VIII. A military career which had previously allowed service in the armies of foreign princes, and an open exchange between military professionals of various nationalities and allegiances both within and beyond the Pale was recast into one which saw the Calais garrison emerge, during the 1540s, as a force comprised of English (and Welsh) men whose allegiance was explicitly and exclusively to the king. While foreign mercenaries proliferated in the Pale during the 1540s, they were consciously set apart, in Gruffudd's eyes at

tion in Calais 1534–1540', *Journal of Ecclesiastical History*, xvii (1992), 152–71; George Bernard, *The King's Reformation: Henry VIII and the Remaking of the Church of England* (New Haven, CT, 2005), 527–32.

[96] Ellis Gruffudd, 'Boulogne and Calais from 1545 to 1550', ed. M.B. Davies, *Fouad I University Bulletin of Faculty of Arts*, xii (1950), 29–31. For Gruffudd's career generally see Thomas Jones, 'A Welsh Chronicler in Tudor England', *Welsh Historical Review*, i (1960), 1–17.

[97] Ellis Gruffudd, 'The Enterprise of Paris and Boulogne', ed. M.B. Davies, *Fouad I University Bulletin of Faculty of Arts*, xi (1949), 65. Not all members of the garrison won the chronicler's praise: one 'Master Hussey', probably John Hussee who had been Lord Lisle's man of business in the 1530s and found a place in the garrison, was characterised by Gruffudd as 'a fat-bellied lump of a man ... lacking in sense and a coward at heart' whose incompetence led him and his men into a French ambush during the siege of Montreuil in 1544: ibid., 62.

least, from both the regular garrison and the English, Welsh and Irish contingents that reinforced the Pale's defences. His derision of the foreign mercenaries was one manifestation of this. Part of the criticism of the mercenaries was their unprofessionalism, in contrast to the regular garrison,. During March and April 1545 the marketplace in Calais was the scene of constant affrays between rival national groups; throughout the Pale

> there were so many depraved, brutish soldiers from all nations under the sun – Welsh, English, Cornish, Irish, Manx, Scots, Spaniards, Gascons, Portingals, Italians, Arbannoises, Greeks, Turks, Tartars, Almains, Germans, Burgundians, Flemings, who had come here … to have a good time under the king of England, who by nature was too hospitable to foreigners.[98]

English soldiers in the Pale, on the other hand, stood in an entirely different relationship to royal authority. Their conduct and conditions of service, as well as being regulated by military discipline and the various provost marshalls, were also conditioned by a new oath sworn by both the captains and soldiers from at least 1541. It reflected the political situation of the time: an embattled England standing alone against those foreign princes still under the yoke of the Papacy. The oath demanded that:

> Ye swere that ye shalbe true and faythfull liegeman to our soveraigne Lord Henry the viij[th] by the grace of God king of England, of France and of Irland, defensour of the fayth and in earth supreme hedde of the Churche of England and also of Irland. And to his heires kynges of England as long as ye shall lyve. Ye shall take his parte ageinst all earthlie ~~princes~~ Creatures. Ye shall not depart from the towne and marches of Calais onlesse that first you ghive a half yeres warnyng. And to your true might and power ye shall ever kepe the sayd N true Englissh and in nowise wear any manner Cognisaunce save onlie the kinges highnesses as long as you shalbe here in Retynue.

Moreover, the soldiers swore to 'observe kepe maynteyne and defend the holle effectes and contentes of all and syngular Actes Statutes … in derogacion extirpation and extinguishment of the Bishop of Rome and his auctoritie'. The oath also regulated the professional conduct of the soldiers, requiring them to promise to keep watch and ward, not to go absent without licence, to maintain discipline and harmony within the garrison, and to report anything which might threaten the security of the town or the realm to the Calais council.[99] It seems likely that these latter clauses drew upon older oaths and customs observed within the Pale, while the stress on the Pale's 'Englishness' echoed fifteenth-century rhetoric, but the stress on the exclusivity of service to the king marked the final move of the professionalism of the Calais garrison, its *esprit de corps*, away from the international fellowship of a profession in arms into a

---

[98] Gruffudd, 'Boulogne and Calais', 15–18. Gruffudd, of course, also reflected a wider, xenophobic discourse of foreign mercenaries during the 1540s: Gunn, Grummitt and Cools, *War, State and Society*, 276–7.

[99] SP1/174, ff. 185–6 (*LP*, XVII, 1188(2)). The surviving copy of the oath is clearly a proforma. The soldiers of the various castles and bulwarks in the Pale were sworn to keep their particular charge, as well as to the more general clauses.

small standing army devoted to the service of the prince and nation.[100] In this the English were, of course, following trends apparent in the rest of western Europe. In the Habsburg Netherlands, for example, Charles V, Philip II and their regents all promulgated bans on Netherlanders serving other princes. By the 1550s the rhetoric behind these had moved from 'the prejudice of the public weal' to the 'defence of their fatherland'.[101]

* * *

Clearly, the Calais garrison provided the most important pool of military expertise in late medieval and early Tudor England. Its soldiers and captains were, for the most part, skilled fighting men who were identified by contemporaries as men of war, and who were defined both individually and as a group by their actions in war. Military knowledge and expertise was brought into Calais by men who had seen service in Normandy, Gascony and the Scottish borders, or in the wars of foreign princes. They were also exported to be utilised in the civil wars of the mid-fifteenth century and elsewhere in both English and foreign service. The professionalism of the garrison – in the dual sense of a collective identity and an *esprit de corps*, and a knowledge of and expertise in the art of war – continued throughout the period. However, in two important ways the nature of this professionalism was changed in the last years of the fifteenth and first decades of the sixteenth centuries.

First, the role of chivalry within the garrison underwent a subtle yet significant transformation. In the fifteenth century notions of chivalry, held in common throughout western Europe, had often determined the conduct of war in the Pale. While chivalric service and deeds of arms in the service of the prince had always played an important role in the garrison's collective identity (as exemplified by *The Beauchamp Pageant*, for instance), they had existed alongside an international view of chivalric practice which allowed for the free exchange of ideas and personnel between the knightly communities of western Europe and beyond. In the fifteenth century this was exemplified by the service of members of the garrison in the armies of Charles the Bold and Maximilian, and by the presence in Calais of men like Gaillard de Durefort and Antonio della Turre. During the early sixteenth century the role of foreigners in the garrison changed. No longer the equals of the knightly English captains of the garrison, the foreign presence became restricted to professionals of lower social status, especially gunners, and mercenaries, distinct from the regular garrison in numerous ways. In contrast, the English knightly captains, such as Sir John Wallop, Lord Grey or Lord Maltravers, retained their chivalric identity, but had it redefined in terms of

---

[100] It appears that this exclusivity of service survived beyond the end of Henry VIII's reign until the demobilisation of the garrison at Boulogne by the terms of the treaty of Boulogne in March 1550. Thereafter, bands of English soldiers sought employment in the Imperial army and several apparently fought with distinction at the siege of Metz in 1552 and against the French in Picardy the following year: Mark Charles Fissel, *English Warfare, 1511–1642* (2001), 18–19. Nevertheless, there is no evidence that soldiers from the ordinary Calais garrison were free to follow the profession of arms with other princes.

[101] Gunn, Grummitt, and Cools, *War, State and Society*, 243–4.

service to the king. While the rhetoric of chivalry (for example, in eulogies and at funerals) remained ostensibly the same, the practice was different. As we have seen in an earlier chapter, the formal nature of the relationship between the king and the captains was redefined at the same time, and the stress on war and acts of chivalry being performed exclusively in the service of the prince was a corollary of this development.

Second, the role of the military professional within the garrison altered according to wider changes within the practice of European warfare. In the fifteenth century men like Andrew Trollope were skilled professionals, able to use years of experience to advise on the art of war. They were noted for their prowess, but also for their appreciation of tactics, logistics and the mechanics of war. Importantly, however, it was the chivalric aspect of their conduct that was, with a few notable exceptions, stressed and held in more esteem by contemporaries. It was this shared culture of chivalry, war and military service that allowed these men to operate within the northwest-European military community. In the sixteenth century, however, this gradually began to change and an appreciation of the practicalities of war gained more recognition. The most successful captains at Calais were those who conducted diplomacy, managed the victualling and supply of the garrison, ensured that the soldiers were properly paid and disciplined, and did all these solely as a servant of the king. In the eulogy for Lord Maltravers, for instance, these qualities were juxtaposed with those of his personal prowess and *largesse*, all contributing to his honourable service to the king. In terms of recognition and recommendation among contemporaries it was the practical aspects of generalship which were privileged over the medieval qualities of the chivalric warrior. This was parcel of a wider European-wide transformation in the art of war, reflected in the production of new military manuals in the middle years of the century. The professionalism of the soldiers was altered too. There remained an *esprit de corps* or 'institutional memory' that had existed in the fifteenth century, but among the garrison the ties to the crown were strengthened. The freedom of movement, the sense that the profession of arms could be followed in a variety of ways and for different employers, which had been characteristic of the soldiers earlier was replaced by an ethos of exclusivity of service to the crown and a delegitimisation of violence and military service in any other sphere. By the 1540s the Calais garrison exhibited some of the salient features of the emergent professional, standing armies which were characteristic of the early modern European state.

6

Weaponry and Fortifications in Calais

Perhaps the most interesting aspect of the records of the English administration of Calais in the fifteenth and sixteenth centuries is the information they provide about the weaponry used by the soldiers of the garrison. Such detailed information on the weapons used by English armies in this period is uncommon. In this chapter the type of weaponry used by the garrison, with special reference to the developments in gunpowder artillery, will be examined. The built defences of the Pale will also be described. In the final part of this chapter the weaponry and fortifications will be set in the wider context of the European 'military revolution' of the sixteenth century. In a time of rapid change in military technology, this insight into developments in English arms and their relationship to those in Europe more generally is especially important. To what extent was England, as illustrated by the experiences of the defence of the Pale, involved in these changes and how far were changes in the Calais garrison indicative of more general trends in English armies?

Weaponry

The Calais garrison was typical of the kind of infantry-based forces that characterised European armies at the end of the Middle Ages. It was, as we have seen, ostensibly divided into men-at-arms and archers for the purposes of administration, but this arbitrary division did not necessarily correspond to the tactical roles of the soldiers themselves, nor the weapons they used. The survival of many of the Calais victuallers' accounts (the official who was responsible from 1436 until 1492 for the supply of weaponry to the garrison) means that the purchases of weaponry for the garrison's use can be reconstructed in detail. After 1492 reforms in the financial administration of the Pale meant that there were no longer separate victuallers' accounts, and for the remainder of the period it seems that the supply of arms and ammunition to the garrison was increasingly taken over by royal commissioners, albeit often working from within the Pale. The records made by these commissions survive only sporadically. Nevertheless, sufficient sixteenth-century material is extant to gain a reasonably clear picture of the arms used by the Calais garrison and other soldiers involved in the defence of the Pale in that period.

Given the prominence of the longbow in the 'infantry revolution' that had characterised English success in the Hundred Years War,[1] the Calais garrison

---

[1] For the 'infantry revolution' of the early fourteenth century see Clifford J. Rogers, 'The

might reasonably be assumed to have been armed predominantly with the bow during the fifteenth century. Indeed men described as 'archers' comprised the majority of the garrison and there is evidence of centrally supplied bows and arrows in the victuallers' account. Between 1434 and 1436, for example, 1,705 bows were sold to the soldiers by the victualler.[2] In 1460–1, another period of intense military activity in the Pale, 380 bows were received by the victualler, of which 147 were 'expended' (that is, they were sold to the soldiers) and the remainder handed over to the new victualler, John Wode.[3] However, as this was the basic weapon of the soldier in the garrison, it is more likely that longbows were procured on a private basis. The demand for bows among the soldiers, and for the repair of existing stocks, probably explains the high incidence of protections issued to fletchers and bowyers to pass beyond the seas in the retinue of the Calais victualler.[4] Moreover, other evidence makes it clear that there were a large number of bows in circulation in Calais outside the garrison. In 1478, for example, the married members of the staple company challenged their bachelor colleagues to an archery competition.[5]

The victuallers' accounts also make it clear that the soldiers of the Calais garrison employed a wide range of other weaponry, most of which was centrally supplied, to meet the particular demands of the defence of the Pale. The most important of these were crossbows. In the fourteenth century the crossbow had not been associated with the English and, indeed, in Calais the core of the forty crossbowmen of the captain's retinue had originally been Genoese.[6] By 1436, however, the crossbow was firmly established in the hands of English soldiers. Given the space restrictions when firing from castles, the crossbow was in many ways preferable to the longbow as a weapon for the defence of the Pale. More-over, in a siege context the crossbow's slower rate of fire was less of a disadvantage than when in the open field.[7] However, the victuallers' frequent purchase of pavises, large shields behind which the crossbowman could reload, suggest that the use of crossbows in the open field may have been more widespread than commonly thought. The fifteenth-century military crossbow, often made from steel, was capable of greater penetrative power than either the longbow or the handgun by virtue of the winding mechanism which imparted great force to the projectile. It was an expensive item of equipment and thus was procured by the royal authorities in Calais before being issued to the soldiers. Before the mid-1460s crossbows were usually bought from English merchants, possibly

Military Revolutions of the Hundred Years War', in *The Military Revolution Debate*, ed. Clifford J. Rogers (Boulder, CO, 1995), 55–93.

2 E364/72, rot. D. See below, pp. 46–8 for a discussion of the contemporary terms used to describe members of the garrison.

3 E101/195/14.

4 For example, Nicholas Robleyns, of London, fletcher, crossed the Channel in the retinue of John Wode, in 1462: C76/146, m. 13.

5 *The Cely Letters 1472–1488*, ed. Alison Hanham (EETS, cclxxiii, 1975), 26–7.

6 E101/180/4, f. 6.

7 Bert S. Hall, *Weapons and Warfare in Renaissance Europe: Gunpowder, Technology and Tactics* (Baltimore, MD, 2002), 16–18.

having been first imported from the Low Countries. In 1458–9, for example, the victualler purchased crossbows, as well as saltpetre, brigandines, lances and longbows, from the London merchants, John Reynolds and William Nicoll.[8] But after the marriage in 1468 of Edward IV's sister, Margaret, to Charles, duke of Burgundy, the Calais victualler was able to take advantage of the flourishing arms trade in Brabant and Flanders.[9] Thus, in the 1470s the victualler, William Rosse, purchased forty-nine wooden crossbows from Henry Derykson of Antwerp and 120 iron ones from William Stenkyn of Brussels, as well as seventy pairs of 'dowble wynches' and forty thousand quarrels.[10] By 1476 there were 121 steel crossbows and forty wooden ones in the wardrobe in Calais castle compared with 1,076 longbows, suggesting that while the crossbow had not supplanted the longbow as the principal English missile weapon, it still constituted a significant part of the armament of the Calais garrison.[11]

The series of inventories of military equipment compiled in the 1470s and 1480s further demonstrates that the Calais garrison had access to a wide variety of weaponry. Besides the longbow, the most important infantry weapon in fifteenth-century English armies was the bill. The inventories reveal that large numbers of bills were stockpiled in Calais, both for the garrison's own use and, due to the importance of Calais as an arsenal for English armies generally, particularly for Edward IV's invasion of France in 1475. In 1481 there were eighty-four 'white' bills and 119 'black' bills in the Calais armoury. Another important weapon was the 'battleaxe', probably the two-handed poleaxe, the favoured weapon of the armoured man-at-arms on foot in the fifteenth century, rather than the smaller battleaxe which could be used on horseback as well as on foot. In the same inventory there were sixty 'gylt' axes and 172 'ungylt' ones.[12] The numbers suggest that in the late fifteenth century the heavy poleaxe was the pole arm of choice for well-equipped English soldiers, replacing the lighter bill. The impact of European tactics on English armies is also suggested by the presence of large numbers of 'spears' or pikes in Calais. It is clear that in the late 1470s and early 1480s the number of 'spears' was increasing. In Guînes in 1476 there were twenty-four 'spears' listed in the inventory; by 1485 this had risen to sixty-seven. In Calais in 1481 there were 941 spear heads awaiting their shafts, as well as twelve dozen headed 'marespikes' or 'moorish pikes' and thirty dozen unheaded.[13] The growing importance of longer pole arms within English armies

8 E101/195/11, f. 3.
9 Grummitt, 'Defence of Calais', 260–1.
10 E101/55/5. Longbows still outnumbered crossbows in Rosse's account by nearly four to one, but longbows continued to be bought from predominantly English sources.
11 E101/198/13, f. 64v. The high number of bows probably represents the remains of the stockpile accumulated for the invasion of France the previous year.
12 E101/198/13, f. 77v.
13 Ibid., ff. 51v, 70, 77v, 79. The precise difference between the spears and 'morispikes' is unclear. By Henry VIII's reign the 'Moorish pike' was the name commonly given to European long pikes in English armies, probably based on the fact that it was believed that their use by the Moors predated that of the Swiss and French: C.W.C. Oman, *The Art of War in the Six-teenth Century* (1937), 291.

may have been a reaction to the success of Swiss pikemen against the armies of Charles the Bold. This trend continued into the Tudor period, a process perhaps made more rapid by Henry VII's first-hand experience of the effectiveness of pikes at Bosworth.[14] Indeed in 1492 the indenture for Henry VII's invasion of France made with Sir Rhys ap Thomas contained a clause for the provision of two hundred footmen armed with 'long spears'.[15] By Henry VIII's reign the pike formed an important part of English armies and by 1547 had become the principal pole arm.[16]

This willingness to adapt continued to be evident in the early sixteenth century and is perhaps most apparent in the garrison's use of handheld firearms. The earliest mention of handguns in the Calais victuallers' accounts is in 1467–8, when one iron and twenty brass guns were bought from various merchants in the Low Countries.[17] This may seem rather late in European terms: Duke John the Fearless of Burgundy could equip four thousand handgunners as early as 1411 and by the first half of the fifteenth century many German towns maintained stocks of *Handbüchsen*. Here, however, it may be that the terminology obscures the fact that the guns purchased in 1467–8 were in fact arquebuses, longer matchlock weapons that first appeared around 1450 and proliferated in most European armies during the last quarter of the fifteenth century. Unlike the 'hakegun', later termed a 'hagbusshe' in the Calais inventories, the arquebus or handgun could be fired unsupported from the shoulder.[18] If that is the case the Calais garrison was not merely playing catch-up with the Burgundians, but was itself at the forefront of developments in European military technology. That these weapons were indeed early arquebuses is attested by the presence in the inventories of the various new paraphernalia needed to load and service them: 'stampers' to ram home the shot, 'cockers', triggers and matchcord.[19] These new 'handguns' continued to exist alongside the older hand-held gunpowder weapons, the 'hake' or hook gun and the hand culverin. By 1474–5 the victualler recorded twenty-five iron and 243 brass handguns alongside fifteen iron 'hakeguns' in his account.[20]

By the early sixteenth century the arquebus had emerged as the most important infantry missile weapon on the battlefield among western European armies in general. The first evidence of its success comes from the Spanish

---

[14] For the presence of French pikemen at Bosworth and their importance at the crucial stage of the battle see Michael K. Jones, *Bosworth 1485: Psychology of a Battle* (Stroud, 2002), 162–70.

[15] E101/72/6/1154.

[16] Gervase Phillips, *The Anglo-Scots Wars 1513–1550* (Woodbridge, 1999), 78–9.

[17] E101/197/3.

[18] Hall, *Weapons and Warfare*, 95–6. The hook gun was so called because of the hook designed to rest the heavier barrel against a castle wall or some other support and absorb some of the weapon's recoil. See the illustration in Christopher Gravett, *Medieval Siege Warfare* (1990), 43 plate J. For the difference in English terminology see *The Anthony Roll of Henry VIII's Navy*, ed. C.S. Knighton and D.M. Loades (Navy Records Society Occasional Publications, ii, 2000), 173–4.

[19] E101/198/13.

[20] E101/198/9, f. 2.

Reconquista, and by the first decade of the 1500s, in the employment of Spanish troops in Italy, it had revolutionised infantry warfare.[21] In 1513 Henry VIII ordered eighty 'handguns with horns' from the Spanish merchant, John de Castro, for his invasion of France.[22] As there are no separate Tudor victuallers' accounts after 1492 it is impossible to chart the growth of arquebuses in the Calais garrison. An inventory made in 1533, however, records only nine old brass 'hagbusshes' and 150 iron ones.[23] By 1539 there were 110 newer handguns in the town itself alongside 142 old 'hagbusshes' and 2,740 longbows; in Calais castle there were twelve handguns alongside 65 iron 'hagbusshes' and seven brass ones, ninety-two bows and nineteen crossbows; in Guînes there were sixty-two handguns as opposed to 202 'hagbusshes', thirty-four crossbows and 310 longbows.[24] The 1540s saw a massive increase in the number of handheld gunpowder weapons within the Pale. The series of inventories compiled at the death of Henry VIII in 1547 makes the extent of this quite clear. It leaves no doubt of the fact that they were widely employed in the defence of Calais. There were enough handguns in the Pale to equip most of the garrison and a good proportion of the reinforcements still stationed there. For example, in 'Thandgoune chambre' alone there were 238 'demi-hackes', and 840 'handgounes of Thitallyon fasshion' that were serviceable, as well as a hundred guns in need of repair. This compared with 279 'hagbusshes' of all descriptions, 1,500 longbows and 110 crossbows. Thus by the end of Henry VIII's reign the number of 'fiery weapons' had reached a parity with more conventional missile weapons.[25]

A similar modernisation of weaponry and adaptability to new techniques and ideas is evident among the larger-calibre gunpowder artillery. The effectiveness of English cannon in the fifteenth century is frequently portrayed as lagging behind that of Burgundy and France in terms of numbers, size and technology. The Calais evidence, however, suggests strongly that this was not the case. In 1436 there were about 130 guns of all sizes in Calais, some of them probably dating as far back as the last quarter of the fourteenth century.[26] In preparation for the Burgundian siege, in March that year, the crown ordered twenty-eight guns, five hundred gunstones and other supplies to be delivered to the treasurer of Calais, Robert Whittingham; four months later £10 was delivered to him 'sur la faissance de divers canons estre ordenez pur la defense de nostre chastell & ville de Cales'.[27] After the siege and for the remainder of Henry VI's reign there is little evidence of any attempt to modernise the Pale's gunpowder weaponry, although it is interesting that the eleven purchases of guns for which a place of origin is recorded were made from the English smiths John and Steven

---

[21] W.H. Prescott and A.J. McJoynt (eds), *The Art of War in Spain: The Conquest of Granada, 1481–1492* (1995), 36–7; Oman, *Art of War*, 52–5.

[22] *LP*, I ii, 1968.

[23] SP1/78, ff. 78–78v (*LP*, vi. 930).

[24] SP1/106, ff. 195–210v (*LP*, XI, 488).

[25] *The Inventory of King Henry VIII: The Transcript*, ed. David Starkey (1998), 120–1.

[26] E364/72.

[27] E404/52/19, 383.

Clampard.[28] Nevertheless, it is clear that there was a decline in the relative quantity and quality of gunpowder weaponry in the Pale during the reign of Henry VI. This was not due to any disinclination on the part of the English to use gunpowder weaponry, rather it stemmed from the political crisis caused by the insufficiency of Henry VI's kingship and the failure to provide royal leadership crucial to the development of new weapons and technology.[29]

This situation was turned around sharply with the accession of Edward IV in March 1461. Edward, along with his brother, Richard, duke of Gloucester, later Richard III, had a personal interest in gunpowder weaponry and this, along with the diplomatic and commercial alliance with Burgundy in 1468, energised the development of these weapons in the Pale.[30] By appointing as victualler a merchant, William Rosse, who already had close contacts in the Low Countries, Edward helped to open the specialised metallurgical industries of Brabandt and Flanders to English markets. Edward's reign was thus marked by such technological innovations as arquebuses and iron 'gunstones'. Moreover, by 1474 at the latest, Rosse was comptroller of the king's ordnance,[31] and along with the master smith of Calais, a Dutchman named Giles van Rasingham (by 1473 also master of the king's guns),[32] he was responsible for assembling an artillery train for the 1475 invasion of France that, in the eyes of one Italian observer at least, was finer than that of the duke of Burgundy. The pride of Edward's train was *The Great Edward of Calais*, which the king took with him to Fauquembergues in Artois where he met his ally, Charles of Burgundy. This piece had cost the huge sum of £515 Flem. As well as *The Great Edward*, Rosse and van Rasingham purchased two long serpentines from the Low Countries, one of them weighing 817 kg, as well as manufacturing another 54 iron serpentines in Calais. With guns brought over from the Tower of London and presumably those already stored in Calais, the artillery train for the 1475 invasion was a formidable one and certainly on a par with that of the duke of Burgundy.[33] The artillery train kept in the Pale amounted to some 233 pieces by the early 1480s and guns made in Calais under the supervision of Rosse and van Rasingham formed the mainstay of the artillery used against the Scots in the campaigns of 1481 and 1482.[34]

---

28 In all forty-eight guns were purchased by the victualler between 1436 and 1456, the largest number, twenty-eight, in 1450–1, as fears of a French or Burgundian attack increased. As Rainey points out, given the diplomatic situation, it is likely that these were made in England: Rainey, 'Defence of Calais', 209.

29 Grummitt, 'Defence of Calais', 256–9. In France the centralisation of the artillery train under the Bureau brothers had benefited from Charles VII's personal interest in military matters. Similarly, the Burgundian dukes showed a real interest in warfare and the tools of war that was conspicuously absent in the kingship of Henry VI.

30 This paragraph is based upon the argument in Grummitt, 'Defence of Calais', 259–67.

31 E405/59, rot. 7.

32 E405/57, rot. 7.

33 E101/55/4, fol. 37v; E101/55/5, 7. There were already some 150 large guns (excluding handguns) in Calais itself in 1475: E101/198/9, f. 3v. Charles the Bold took at least 150 guns from the ducal arsenal at Lille with him to Nancy in the same year: R.D.S. Smith and Kelly de Vries, *The Artillery of the Dukes of Burgundy, 1363–1477* (Woodbridge, 2005), 340–2.

34 Grummitt, 'Defence of Calais', 266.

During Henry VII's reign there is little evidence of any augmentation or modernisation of the Pale's gunpowder weaponry. The most important development was that the centre of English artillery manufacture and storage was moved away from Calais back to the Tower of London.[35] Henry VIII's personal interest in artillery, however, and his desire to invade France ensured that the armament of Calais once again came under the royal spotlight after 1509. In 1510 Henry employed the services of the leading German expert in the manufacture of ordnance, Hans Poppenruyter of Malines. Further foreign craftsmen were encouraged to come to England in preparation for the French expedition of 1513 and the king established a foundry for them in Houndsditch.[36] The inventories of the Pale's artillery demonstrate how Henry's efforts to attract the best German, Dutch and Italian gun-manufacturers to England helped improve the quality and quantity of ordnance in the Pale.[37] For example, the largest piece in Guînes in 1537 was a 'Nowenborow [Nuremberg] culverin of bras', while there were several brass sakers of 'houndiche [Houndsditch] makyng'. In Calais there were brass Nuremberg culverins and bastard-culverins, as well as a 'bras culveryn of Hans Popenrunders makyng'.[38]

The fruits of this investment in developing a modern facility to manufacture artillery within England can be seen in the revitalisation of the Calais foundry in the 1530s and the council of Calais's patronage of John and Robert Owens, the town's resident gun-founders. As we have seen, a foundry had existed in Calais since at least the early 1470s. It was during Lord Lisle's term as deputy

---

[35] Ibid., 267–9.

[36] *LP,* I i, 287, 145–6, 709; I ii, 1472.

[37] There were four Henrician artillery inventories for the Pale. The 1533 survey of the town of Calais was taken on Lord Lisle's arrival as deputy: SP1/78, ff. 78–81 (*LP,* vi. 930). The 1537 survey was taken by Sir Christopher Morris, master of the ordnance; it is more extensive and survives in two copies: the first is among a general book listing the king's ordnance dated 1539 and covers Guînes: E101/60/3, ff. 26–30, Hammes (ff. 31–33) and Rysbank Tower (f. 34); the second copy among the State Papers is the same but also includes the town of Calais and Newembridge: SP1/106, ff. 195–210v (*LP,* XI, 488). The 1542 survey of Rysbank Tower was sent to the privy council by the council of Calais as part of a general reinforcement of that fortress: SP1/173, ff. 43–44v (*LP,* XVII, 829). The most extensive survey, however, was taken in December 1547 and forms part of the massive inventory ordered on the death of Henry VIII. It includes the town of Calais, all the fortresses and the three bulwarks recently completed in the county of Guînes. The description of guns raises some major problems of interpretation. A glossary of the terms used in the inventories is available in H.C. Blackmore, *The Armouries of the Tower of London*: I *The Ordnance* (1976), 215–48. See also the excellent description of the various types of Burgundian gunpowder weaponry in Smith and De Vries, *Artillery of the Dukes of Burgundy*, 203–60. The various sizes of cannon, usually muzzle-loading, ranged from cannons, through culverins, sakers and falcons, to the bass, 'the smallest of the standard cannon-types'. Related to these was the serpentyne, apparently an older term for any gun that had a long barrel length in relation to its calibre. The other main type of piece was comprised of various fowlers, 'port-pieces' and slings. These, at least in the Calais context, seem to relate to breach-loading, swivel mounted guns with one or many 'chambers'. The diversification of gun-types in the sixteenth century shows that guns were evolving different forms to perform specific tactical roles. For full definitions of these and the other pieces listed in the inventories see Blackmore's glossary.

[38] E101/60/3, ff. 26, 26v; SP1/106, ff. 195, 195v (*LP,* xi. 488).

(1533–40), however, that the number and quality of pieces cast there rapidly improved. This was clearly in part a response to the king's personal interest, but was also due to the realisation of the need to modernise the defences on the part of the Calais council. Given its members' own military credentials and experiences and contacts with the French and Imperial military classes this should come as no surprise. In May 1535 Lisle reported to the king that Henry Johnson, surveyor of the ordnance in the Tower of London, had cast thirty-two guns in Calais, while a further twelve were almost completed.[39] Soon the council, and especially Lisle, emerged as the key dynamic in the modernisation of the Pale's ordnance. Lisle, at the behest of Sir Christopher Morris, master of the ordnance in England, employed the Owens brothers – experienced founders who had previously been employed at Houndsditch – to cast guns at Calais.[40] The result of the re-establishment of the Calais foundry was an increase in the number of modern brass pieces in the Pale. For example, between 1533 and 1537 the number of brass pieces on the walls of Calais rose from thirty-one to 110, an increase of 58 per cent in the proportion of such guns. Nevertheless, the reduction in the number of older iron pieces left the amount of ordnance less than that thought necessary by the council in 1533.[41] However, by 1547 the amount of ordnance exceeded even this estimate. Alongside these developments was a change in the way the ordnance within the Pale was organised and maintained.

From the late 1530s the ordnance was kept by local 'quartermasters', presumably under the overall supervision of the master of the ordnance at Calais. This system was indicative of the privy council's willingness to delegate responsibility for the defence of Calais to members of the garrison and local men. When under local command, as opposed to central command from Westminster, the ordnance in the Pale could quickly be moved to meet the threats that arose on the borders. The council of Calais appointed George Browne, master of the ordnance in the Pale, to oversee the augmentation and modernisation of its defences. In January 1546 he indented with Sir Thomas Seymour, master of the ordnance in England, for ten new brass pieces and forty iron pieces, as well as sufficient stores and ammunition. Moreover, the privy council noted that letters were to be sent to the council of Calais forbidding the 'delyvery of any parcell of the municion under his charge to any persone privately', but only to Browne himself.[42] In the town of Calais itself, the council appointed quartermasters corresponding to the existing municipal divisions: for example, in December 1547 the ordnance in 'Bulleyn Welle' quarter was in the charge of William Assheton. Assheton appears as one of the vinteyne in the 1540 muster roll and in 1552 his widow held a mansion within the town.[43] The effectiveness of this

---

[39] *Lisle Letters*, ii. 385. In 1534 Johnson had been commissioned to bring all the broken brass pieces in the Pale to the Tower to be recast: *LP*, vii. 97.

[40] *Lisle Letters*, iii. 650, 687.

[41] SP1/78, f. 81. In 1533 the council considered that the walls needed to be augmented by a saker, a demi-culverin, seven falcons, twenty-nine serpentines and thirty-two fowlers.

[42] *APC*, i. 316–17.

[43] Society of Antiquaries MS 129B, f. 293v; *Lisle Letters*, i. 681; BL, Harl. MS 3880, f. 154. Other 'quartermasters' included John London, an archer at 6*d.* per day in 1540; Bernard

system is underlined by the council's ability to reinforce the areas under the most constant threat of attack, notably around Guînes. In 1547 there were 178 pieces at Guînes compared to 124 in 1537, although most of these were of the older iron type.

As well as the augmentation of the ordnance itself, the council was responsible for the bulwarks constructed to guard the Pale against incursions from the French castle at Ardres. Ellis Gruffudd describes how the original planning and construction of these between 1540 and 1542 was carried through by the council with the minimum of interference from Westminster.[44] In Decembee that Harway Bulwark was sufficiently furnished with ordnance.[45] By 1547 there were ten pieces in Harway, sixteen pieces in Bellingham and fifteen in Bootes bulwark.[46] The reinforcement of the borders of the Pale nearest the French fortress at Ardres demonstrates the effectiveness of the council in exercising control over the defences and its ability to react swiftly to changes in the military situation. Moreover, the council also took measures to improve the quality of gunnery within the Pale. In 1542 they wrote to the privy council requesting that the extraordinary gunners then in Calais and Guînes be put in their own wages – that is, made a permanent part of the garrison – to encourage excellence in gunnery among the soldiers.[47] Moreover, gunners were added to the establishment of the outlying forts and bulwarks. At Rysbank there were eight men called 'gounners' at 6*d.* a day, while at Newembridge there were three *vibrellatores* ('bombadiers') and a gunner at each of the new bulwarks. Moreover, the accounts make it clear that they were Englishmen.[48]

Fortifications

In 1347 the town of Calais was fortified by a complete, high stone curtain wall, punctuated by six round towers and four gates, all built in the thirteenth century by the count of Boulogne. In the north-western corner of the town was a castle of similar vintage, consisting of a circular donjon with a rectangular bailey, studded with six round towers and a gatehouse.[49] The upkeep of the fortifications in Calais was necessary to defend the town and marches against attack from hostile princes, but also against the more frequent assault of the sea and the other elements. While, through the opening of the sluices around Calais, water provided the surest means of defence against any attacker, it also proved a constant danger to the vitality of the Pale. The unceasing battle to shore up

---

Borowe, who in 1540 served in the vinteyne; and George Hall, who was presumably related to the comptroller, Francis Hall.

[44] Colvin, *The King's Works*, iii. 374.

[45] SP1/174, f. 181 (*LP,* xvii. 1188).

[46] Society of Antiquaries MS 129B, ff. 318v–320.

[47] SP1/173, f. 41 (*LP,* xvii. 829); *LP,* xvi. 174, 197, 759; xvii. 691.

[48] E351/530, rot. 3; 535, rot. 4–5.

[49] Colvin, *The King's Works*, i. 423, 445. This section is largely based on the extensive survey of the fortifications of the Pale in the relevant volumes of *The History of the King's Works*, supplemented by my own research.

walls, harbours and jetties is not the concern of this section, however; instead, the efforts of successive English administrations to meet the purely military problems of Calais's built defences will be examined.

Colvin divides the history of Calais's fortifications in the fifteenth century into three distinct phases. First, the period from 1422 until 1441 saw a neglect of the Pale's fortifications brought about by a crisis in morale occasioned by set-backs elsewhere in Lancastrian France, the ineffectiveness of Henry VI's rule, the general shortage of money and the maladministration and corruption of two successive treasurers, Richard Buckland and Robert Whittingham. Second, the period 1441–60 saw a revitalisation of the defences in which 'more money was spent on the defences of Calais by land and sea than on any other military construction since the time of Edward I'. Finally, the rule of Edward IV and Henry VII saw a period of sound financial administration under the act of retainer during which time the fortifications were regularly repaired and updated.[50] This continued until the major programme of refortification embarked upon by Henry VIII.

Although the first period was characterised by wholesale corruption on the part of the treasurers which left the defences 'ful ruinous and ... in grete mischeff for default of reparacion',[51] the town did survive the Burgundian siege of 1436. Moreover, the siege showed the first signs of the defences of Calais being adapted to meet the threat posed by the 'artillery revolution' and Philip the Good's formidable artillery train. To meet the threat posed by the Burgundian guns earthen bulwarks, designed to accommodate the garrison's artillery, were built outside the town's gates. The slow adaptation of the town's defences to take account of the threat posed by modern siege guns continued after the Burgundians' defeat: in 1438–9, for instance, 'a great timber loop' was made in the east curtain wall for bombards to fire upon would-be attackers. Nevertheless, the siege, along with the occasion in 1439 when large portions of Calais castle appear to have fallen into the sea, convinced even Henry VI's hard-pressed government that something needed to be done to overhaul the Pale's built defences.

The period from 1441 until 1451 was characterised by extensive attempts to modify the medieval fortifications to meet the growing threat from effective gunpowder artillery. Between 1448 and 1450 the earthen bulwarks outside the gates of Calais were rebuilt in stone and mortar and another earthen bulwark was constructed outside the Postern Gate. They were then rebuilt in brick in 1453–4. As Colvin observes, these were the 'earliest examples of their kind known to have been constructed by English masons' and predated the first purpose-built artillery fortifications in England by some thirty years.[52] Many town fortifica-

---

50 Colvin, *The King's Works*, i. 431–2.
51 E101/193/5, the depositions taken in 1442 regarding Buckland and Whittingham's corruption. The state of the town's walls cannot have been helped by the fact that Whittingham dismissed the town's masons and carpenters, pocketing their wages.
52 Colvin, *The King's Works*, i. 449; J.A. Donnelly, 'A Study of the Coastal Forts built by Henry VIII', *Fort*, x (1982), 107.

tions and castles in England had, of course, already been adapted to house guns and offer a defence against gunpowder weapons by this date, but the Calais fortifications were the first to adopt the low, solid bulwarks that were a feature of the development of artillery fortifications in Italy.[53] Similarly, at Guînes, where the old medieval castle had been adapted to accommodate artillery in 1438–9, a new brick bulwark was built between 1445 and 1450. Moreover, the banks of the ditches which surrounded the town itself were raised in height at the same time. That the 1440s and 1450s were important for the fortification of Guînes is shown by the fact that the bulwarks there were known in Henry VIII's reign as 'Purton's' and 'Whetehill's' bulwarks after the castle's commanders in the mid-fifteenth century. When the earl of Warwick became captain in 1455 he took command of 'a fortress which was once more in a state to serve as an effective military base'.[54]

Given Edward IV's commitment to the modernisation of the Pale's gunpowder weaponry, it is no surprise that similar efforts were made to update and augment the built defences. He added 'false brayes' and 'murderers' to the defences of Calais, but once again the most intensive programme of new works was at Guînes. Here, between 1462 and 1474, 'a new bulwark of brick and hardstone with gunports all round' was built in the north-western corner of the castle. Moreover, 'three stone vaults called murderers situated in a certain earthen bank formerly made between the two ditches on the south-side of the castle for guns to shoot out of' were built. With its permanent, turfed banks and advanced parapets, the fortifications at Guînes resembled those that were developing in Italy and which proliferated there after the French invasion of 1494. Indeed, Guînes was not only 'one of the earliest fortresses under English control to be adapted for the needs of artillery warfare', but was one of the first such projects in north-western Europe.[55] Clearly the potential for modern fortifications was present in late fifteenth-century England but, as we shall see, on the whole the political and military situation militated against it. The very strength of Calais in the late fifteenth century (not to mention the internal problems of the French crown) made the prospect of a French assault a distant one and during the reign of Henry VII there is no evidence of any attempts at refortification of the existing defences. Annual expenditure on the fortifications fell from an average of £1,700 under Edward IV to less than £400 in the last decade of Henry VII's reign. This was not primarily due 'to the parsimony of the king',[56] but merely to the lack of a military imperative to do otherwise.

That was to change, however, in the reign of Henry VIII as Calais again became the focus of English military ambitions in France. Later, as the dangers of attack from the hostile Catholic powers of Europe increased, there was a

---

[53] For the contemporary development of gunpowder fortifications in English Gascony, which did not yet include 'permanent stone defences' see Malcolm Vale, *War and Chivalry: Warfare and Aristocratic Culture in England, France and Burgundy at the End of the Middle Ages* (1981), 132–3.

[54] Colvin, *The King's Works*, i. 448.

[55] Colvin, *The King's Works*, i. 452–3.

[56] G.A.C. Sandeman, *Calais under English Rule* (Oxford, 1908), 37.

renewed imperative to reform the built defences of Calais. Thus, from 1511, and especially from the mid-1530s, a concerted attempt was made to adapt and modernise the Pale's fortifications. There were two main periods of rebuilding, 1511–15 and 1538–44; both coincided with increased government interest in Calais as a base for the king's French expeditions. Between 1511 and 1515 the western end of the town was further strengthened by bulwarks designed for artillery to supplement the existing towers.[57] However, as the government's energies were directed, first, into the search for a lasting European peace and the maintenance of Tournai and, secondly, into obtaining the king's divorce, the defences were neglected. In 1518 the lord privy seal, Bishop Fox, then in Calais on diplomatic business, complained to Wolsey of the 'ruynes and deceyes' of the fortifications. The only significant works during the 1520s were on the new fortress at Newembridge. Newembridge was strategically vital to the defence of the Pale: the sluices it controlled could be opened to inundate the Low Country. In the fifteenth century the bridge itself had a fortified gate house, where tolls for entry to Calais were collected, and in Henry VII's reign a bulwark for artillery appears to have been built there. Beginning in 1521 more extensive works were put in train: a new tower, earthen bulwarks, a gate and 'gallery', a 'great mount' for artillery and accommodation for a garrison had been installed there by 1526.[58] On the whole the defences of Calais suffered during the long period of peace after 1523. On his visit to the Pale in 1527 Wolsey himself found them to be 'in noo litell disordre, and, for lak of reparations, in marvelous decaye, clerely unfurnished of tymbre, ston, borde, and of every other thing requisite for the same'. This was despite over £10,700 having been spent on the king's works between 1515 and 1525, albeit a large proportion of that sum was used to stop the encroachments of the sea.[59]

When Henry visited Calais in 1532 the reformation and modernisation of the town's medieval fortifications were subjects that attracted personal royal attention.[60] The remaining tall, thin, stone towers were to be replaced with smaller, compact bulwarks designed to accommodate artillery. However, as Colvin points out, there is little evidence of any serious work being carried out before 1538. As in the reform of military service in the Pale and other aspects of the defence of Calais, it is clear that the late 1530s mark an important juncture in the government's attitude. A renewed commitment was apparent in the conduct of the king's works. Under the supervision of the surveyor, Sir Richard Lee, 'the acknowledged English expert on military engineering',[61] attempts to modernise the defences were carried out at Calais, Guînes, Rysbank, Newembridge and Hammes. In Calais the old Beauchamp and Dublin Towers were replaced with

57 Colvin, *The King's Works*, iii. 341–3.

58 Colvin, *The King's Works*, iii. 362–3.

59 Colvin, *The King's Works*, iii. 343–4, 361; *LP*, iv. (2) 3254. The neglect of Calais should be contrasted with the ultimately futile efforts expended on the defence of Tournai in the same period: C.G. Cruickshank, *The English Occupation of Tournai 1513–1519* (Oxford, 1971), 104–28.

60 The king's own scheme for the fortifications is printed in full in *Chronicle of Calais*, 125–9.

61 Colvin, *The King's Works*, iii. 356.

more modern bulwarks. At Guînes spending on the works ran at £1,500 a month in 1539–41. The fortress at Newembridge was also completely overhauled. In 1536 only one piece of artillery was recorded there and in 1539 Robert Seymour, the lieutenant, reported to Cromwell that he considered the fortress untenable.[62] However, by 1547 there were fifty pieces of artillery listed along with sufficient ammunition and 'necessaries' to equip the regular garrison, as well as a squadron of cavalry and a hundred extra infantry housed in a modernised fortification.[63] At both Calais and Guînes Lee designed and built trefoil-shaped bulwarks, clearly showing some awareness of the principles of the new artillery fortifications. The importance the government attributed to the defence of Calais in the last decade of Henry VIII's reign, and the strenuous efforts made to ensure its effectiveness, are evident from a surviving contemporary estimate of the cost involved. Between September 1538 and January 1547 the government spent £120,675 on building materials in Calais, as well as a similar amount on the wages of men employed in those works.[64]

The Treaty of Camp in June 1546 brought an end to open hostilities between England and France and the concentration on war with Scotland ensured that work on the defences during Edward VI's reign consisted of little more than a continuation of the projects embarked upon under Henry VIII and the constant battle against the elements. New works were begun at Newembridge and Guînes only in 1550 when the surrender of Boulogne again meant a renewed military necessity to look at the Pale's defences. At Newembridge work included 'a square tower of sixty foot platform' (presumably as important as a watch-tower as it was a defence against artillery) and a strengthening of the walls. At Guînes the trefoil bulwark had apparently sunk into the moat: its remains were to be demolished and the stone used to raise the height of the old keep. In 1552 a new plan of fortification for Guînes was put into action and by 6 July the following year £6,627 had been spent. The nature of the works, however, is obscure.[65] In 1556 the privy council appointed John Rogers, probably the leading exponent of artillery fortifications in England, as surveyor of the works at Calais and the following year he embarked upon a major series of refortification at both Guînes and Calais.[66] This work, however, was probably never begun as in January 1558 the Pale fell to the French army of the Duc de Guise.

---

[62] SP1/106, f. 210v (*LP*, xi. 488); *LP*, xiv. (1) 428.

[63] *Inventory of King Henry VIII*, 122–3; Colvin, *The King's Works*, iii. 363.

[64] SP10/15/11 (*Calendar of State Papers, Domestic, Edward VI 1547–1553*, ed. C.S. Knighton (revised edn, 1992), 721). In all between 30 September 1538 and 31 July 1552 the government spent £371,428 18s. 9d. on maintaining the defences of Calais: £151,412 12s. on fortifications and £220,016 6s. 9d. on wages and diets. See below, p. 156.

[65] Colvin, *The King's Works*, iii. 352–3, 363.

[66] For Rogers see L.R. Shelby, *John Rogers, Tudor Military Engineer* (1967). For the constrasting social status of Rogers and the military engineers and architects in contemporary Italy, see Simon Pepper, 'Artisans, Architects and Aristocrats: Professionalism and Renaissance Military Engineering', in *The Chivalric Ethos and the Development of Military Professionalism*, ed. D.J.B. Trim (Leiden, 2003), 136–8. His colleague at Calais, Sir Richard Lee, was, however, of equal standing to continental engineers ('an international soldier, courtier and fortification expert': ibid., 137).

Calais and the 'military revolution'

The 'military revolution' debate is now almost half a century old. Since Michael Roberts's seminal article, first published in 1956, where he identified the military innovations of Maurice of Nassau during the 1590s and Gustavus Adolphus during the Thirty Years War as introducing a new period when changes in tactics and army composition heralded an age of centralisation and state formation driven by the demands of war, the chronology of the military revolution, and even whether it took place at all, have been hotly debated.[67] Nevertheless, few historians have attempted to look at the English evidence in the context of the military revolution. David Eltis's important work has more to say on the theory than the practice of war in sixteenth-century England, while recent studies by Tom Cogswell and Michael Braddick have examined the 'military–fiscal' revolution of the early seventeenth century and its effects on the development of political and administrative institutions.[68] What work has attempted to address the question of England's role in the 'military revolution' has concluded that during the fifteenth and sixteenth centuries the English became increasingly marginalised from mainstream European developments in weaponry, tactics and fortifications.[69]

In an important article on military change during the Hundred Years War, Clifford J. Rogers has posited a new conceptual framework within which to analyse changes in war and its wider impact. The concept of 'punctuated equilibrium evolution' allows there to have been more than one military revolution: several short periods of intensive change reacting to more of a gradual, incremental evolution of the art of war and military institutions.[70] Thus of the four periods of military revolution between the early fourteenth and the seventeenth centuries two – the artillery revolution of the early fifteenth century and the artillery fortifications revolution of the early sixteenth century – are directly covered by this study of the Calais garrison. Examined in this context, it becomes clear that the Calais garrison was by no means isolated from European

---

[67] Michael Roberts, 'The Military Revolution, 1560–1660', in *Essays in Swedish History*, ed. Michael Roberts (Minneapolis, 1967), 195–225; Geoffrey Parker, 'The Military Revolution, 1560–1660 – a Myth', *Journal of Modern History*, xlviii (1986), 241–78 (both are reprinted in *The Military Revolution Debate*, ed. Clifford J. Rogers (Boulder, CO, 1995)); Parker, *The Military Revolution: Military Innovation and the Rise of the West, 1500–1800* (Cambridge, 1988).

[68] David Eltis, *The Military Revolution in Sixteenth-Century Europe* (1998); Michael J. Braddick, *The Nerves of State: Taxation and the Financing of the English State, 1558–1714* (Manchester, 1996); Tom Cogswell, *Home Divisions* (Manchester, 1998).

[69] Gilbert John Millar, *Tudor Mercenaries and Auxiliaries, 1845–1547* (Charlottesville, VA, 1980); Parker, *Military Revolution*, 26–7; Kelly de Vries, 'Gunpowder Weaponry and the Rise of the Early Modern State', *War in History*, v (1998), 127–45. Recent writing, however, has began to question this view: see Phillips, *Anglo-Scots Wars*, 42–103 and Luke MacMahon, 'Chivalry, Professionalism and the Early Tudor Army in Renaissance Europe: A Reassement', in *The Chivalric Ethos and the Development of Military Professionalism*, ed. D.J.B. Trim (Leiden, 2003), 184–210.

[70] Rogers, 'Military Revolutions', 76–7.

developments and, moreover, that these changes were not restricted to the unique circumstances of the Pale but were adopted widely throughout English armies.

The artillery revolution

Guns, as Clifford Rogers observes, had been a feature of English and European armies for almost a hundred years before they revolutionised the practice of war in the years between 1420 and 1450.[71] Edward III had employed at least ten cannon at the siege of Calais in 1347, of which two were said to be 'large', alongside other 'great engines', probably older-style siege weapons such as the trebuchet.[72] Fourteenth-century cannon, however, were simply not large enough to dominate the battlefield, and more importantly, siege warfare as they were to do by the mid-1400s. It was not until the 1420s that three related developments allowed gunpowder weaponry to revolutionise warfare. First, longer barrel lengths increased the destructive power of guns; second, new manufacturing techniques were developed, enabling guns to be made by binding long staves of iron together to form the barrel; and third, limestone added during the refining of iron ore made available large amounts of cheaper, stronger iron.[73] Coupled with these developments of the guns themselves was a change in the process of making and storing gunpowder. Rather than the three ingredients of gunpowder – charcoal, saltpetre and sulphur – being mixed together when dry, they were wetted and combined. This 'corned' powder retained its explosive qualities longer (its constituents did not separate out during storage) and allowed the production of powder with as much as three times the explosive power of its sifted counterpart. Together these factors transformed the power of gunpowder weaponry in warfare. The gun reversed the superiority of the defender in sieges during the period from 1400 to 1430 and, by the middle of the fifteenth century, corned powder had allowed the development of effective hand-held guns. By the end of the fifteenth century improvements in casting techniques, particularly with regard to bronze, were beginning to make the gun the infantry weapon *par excellence*.[74]

In many accounts it is with the artillery revolution that the English army and English way of waging war begin to appear backward and old-fashioned when compared with continental Europe. In the fourteenth century the quality and quantity of English gunpowder weaponry was equal to or better than its main continental rivals, Burgundy and France. But by the mid-fifteenth century the artillery train of the duke of Burgundy and the reforms of Jean and Gaspard Bureau, respectively treasurer and master of artillery in France from about 1440, had, it is argued, relegated England to the second division in terms of military technology. Some historians have gone even further, arguing that firearms were of paramount importance in allowing the states of continental Europe to expand

---

[71] Ibid., 64.
[72] T.F. Tout, 'Firearms in England in the Fourteenth Century', *EHR*, xxvi (1911), 673.
[73] Rogers, 'Military Revolutions', 68–72.
[74] Hall, *Weapons and Warfare*, 67–100.

politically and geographically and to allow princes, such as the kings of France and Ferdinand and Isabella of Spain, to assert their authority effectively both within and beyond their realms.[75] Indeed, it is asserted that in England exactly the opposite to the European model of increasing state control over firearms and the resulting increase in central authority occurred: 'after nearly a century and a half of strong royal control over gunpowder weaponry in England, such weaponry had almost disappeared by the middle of the fifteenth century and would not reappear until the middle of the sixteenth century'.[76]

It is clear from the Calais evidence, however, that this was not the case. Guns were a constant feature in the defence of Calais throughout the fifteenth century and from the 1460s the crown made systematic attempts to augment and modernise its holdings of such weapons. Moreover, under the first two Tudors the crown increasingly asserted its monopoly over the manufacture and ownership of the larger pieces of ordnance. The artillery maintained at Calais played an important role in this royal monopoly: in 1491, for instance, the chamberlain of Rye paid 4s. 10d. for a set of wheels for the 'great gun' that was had from Calais.[77] Since there is no record of the purchase of this gun in the town accounts and there is other evidence of Calais's artillery being moved around the kingdom, it is reasonable to assume that the crown was deliberately augmenting the weaponry available for this strategically important Sussex port. For the 1497 Scottish campaign 237 guns were sent north, mainly from the Tower. Some of these guns may have been moved from Calais: a brass 'curtowe' called *Cales* and two brass 'demi-curtowes', *Ruysbanke* and *Guysnes*, were shipped north.[78] Similarly, Henry VIII took steps to ensure that the quality of English ordnance remained comparable to that of his European counterparts, especially that of the emperors Maximilian and Charles V, by importing foreign gunmakers to work at his foundries. This patronage of foreign gun-founders has been cited as evidence that England 'adopted new ideas and new weapons more slowly than the rest of Europe'.[79] However, that is to misunderstand the nature of technological change in early modern Europe. English gunmakers were well established in England by 1509 and in 1513, as the Venetian ambassador observed, they were employed 'by day and night and on all festivals' to make cannon.[80] The employment of foreign craftsmen was evidence of Henry VIII's willingness to adopt new, European ideas about gun-founding, particularly brass founding, and use them to improve and modernise existing English technology. In early modern Europe

---

[75] Parker, *Military Revolution*, 8.

[76] De Vries, 'Gunpowder Weaponry', 142–4.

[77] East Sussex Record Office, Rye 60/3, f. 90.

[78] Grummitt, 'Defence of Calais', 269. The 'curtow' and 'demi curtows' probably came from Calais in preparation for the invasion of France in 1492. Eight 'demy-curtows' and a 'curtow' were shipped from Calais to Sandwich by Sir Sampson Norton. At the conclusion of the campaign only seven of the 'demi-curtows' returned to Calais, the remainder were transferred to the Tower: E36/15, ff. 4v, 33v.

[79] C.G. Cruickshank, *Henry VIII and the Invasion of France* (Stroud, 1990), 64.

[80] *Calendar of State Papers, Venetian*, ed. R. Brown, C. Bentinck and H. Brown (9 vols, 1864–98), ii. 219.

ideas and technical expertise were not nationalised and 'owned' by the state and the free exchange of military knowledge characterised the relations between England and the territories of the Empire as they had done England and Burgundy in the fifteenth century. Although England's development of its larger gunpowder weaponry in the sixteenth century may have been largely reactive, it does not follow that its quality or usage differed from those of its continental counterparts.

It is in relation to handheld guns, however, that the Calais evidence suggests a re-evaluation of English military technology in the late fifteenth and early sixteenth centuries. England has long been assumed to have been slow in adopting handheld firearms. Thus, it is argued, during the Wars of the Roses their use was restricted to foreign mercenaries, as with the earl of Warwick's employment of Flemish handgunners at the second battle of St Albans in 1460.[81] In the sixteenth century the traditional English attachment to the longbow meant that Henry VIII was forced to recruit foreign mercenaries in order to make good the lack of handguns in his armies. According to Millar, in 1544, 'those soldiers equipped with firearms were invariably Italians or Spaniards'.[82] Again, the Calais evidence shows this to be an erroneous opinion. The Calais garrison used handheld firearms from the first half of the fifteenth century and by the late 1460s they had stocks of the newer, matchlock arquebuses. This development, then, was contemporaneous with the adoption of these weapons in the armies of the Valois dukes of Burgundy and kings of France. However, these weapons remained a relative rarity in English armies as they did in those of the French king. It was not until the success of the Spanish handgunners in northern Italy that the arquebus became the principal missile weapon of northern European infantry: not until after the battle of Pavia in 1525 did the French, for example, begin to adopt the arquebus in great numbers.[83] Nor should the English use of mercenaries be considered as a necessary measure to compensate for the lack of specific military skills. The use of mercenaries was universal in European armies, indeed those of Charles V consisted almost entirely of them, and in employing mercenaries Henry VIII was merely following a general European trend.[84]

The use of arquebuses by Englishmen was widespread from at least the early 1540s. As early as 1476 the victualler had paid for two 'butts' or firing ranges to be constructed in Calais for practising with 'hakeguns' and for determining

---

[81] *The Historical Collections of a Citizen of London in the Fifteenth Century*, ed. J. Gairdner (CS, new series, xvii, 1876), 213. For an extreme (and mistaken) view that the loss of royal control over gunpowder weaponry was a factor in the domestic turmoil of the mid-fifteenth century see Kelly de Vries, 'The Use of Gunpowder Weaponry in the Wars of the Roses', in *Traditions and Transformations in Late Medieval England*, ed. Douglas Biggs, Sharon D. Michalove and Albert Compton Reeves (Leiden, 2002), 21–38.

[82] Millar, *Tudor Mercenaries*, 22, 44, 90.

[83] Oman, *Art of War*, 223; *Histoire militaire de France*, ed. Philippe Contamine, i. *Des origines à 1715* (Paris, 1992), 217–18, 245.

[84] David Potter, 'The International Mercenary Market in the Sixteenth Century: Anglo-French Competition in Germany, 1543–50', *EHR*, cxi (1996), 24–58.

which of the archers was to be promoted to a gunner with an extra 2*d*. per day.[85]
From 1544 large numbers of the Englishmen stationed in the Pale and at
Boulogne were armed with handguns of one sort or another. Among the garrison
at Boulgone, for instance, Sir John Bridges, lieutenant of the castle, had thirteen
English 'hacbuters', twenty were under the command of the master of the
ordnance, John ap Richard commanded two hundred, Henry Dudley and
Thomas Inguter a hundred each and John Store ninety-seven. In the adjoining
bulwark, the Base Boulogne, Sir Thomas Poynings had a hundred, Henry Wyatt
forty, Thomas Dierer ninety-three and Edmund Bowes forty. Indeed, of the total
of 1,353 'hacbutteres', 945 were Englishmen.[86] The use of arquebuses within
English armies was notable enough to attract the attention of an Italian mercenary who described how the English arquebusiers stood behind the pikemen,
firing over their heads. When drawn up for battle the arquebusiers joined with
their archers to flank blocks of pikemen in a adaptation of the English tactic that
had prevailed during the Hundred Years War. Moreover, they may have used
their arquebuses at similar ranges to the longbow, much shorter than the French
were accustomed to.[87] As Gervase Phillips has recently pointed out 'the English
had been using bows in this fashion for centuries, so gunpowder weapons
offered little that was tactically innovative'; the transition from bow to arquebus
was therefore a relatively painless experience for soldiers in the field, achieved
over more than fifty years of gradual adoption of the gun. Indeed, arquebuses
and bows continued to deployed side-by-side in English armies throughout the
period.[88] Nor was this adoption of the arquebus and handgun limited to the
Calais Pale with its constant exposure to continental ideas and those armies that
fought on the continent. A contemporary picture of the English victory over the
Scots at Pinkie shows English handgunners skirmishing in front of the Scottish
pike blocks.[89] In 1549 the privy council requested unmarried men from York to
learn shooting of the arquebus, while the spread of new weaponry is evident
from the muster certificate of Exeter twenty years later: the commissioners
returned the names of 447 able men, 111 archers, 112 pikemen, 106 billmen
and, significantly, 118 men armed with arquebuses.[90]

---

[85] This may explain the seven-fold increase in powder consumption in the last half of the fifteenth century: Rainey, 'Defence of Calais', 207, 214.

[86] SP1/196, ff. 43–6. Of the foreign handgunners, eighty-eight were Italian and 398 Spanish.
The total size of the garrison at this time was some 5,500: see above, pp. 54–5.

[87] J.R. Hale, *Renaissance War Studies* (1983), 267; Paul E.J. Hammer, *Elizabeth's Wars*
(Basingstoke, 2003), 29–30.

[88] Gervase Phillips, *Anglo-Scots Wars*, 70–2; Phillips, 'Longbow and Hackbutt: Weapons
Technology and Technology Transfer in Early Modern England', *Technology and Culture*, xl
(1999), 576–93. While the transition was not painful for ordinary soldiers, it clearly alarmed
traditionalists who saw in the decline of the bow evidence of the decline of English military
strength: Jeremy Goring, 'Social Change and Military Decline in Mid-Tudor England',
History, lx (1975), 185–97.

[89] Reproduced in Oman, *Art of War*, 284.

[90] *York Civic Records*, vol. iv, ed. Angelo Raine (Yorkshire Archaeological Society Record
Series, cviii, 1943), 181–2; *The Devon Muster Roll for 1569*, ed. A.J. Howard and T.L. Stoate
(Bristol, 1977), 246–9.

The artillery fortress revolution

The development of effective gunpowder weaponry in the first half of the fifteenth century spelt the end for the quintessential medieval fortress with its high, thin curtain walls. In the 1440s, although his work remained unpublished until 1485, the Italian humanist, Leon Battista Alberti, argued that fortifications needed to be 'built in uneven lines, like the teeth of a star' if they were to withstand gunpowder artillery.[91] It was the French invasion of Italy in 1494, when Charles VIII fielded what appeared to contemporaries as the largest and most modern artillery train then seen, that proved the catalyst for the development of fortifications on a massive scale that were designed to withstand bombardment. By the early sixteenth century low angled bastions combined with wet or dry ditches were appearing in northern Italy. This system of fortifications, reliant on overlapping fields of fire and low, solid artillery platforms, was known as the *trace-italienne* and by the middle of the sixteenth century had spread to north-western Europe. By 1559 twelve towns in the Low Countries possessed a completely new circuit of fortifications based on the principles of the *trace-italienne*, while eighteen more were partially fortified.[92] By mid-century, then, the balance in siege warfare had once again been tipped in favour of the defenders. The *trace-italienne* resulted in escalating costs, both for the defender in terms of building and maintaining the new fortifications, and for the attacker, in terms of the expense of investing fortresses and maintaining large armies to continue lengthy sieges. Sieges became the dominant feature of early modern European warfare until the end of the eighteenth century; indeed, Parker argues that 'battles [were] more or less irrelevant in all the areas where the new fortifications were built'.[93] The artillery fortress revolution, it is argued, more or less passed England by. It was not until 1545, in reaction to the French attack in the Solent, that Henry VIII began to use the new technology in England.[94] Before this time what few English fortifications existed were old-fashioned and, if tested, would have proved inadequate to the rigours of modern warfare. Indeed, *trace-italienne* fortifications played little or no part in the British Civil Wars of the seventeenth century and it was only from the 1670s that any attempt was made to develop modern fortifications and then only in the peripheries of the realm, such as Fort Kinsale in Ireland. Even these failed to meet European standards and 'the full *trace-italienne* only came to Ireland – and to Scotland – in the eighteenth century'.[95]

Historians, led by Geoffrey Parker, have, however, been unnecessarily gloomy in their assessment of the military fortress revolution in an English context. As we have seen, attempts were made in Calais to adopt new methods of fortification which addressed the problems caused by the increasing potency of gunpowder weaponry. Periodically from the 1440s the high curtain walls of

---

[91] Parker, *Military Revolution*, 8–9.
[92] Hale, *Renaissance War Studies*, 1–29; Parker, *Military Revolution*, 12.
[93] Parker, *Military Revolution*, 16.
[94] Donnelly, 'Coastal Forts', 105–26.
[95] Parker, *Military Revolution*, 27–32.

Calais were lowered and bulwarks built to create artillery platforms. These changes were again reactive: the works at Calais and Guînes between 1448 and 1454 were doubtless a response to the efficacy of French cannon demonstrated by the fall of English-held castles in Normandy and Gascony. This should not lessen, however, their importance with regard to Englishmen's knowledge and adoption of the principles of the artillery fortress revolution. The works in the Calais Pale during the mid-fifteenth century were contemporaneous with the beginnings of such works in Italy.[96] Similarly, it would be wrong to conclude, as Parker seems to, that the failure of Henry VIII's government to adopt fully *trace-italienne* style fortifications in Calais shows that such ideas were unused in English fortifications. The works at Guînes and Calais from the late 1530s demonstrate that the English crown could and did commission the construction of bastions with overlapping fields of fire. Moreover, contemporary criticisms of the Henrician fortifications in the Pale have been quoted out of context. Parker uses a Portuguese engineer's criticism of the works at Guînes to dismiss Henry VIII's coastal fortifications of the late 1530s and early 1540s as 'outdated even before they were completed' due to his reliance on native craftsmen.[97] Having inspected the works in the spring of 1541 the engineer reported that they were of little military value. Henry VIII's response, apparently, was to call the man an ass who did not know his business. But according to the account of the incident by the imperial ambassador, Chapuys, the problem was not the quality of the fortification but rather the natural situation of Guînes itself. The town could not be 'fortified efficiently owing to two hillocks commanding the avenues and streets' thus giving a huge advantage to the attacking force.[98]

These natural disadvantages reveal why the *trace-italienne* was never fully adopted in the Pale and throughout the English realm. Calais's principal defence had always been the sea. Throughout the period the maintenance of the water-ways of the Pale remained a high priority, witnessed by the frequent issuing of commissions of the sewers. Concerns were often raised about the drainage of the Low Country by farmers and the dangers posed by the draining of the marshes reached a crisis in 1534 with the decision to flood the Meane Broke. This large area of marshland had been granted to Sir Robert Wingfield, a former deputy of Calais, in 1529 and he had duly settled it with his tenants.[99] In the 1540s the importance of the water defences was underlined by the plan to build a great dyke called the 'New Ryver' which would run like a great moat from Gravelines to Guînes. Therefore, while the built defences of Calais were important, they were only one part of a system of defence which relied equally upon the

---

[96] For England see John R. Kenyon, 'Coastal Artillery Fortifications in England in the Late Fourteenth and Early Fifteenth Centuries', in *Arms, Armies and Fortifications in the Hundred Years War*, ed. Anne Curry and Michael Hughes (Woodbridge, 1994), 145–9. For Italy see Hale, *Renaissance War Studies*, 13–14.

[97] Parker, *Military Revolution*, 26–7.

[98] *LP*, xvi. 733, 762.

[99] The council of Calais informed Cromwell that the Pale was strengthened by the flooding of the marsh to the tune of ten thousand men: *LP*, vii. 1511. The dispute over 'Wingfield's marsh' is covered by *LP*, vii. 431, 1362, 1502, 1565.

elements and natural obstacles to an attacking force. The evidence of foreign observers is also a poor guide to the defensive capabilities of the Pale. While the Portuguese observer questioned the viability of Guînes's defences in 1541, forty years earlier the Venetian ambassador doubted if 'the castle of St Peter at Rhodes is more strictly defended against the Turks as Calais is against the French', and in 1554 and again in 1557 his successors reported on Calais's strength.[100] Moreover, the importance of *trace-italienne* fortifications in north-western Europe in the sixteenth century has been overstated. Although twelve towns in the Low Countries might have had full circuits by 1572 this meant, as David Eltis has observed, that some two hundred walled towns did not.[101] Calais, as we have seen, was well furnished with artillery and had adapted its fortifications to take account of gunpowder weaponry well before 1500 and, as one Spanish engineer observed, an advantage in artillery tended to make the defenders of besieged towns and fortresses invulnerable.[102] Moreover, as with weaponry, the English continued to adapt new technology and methods of fortification to meet their particular needs. The continued existence of high towers in both the Pale and the new series of coastal fortifications constructed in England during the late 1530s and 1540s was testimony to their importance as lookouts to give advance warning of enemy incursions, not of a general English reluctance to adopt the latest military technology.[103] Calais, as we shall see, did not fall in January 1558 due to the failure of the English to adapt to the demands of the 'artillery fortress revolution'.

* * *

As England's premier military establishment in the fifteenth and sixteenth centuries the Calais garrison provides a telling comment on the state of English military technology *vis-à-vis* the rest of western Europe. The Calais victuallers' accounts of the fifteenth century and the various sources relating to the sixteenth century show that the English in the Pale were willing to adopt new weaponry, technology and tactics to meet the changing demands of war. While there are few instances of real innovation in the garrison (although the artillery fortresses built in the first half of the fifteenth century were contemporaneous with the earliest examples elsewhere in Europe), it is clear that, where there was a military imperative, the English were not backward in accepting new ideas. The various changes which constituted a military revolution in western Europe in the hundred years after 1450, principally the adoption of firearms and the tactical changes they forced upon armies, were known and employed by the English in Calais. This is clear in the forces that defended the Pale from French attack during the mid-1540s: the increasing size of these forces, their weaponry, tactics and the fortifications they defended were all products of the European military

---

[100] *A Relation, or rather a True Account, of the Island of England*, ed. C. Sneyd (CS, old series, xxxvii, 1847), 45; *CSP, Venetian*, v. 584, vi. (2), 1050.

[101] Eltis, *Military Revolution*, 29.

[102] Hale, *Renaissance War Studies*, 16.

[103] Ibid., 77.

revolution. Rather than being isolated from the rest of Europe in terms of military change, England experienced the developments at a comparable rate to the rest of western Europe. The defence of the Calais Pale, England's bridgehead on the continent, was naturally the clearest manifestation of them.

7

Financing and Supplying the Garrison

Separated from the mainland by the English Channel and surrounded by poten-
tially hostile territory, the Calais Pale relied upon constant supplies of food,
clothing and building materials to maintain its viability as a military frontier.
Moreover, the garrison needed to be paid and the difficulties of providing the
necessary cash to meet the costs of the defence of Calais remained a constant
problem for English governments between 1436 and 1558. Their success in
tackling the related problems of finance and supply has been a recurrent theme
in discussions of Calais under English rule. Central to the problems of finance
was the relationship between the crown and the merchants of the staple, the
company of merchants granted a monopoly of English wool exports to the
markets of the Low Countries through Calais. The costs of the defence of Calais
were met by the profits of the English wool trade; indeed, the decision to move
the wool staple to Calais in Edward III's reign was governed by the need to pay
for the newly acquired Pale and was greeted by protests from the English
merchant community. As will become clear, the defence of Calais was, on the
whole, paid for by a successful partnership between the crown and the staplers;
only in periods of political crisis did this system come under strain. The decline
of the wool export trade in the early sixteenth century forced a reappraisal of the
way in which the crown met the costs of the defence of Calais. Similarly, the
supply of the food and other necessaries to the garrison was achieved by a partnership between the crown and private merchants. The way in which Calais was
financed and victualled in the fifteenth and sixteenth centuries was indicative of
the crown's more general ability to mobilise its subjects' resources to meet the
demands of military action. The crown's response to the escalating costs of the
Calais garrison during our period amidst a shift in the traditional commercial
patterns which had previously underpinned its finances therefore provides an
important comment on the way in which the English polity responded to war.

The crown and the merchants of the staple

In financial terms the defence of Calais was a mammoth undertaking. In
1371–2, for example, a year typical of the late fourteenth century, the treasurer
of Calais spent £20,264, the vast majority of that (£18,617) on the wages of the
garrison. This made Calais one of the largest items of crown expenditure in
Edward III's reign after 1347, second only to the royal household.[1] By the first

---

[1] Edouard Perroy, 'L'Administration de Calais en 1371–2', *Revue du Nord*, xxxiii (1951),

decade of the fifteenth century the annual wage bill was still around £16,000 per annum. At the same time the crown's net annual revenue, excluding lay and clerical subsidies, averaged only a little over £52,000.[2] In 1421 the defence of Calais was estimated to account for a third of the crown's regular annual income.[3] By the 1430s the cost of Calais had fallen as a proportion of national expenditure, as the spending on the king's household, Ireland and Gascony increased: in 1433 the treasurer of England, Ralph, Lord Cromwell, estimated the annual expenditure at Calais to be £11,931, about a sixth of the crown's annual income.[4] This cost remained fairly constant throughout the remainder of Henry VI's reign, but the financial chaos which characterised the 1440s and 1450s meant that the wages of the garrison were often in arrears, resulting in mutinies in 1442 and 1454.[5] By the mid-1460s the annual cost of the garrison had been reduced and standardised at £10,022 4*s.* 4*d.* per annum, about a seventh of total royal income.[6] This figure remained the nominal cost of the garrison until the 1530s. In reality, however, the garrison regularly survived on half this amount. By 1500 the crown's annual ordinary income (that is, excluding extraordinary taxation) was in excess of £100,000.[7] The defence of Calais, therefore, probably consumed less than a tenth of the crown's annual income at the beginning of the sixteenth century.

The proportion of total royal income consumed by the defence of Calais in peacetime continued to fall under Henry VIII. Any attempt to calculate the total income of Henry VIII is doomed to failure because of the proliferation of bodies which handled royal finance, and the gaps in the accounts. Although his revenue from lands, the customs and other traditional sources was probably little more than his father's, other sources, including the French Pension and, from the mid-1530s the fruits of his attack on the resources of the Church, meant that by the late 1530s Henry VIII's total revenue, excluding taxation, probably exceeded £250,000 per annum.[8] At the same time, the treasurer of Calais's expenses rarely exceeded £10,000 per annum. In war, however, the cost of defending Calais rose

---

218–27, esp. p. 224. In the period 1360–77 Edward III spent on average £32,000 per annum on his household: Chris Given-Wilson, *The Royal Household and the King's Affinity: Service, Politics and Finance in England 1360–1413* (New Haven, CT, 1986), 94.

2   David Grummitt, 'The Financial Administration of Calais during the Reign of Henry IV, 1399–1413', *EHR* cxiii (1998), 277–99; T.E.F. Wright, 'Royal Finance in the Latter Half of the Reign of Henry IV of England' (DPhil thesis, University of Oxford, 1984), 374, table 42a.

3   J.L. Kirby, 'The Financing of Calais under Henry V', *BIHR*, xxiii (1950), 165–77.

4   *PROME*, xi. 102–13; J.L. Kirby, 'The Issues of the Lancastrian Exchequer and Lord Cromwell's Estimates of 1433', *BIHR*, xxiv (1951), 121–51.

5   For the financial weakness of the Lancastrian regime see Griffiths, *The Reign of Henry VI* (2nd edn, Stroud, 1998), 376–94; G.L. Harriss, 'Marmaduke Lumley and the Exchequer Crisis of 1446–9', in *Aspects of Late Medieval Government and Society: Essays Presented to J.R. Lander*, ed. J.G. Rowe (Toronto, 1986), 143–78.

6   Charles Ross, *Edward IV* (2nd edn, New Haven, CT, 1997), 385.

7   B.P. Wolffe, *The Royal Demesne in English History: The Crown Estate in the Governance of the Realm from the Conquest to 1509* (1971), 216–17.

8   For the problems of estimating Henrician financial resources see Richard Hoyle, 'War and Public Finance', in *The Reign of Henry VIII*, ed. Diarmaid MacCulloch (Basingstoke, 1995), 75–84; Sybil Jack, 'Henry VIII's Attitude towards Royal Finance: Penny Wise and Pound

dramatically: more than a tenth of the £3,501,453 spent on war and defence between 1538 and 1552 was spent on the Calais Pale.[9] Nevertheless, it never consumed the proportions of total royal income that it had done during the fifteenth century. During Mary's reign the crown's ordinary annual income has been estimated to have been in the region of £130,000; taxation boosted this figure to over £200,000, but this is almost certainly an underestimate of the crown's financial resources.[10] At the same time the cost of defending the Pale was about £20,000 per annum.[11] This suggests that, at the time of the town's fall to the duke of Guise, the defence of Calais was well within the financial resources of the English crown.

The history of the financing of Calais throughout the period 1436 to 1558 is inextricably linked with the history of the merchants of the staple. The merchants of the staple were the English company to whom Edward III had granted a monopoly over the trade in English raw wool to the Low Countries, provided that all exports were carried to Calais before being sold in the marts of Flanders and Brabandt.[12] In the late fourteenth century the importance of Calais and its military establishment had been guarenteed by the confirmation of the town as the wool staple and, in 1363, a mint had been established to turn the profits of that trade into coin with which to pay the garrison. By the reign of Richard II reservations, determined in parliament, of a proportion of the wool customs for the defence of Calais ensured stability, but in the financial crisis of the first part of Henry IV's reign this was abandoned, leading to arrears in the wages of the garrison and resulting in mutiny in December 1406. This crisis was solved by large loans from the staplers and the system of reservations was quickly readopted.[13] Flexibility remained the key to the financing of the Calais garrison. J.L. Kirby has shown how, during the reign of Henry V, the treasurer of Calais, Roger Salvayn, was able to organise a system of credit that, despite the closure of the mint, allowed the merchants to pay their customs in Calais direct

---

Foolish?', in *François Ier. Deux princes de la renaissance (1515–1547)*, ed. Charles Giry-Deloison (Arras, 1997), 145–64.

9 SP10/15/11; *Calendar of State Papers, Domestic, Edward VI 1547–1553*, ed. C.S. Knighton (revised edn, 1992), 721. On average some £24,762 was spent per annum on the defence of Calais in these years. This did not include the whole cost of the garrison, much of which was still paid for by the wool merchants as explained below. The total cost, then, of the defence of Calais was probably more than £30,000 per annum in the 1540s.

10 David Loades, *The Reign of Mary Tudor: Politics, Government and Religion in England, 1553–1558* (Harlow, 1991), 239, 242–3.

11 E351/534–5.

12 There is no comprehensive history of the wool staple but for its establishment and early history see Eileen Power, *The Wool Trade in English Medieval History: Being the Ford Lectures* (Oxford, 1941) and T.H. Lloyd, *The English Wool Trade in the Middle Ages* (Cambridge, 1977).

13 Grummitt, 'Financial Administration', 278–92. Reservations entailed a specific part of the wool customs and subsidy being reserved for the wages of the Calais garrison. These agreements were usually made in parliament with the assent of the merchants. In effect, this meant that the staplers could pay a proportion of their customs directly in cash to the treasurer of Calais, providing paper obligations to the collectors of customs in the English outports with which the latter were able to gain their discharge at the exchequer.

to the captains of the various retinues. These were a continuation of the arrangements of the previous reign. The bonds by which the merchants agreed to pay their customs in Calais, instead of in the port from which the wool was exported, were arranged on pain of forfeiture of the merchants' wool stocks. This system was beneficial to both parties: the soldiers were paid promptly or, if not, they had the insurance of the wool stocks; the merchants, on the other hand, could avoid paying their customs until after the wool had been sold. This also cut out any delays in transporting money from the outports to the exchequer and on to Calais.[14] In effect it duplicated the system in operation when the Calais mint was working, allowing the transfer of cash directly between the merchants and the soldiers.

The financial pressures due to the costs of the campaign in Normandy in the last years of Henry V's reign and the weak government of Henry VI's minority brought new difficulties for the Pale. Fortunately, however, the period between 1421 and 1429 was a relatively quiet one for the Pale: warfare abated, trade prospered and the Calais mint served its purpose. On 20 July 1422 English coin once again began to flow from the mint in response to a petition from the staplers.[15] However, by the late 1420s diplomatic events and another shortage of bullion were placing an increasing burden on the administration of Calais. In 1429 the siege of Orléans brought a renewal of open warfare and an increase in the cost of maintenance of Calais's defence. In response parliament passed a ordinance known as the Calais staple Partition and Bullion Ordinance. Merchants were required to deliver bullion to the value of one third of the wool price to the Calais mint after each sale.[16] The crown's bullionist policy, manifested through its insistence that the staplers pay for the garrison by delivering bullion to the Calais mint, was thwarted by the century's second great bullion famine. Between 1440 and 1460 there was 'almost no gold or silver to be had' anywhere in Europe.[17] Thus the crown was forced to alter its relationship with the staplers. From the 1440s the government, as well as the commanders of the garrison in Calais themselves, were forced to resort to borrowing money directly from the merchants, repayable by shipping wool free of customs. This, in effect, was an anticipation of future customs yields.

The crisis in Calais's finances that this precipitated arose not from structural problems inherent in the system of paying for the defence of Calais, but rather from the combination of European economic problems and the weak royal leadership provided by Henry VI. During the 1430s, as Ralph Griffiths has argued, 'the gap between the crown's resources and its commitments … widened

---

[14] Kirby, 'The Financing of Calais under Henry V', 165–77.

[15] Stanley Walker, 'The Calais Mint 1347–1470', *British Numismatic Journal*, 2nd Series, vi (1922), 77–90; Peter Spufford and Peter Woodhead, 'Calais and its Mint', in *Coinage in the Low Countries*, ed. N.J. Mayhew (Oxford, 1979), 177.

[16] Munro, *Wool, Cloth and Gold*, 84–93.

[17] Spufford and Woodhead, 'Calais and its Mint', 178; H.L. Gray, 'English Foreign Trade from 1446–1482', in *Studies in English Trade in the Fifteenth Century*, ed. E.E. Power and M.M. Postan (1933), 20–38; P. Nightingale, 'England and the European Depression of the Mid-Fifteenth Century', *Journal of European Economic History*, xxvi (1997), 631–56.

alarmingly.'[18] By the mid-1430s the crown relied upon large loans, principally from Cardinal Henry Beaufort, the city of London and the group of individuals whom Henry V had enfeoffed with the duchy of Lancaster lands, to meet the everyday costs of government. Moreover, policy was frequently constrained by the need to meet the crown's outstanding debts – already £164,000 in 1433 – and the fact that the most reliable sources of income were often assigned to meet the demands of the crown's creditors. Beaufort alone lent £91,500 between 1432 and 1442 and at times secured repayment from the customs, a source of revenue which should have been available to meet the costs of Calais.[19] Although some individuals tried manfully to maintain effective government amidst this financial chaos, the failure of Henry VI to provide strong royal leadership ensured that the regime's financial priorities were not always effective administration and the defence of the realm. In fiscal affairs, as in other areas of government, the king failed to exercise the authority needed to prioritise the regime's commitments.[20] As far as Calais and the staple were concerned, the king exacerbated an already difficult situation by frequently granting licences to individuals to bypass the staple or ship wool free of customs. Even after the loss of Normandy in 1450, the duke of Somerset was able to exploit his influence over the king in order to ensure that priority was given to the payment of his debts by the exchequer, rather than the more pressing needs of defence and the repayment of loans by the staple company and others. In the early 1450s both Somerset and the duke of York obtained assignments on the wool customs for the payment of debts due to them.[21]

In the first half of the fifteenth century the crown's policy for the financing of Calais appears to have been determined by the king's council and, above all, in parliament. This demonstrated the wider fact that, during this period, the determination of fiscal policy was something that involved the whole political nation; the crown negotiated with its subjects the ways in which money was to be raised and spent. This was nowhere more apparent than in the funding of the Calais garrison. The crucial importance of the staplers to financing the defence of Calais was reflected in the frequent parliamentary petitions that were submitted on the company's behalf to maintain their trading privileges. In 1433, for example, a petition that staple goods shipped elsewhere than to Calais should be

---

[18] Griffiths, *Henry VI*, 121.

[19] Although most of Beaufort's loans were repaid from direct taxation, the customs in Southampton were often diverted to meet his claims. At times the wool customs in other ports were assigned to repay his debts: in 1438, for instance, two thousand marks from the customs in London were assigned for repayment of a loan of £7,333 6s. 8d. made that year: G.L. Harriss, *Cardinal Beaufort: A Study of Lancastrian Ascendancy and Decline* (Oxford, 1988), 401–6.

[20] John Watts, *Henry VI and the Politics of Kingship* (Cambridge, 1996), 195–9; Christine Carpenter, *The Wars of the Roses: Politics and the Constitution in England, c. 1437–1509* (Cambridge, 1997), 95–6.

[21] Bill Smith, 'The Financial Priorities of Lancastrian Government, 1450–55', in *Social Attitudes and Political Structures in the Fifteenth Century*, ed. Tim Thornton (Stroud, 2001), 168–83.

forfeited had met with only partial success; two years later, amidst growing fears of a Burgundian assault on the Pale, a petition for the maintenance of the bullion ordinances and the privileges of the staplers was successful. This was almost certainly connected to the staplers' underwriting the duke of Gloucester's captaincy which was confirmed in the same parliament.[22] In the following parliament, which assembled at Westminster in January 1437, the settlement of the wages due to Gloucester was an important matter of business. It was agreed that the feoffees appointed by Henry V to administer part of the duchy of Lancaster should lend two thousand marks. Gloucester probably felt that this was insufficient and petitioned parliament for further remedy. In March the commons agreed that 20s. of wool subsidy on every sack of wool paid by native merchants should be diverted to the garrison for the next three years, prompting a second successful petition by Gloucester that, because a downturn in trade could lead to a shortfall in the customs, the treasurer of England might be allowed to make payments from other funds. As in previous years, the king also agreed parliamentary petitions in favour of the staplers and their privileges.[23] Similarly, in the parliament of February 1449, petitions in favour of the staplers coincided with deliberations over the financing of the garrison. In parliament's third session it was again agreed that 20s. of the wool subsidy payable on each sack should be reserved for the garrison.[24]

The discussion and settlement of Calais affairs in parliament was partly facilitated by the presence, as MPs and lords, of many of those with a vested interest in the Pale. Noble captains, like Gloucester, would, of course, have attended and presented their views, and have represented those of the soldiers, to the lords and commons. More important, perhaps, was the presence of many office-holders and staplers as members of the commons. Since the late fourteenth century individual staplers, elected to represent various shire and borough constituencies, had formed an influential and cohesive lobby group in the commons.[25] During parliaments in which Calais business loomed large, the staplers would doubtless have participated in the deliberations with the crown. In 1435, for example, the stapler interest was represented by three of the company's leading members, Robert Large, representing London, Robert White, sitting for Sandwich, and Hamon Sutton, elected to represent Lincoln. Other staplers, like William Cantelowe, victualler of Calais from 1436 until the late 1440s, who was one of the London MPs in the parliaments of 1453 and 1455, would have been an important source of experience during Calais debates. On at least one occasion a parliamentary election was manipulated to ensure the return of a MP with a Calais agenda. In 1455 the sheriff of Kent and victualler of Calais, Sir John Cheyne, altered his return to ensure that his friend and the treasurer of Calais,

---

22 *PROME*, xi. 146, 168–70, 182–3; Griffiths, *Henry VI*, 201.

23 *PROME*, xi. 204, 209–10, 217–19, 228–9; E28/58/46.

24 *PROME*, xii. 51–2, 57–8; *CPR, 1446–52*, 219.

25 Gwilym Dodd, 'The Calais Staple and the Parliament of May 1382', *EHR*, cxvii (2002), 94–103; J.S. Roskell, L. Clark and C. Rawcliffe (eds), *The House of Commons, 1386–1421* (4 vols, Stroud, 1993), iii. 49.

Sir Gervase Clifton, was named as one of the knights of the shire. As well as securing guarantees of his own and Cheyne's position in relation to fines levied on them for failure to render account, Clifton sat on the committee of lords which discussed the settlement of the garrison's wages and probably also ensured Cheyne's involvement in their deliberations.[26]

Nevertheless, the increasing inability of the crown to meet its financial obligations to the merchants of the staple eventually forced them to assume direct responsibility for the financing of the Calais garrison. As we have seen, from 1437, following earlier practice, 20*s.* of customs on every sack of wool exported to Calais had been regularly reserved for the garrison.[27] Nevertheless, this had little effect on improving Calais's finances. In August 1442 the king's council had written to the staplers asking them to lend £500 to Sir William Pirton, captain of Guînes, and to Pirton and his retinue asking for their forbearance. At the same time the garrison in Calais resorted to mutiny, seizing the merchants' wool and selling it at a reduced price to realise their arrears, prompting an appeal by the captain of Calais, the duke of Buckingham, to be allowed to go to the Pale to restore order.[28] During the 1440s successive treasurers of Calais left a total debt of over £30,000 outstanding on their accounts in the form of bills promising payment to captains and individual soldiers. By 1449 the situation was again critical. Throughout the decade the staplers had been regular creditors of the crown, but in 1449 they demanded action to stem the chaos reigning in Calais. A petition presented to parliament that year complained of the widespread practice of granting licences to bypass the Calais staple and of the corruption of customs officials. These problems, they explained, had reduced the yield from the wool customs from as much as £68,000 per annum in Edward III's reign to only £12,000. As a result their fellowship was diminished, the soldiers were unpaid and the defences of Calais 'like to be uttirly destroied'.[29]

Although the king assented to their petition and the staple's privileges were renewed, there was little immediate improvement in Calais's finances. Exemptions granted to the duke of Suffolk and Queen Margaret lessened the concession's force, and the crisis in Normandy and Gascony between 1450 and 1453 placed further pressure upon the crown's fiscal resources. During the 1450s the staplers gradually assumed greater responsibility for the financing of Calais by contributing large loans repayable from the wool customs. Nevertheless, this was not the system of reservations that had operated earlier and other creditors also had claims on the wool customs, delaying repayment of the staplers' loans. In 1454 the duke of York, protector of the realm during Henry VI's first bout of madness, was forced to relax further the bullion laws in return for a loan from the staplers of over £17,000. This was in response to another mutiny by the

---

[26] *POPC*, vi. 247–9; *Six Town Chronicles of England*, ed. R. Flenley (Oxford, 1911), 142.

[27] *PROME*, xii. 57–8; A. Haward, 'The Relations between the Merchants of the Staple and the Lancastrian Government from 1449 to 1461', in *Studies in English Trade in the Fifteenth Century*, ed. E.E. Power and M.M. Postan (1933), 301–2.

[28] *POPC*, v. 200–1, 203–4.

[29] *PROME*, xii. 57–8; Haward, 'Relations', 293–301.

garrison between May and July that year. By February 1456 further loans meant the crown was indebted to the merchants of the staple to the tune of some £39,000, roughly equal to four years' cost of defending the Pale. The settlement negotiated between the crown, the merchants and the soldiers in that year appears to have eased the problems: up to March 1456 the staplers advanced a further £40,000 to the treasurer of Calais to discharge the garrison's arrears.[30] Although, as A. Haward points out, the lack of treasurer's accounts after 1456 makes it impossible to ascertain how the garrison was financed in the last years of Henry VI's reign, problems clearly remained. In December 1458 the king again agreed to refrain from selling licences for four years giving exemption from the staple in return for further loans.[31]

As the struggle for control of Calais emerged as one of the key areas for the battle between York and Lancaster, the staplers found themselves elevated to a new position of political importance. The staplers' decision, in early 1456, to finance the earl of Warwick's takeover of Calais immediately identified them with the Yorkist lords.[32] Historians agree that it was not due to partisan support for the rebel lords' policies that the staplers agreed to bank-roll Warwick; rather they had decided that it was the prospect of a Yorkist victory that offered the best opportunities for the repayment of previous loans and favourable terms for the provision of future ones. A sound relationship with the government would ensure the security of Calais and thus the merchants' trade. Indeed, after 1461 the relationship between the Yorkist government and the staplers quickly evolved to the point where they took on responsibility for the entire financial administration of Calais, thus solving the problems caused by the failures of Henry VI's administration.

Between August 1461 and March 1465 the merchants of the staple lent Edward IV almost £55,000, redeemable from the revenues of the customs and subsidies on wool.[33] Moreover, ever mindful of the importance of stapler cash to his regime, Edward even agreed to repay Henry VI's debts to the company. Nevertheless, the treasurer of Calais still continued to plead for money to pay the garrison's wages. This was probably due to the fact that the staplers were acting as general crown creditors, delivering much of the cash not direct to Calais, but to the exchequer where it could easily be appropriated for some other purpose. In March 1465, for example, the company lent £11,728 19s. 2d., of which it delivered £3,756 11s. ½d. to the treasurer of Calais, and the remainder to Westminster. Various means were tried to solve this problem: in 1463 the treasurer of Calais had been given £20,000 with which to trade in wool and use the profits to discharge the garrison's arrears. The problems of Calais also affected royal policy more generally. The following year Edward IV failed to press home

30 Ibid., 304–7; G.L. Harriss, 'The Struggle for Calais: An Aspect of the Rivalry between Lancaster and York', *EHR*, lxxv (1960), 30–53.
31 P.A. Johnson, *Duke Richard of York 1411–1460* (Oxford, 1988), 138; *CPR, 1452–61*, 500–1; Haward, 'Relations', 306, 312–13.
32 Harriss, 'The Struggle for Calais', 44–8.
33 *CPR, 1461–7*, 54, 220, 222, 271, 378, 438.

his military advantage against the Scots, as most of that year's subsidy and a grant from convocation were directed to meeting the costs of the defence of Calais.[34] What was needed was an agreement by which the staplers would assume formal responsibility for what they had been doing in an ad hoc manner for the last century or so, paying the garrison from the profits of the English wool trade.

In 1466 the crown entered into the first act of retainer with the merchants of the staple. Significantly, and reinforcing the fact that this was a private agreement, the act was not made in parliament, but took the form of an indenture between the staplers and the king and was only later ratified by the lords and commons. By this agreement the merchants agreed to collect and retain the wool customs nationwide and the revenues of Calais and in return to pay £10,022 4s. 8d. annually for the wages of the garrison until the crown's debt to them of £32,861 was repaid. The mayor of the staple assumed the office and responsibilities of the treasurer and victualler of Calais and surveyor of the king's works. Because of Henry VI's brief Readeption in 1470–1, the act of retainer was not passed in its final form until 1473. This time the agreement was in the form of an act of parliament. It was presented to parliament because it also provided for the repayment of loans made to Edward in exile by a group of staplers. As well as the agreements made in 1466, the staplers additionally agreed to pay annually £100 for the wages of the customers of the port of London, and a thousand marks for the wages of the royal judges, and to provide enough money for the safe conduct of the wool-fleet between England and Calais. The 1473 act of retainer highlighted the special relationship between the staplers and the Yorkist regime. By this time the crown's debts to the staplers appear to have been settled. The act specified a period of time, sixteen years, during which both parties would act for the benefit of the other: the king 'retained' the services of the merchants as the financiers of his town and marches; in return the staplers received royal protection for their trade and, as far as possible, a foreign policy favourable to mercantile interests. The act of retainer demonstrated the ability of a regime supported by the mercantile classes to meet its financial and military commitments in the Pale.[35] It is clear that this arrangement transformed the management of the Pale's finances. From 1467 until 1483 the treasurer returned an average annual surplus of £705 to the exchequer. Moreover, in that period the exchequer did not issue any money for the ordinary costs of Calais. Even in times of crisis – 1468, 1470–1 and 1475 – the staplers continued to provide enough money to maintain the garrison. Far from being a burden, by the late fifteenth century Calais was actually returning a sizeable annual profit to the crown.

Under Henry VII, however, a different set of priorities, other than the effective financing of the defences of Calais, governed the relationship between the

---

[34] Ross, *Edward IV*, 55; J.R. Lander, 'Council, Administration and Councillors', *BIHR*, xxxii (1959), 139–42.

[35] *PROME*, xiv. 119–31; *CPR, 1467–77*, 270; Eileen Power, 'The Wool Trade in the Fifteenth Century', in *Studies in English Trade*, ed. Power and Postan, 74–5.

crown and the merchants of the staple.[36] For the first ten years or so of the reign the staplers continued to fulfil their obligations under the act of retainer. From about 1495, however, the crown shifted its priority to the prompt payment in coin of the merchants' surplus to the king once their account had been rendered. By the end of the century the arrears of their surplus had exceeded £13,000 and the merchants were forced to enter into bonds to ensure their payment to the king. This prioritisation of the payment of the surplus lessened the amount available to the pay the wages of the garrison. Between April 1505 and April 1509 the merchants paid, on average, only £5,784 of the £10,022 due under the terms of the act of retainer every year for wages. During the same period an average of £4,020 was paid annually to the king.[37] Between 1500 and 1509 almost £32,000 was paid to the king. In 1504 the act of retainer was renewed for a further sixteen years. The staplers, as before, were allowed to retain the wool customs and pay the garrison, returning any surplus to the king. The agreement was, for the first time, enshrined in statute.[38] Nevertheless, the crown's principal concern during the last five years of Henry's reign was that the staplers deliver cash to the king's chamber. Despite Henry VII's avarice the military effectiveness of the garrison does not seem to have suffered: the first decade of the sixteenth century was one of peace and it may be that the numbers of the garrison were reduced to save costs. Certainly the soldiers' credit among Calais's merchant community remained strong and the garrison's finances could even withstand peculation by the lieutenant, Giles, Lord Daubeney.[39]

Under Henry VIII the crown's exploitation of the merchants of the staple continued. However, as with the rest of his father's 'chamber system', it was put on a more secure legal footing. Both the Yorkist kings and Henry VII had used the informal machinery of the king's chamber as an important department of national financial administration. The informality of this system had led to accusations of corruption and extortion by the king's ministers, and Henry VIII's council and first parliament were anxious to restore confidence in the royal administration. The Court of General Surveyors, the conciliar body which had overseen the treasurer of Calais's and the staplers' dealings with the crown, was

---

[36] This paragraph is based mainly on Grummitt, ' "For the Surety of the Towne and Marches": Early Tudor Policy towards Calais 1485–1509', *Nottingham Medieval Studies*, xliv (2000), 193–6.

[37] My own figures derived from a summary of staple accounts in E101/201/28.

[38] 19 Hen VII, c. 27: *Statutes of the Realm*, ed. A. Luders et al. (11 vols, 1810–28), ii. 667–9. The 1473 agreement had been presented in parliament and enrolled on the Parliament Roll but had not become a statute. Why the 1504 agreement became a statute is unclear but the act was accompanied by a proviso restricting which merchants could have a voice in the staple court. This may have been prompted by an attack on the company's liberties by the merchant adventurers, resulting in an appearance before the king's council later that year: *Select Cases in the Council of Henry VII*, ed. C.G. Bayne and William Huse Dunham (Seldon Society lxxv, 1956), 149–51. The renewal of the act of retainer may, therefore, have given a welcome opportunity to confirm the staplers' privileges by statute.

[39] A schedule of charges against Daubeney, dated in Henry VII's twenty-first regnal year, details nearly £7,000 that he had received for positions in his retinue at Calais that had been vacant since 1486: E101/640/5.

made subject to the full exchequer procedure and deprived of its use of the privy seal. In July 1511 the king appointed Sir Robert Southwell as chief auditor of the exchequer. His charge included those accounts previously under the General Surveyors and those, including the staple, audited by the foreign auditors of the exchequer.[40] However, the surplus of the merchants' account continued to be paid directly into the chamber,[41] or assigned by the king from the chamber,[42] and this remained the priority for both the crown and the staplers. In 1515 the act of retainer was extended by act of parliament for a further twenty years from April 1516. This enshrined the royal manipulation of the staplers in statute. The £10,022 4s. 8d. payable for the wages of the garrison was divided, half to the soldiers and half to the king 'in his Chambre, his exchequer in Westminster or ellis where in suche place and to suche persons as his Grace shall appoynte to his use'.[43] It is evident that the initial conception of the act of retainer – a means of farming out the difficult task of paying the garrison and discharging royal debts – had been superseded. The king now saw the merchants of the staple and the act as an easy way of collecting the wool customs and providing a regular supply of foreign specie which he could hoard or assign as the need dictated.

This arrangement continued into the 1520s. For the first thirteen years of Henry VIII's reign the staple showed, on average, a surplus of £1,400 per annum.[44] The wealth of the merchants was not questioned nor the ability of the wool trade in general to withstand its subjugation to political whims. For example, at some point between May 1523 and January 1524 the staplers were forced to contribute a loan of £6,500 towards the costs of the French campaigns of 1522–3.[45] However, the 1520s were also a decade of crisis for the English wool trade. A declining share of overseas trade coincided with an unfavourable foreign policy to destroy the act of retainer and the merchants' ability to continue to contribute to the early Tudor regime in general. However slow the payment of the surplus of their accounts into the chamber, the staplers had consistently fulfilled their most important role: the prompt payment of the Calais garrison. When this stopped the government was forced to reconsider its attitude towards the company and the financial administration of Calais.

The decline of the English wool export trade is well known and well documented.[46] The staplers suffered from the growing demand in their Flemish markets for fine quality Spanish wool and the instability of the exchange rate. This was coupled with the growing economic and political importance of the

---

[40] Wolffe, *The Crown Lands*, 77; *LP*, I i, 709/4.

[41] For example, BL, Add. MS 21481, f. 324. £1,500 paid 20 December 1511 and £2,500 paid 9 July 1513 of their surplus from 1509–10.

[42] Ibid., f. 328. An assignment in August 1513 of £1,200 of their surplus from 1510–11, most probably to John Daunce, treasurer of war.

[43] 7 Hen VIII, c. 10 (*Statutes of the Realm*, iii. 199–202).

[44] E101/202/18; 203/14; 696/32.

[45] *LP*, IV iii, A37; Hoyle, 'War and Public Finance', 89. The original does not give an exact date, merely stating that the loan was delivered to Peckham as treasurer of the king's chamber.

[46] Power, 'The Wool Trade in the Fifteenth Century', 39–90; *The Ordinance Book of the Merchants of the Staple*, ed. E.E. Rich (Cambridge, 1937), 5–20.

merchant adventurers. Throughout Henry VII's reign the two companies had been locked in a struggle for rights of trade in the Low Countries, culminating in the famous case before the king's council in 1505.[47] Nevertheless, it is too easy to blame the company's difficulties in the early sixteenth century on purely economic factors. The average value of the customs and subsidy yield, the important figure as far as the act of retainer was concerned, as opposed to the actual volume of wool exported declined by only 16.5 per cent from the first five years of Henry VII's reign to the last five years.[48] As I have argued above, the staplers' difficulties in meeting the garrison's wages were caused more by Henry VII's rapacity and his demands that the surplus of their accounts be paid promptly into his chamber in cash than by any remorseless decline in the value of their exports. Nevertheless, it is clear that during the reign of Henry VIII the English wool export trade finally lost its medieval supremacy to the cloth trade.

The crisis came in 1523–4. That year the payments to the crown and to the garrison exceeded the value of the customs collected by some £2,150.[49] This may have been precipitated by the renewal of war between England and France in 1522. Wolsey's foreign policy had moved towards a *rapprochement* with the Empire culminating in Charles V's visit to England and the treaty of Windsor in June of that year. This committed England and the Empire to war to curb 'the ambition of the king of France' and arranged a marriage treaty between Charles and the Princess Mary.[50] The favourable trading conditions for the staplers may have been sacrificed in the name of Tudor diplomacy.[51] In 1527 the staplers made a plea to the king to reverse their decline. They complained that Calais was a military, not commercial, base and that continual war had prevented them reaching their markets and had isolated the town. Their decline is evident from the particulars of the wool custom accounts for London. In 1517–18 there were 113 staplers shipping wool. By 1536 this number had declined to just forty.[52]

The crisis of the English wool trade meant that the wages of the Calais garrison fell into arrears. In 1528 the deputy of Calais, Sir Robert Wingfield,

[47] *Select Cases in the Council of Henry VII*, clxiii, 38, 42–3, 149–51; Anne F. Sutton, *The Mercery of London: Trade, Goods and People, 1130–1578* (Aldershot, 2005), 338–41.

[48] An average yield of £13,794 per annum between 1485–6 and 1489–90 and £11,520 between 1505–6 and 1509–10, see table 5.1 below. This is at odds with Peter Ramsey's assertion that the export of wool declined by 30 per cent during Henry VII's reign, while cloth exports rose dramatically by 61 per cent: 'Overseas Tade in the Reign of Henry VII: The Evidence of the Customs Accounts', *EHR*, 2nd series, vi (1953–4), 179.

[49] E101/696/32, rot. 3.

[50] *LP*, III ii, 2322, 2333.

[51] J.D. Mackie, *The Earlier Tudors, 1485–1558* (Oxford, 1952), 310–15. However, the invasion of France in 1513 had a much less dramatic effect on wool exports than either the campaign of 1522 or that of 1523. In 1513 the staplers' payments exceeded their charge by only 44s. 6d.: E364/120, 2 Hen VIII, rot. A. It may be that sheep diseases also cut the amount of wool available for export in the early 1520s. However, I have found no conclusive explanation of why the staplers' trade should have collapsed in this year.

[52] *Tudor Economic Documents*, ed. R.H. Tawney and E.E. Power (3 vols, Oxford, 1924), ii. 26; E122/204/3; 204/7. In 1527 the staplers claimed that the total number of shippers throughout England was only fifty-three: SP1/239, ff. 98v–101v (*LP*, Addenda I i, 958).

and the treasurer, Sir Richard Weston, complained to Wolsey that the staplers had no money and did not know when they would.[53] However, indentures continued to be made between the treasurer of Calais and the staple for payment of the wages.[54] This resulted in the company falling more and more in debt to the crown. The decision to prioritise the payment of the garrison's wages over the merchants' surplus to the king was probably taken by the authorities in Calais in consultation with the lieutenant and constables of the staple. By 1532 the company's debts to the crown, principally for their arrears of their surplus but also for their failure to meet the standing charges of the garrison, had reached £22,163 9s. 10d.[55] Finally, in March 1533 the staple was suspended and the merchants were prevented from trading with the Low Countries.[56]

From 1533 until 1535 the re-establishment of the Calais staple and some form of act of retainer were high on the political agenda. That it occupied much of the time of Thomas Cromwell, the king's secretary and chief minister, is evident from his lists of 'remembrances' preserved among the state papers. In 1533 the council presented a list of proposals to the staplers. They were to repay all outstanding debts to the crown; the custom on a sack of wool was to be increased by 13s. 4d. and by a half-penny for every fell; they were to be required to import bullion as required by statute; and the king was to have their lands in Calais. In return the merchants were 'to contynew thayr companye accordinglye and to pay for no more wolles & felles than they shall shipp'.[57] This was followed by much negotiation between Cromwell, the council and the staplers. The negotiations reveal that the staplers felt under attack by the government and the act of retainer, 'not induced by them nor yet in ther powers to remove'. Proposals made by the council at Greenwich were, on reflection, rejected by the merchants.[58] However, the longer the negotiations continued the weaker the merchants' position became. The government held the upper hand, for it was the individual staplers who depended for their prosperity on the export trade with

---

[53] *LP*, IV ii, 4887, 5051; iii, 5420, 5433.
[54] For example, E101/205/10. Indentures were made on 24 November 1531 and 11 July 1532 between the staplers and Robert Fowler, under-treasurer of Calais, for £8,185 6s. 7d. However, the total charge of the staple amounted to only £5,918 5s. 4d.
[55] E101/696/32, rot. 6.
[56] This cessation in trade precipitated a mini-crisis in Anglo-Imperial relations. In July 1533 the Imperial secretary, Jehan de la Sauch, presented a letter from Margaret, the regent of the Netherlands, expressing Imperial concern: *LP*, VI, 820 and 918. De la Sauch and Chapuys, the Imperial ambassador, had their meeting with Henry VIII some time before 13 August. Chapuys told the king that 'seeing that the staple of Calais had been set open from all antiquity, and had been wont to supply the Low Countries with wool, it was a new thing, and at times very suspicious to close it, as trade was a great bond of mutual amity': *LP*, VI, 975, 1018. The king's chief minister, Thomas Cromwell was, at this time, favouring a generally pro-Imperial foreign policy and the collapse of the Calais staple must have strained this.
[57] SP1/76, f. 4 (*LP*, VI, 423). A clear reference to the fact that payments to the garrison had regularly exceeded the staplers' charge.
[58] SP1/100, ff. 176–91v (*LP*, IX, A18). The king's council also assessed the viability of the English wool trade. Their conclusions were generally unfavourable to the staplers, suggesting that the lack of profit to the king was in part due to the staplers' duplicity: E101/207/14.

the Netherlands.[59] The staple was open again by mid-November 1533,[60] but it was not until 1535 that the new agreement between the crown and the merchants of the staple was formalised. An indenture made on 31 October released the staplers from the 1515 act of retainer. By the terms of this new agreement they were licensed to trade for five years and acquitted of almost £15,000 of their debts; in return they released Henry from repayment of £10,000 they had lent him some ten years earlier. Their lands in Calais, with the exception of Prince's Inn and the Staple Prison, were resumed by the king. They were to repay debts of £10,000, in one lump sum of £6,000 and bi-annual payments of £1,000.[61] This agreement represented a small victory for the staplers. Its terms were slightly better than the 'extreme Acte of Reteignour' they had rejected two years earlier.

Nevertheless, despite their obvious decline from their position of national importance during the first half of the fifteenth century, the staplers continued to play an important role in the defence of Calais and the management of the English war effort in the 1540s and 1550s. Soon after the new agreement of 1535 the merchants were again contributing substantial, if irregular, amounts for the garrison and works in the Pale. In 1539, for instance, these came to £6,703. During the mid-1540s they contributed around £5,500 per annum towards the ordinary costs of the Calais garrison.[62] During the reigns of Edward VI and Mary these payments increased further. In May 1554 the lieutenant and constables of the staple delivered £7,136 to the treasurer of Calais and a further £4,116 the following July.[63] Moreover, members of the staple company continued to be at the centre of the financial administration of Calais into the 1550s. During the 1530s Robert Fowler, a man with a long pedigree in both royal administration and the wool trade, acted as treasurer alongside his brother, Thomas, another prominent merchant. During the 1540s and 1550s Francis Hall, a Lincolnshire stapler and comptroller of Calais between 1545 and 1552, was involved in both the financial administration of Calais and the wider procurement of arms and supplies for the English war effort. Like his fifteenth-century predecessors, Hall was able to use his commercial contacts in the Low Countries to good effect on the crown's behalf.[64] Moreover, the merchants of the staple continued to provide

---

[59] In December 1533 the staplers approached Mary of Hungary, Charles V's regent in the Low Countries, in an attempt to reopen trade: *LP,* VI, 1510.

[60] *Calendar of Letters, Despatches, and State Papers, relating to the Negotiations between England and Spain, Preserved in the Archives at Simancas and Elsewhere* (13 vols, 1862–1954), ii. 889.

[61] SP1/98, ff. 116v–69 (*LP,* IX, 716).

[62] E101/206/5; *LP,* IX, 26, 552; XV, 749; Royal Commission on Historical Manuscripts, *Calendar of the Shrewbury and Talbot Papers in Lambeth Palace Library and the College of Arms* (2 vols, 1966–71), ii. 341. For the 1540s see E351/530–2.

[63] E351/534–5.

[64] For the Fowlers see Grummitt, 'Calais 1485–1547', 123, 191–2. For Hall see S.T. Bindoff (ed.), *The History of Parliament: The House of Commons 1509–1558* (3 vols, 1982), ii. 279–8.

private loans to members of the garrison which offset any delays in the payment of their wages.[65]

The decline of the staple and its members' inability to meet the costs of Calais's defence forced the crown to look for new methods of finance to avoid the situation of the mid-fifteenth century. That the early Tudors succeeded in paying for the defence of Calais without a rerun of the mutinies of the garrison that had characterised the various financial crises of the fifteenth century is evidence of their success in meeting the new challenges posed by the changing economic conditions of early sixteenth-century Europe and the escalating cost of early modern warfare. The ordinary costs of Calais, the regular payment of the garrison and the upkeep of the defences that had been covered by the act of retainer were met by a mixture of financial retrenchment and administrative innovation. From the 1530s a strict priority of payments, headed by the wages and works, was imposed. Thus, when pursuing his master's annuity, Lord Lisle's agent could warn: 'they saythe that the Treasorer of the chamber is often without mony and the Joyell Howse, Augmentations, and fyrst frywtte is as ill, and the Checker warsst, and to be payde at Caleys by the treasorer or the receyvor is warst of all'.[66] This was not due to the fact that there was no money at all in Calais; rather, a strict priority was assigned to payments and there was simply no spare money for Lisle's annuity. There is also evidence that the administration attempted to increase the yield from local sources at this time. This was evident as early as 1500 when Henry VII ordered a commission to investigate the sources of revenue in the Pale and to maximise their profitability to the crown.[67] In the 1520s and 1530s the administration made efforts to maximise the rents due from the marshy areas of the lordships of Marke and Oye through drainage and a new survey of rental values. By 1540 the lordships of Marke and Oye were worth about £4,400 per annum compared to only £400 during the reign of Henry VI.[68]

The crown also tied the defence of Calais into a national system of finance that exploited the new sources of revenue available from the mid-1530s for the purposes of war. Richard Hoyle has recently argued that two new agencies, the Courts of Augmentations and First Fruits and Tenths and the profits of the dissolution of the monasteries which they handled, probably doubled the crown's annual income. He has estimated that First Fruits and Tenths provided as much £42,000 per annum and the dissolution of monastic houses swelled the royal

---

[65] *Lisle Letters*, v. 1280. The staplers had, of course a long history of lending sums privately to members of the garrison: Alison Hanham, *The Celys and Their World: An English Merchant Family of the Fifteenth Century* (Cambridge, 1985), 236–7.

[66] SP3/4/94.

[67] C76/181, m. 2. It is not clear whether or not this commission actually served its purpose. In October 1508 William Yong, a clerk in the Calais exchequer, claimed that the commissioners had hidden their evidence from the king and thus defrauded the royal revenue by some one thousand marks per annum: SC1/52/65. However, Yong's testimony must be treated with caution: he harboured a grudge against the Calais council because he thought they had deprived him of his office of chief-surveyor and keeper of the records: *LP,* I ii, 3595.

[68] E101/206/12, f. 1; Morgan, 'Government of Calais', 170–2.

coffers by 'a little less than £50,000'. It is evident that a significant proportion was made available for the programme of refortification and the costs of warfare. John Gostwick, treasurer of First Fruits and Tenths, for instance, paid out £175,000 on military expenses between 1535 and 1540.[69] In 1540 the treasurer of Calais received £5,416 13s 4d from Gostwick towards the ordinary expenses.[70] From 1538 payments from the Court of Augmentations were directed towards the costs of the king's works in the Pale – a total of £3,000 in 1543 alone – but were also employed in meeting the wages of both the ordinary garrison and the various crews in the Pale. For example, in December 1540 the treasurer of Augmentations paid £636 7s. 10d. for the garrisons of the bulwarks around Guînes.[71] In the absence of systematic accounts for the late 1530s, 1540s and 1550s it is impossible to assess accurately the amount of money received at Calais from these new revenue agencies. However, along with the funds coming from the staplers and other established revenue sources in England, such as the exchequer and king's chamber,[72] the government, both in England and the Pale, ensured that there was almost always money available and thus avoided the periods of absolute poverty and desperate measures that had characterised much of the fifteenth century.

The success of the regimes of Henry VIII and Edward VI in meeting the costs of war between 1538 and 1552 is shown in a declaration drawn up by the government of John Dudley, duke of Northumberland, itemising the monies spent on military matters in that period. In all, the wars against France and Scotland, the capture of Boulogne, the defence of Calais, fortifications in England, the defence of the seas and the suppression of the 1549 rebellions cost some £3,501,453. Of this sum, in the reign of Henry VIII £276,766, and in that of Edward VI £94,664, was spent on the defence of Calais.[73] As Richard Hoyle has observed: 'It was possible to fund war on this scale only because of the most breathtaking acts of will by the king and by the subordination of every aspect of government finance to the imperative of war.'[74] The financing of the defence of Calais, therefore, became part of a wider fiscal system designed to meet the costs of war. As a proportion of spending on military matters, and of crown expenditure generally, the relative cost of Calais was declining during the first half of the sixteenth century. The development by the early Tudors of new institutions of crown finance to fund war (such as the Tudor subsidy and the new revenue courts of the 1530s) enabled the dependence of the garrison upon the merchants of the staple to be broken. By incorporating Calais into a wider programme of military expenditure, the crown was able to offset the effects of the decline of the English wool export trade.

For most of the period of English occupation the history of the Calais garrison and the English wool trade were inextricably linked. The merchants of

[69] Hoyle, 'War and Public Finance', 83–4, 88.
[70] E101/206/12.
[71] *LP*, XVI, 745; XVII i, 436; XVIII ii, 231.
[72] BL, Arundel MS 97, f. 85v (*LP*, XIV ii, 781); *APC*, i. 285, 382.
[73] SP10/15/11 (*CSP, Domestic, Edward VI*, 721).
[74] Hoyle, 'War and Public Finance', 91.

the staple had a vested interest in ensuring that the Calais garrison was well paid and the Pale well defended. Unfortunately, before 1466 other demands on the wool customs and political crises meant that the finances of Calais were frequently in a parlous state. The act of retainer, which ensured that Calais was adequately financed for nearly sixty years, was the product of both the crown's and the merchants' determination to prioritise the defence of Calais. The situation was further eased by the fact that the cost of Calais declined in relative terms as the crown consolidated and expanded its fiscal resources in the late fifteenth century. The establishment in the Pale was able to survive the decline of the wool trade from the 1520s for precisely this reason. By the last decade of English rule in the Pale the defence of Calais was just one part of much larger military budget. Ironically, the finances of Calais were probably as healthy as they had been for any period under English occupation when the town finally fell in January 1558.

Supplying the garrison

The provision of money to provide for the garrison's wages and the costs of maintaining the defences of the Pale was only part of the wider question of supply. The area conquered by Edward III in 1347, although extensive, was neither large enough nor fertile enough to provide for the military establishment in Calais. Although the arable land of the Calais Pale produced grain for the garrison's use, the great majority of victuals had to be supplied from the English mainland or through trade with England's continental allies. Naturally, this latter means of supply was an unreliable one, subject to the fortunes of war and shifting alliances, and so the supply from England was the Pale's most important source of victuals. The previous chapter looked at the question of the supply of weaponry to the Pale, here the emphasis will be on the other necessaries – principally food and clothing – that allowed the garrison to function as an effective military force.

During Edward III's reign the traditional system of purveyance – the compulsory purchase of food at fixed prices by royal officials – was used extensively to victual the Calais garrison.[75] Between 1347 and 1361 over thirteen thousand quarters of wheat, almost four thousand quarters of malt, 6,700 quarters of oats and 2,814 cattle and pig carcasses were purveyed for Calais. The distribution of supplies to the soldiers was placed, after about 1353, in the hands of local keepers of victuals. Alongside the system of purveyance, English merchants were also licensed to trade with Calais and stores were taken in raids against the French. As a proportion of total receipts these latter two methods probably accounted for less than 10 per cent of all victuals received. From the later fourteenth century, however, the proportion of victuals supplied by private merchants trading to Calais, selling their wares to the victualler, increased,

---

[75] Much of this paragraph is based upon S.K. Burley, 'The Victualling of Calais', *BIHR*, xxxi (1958), 49–57.

amidst extensive complaints about the practice of purveyance.[76] From the reign of Richard II merchants bringing victuals to Calais were absolved from the payment of custom on entry to the town, a practice designed to encourage the victualling of the town by private means.[77]

By the 1430s the vast majority of the garrison's supplies were provided by private merchants receiving various concessions for agreeing to trade in victuals with the garrison. The immunity from customs granted in Richard II's reign appears to have lapsed and the treasurer of Calais collected customs levied on goods entering the town. This 'privatisation' of the supply services clearly reduced the amount of food entering the town because on 15 May 1436, faced with an imminent Burgundian attack, the king restored the freedom from customs for those resorting to Calais to victual the garrison provided the carrier obtained letters testimonial from the mayor of Calais stating the quantity of goods so delivered.[78] This was a short-lived expedient by the hard-pressed Lancastrian regime eager to maximise all immediate sources of revenue: the customs on victuals entering the town were certainly being collected once more by December 1441 when their proceeds were used to meet the arrears of pay in the garrison.[79] Changes to this system were only apparent during times of crisis. In May 1449, for example, certain parts of Kent, including the Isle of Thanet, the hundreds of Maidstone, Hayhorn and Twyford, and an area between Canterbury and the coast, were reserved for victualling Calais and Dover, amidst fears of a French attack.[80]

The question of what quantity of victuals the fifteenth-century garrison actually consumed is almost impossible to answer. During times of peace the amounts of food and other supplies purchased by the victualler were not impressive. In 1445–6, for example, Robert Manfeld recorded the purchase of only 274 quarters of wheat, just over three tuns of white wine, 131 live cattle, four hundred sheep, 135 sides of bacon and two thousand stockfish. This picture is almost certainly incomplete, as it does not take into account the large amount of private trade not recorded by the victualler.[81] Most of the garrison's food was presumably supplied by private merchants resorting to Calais to trade directly with the soldiers, bypassing the official victualler while the royal authorities collected a tax from the merchandise sold. But during times of war the amount of stuff bought directly by the victualler increased greatly. Between July 1436 and November 1439, for example, William Cantelowe purchased huge quantities of grain, beer and wine, dried fish and meat and spices. In all he spent £6,635,

---

[76] For contemporary complaints about purveyance, usually for the royal household but also encompassing other government expenditure such as Calais, see Given-Wilson, *The Royal Household and the King's Affinity*, 111–13, 259–60.

[77] SC8/10582; J.F. Baldwin, *The King's Council in England during the Middle Ages* (Oxford, 1913), 505–7.

[78] E364/77, rots 7–8.

[79] E364/80, rot. 4.

[80] *CPR, 1446–52*, 244. The grant was apparently 'pursuant to the ordinance of the king's progenitors' but what that ordinance was is not clear.

[81] E101/194/6.

more than five times the amount bought in peacetime.[82] These supplies were augmented by whatever could be stolen from the enemy. During the duke of Gloucester's *chevauchée* into Burgundian territory following the relief of the 1436 siege, the English drove thousands of cattle back to the Calais Pale, even bartering them on the way back in return for bread.[83]

The majority of the trade in victuals was between Calais and London and the south-east of England. Cattle, for example, were usually purchased at Dover and Sandwich; occasionally the victualler sent his agents further afield, as in 1471–2 when twenty cattle were driven from Sheffield to Sandwich before embarkation for Calais.[84] Before the fall of Normandy and Gascony victuals were often bought in the other English possessions on the French mainland. In 1445–6, for instance, the victualler purchased wheat from Rouen and wine from Brittany.[85] Between 1450 and 1466 there is no evidence of trade between Calais and Normandy, but after that date, due to the earl of Warwick's cordial relations with the French, contact was resumed. In 1466–7 both wheat and wine were supplied to the garrison by French merchants.[86] Nevertheless, in the late fifteenth century the vast majority of victualling was carried out by English merchants, witnessed by the large number of protections issued to cross the Channel in the victualler's retinue. By the late 1470s, with the return of war to Picardy and Artois following the death of Duke Charles of Burgundy in 1477, the reliance on English merchants had become almost total. Licences to ship victuals to Calais free of customs were routinely granted both to English merchants and to soldiers and captains in the garrison.[87]

This system continued into the reign of Henry VII. There is no evidence of any shortages of supplies in the Pale between 1485 and 1509. In 1492 Henry VII reformed the financial administration of the Pale, removing the treasurer of Calais's account from the exchequer. From that date the victualler, William Rosse, also no longer rendered a separate account, highlighting the ease with which the victualling arrangements were operating and the fact that the crown no longer delivered money directly to Calais to buy victuals.[88] By this date the provision of supplies was almost exclusively in private hands, and the needs of the garrison were catered for by those merchants granted safe conducts to cross

---

[82] E101/192/10. The inventory of foodstuffs was as follows: 3,484 quarters of wheat; 2,863 quarters of malt; a measly two quarters of barley; thirty-eight quarters of beans; sixty-two quarters of peas; thirty-three quarters of flour; one pipe of flour; two hundred quarters of oats; 193 quarters of coarse salt; one pipe of ale; 282 pipes of beer; eighty-two tuns of French red wine; eight tuns of French white wine; twelve tuns, one pipe of red Gascon wine; three 'fattes' of Rhenish wine; six pipes of vinegar; eight pipes of olive oil; 30¼ beef carcasses; ninety-three live cattle; 1,965 saltfish; 5,459 stockfish; sixty-five barrels of salted salmon; two lasts, four barrels and three firdekyns of white herring; sixty-two cades of herring; twelve 'sades' of sprats; 4,041 lbs of almonds; forty-three lbs of pepper; sixty lbs of ginger; 2¼ lbs of sugar; 1 lb of saffron; and 120 whey cheeses.

[83] *The Chronicles of Enguerard de Monstrelet*, ed. Thomas Johnes (1840), 43.

[84] E101/197/14, f. 11. The cattle were then put to pasture around Guînes.

[85] E101/194/6.

[86] E101/196/17; 196/19, f. 24.

[87] See, for example, the licences enrolled in C76/165, ms 6–8, 14; 166, ms 6–8, 10, 12.

[88] *CPR, 1494–1509*, 140; E159/268, *brevia directa baronibus*, Michaelmas, rot. 17.

the Channel to victual the garrison. The lack of accounts makes the extent of this trade almost impossible to trace; the only evidence is the so-called 'increment of victuals', a tax of 40*d*. in the pound, collected by the treasurer of Calais from all victuals sold to the garrison. This system of victualling even meant that the establishment and arrangements made at Calais were entirely separate from those at Hammes and Guînes. The practice of leaving the victualling of military establishments to private enterprise by encouraging merchants to trade with garrisons became standard in the early sixteenth century. As Cliff Davies and Charles Cruickshank have shown, Henry VIII's first French campaign and the English garrison at Tournai followed the example of Calais and relied for their victuals on private merchants from England, France and the Low Countries.[89]

The problem with this system was that it was reliant on two factors: first, the ability of the soldiers to pay for their victuals or at least have a good credit rating among the mercantile community; second, upon a favourable trading climate that allowed relatively uninterrupted trade between England and its principal markets in the Low Countries. The first indications that there were serious shortages of victuals in the Pale came in 1521. Amidst fears of French aggression, the deputy, Sir Robert Wingfield, wrote to Wolsey in November of that year complaining of how poorly Calais was supplied.[90] This led to a 'searche of vitaylls' which reported that the stores maintained by the officers of the garrison and in the outlying castles were deficient in many of the thirteen basic items of food, drink and fuel.[91] The following year the situation worsened as border warfare between France and the Habsburg Low Countries led to widespread burning and destruction of crops throughout Flanders and Picardy.[92] Part of the problem was that the Calais garrison was just one small part of a massive military presence in north-western Europe at this time, including the English army assembled in the Pale under the earl of Surrey to raid French Picardy, as well as the French and Habsburg armies. This led to an unsustainable demand for victuals. Moreover, as we have seen, in 1523–4 the staplers' trade collapsed. This led to a shortage of cash to pay the garrison's wages and a subsequent collapse of the credit arrangements with victuallers that had previously sustained the garrison during periods of poverty. This had a knock-on effect throughout the Pale: the collapse of the wool trade meant a shortage of coin at Calais, while the insolvency of the garrison led to dire problems for the merchants making their living by selling victuals to the garrison.[93] In 1527 the shortage of victuals was further exacerbated by bad harvests, plague and floods which destroyed some of

---

[89] C.S.L. Davies, 'Supply Services of the English Armed Forces, 1509–1550' (DPhil thesis, University of Oxford, 1963), 167–9; Charles Cruickshank, *Henry VIII and the Invasion of France* (Stroud, 1990), 51–60. The reliance upon private victuallers in Tournai caused problems as the townsmen were reluctant to sell food to an occupying army: Cruickshank, *The English Occupation of Tournai 1513–1519* (Oxford, 1971), 70.

[90] *LP,* III ii, 1777.

[91] E36/270, ff. 607–42; Morgan, 'Government of Calais', 193–4.

[92] *LP,* III ii, 2376.

[93] *LP,* V, 1510. Although this list of complaints from the burgesses of Calais dates from 1532 the problems are indicative of those experienced throughout the previous ten years.

the best grain-producing areas of the Low Country. In addition, Wolsey's visit to the town in the summer of that year had exacerbated the situation: his large retinue had overstayed its welcome and helped itself to victuals destined for the garrison.[94]

The government's answer to the problems of victualling Calais was short-sighted. Between 1529 and 1532 the crown attempted to make the Pale self-sufficient, by banning imports from England and developing food production in the Pale. The perception that the Palesmen were too eager to sell their produce and victuals for a profit to the Low Countries was met with vehement denials from the civilian and military authorities in Calais.[95] By 1533 the victualling of Calais was in crisis: the high price of wheat in England meant that no merchants were willing to travel to Calais to sell it there and some of the food stored in the town was four years old and quite rotten.[96] Although these strict prohibitions were lifted in 1534, the government continued the ban on re-export from Calais and the authorities found it very difficult to persuade merchants to resort to the Pale.[97] The problems of victualling Calais in the 1520s and early 1530s were indicative of a wider malaise in the government of the town and marches and the crown's attitude towards the Pale. The extended periods of peace between 1514 and and the mid-1530s meant that there was no longer a military imperative to make the efficient supply of the Pale a priority. Moreover, as Henry VIII sought to extricate himself from his marriage to Catherine of Aragon the energies of government were increasingly drawn away from Calais. This led to the crown's neglect of the government of Calais and its military importance.

This neglect was recognised and attempts made to correct it by Sir William Fitzwilliam's commission sent to the Pale in August 1535. As we have seen, as a result of the commissioners' findings the Reformation Parliament passed the so-called Calais Act in the following year.[98] The Calais Act, despite making provision for members from Calais to sit in the English parliament, was principally a set of ordinances for the better government of the town and marches, designed specifically to restore the division between the military and civilian communities in Calais and, by reviving ancient customs fallen into abeyance, restore the garrison to a model of military efficiency. As well as the reformation of military service in the garrison itself, the overhaul of the system of victualling was one of the act's main concerns. The deputy assumed overall responsibility for the victualling of the garrison, while the civilian authorities were given responsibility for the 'mayor's garner' filled with a thousand rasers of corn.[99] Moreover, each householder was to keep supplies sufficient for six months in his

---

[94] Morgan, 'Government of Calais', 195.
[95] Ibid., 196–7.
[96] *Lisle Letters*, i. 41–2; *LP*, VI, 1026.
[97] Morgan, 'Government of Calais', 197.
[98] The act, 27 Hen VIII, c. 63, was actually entitled 'An Acte declaryng certeyn Ordenances to be observyd in the Towne of Calis and Marches of the same' but the title 'Calais Act' will be adopted here for convenience. The text of the Calais Act is printed in *Statutes of the Realm*, iii. 632–50.
[99] A raser contained about four bushells of corn.

house. The act further delineated the boundaries between soldiers and civilians: the involvement of the men of the garrison in retail trade was limited to buying their own horses, brewing beer solely for their own household and a restricted part in the herring trade. No soldier was to keep a shop, except within the castle walls, nor act as a victualler. Even then, members of the garrison were only able to indulge in trades directly linked to military needs – for example, smith and armourer – with a few exceptions for partnerships allowed. The Calais Act also stated that too much corn was used for brewing and restricted the number of breweries outside the wall of Calais to four. Tolls on victuals being brought to Calais were relaxed to encourage merchants, and there is evidence of a greater number of French merchants supplying the Pale with victuals. Although the initial impact of the Calais Act was an adverse one, causing friction between soldiers, victuallers and brewers,[100] it demonstrated that the crown was willing to tackle the problems of supply and adopt a more interventionist stance in victualling the garrison.

This interventionist stance, indicative of a new willingness of the crown to deploy national resources to sustain the garrison, was most evident during the wars of the 1540s and 1550s. In some ways the system of victualling with which the governments of Henry VIII and Edward VI maintained their wars with France and a vastly augmented garrison in the Pale was similar to that used in the fifteenth century. From 1543, with the resources of government behind it, the Calais garrison was adequately victualled. Two methods were used to ensure this. The first, and least important of the two, was that the Pale (along with, from 1544, Boulogne) was exempted from the general prohibition of exporting foodstuffs from England. Private merchants, therefore, were encouraged to come to Calais to trade in victuals with the garrison. In September 1545, for example, the mayor of London was instructed to issue a proclamation that the king's subjects could ship 'wheat, malt, rye, oats, beans, peas, beefs, mutton, bacon, bread, beer, butter, cheese' and other necessaries to Calais.[101] Second, the crown gave large amounts of money to appointed purveyors of victuals with which to buy food and other supplies and then to sell it on to the garrisons, rendering account for the profits at the exchequer.[102] On the whole, it seems this system worked, ensuring that the soldiers of the Pale were well fed and supplied throughout the period of war with France. The soldiers' confidence in their supply lines from England even encouraged them to lay waste to the grain-producing areas of Picardy so vital to the supply of their peacetime needs.[103] Despite the success in providing victuals, the chronicler Ellis Gruffudd, described the huge wastage by the English purveyors of victuals and the considerable profits made by private merchants. These claims are borne out by other evidence: between September

---

100 *LP*, XI, 575, 1359, 1388; XII i, 186. In fact, the benefits of the provisions of the Calais Act were not really felt until the early 1540s because of an agricultural slump which affected Flanders between 1538 and 1540: Morgan, 'Government of Calais', 200.

101 *LP*, XX ii, 271.

102 Davies, 'Supply Services', 167–8, 188–9.

103 Described in the chronicle of Ellis Gruffudd, a soldier of the garrison: Morgan, 'Government of Calais', 203–4.

1544 and October 1546, for instance, £26,000 worth of food was delivered to Boulogne of which a massive £11,191 was written off as waste. In 1545 the privy council feared that claims of shortages at Calais were mere profiteering, designed to ensure a surplus that could then be sold for profit. The council sent over its own man and no further complaints were heard.[104] The crown certainly made no great profit from selling victuals to the garrisons in the Calais Pale. Between June 1550 and March 1551, for instance, the purveyor of victuals at Guînes received £4,042 7s. 3½d. to buy victuals; these he sold to the soldiers for £4,105 2s.[105] Nevertheless, the shortages of victuals that had characterised the 1520s and 1530s were no longer present and the success of the supply system of the 1540s is evidence of the ability of early Tudor government to meet effectively the short-term demands of war.[106]

The end of the war with France brought an end to the period of the government's intense interest in the victualling of Calais. The return to peace meant a return to the private victualling arrangements that had always been the crown's preferred means of meeting the demands of the garrison for food and other supplies. In 1552 a commission was sent to the Pale in order to reform some of the abuses that had occurred during the treasurership of Sir Maurice Denys. This included an attempt to increase the food production and efforts to reform the victualling trade, in particular to prevent it from falling entirely into the hands of the wool merchants.[107] This attempt to decrease the amount of money spent on victualling Calais was only partly successful: in 1554 bad harvests led to a serious dearth in the Pale, but during Mary's reign the crown spent only £2,000 per annum on average on victuals compared with some £15,000 annually during the early 1540s. Nevertheless, as Morgan points out in his analysis of the victualling arrangements, although the garrison officials were reluctant to flood the lands around Calais when the duke of Guise attacked because they had already been sown with that year's corn, a lack of victuals and other supplies was not considered a major factor in the fall of Calais in 1558.[108]

* * *

In the mid-seventeenth century the historian Thomas Fuller, writing of England's last continental possession, wrote: 'But now it is gone, let it go; it was but a beggarly town, which cost England ten times yearly than it was worth in keeping thereof, as by the accounts of the exchequer doth plainly appear'.[109] His sentiments have been followed by most modern commentators on the financial cost of maintaining the Calais garrison. However, this chapter has shown that this is an overly simplistic analysis. By exploiting the relationship between the

---

[104] Morgan, 'Government of Calais', 204; Davies, 'Supply Services', 286; *LP*, XX ii, 558; *APC*, i. 189, 197.

[105] E351/199; Davies, 'Supply Services', 189.

[106] The statement, made by Ellis Gruffudd in 1550, that the state of victuals had never been worse must be treated with caution: Morgan, 'Government of Calais', 205.

[107] E101/540/51; *APC*, iv. 107, 144, 272, 373; *CPR, Philip and Mary*, ii. 11.

[108] Morgan, 'Government of Calais', 206–7.

[109] Thomas Fuller, *The Church History of Britain: From the Birth of Jesus untill the Year 1648* (6 vols, 1655), ii. 428.

crown and the merchants of the staple, the English administration in Calais actually returned a profit to the crown for much of the period between 1436 and 1558. In other words, the profits of the English wool export trade, based in Calais, were employed effectively to meet the costs of the Pale's defence. When the finances were in crisis this was due either to political incompetence or a breakdown of the vital relationship between the crown and the wool merchants. During the 1540s, when war on a scale demanded by the new technologies and tactics driven by the military revolution led to unprecedented demands for money and supplies, the Tudors showed what could be achieved by a government supported by the political nation and united in a common goal. Similarly, for the most of the period the crown ensured that the soldiers of the garrison were well fed and supplied with cloth, weapons and all other necessaries. The financing and victualling of the Calais garrison also shows, however, the limitations of late medieval and early modern governments in meeting the demands of war and recurrent military expenditure. To pay the garrison and supply it the crown relied upon the goodwill and prosperity of the merchant community; its taxes and customs paid for military expenditure, while the merchants themselves supplied most of the garrison's food by trading directly with the soldiers in their capacity as private individuals. This was a precarious balance and when that balance was upset, as in the 1430s or late 1520s, crisis ensued with dire consequences not only for the Pale but for the wider polity as well.[110] It would take until the middle of the seventeenth century before the English government devised a system of fiscal administration whereby the state assumed the sole responsibility for funding and fighting wars.[111]

[110] Wolsey's pro-French policy of the late 1520s and banning of English merchants from the Brabantine fairs in 1527, leading to war with the Netherlands the following year, largely explains the cardinal's deep unpopularity in the early stages of the Reformation Parliament: S.J. Gunn, 'Wolsey's Foreign Policy and the Domestic Crisis of 1527–8', in *Cardinal Wolsey: State, Church and Art*, ed. S.J. Gunn and P. Lindley (Cambridge, 1991), 149–77.

[111] James Scott Wheeler, *The Making of a World Power: War and the Military Revolution in Seventeenth Century England* (Stroud, 1999), 216.

8

The Fall of Calais in 1558

As every schoolboy used to know, Calais fell to the French in January 1558. It was an event of international importance. To Mary Tudor it was a disaster, trumpeting stark evidence of the failure of her policies and especially the alliance with Spain. Whether or not the queen really declared that the word 'Calais' would be engraved on her heart for ever we shall never know, but the loss of the town and marches was a bitter blow to her regime politically and to the English national psyche generally. Moreover, for Protestant contemporaries and later observers, the fall of Calais became synonymous with the national decline caused by Mary's rejection of her father's religious policies.[1] To more rational observers, the town's capture still illustrated the decline in English martial abilities during the sixteenth century and the futility of a geopolitical policy based on the continental mainland. The loss of a town which had symbolised the conquests of Edward III and Henry V was, in reality, no loss at all. By forcing English monarchs to abandon their pretension to the French throne, it opened the way to the exploration of the New World and the development of an oceanic outlook in which lay the origins of England's status as a 'Great Power'.[2]

As will have become clear from the arguments presented thus far, this view is overly simplistic. Militarily there was no reason why the French should have automatically triumphed over the English garrison of the Pale. Culturally, economically and politically too, Calais still played an important role in the mid-Tudor polity. How, then, did it fall so quickly to the duke of Guise in the winter of 1558 and why were the English unable to recover it? The reaction to the siege and subsequent loss of Calais also allows us to consider the extent to

---

[1] Robert Bell Calton, in his history of Calais, spared only two pages to the events of January 1558 concluding: 'Thus ended our tenure of Calais under probably the most odious of its English chatelains, namely, the bigoted and intolerant Romish Queen Mary': *Annals and Legends of Calais* (1852), 160.

[2] Thomas Fuller observed: 'But now it is gone, let it go; it was but a beggarly town, which cost England ten times yearly than it was worth in keeping thereof, as by the accounts of the Exchequer doth plainly appear': *The Church History of Britain: From the Birth of Jesus untill the year 1648* (6 vols, 1655), ii. 428. For other similar assessments see G.R. Elton, *England under the Tudors* (1955), 222; J.D. Mackie, *The Earlier Tudors 1485–1558* (Oxford, 1952), 558–9. J.B. Black in the Oxford History of England series, wrote that the loss of Calais helped England 'to launch out on her true destiny as an island kingdom': *The Reign of Elizabeth 1558–1603* (Oxford, 1959), 35. For a French view of the fall of Calais as the stimulus for the English to grasp their maritime destiny see Fernand Braudel, *Civilisation and Capitalism, 15th–18th Centuries*, trans. Siân Reynolds (3 vols, Berkeley, CA, 1992), iii. 353–6. See also David Reynolds, 'At Calais Gate', in *Premodern Places* (Oxford, 2004), 70–1.

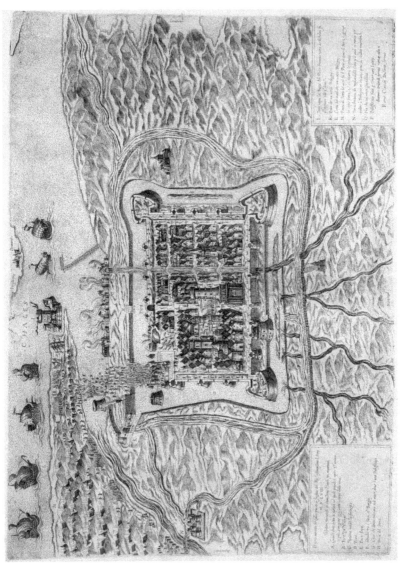

Fig. 3 The Siege of Calais, 1558. Eighteenth-century lithograph reproduced from G. Lefebrve, *Histoire générale et particulière de Calais et du Calaisis* (2 vols, Paris, 1766). This shows the French assault on Calais castle, although the representation of the town's fortifications probably reflect the eighteenth-century imagination rather than sixteenth-century reality.

which views on war and military service had changed since the early fifteenth century. How did Englishmen and women react to the defeat and find explanations for it?

The campaign

The marriage of Mary Tudor to Philip II of Spain in July 1554 always threatened to embroil England in the dynastic struggle between the houses of Habsburg and Valois. A measure of the domestic disquiet raised at this prospect was the clause in the marriage treaty which specifically stated that England was not to be involved in Philip's ongoing wars. The truce of Vaucelles in February 1556 between Henry II of France and Philip seemed to offer some basis for hope that the long Habsburg–Valois wars were at an end, but the intervention of Pope Paul IV in the affairs of Naples in the summer of that year upset the delicate balance. In September Philip's viceroy in Naples, the duke of Alva, invaded the Papal States provoking a reaction from the French who dispatched an army under the duke of Guise. In January 1557 the French unsuccessfully attacked Douai and by the end of the month Philip and Henry were, once again, formally at war. The English were unsure of their next move: did the 1554 marriage treaty extend only to wars in progress at that time? Moreover, in the same year the English had reaffirmed their treaty obligations to come to the aid of the Netherlands if attacked. Finally, the support given by the French to English rebels, notably Thomas Stafford who landed at Scarborough in April 1557, forced the council's hand and war was declared against Henry II on the following 7 June.[3]

Despite initial reservations about the cost and subordination of English interests to those of Spain that involvement in Philip's war threatened, the campaign of 1557–8 demonstrates again how war could mobilize the political community in a national effort. Philip himself remarked that with the coming of war he found 'such goodwill among everyone in his kingdom'. This was particularly marked in the summer of 1557 as those opposed to the Marian regime, principally on religious grounds, and those who had been involved in Wyatt's rebellion three years earlier, rushed to join the army. The leader of the expeditionary force which crossed the Channel in July was William Herbert, earl of Pembroke. Pembroke, while a supporter of Philip, had clashed with other councillors, notably Stephen Gardiner, bishop of Winchester, over religious policy, and service in war provided the perfect opportunity to restate his loyalty and case for reward and political influence. A similar motivation can probably explain the involvement of Viscount Montague and the committed Protestant, Henry Manners, earl of Rutland. Similarly, Francis Russell, earl of Bedford, returned from religious exile to take part in the expedition. Lower down the political and social ladder, the three surviving sons of John Dudley, duke of Northumberland,

---

[3]   The best account of the war of 1557–9 is C.S.L. Davies, 'England and the French War, 1557–9', in *The Mid-Tudor Polity* c. *1540–1560*, ed. Jennifer Loach and Robert Tittler (Basingstoke, 1980), 159–85. See also Paul Hammer, *Elizabeth's Wars* (Basingstoke, 2002), 48–53.

took part, as did several of those involved in Wyatt's rebellion. Indeed, Robert Dudley even took command of Pembroke's artillery train.[4] In July Pembroke crossed with 1,200 horsemen, four thousand foot soldiers, 1,500 pioneers and two hundred miners. The cost was met by Philip, who insisted on leading them personally into battle. While there was some debate about the effectiveness of their equipment, they certainly did not lack enthusiasm. On 10 August a French attempt to relieve the Spanish siege of St Quentin ended in disaster with over three thousand of their soldiers killed, and seven thousand captured, including their commander Anne de Montmorency, the constable of France. While the English missed the battle, they did arrive in time to storm the town of St Quentin itself, still holding out under Gaspard de Coligny. Two thousand Englishmen took part in the final assault and, according to the report sent back to Queen Mary, they were the first through the breach. The English had acquitted themselves well: the domestic response was one of pride and celebration, while the six hundred or so casualties testified to the fierceness of the fighting in which they had been involved.[5]

The outbreak of war also led to the reinforcement of Calais. Rumours of French plots to capture the town had led to a contingent of men being sent to the Pale in January 1557 under the command of the earl of Pembroke, but it was not until the summer that the prospect of war led to a more thorough reassessment of the Pale's defences.[6] Internal politics among the Calais council and garrison and financial pressures in England may have weakened the town's defences since 1553 and a French diplomat, returning to France and travelling through the Pale in June 1557, reported the built defences to be in a hopeless state.[7] In July Calais was reinforced with a small force and a crew dispatched to Guînes. This was part of a much wider domestic military effort with a large fleet also deployed in the Narrow Seas. Moreover, some twenty thousand men from England and Wales were mobilised to resist any French invasion.[8]

By October 1557 it appears that Henry II had decided upon an attack on Calais. The defeat at St Quentin appears to have had a marked effect on the French king, galvanising him to embark upon some military adventure by which the honour of France could be assuaged. The duke of Guise was recalled from Italy, as were his best troops, and by the second week in October he had received

---

4   Davies, 'England and the French War', 162–3; Simon Adams, 'The Dudley Clientele', in *The Tudor Nobility*, ed. G.W. Bernard (Manchester, 1992), 247–53; Glyn Redworth, '"Matters Impertinant to Women": Male and Female Monarchy under Philip and Mary', *EHR*, cxii (1997), 611–12.

5   Davies, 'England and the French War', 165–6; BL, Stowe MS 571, f. 95. In all the army suffered some 18 per cent casualties, mainly from sickness and disease: Hammer, *Elizabeth's Wars*, 49. For the lighting of bonfires at Bristol, Cambridge, London and Norwich in celebration of the victory at St Quentin see Steven Gunn, 'War, Dynasty and Public Opinion in Early Tudor England', in *Authority and Consent in Tudor England: Essays Presented to C.S.L. Davies*, ed. G.W. Bernard and S.J. Gunn (Aldershot, 2002), 133, 137.

6   Morgan, 'Government of Calais', 239–46.

7   R.A. de Vertot, *Ambassades de Messieurs de Noailles* (5 vols, Leiden, 1763), i. 35–6.

8   *Calendar of State Papers, Domestic Series, Mary I, 1553–1558*, ed. C.S. Knighton (1998), 626, 640.

his commission as *lieutenant-général du Roi*. Guise held several councils of war in the presence of the king. On 2 November, at one such meeting, Henry put forward a concrete proposal to attack the Pale. At first, it seems, Guise and the other counsellors were cautious, but on the next day the governor of Boulogne, Jean de Senarpont, was sent to reconnoitre the town and marches. On 20 November news came of the withdrawal of the Spanish field army from Picardy and on that day the king decided to invest Calais. Guise was still cautious and doubtful whether the forces required for a successful attack could be assembled in time. By early December, however, a large army had been massed at Compiègne. It marched north to Pontoise and reached Abbeville on the 12th of that month. Intelligence confirmed the French suspicions that the Pale was poorly guarded and that communications between Calais and London were in some disarray. The French, on the other hand, had mobilised a large army with impressive speed. By the end of December the English were finally aware of an army of some eight thousand Swiss, eight thousand Germans, eight thousand French infantry and three thousand cavalry encamped between Marquise and Ambleteuse.[9]

The English response to an increasingly obvious French military build-up was both slow and inadequate. Certainly, by early December the French plans were well known. On the 6th of that month the Venetian envoy sent details on the descent upon the Pale back to the Doge, and both Flemish and Spanish spies were reporting Guise's movements to their masters.[10] The Calais council, however, seem to have been blissfully unaware of the magnitude of the situation. The treasurer, Sir Thomas Cornewallis, had returned to England at the beginning of December, and John Highfield, master of the ordnance, had been in England since May reporting on the state of the town's artillery. There had been very little communication between London and Calais since June, when William, Lord Grey de Wilton, had asked for reinforcements. In August the privy council had interfered over the election of the mayor of Calais and in November the last remnants of Pembroke's expedition army had returned to England, but there had been no communication between Lord Wentworth, the deputy of Calais, and the government concerning the duke of Guise's activities.[11] On 16 December Vendeville, the governor of Gravelines, passed the news that the French were baking large quantities of bread at Ardres, as well as information received from Spanish spies in France. At the same time, De Noyelle, Flemish governor of Hesdinfert (known to the English as 'New Hesdin') in Artois, told Wentworth

---

[9] The fall of Calais is described from the French perspective in D.L. Potter, 'The Duc de Guise and the Fall of Calais, 1557–8', *EHR*, xcviii (1983), 481–512. See also P. van Dyke, 'François de Guise and the Taking of Calais', *Annual Report of the American Historical Association*, 1912–1913, cxvi (1913), 99–109 and Morgan, 'Government of Calais', 256 for the size of the French army in December. By the end of the campaign Guise had between thirty and thirty-six thousand men in the field: Potter, 'Fall of Calais', 495.

[10] *Calendar of State Papers, Venetian*, ed. R. Brown, C. Bentinck and H. Brown (9 vols, 1864–98), vi. 1098; Morgan, 'Government of Calais', 250–1.

[11] *APC*, vi. 112, 149, 217; *An English Garner*, ed. Edward Arber (1909), 312; Morgan, 'Government of Calais', 251; van Dyke, 'Taking of Calais', 104–5.

that his spies had uncovered a detailed French plan to take Newembridge and Rysbank Tower, and then invest the town of Calais itself. Wentworth replied that the defences of the Pale were well attended to and that the Flemings should mind their own business.[12] Wentworth also failed to inform Lord Grey at Guînes of the Flemish fears. Only on 22 December did Grey hear of the French build-up, from du Bugnicourt, the governor of Artois, whereupon he immediately warned London. On the same day Wentworth was warned by an English spy that the French army was at Abbeville, possibly bound for the Pale. It was only now that the deputy thought fit to inform Queen Mary. There was another delay before, on 27 December, Wentworth and Grey held a council of war with the other members of the Calais council. They noted that the Pale was desperately short of both men and victuals (indeed there were none at all at Newembridge and the Rysbank) and that the dearth in England had prevented victuallers from trading with Calais. They concluded that there was no way of preventing the French from overrunning the Pale and, rather than offering open battle, they decided that the meagre defenders should be concentrated in the Pale's various castles and bulwarks. Ominously they also noted that 'this hard and frosty weather, if it continue, will give the enemy great advantage' by restricting the effectiveness of the Pale's water defences.[13]

The crown's reaction to the news from the Pale was to issue commissions of array for the southern counties. The earl of Rutland was named commander of the army, the earl of Pembroke having excused himself with some indisposition. What was bound to be the slow process of raising men and assembling a fleet was further complicated on 29 December by another letter from Wentworth who assured the queen that the French meant to attack the Flemish-held castle of New Hesdin rather than the Pale. Mary cancelled the general muster, but two days later Lord Grey raised the alarm again. His men were already skirmishing with French troops at Licques (just south of Guînes) and a French fleet was approaching from Boulogne.[14]

On New Year's Eve French cavalry appeared on the hills above Calais. Simultaneously, the Boulogne fleet moved to cut Calais off from England.[15] The following day part of the French army, under the command of the duke of Nevers, drew up before Newenham Bridge. The small bulwarks built along the banks of the Hammes river were quickly overwhelmed, as was the partially rebuilt castle at Sandegate. At 9 o'clock in the evening of 1 January 1558

---

12 Anon., 'The Loss of Calais', *North British Review*, xlv (1866), 445; *Calendar of Letters, Despatches, and State Papers, relating to the Negotiations between England and Spain, Preserved in the Archives at Simancas and Elsewhere* (13 vols, 1862–1954), xiii. 331.

13 *Calendar of State Papers Preserved in the Public Record Office, Foreign Series, Mary 1553–1558*, ed. W.B. Turnbull (1861), 695–9, esp. p. 698; Anon., 'The Loss of Calais', 447.

14 Morgan, 'Government of Calais', 258; *CSP, Mary 1553–1558*, 702, 703.

15 The best modern narrative of the campaign to capture Calais and Guînes from an English point of view is Morgan, 'Government of Calais', 258–68. See also Anon., 'The Loss of Calais' and Davies, 'England and the French War', 168–75. For the various sixteeenth-century English eye-witness accounts of the campaign see *Tudor Tracts*, ed. A.F. Pollard (1903), 291–300, 312–16, 321–30.

Wentworth wrote again to the queen. He explained how the defenders had retired to Newembridge in the face of the French advance. Horsemen from Calais had sallied out to skirmish with the French infantry, but little contact had been made. Wentworth then described a skirmish between two hundred French arquebusiers and a troop of English horse under the command of the marshall of Calais, Sir Anthony Aucher. Seeing the English horse, the French came on 'marvellously hotly'. The English retreated to Newembridge, whereupon the garrison there 'bestowed divers shot upon the enemy, and hurt some. Of ours, thanked by God! None slain nor hurt, save a man-at-arms stricken in the leg with a currion.' Despite this stirring encounter, and the stalwart defence of the bulwarks at Froyton and Nesle, by the end of the day there were some twelve thousand French soldiers lodged in the Pale awaiting the arrival of the duke of Guise himself. Wentworth concluded: 'This having set all things in the best order I can, I make an end of three days' work; and leave your Majesty to consider for our speedy succour'.[16]

At this point the French hesitated. Instead of making straight for Newembridge, their forces divided into two: half made their way across the dunes to the Rysbank and the other half made towards the marshes of the Low Country to intercept Spanish forces expected from Gravelines. Despite advice from the Calais council, Wentworth refused to open the sluices until the following day (2 January) allowing the French valuable time to place their men. On 4 January two thousand French foot soldiers and four thousand cavalry moved around to the Isle of Colham to cut the town of Calais off from Spanish troops coming from Gravelines. At this point the defenders' nerves began to fray. Wentworth allowed the commander of the garrison at Newembridge, Nicholas Alexander, to surrender the fort without a shot being fired. Similarly at Rysbank Tower the captain, John Harlestone, decided he could not withstand a French artillery barrage and abandoned the fortress. This was a vital loss and effectively closed the haven to English shipping and any realistic prospect of immediate reinforcements from England. The French were quick to take possession of Rysbank Tower and battered the walls of Calais from this vantage point. A battery of some sixty cannon was also set up on the dunes in front of the town, concentrating their fire on the walls of the old castle. John Highfield, in his account of the French attack, states that he was unable to train the defenders' own guns on the French battery, but that, nevertheless, the old medieval curtain walls of Calais withstood the bombardment reasonably well and the defenders were able to fill any breaches with 'timber, wool, and other matter sufficiently'.[17]

On the night of 5/6 January the French made their assault on the town itself. Four hundred men, led by Piero Strozzi, marshall of France, and the marechal de Grammont, crossed the estuary and, under a covering artillery barrage, climbed up to the base of the old castle walls. At the Lanterngate the English were assailed by more men, while the Gascon contingent penetrated the breaches in the castle walls, forcing the defenders back across the bailey into the towers

---

[16] *Tudor Tracts*, 306–7.
[17] Ibid., 314–15.

which divided the castle from the town. According to John Highfield, the French entered the old castle unresisted at 8 o'clock on the night of 6 January. Lord Wentworth ordered three cannons and a saker to be brought up and fired upon the castle, hoping to prevent the French from entering the town. This was unsuccessful and Sir Anthony Aucher, who had already distinguished himself in the skirmishing on 1 January, now led a contingent of the garrison and engaged the French in hand-to-hand combat, driving them back into the castle. During this battle, however, Aucher, his son, and fifteen or sixteen other Englishmen were killed. The French continued to reinforce the castle through the night, and by the early morning it was clear to the defenders of the town that they could not resist Guise's forces. A meeting of the council was held in the house of the waterbailiff, Edmund Peyton, and, if Highfield is to be believed, Lord Wentworth dismissed calls from the other councillors to fight to the death. Instead the deputy dispatched Guînes Pursuivant to the duke of Guise seeking terms of surrender. Before dawn Wentworth and representatives from the burgesses, garrison and merchants of the staple met with Guise's representative, Monsieur D'Estrées, in the castle. At six o'clock on the morning of 7 January Wentworth accepted Guise's terms: the town, with its artillery, munitions and victuals, were to be surrendered to the French king; the lives of the inhabitants were to be spared and they were provided with safe conducts to leave Calais; Wentworth and fifty others were to remain as prisoners to be ransomed. At three o'clock in the afternoon the following day the 4,200 surviving inhabitants of Calais emerged from St Mary's and St Nicholas's churches and from the warehouses of the staplers and, refusing Guise's offer of accepting allegiance to Henry II, departed from the town.[18]

While Wentworth was busy negotiating the town's surrender, ever more frantic military preparations were being made across the Channel. On Sunday, 2 January signet letters were sent out to leading noblemen and gentlemen ordering them to levy their 'servants, tenants, friends and others within your rules or offices' and be at Dover on the following Friday or Saturday. The next day large quantities of arms and armour were delivered from the royal arsenal at the Tower of London to Dover to strengthen the defences of the Channel ports.[19] On 4 January five hundred men were raised by the city of London and each trade was ordered to provide arms and armour at their own cost. A week later the wards contributed a thousand men, each clothed in white jackets adorned with the red cross of St George.[20] On the very day that Wentworth surrendered Calais, commissions of array were appointed in every county to raise men to form a relief army for the Pale. The crown hoped to raise between 26,700 and 27,200 men in total. The commissioners were given extraordinary powers and ordered

---

18 Ibid., 291–3, 314–16. According to one contemporary Italian source some of the inhabitants died of hunger and suffocation amidst the rotting skins in the staplers' warehouses where they had taken shelter from the French attack: Morgan, 'Government of Calais', 265.

19 *CSP, Domestic Mary I*, 678; *CSP Foreign, Mary 1553–1558*, 708–10; BL, Harley MS 7547, f. 7v.

20 *The Diary of Henry Machyn, Citizen and Merchant-Taylor of London, from A.D. 1550 to A.D. 1563*, ed. J.G. Nichols (CS, 1st series, xl, 1848), 162–3.

not to exempt 'any liberties or franchises or any city or town a county of itself' from the responsibility to provide men. Thomas Howard, duke of Norfolk, for example, was instructed to raise 1,500 men from Norfolk and a further two thousand from Suffolk. Ten days later the demand was reduced to a thousand for each county to 'preserve Guînes and recover Calais', with the soldiers to be sent to Dunkirk to join the relief army commanded by the earl of Rutland.[21]

The city of Norwich's reaction to the demand for troops shows the lengths to which some communities and individuals went in the opening days of 1558 for the relief of Calais. Norwich's magistracy may have, in part, been motivated by their desire to court the favour of their powerful patron, the duke of Norfolk, but their response is reminiscent of the national response to the siege of Calais in 1436, possibly indicating a genuine wish to save the town and marches from the French, and is probably typical of the experience of other towns. The city agreed to send thirty men for the relief army and the magistrates imposed a special local tax on their fellow citizens, raising £68 7s. The men were clothed in both the Tudor livery and that of the city, waged at 6d. a day for five days and given 20d. for their expenses in marching the forty miles to the muster point at Ipswich. They were armed with a typical assortment of longbows, swords, and black bills and the city's store of eleven handguns was also made available for the expedition. The soldiers were entertained to a civic breakfast before marching out of Norwich under the command of their local 'conductors'. They arrived in Ipswich to the sound of a drum, specially purchased by the city chamberlains for the occasion. The soldiers remained at Ipswich for two or three days before news arrived of the fall of Guînes and of the decision that there would be no expedition to relieve Calais after all. By 29 January they had been sent home with 'hearty thanks for their travail and good will'. All but three of the Norwich men (who 'went ther waye with all thinges that thei were sette forthe withall' and were never seen again) made the long trek home, doubtless disillusioned and disappointed that their 'settyng forthe' had come to nought.[22] On 12 January the queen wrote to the warden of the Cinque Ports, Sir Thomas Cheyne, and the earl of Pembroke at Dover informing them that Calais had fallen. Moreover, a storm had 'so weather-beaten and distressed' the fleet assembled to carry the army across the Channel that it now 'cannot serve'. They were to discharge the men then arriving at Dover for the relief of the town 'with our thanks', retaining only a thousand or so for the defence of Dover castle.[23]

It was not until 13 January that the French began to move on Guînes.[24] There

---

[21] *CSP, Domestic Mary I*, 681–2, 699.

[22] Norwich Record Office, Norwich Chamberlains' accounts 1551–67, ff. 107–8, 125–35v; *CSP, Domestic Mary I*, 711, 713–14. For the, at times, delicate relationship between the citizens of Norwich and the dukes of Norfolk in this period, frequently mediated through the crown's military demands, see Steven Gunn, David Grummitt and Hans Cools, *War, State and Society in England and the Netherlands, 1477–1559* (Oxford, 2007).

[23] *CSP, Domestic Mary I*, 696. On the same day letters were also sent to the local commissioners informing them of the 'extreme tempest' that had disrupted the fleet's preparations and instructing them to keep the soldiers on a hour's standby in their counties: ibid., 697.

[24] Two extraordinary English eye-witness accounts survive of the French attack upon Guînes. The first was compiled by Lord Grey's son, Arthur, probably at the request of the Elizabethan

had been some debate in the French camp over whether to move against Guînes or Gravelines. The former, it was decided, posed the more immediate threat and Guise considered, quite rightly, that a counter-attack by Imperial troops from Gravelines was unlikely. The start of the siege was also delayed by a shortage of pioneers.[25] Grey had some eight hundred men at Guînes and a large quantity of artillery, and he had dispatched his wife to Bruges to seek assistance from Emmanuel Philibert, duke of Savoy, Philip II's governor of the Netherlands. On 4 January Grey had written to the queen informing her that there was now no 'other way for the succour of Calais' and the rest of the Pale but men from either England or the Low Countries. He assured her that 'I will not fail to do the duty of a faithful subject and Captain, although the enemy attempt never so stoutly; according to the trust reposed in me'.[26] Grey was therefore resolved to stand, fight and die in Guînes; unlike their fifteenth-century predecessors, whose indentures had allowed them to abandon the town if not relieved by a certain day in the event of a siege, in the 1550s captains were expected to defend their charges to the death or face charges of treason and cowardice. Realising that he had insufficient men to defend the whole town, Grey retired into the castle, leaving 150 English soldiers in the trefoil-shaped Mary Bulwark beyond the moat on the south side of the castle. Moreover, the fortifications generally were the most modern and well maintained in the entire Pale. The English defenders prepared themselves for the French onslaught by burning many of the houses surrounding the castle to provide clear lines of fire for the defenders' guns. By the morning of the 13th the Spanish commander at Gravelines, Vendeville, had managed to send some five hundred Walloon and Spanish soldiers to reinforce the garrison at Guînes and these Grey appears to have sent to the Mary Bulwark. The initial French assault was hampered by the fact that most of their heavy artillery was still at Calais and by constant sallies from the defenders in the castle (during one of these Guise himself was almost captured), and it was not until the 17th that they began to batter the walls. Initially this met with little success and it was not until some Italian engineers constructed pontoons that the attackers were able to cross the moat and begin their assault upon the castle and the bulwark.

The fighting for Guînes would concentrate on the Mary Bulwark, the modern brick fortification guarding the approach to the castle's keep, and would witness the most savage fighting of the entire campaign. The bulwark was, in Churchyard's words, 'far from succour from any' because the gates of the castle had

---

chronicler, Raphael Holinshed, between 1562 and 1577: *A Commentary of the Services and Charges of Lord Grey de Wilton, K.G....*, ed. Sir Philip de Malpas Grey Egerton (CS, old series, xl, 1847–8), 18–39. The second is by the English poet, Thomas Churchyard, who published in his *A General Rehearsal of Wars &c.* (1579) an account of his own experiences in the Mary Bulwark: *Tudor Tracts*, 321–30. Another English account, drawing on the French account of François de Rabutin published in 1559 as well as other English ones, is by George Ferrers. Written in 1568, it became well known through its inclusion in Grafton's *Chronicle* published in the following year: ibid., 294–9.

25 Potter, 'Fall of Calais', 494.

26 *CSP Foreign, Mary 1553–1558*, 711.

been boarded up and the approaches to the Mary Bulwark had been turned into a killing zone by the French guns.[27] The French cannon fire was so fierce that it quickly silenced the English guns and made a breach in the walls of the bulwark. The defenders also suffered heavy losses and Grey's deputy, Sir Henry Palmer, lost a leg to a cannonball. At 11 o'clock in the morning of 18 January the French began their assault on the Mary Bulwark. Some 450 English, Spanish and 'Burgundian' soldiers withstood a vicious French assault; most of the officers were killed or wounded (mainly it seems from gunfire) and by the nightfall some 150 of the defenders had been killed. The following day the French opened fire on the castle from the marketplace and renewed their assault on the bulwark. The defenders, exhausted through constant alarms during the night, again resisted stoutly and caused the French heavy casualties.[28] Grey himself had been wounded during his last visit to the bulwark (according to his son by an unsheathed sword which he had accidentally trodden on). After another night of constant alarms and 'politic practices', the French launched a third assault on the bulwark and the brays surrounding it on the morning of the 20th. Grey had sent another two hundred from the castle into the bulwark and brays, but on this occasion the attackers' numerical strength prevailed and the defences were over-come. The Spaniards manning the brays and the Netherlanders in the bulwark were slaughtered by the French and of over four hundred defenders only fifteen, including Thomas Churchyard, managed to make their escape to the castle. On seeing the fall of the Mary Bulwark, the defenders of the two smaller fifteenth-century bulwarks around the castle and the base court abandoned their positions too and fell back to the keep.[29] By nightfall the remaining garrison of Guînes was trapped within the keep with no prospect of relief or of driving Guise's men away.

At this point the defenders' resolve began to ebb away. The surviving Span-iards began to threaten mutiny and their murmurings began to spread to the English and they threatened 'to fling my Lord Grey over the walls' if some agreement with Guise was not reached. On the morning of the 21st Grey sent out messengers, including Thomas Churchyard, to ask for a truce and terms. The terms offered reflected Grey's own determination to salvage his reputation and those of his men from the wreck of the Pale's defences: the garrison were to be allowed to leave flying their ensigns in full battle array. Guise told the English delegates that 'this was a stout brag, to seek a capitulation with such advantage upon' considering that the defenders' ordnance had been lost and they could offer the French no 'malice'. Eventually it was agreed that the soldiers might leave with their baggage, but that the captains would remain to be ransomed. Once Churchyard returned to Guînes he claimed that the soldiers would have 'cut my throat' had he not communicated Guise's offer to Grey. By this point the

---

[27] *Tudor Tracts*, 325.
[28] Ferrers's claim that eight or nine hundred were killed and Churchyard's statement that the French lost a thousand 'by their own confession' seem extraordinarily high, but testify to the savagery of the fighting for the bulwark: ibid., 296, 327.
[29] *Lord Grey de Wilton*, 28, 31.

German landsknechts among the attackers had already entered the castle and Grey threatened to fire the few cannon remaining in English hands 'if the Law of Arms were not better observed'.[30] According to his son, Lord Grey attempted to rally the defenders one more time, but the garrison had decided 'that theyr lyves in oother servyce myght yet avayle theyr prynce and countrie' and they were not about to be slaughtered there to satisfy Grey's honour. Grey wisely agreed and offered himself, Sir Henry Palmer and the other captains to Guise, who personally received the castle keys from its former commander.[31] At this point only the ancient castle of Hammes remained in English hands. On the night of 22 January its commander, Edward, Lord Dudley, on the advice of his soldiers and seeing that no aid was forthcoming, led the garrison in escape across the marshes of the Low Country to St Omer.[32]

Explaining defeat

Three weeks after the start of Guise's campaign, Calais and the whole English Pale was in French hands. The news was received at the French court with great joy; bonfires were lit and *Te Deum* sung throughout the realm. In the last week of January Henry II himself arrived in Calais to formally receive the town into French allegiance. In England the news was met with despair. According to the Spanish ambassador the people refused to go to mass on hearing the news, while the London chronicler, Henry Machyn, remarked it was 'the hevest tydyngs to London and to England that ever was hard of'.[33] Although there were, as we shall see, many reasons advanced by contemporaries for such a 'marvel', the immediate reasons were military and centred upon a combination of the inadequate response of Lord Wentworth and the energy and dynamism of the duke of Guise. Looking at the broader perspective and especially how contemporaries explained the defeat reveals much about the role of war and military service in the political culture of mid-Tudor England. How far did explanations of defeat form part of a wider discourse concerned with military decline and the effectiveness of English arms? More importantly in terms of illustrating the ways in which perception of war and military service had changed since the beginning of our period, how was the loss of Calais explained in confessional terms; to what extent was it another rhetorical weapon in the battle for the souls of Tudor Englishmen? Finally, what do the various English accounts of the fall of Calais tell us about the way in which soldiers perceived themselves and were perceived by others in the last half of the sixteenth century?

From the purely military point of view, as David Potter has shown, Guise's

---

[30] *Tudor Tracts*, 327–9.
[31] *Lord Grey de Wilton*, 35–7.
[32] *Tudor Tracts*, 299.
[33] In fact one of the bulwarks on the eastern-most edge of the Pale near Gravelines remained in Spanish hands and was still a cause of dispute in the mid-1560s: Morgan, 'Government of Calais', 269; Potter, 'Fall of Calais', 493. For the reaction in England see *Diary of Henry Machyn*, 163; *CSP, Spanish*, xiii. 351.

generalship stood in stark contrast to that of Wentworth and the other English commanders. The duke was the epitome of the successful Renaissance commander: he realised that logistical support and money, rather than prowess and chivalric behaviour, were the determinants of military success. His co-operation with his uncle, the cardinal de Lorraine, ensured that the army was raised and money made available so soon after the defeat at St Quentin. He was able to use his personality and power as lieutenant-general to squeeze money from the Amiens municipality when central funds ran low and succeeded in getting local communities to provide food for his soldiers. Indeed, the maintenance of the food supply throughout the cold winter months was Guise's main concern and was a problem he met with extraordinary success. He also ensured that powder and shot was made available from local sources when the central reserves of *maître de l'artillerie* ran low. Immediately after the victory, Guise, rather than resting on his laurels, prepared the Pale to resist an Anglo-Spanish army expected imminently in an attempt to recapture the lost possessions. Once he had returned to court in February, Guise also ensured that the new governor of Calais, Paul de Termes, was provided with money for new fortifications and for wages. The capture of Calais 'was due largely to the precise planning and energetic efforts' of Guise and, in the immediate context of January 1558, it was this, rather than any deep-rooted structural failures on the part of the English, that explains the defeat.[34]

On the whole, however, Tudor Englishmen were, unsurprisingly, unwilling to explain the defeat by crediting it to Guise's abilities as a commander.[35] Treason, broadly conceived and having different meanings to different parts of the polity, was the most convenient explanation and appealed because it deflected blame from the accuser. On 28 January Sir Edward Carne wrote to the queen from the papal Curia: hearing that the town had been surrendered without a shot being fired by those appointed to defend it, Carne considered it 'the most abhomynable treason that ever man heard of' and was convinced that other traitors lurked to betray the entire realm to the French.[36] Similarly, the duke of Savoy suspected the master of the ordnance, John Highfield, and had him imprisoned on his arrival in Bruges.[37] Henry Machyn probably reflected popular sentiment in London when he wrote that 'lyke a trayter yt was sold and delivered unto them'.[38] In the general pardon offered at Elizabeth's coronation in January

---

[34] Potter, 'Fall of Calais', 496–512. For the increasing importance of an understanding of logistical and financial matters in determining the success of individual commanders in the sixteenth century see above, pp. 112–13.

[35] Although by the 1560s Guise's reputation as a military commander was well established in England and this was reflected in the narrative accounts of the campaign of 1558. George Ferrers stated that the duke approached the capture of Calais with 'marvellous policy' and indeed Guise's agency is constantly stressed throughout his account. Similarly, Thomas Churchyard described him as a 'noble Prince and faithful captain': *Tudor Tracts*, 290–301, 329.

[36] SP69/12/727 (*CSP, Foreign Mary 1553–1558*, 727).

[37] *CSP, Foreign Mary 1553–1558*, 735.

[38] *Diary of Henry Machyn*, 163.

1559 offences and treasons committed in Calais or connected to its loss were specifically exempted.[39] Initially the crown looked to those captains responsible for the immediate defence of the Pale. On 2 July 1558 a London jury indicted Lord Wentworth, Edward Grimstone, the comptroller of Calais, John Harlestone, Nicholas Alexander and Ralph Chamberlain, the lieutenant of Calais castle, all then still languishing in French prisons. The jurors stated that the accused had conspired on 26 December 1557 to deliver the fortresses of the Pale to the duke of Guise, servant of the French king. Guise had appeared before Calais with 15,000 men and, despite being well-furnished with men and munitions, Alexander had delivered Newhambridge to Guise without a fight on 3 January 1558. Harlestone had done likewise at Rysbank Tower. Then, in Calais itself, Wentworth, Grimstone and Chamberlain had met with one of Guise's heralds and allowed the French to enter the town by the Boulogne Gate. As well as the loss of the town itself and the weapons and munitions contained within it, the conspirators' treason had led to the loss of goods and chattels valued at £200,000.[40] Their trials early in Elizabeth's reign allowed the reasons for the loss of Calais to be debated in public.

Wentworth's return to England in the spring of 1559 to answer these charges developed into something of a cause-célèbre and there was clearly a great deal of public interest in the man who had surrendered Calais. In May a London stationer was fined 2s. for printing 'a ballett of Lorde Wenfurthe w^tout lycense'.[41] The text in question was John Markant's *The Purgacion of the Ryght Honourable Lord Wentworth, concerning the crime laid to his charge ...* This ballad, of nineteen four-line stanzas and ostensibly written in January that year by Wentworth while he awaited his return to England to answer his accusers, states that 'wycked men/which haue ungodly hartes' had conspired to make him a scapegoat. Instead the former deputy of Calais boasted:

> My service true is knowen,
> howe ready I haue bene:
> Both with my body and my goodes,
> to serue the Kyng and Quene ...

> Yet shall my truthe appeare,
> whych they would fayne conceale:
> And my obedience to the crowne,
> and to the common weale.[42]

Instead of his faithful service being remembered and rewarded, Wentworth, 'a noble pere, a subiect true' was 'rewarded thus with hate'. The ballad ends with

---

[39] K.J. Kesselring, *Mercy and Authority in the Tudor State* (Cambridge, 2003), 67.

[40] KB8/38.

[41] *Extracts from the Register of the Stationers' Company from 1557–1587*, ed. J. Payne Collier (1853), 22–3.

[42] John Markant, *The Purgacion of the Ryght Honourable Lord Wentworth, concerning the crime laid to his charge, made the x. of Januarie. Anno MDLviii* (1559). Wentworth had, of course, distinguished himself in Henry VIII's French campaigns in the mid-1540s and especially under Protector Somerset in Scotland in 1547.

an exhortation to subjects to be loyal to Queen Elizabeth, perhaps a foreshadowing of Wentworth's scaffold speech should he be found guilty. Clearly the ballad drew upon a popular perception that he had been made a scapegoat; although it does not name those responsible for the loss of Calais or his accusers, Wentworth's perceived innocence is explicit. Indeed his trial which began on 22 April, six days before the ballad was printed, established the former deputy's innocence. Wentworth was tried on the indictment made at the London Guildhall on 2 July the previous year. He was tried by his peers, headed by William Parr, marquess of Northampton, in his capacity as steward of England. Asked individually in turn, each of the twenty-six noblemen present declared that the former deputy was not guilty of the treasons laid against him.[43] Political considerations may well have been at play here: Northampton had suffered forfeiture in 1554 for his support for Lady Jane Grey and had only been restored to the privy council and his title on Elizabeth's accession. Certainly, Wentworth's acquittal was greeted with some rejoicing, at least in London. Henry Machyn observed that he 'quytt hym-seylff, thanke be God, and clen delevered'.[44]

The acquittal of the leading defendant, however, may have served only to confirm by implication what many Englishmen already suspected: that Queen Mary and her councillors were to blame for the loss of Calais. Moreover, this was not merely a result of their negligence, but also a divine retribution for the nation's abandonment of true religion and England's return to the Roman Church. The loss of Calais had in fact been prophesied in these terms by Robert Pownall in April 1557. Written in exile and taking the form of an open letter addressed to the council of Calais, Pownall's tract was scathing of the queen who had shamefully and treasonably neglected the defence of the realm: 'thy mother the staffe of thy defence, is now so debilitated & weakened as wel in worthy Captaines & valiante Soldiours, as in mony, monitions & victail, that she is scant able to defende, & releve hir selfe.' Nevertheless, Calais (and by extension the realm) could be saved if the town turned 'unto the Lorde thy God with al thy hearte'.[45] The explanation for the loss of Calais as a divine punishment was made more strongly in the spring of 1558 by another exile, Bartholomew Traheron. Traheron's *A Warning to England to Repente, and to Turn to God from Idolatrie and Poperie by the Terrible Exemple of Calece* was an important piece of Protestant polemic, not least as it came from the pen of one of the leading Marian exiles. Traheron placed the blame firmly on the queen's shoulders: 'Thy ruler not only being warned of imminent daunger left that toune purposely spoiled of good soldiars, and warlike stronge men, to a make for hir lust in meaning to give it up to another.' The accusation of purposeful neglect mirrored the crown's own accusations levelled at Wentworth and the other captains of the garrisons. The privy council's inactivity – those 'cruel wolves, ravening beares' – were contrasted with the valiant efforts of the Calais council, 'who were not

---

[43] KB8/38.
[44] *Diary of Henry Machyn*, 195.
[45] Robert Pownall, *An Admonition to the Towne of Callays* (1557), *RSTC* 19078.

notoriously nawghtie men'.[46] Like Pownall, Traheron's final point was, however, a religious one: that the loss of Calais was an example of the misfortune that will inevitably befall the realm as a result of its turning away from Protestant reform.

Both Pownall's and Traheron's tracts also drew their rhetorical force from the fact they were part of a much wider discourse on the nature and problems of Mary's rule. Pownall's denounced her as

> a most wicked & idolatrous Quene. A very Iezebel, that is, a frinde to Baal & his priests, & an utter enemie to god & his people. Yea another Athalia, that is, an utter destroier of hir owne kinerede, kyngdome & countrie, a hater of hir owne subiectes, a lover of strangers, & an unnatural stepdame both unto them & to the mother Englande.[47]

Similarly, Traheron seized upon Mary's supposed subordination of her husband Philip's wishes to her own and those of her subjects. It was the queen and her Spanish husband, rather than the French, who were the real enemy: Mary 'hath also studied these 4. yeres to betraie the o' Englande into the handes of a straunger, and of a nation most defamed in al the world for pride, and crueltie'.[48] To opponents of the regime this was the inevitable consequence of female monarchy. England's interests were bound to be subordinate to those of Spain, just as a wife's interests were bound to be subordinate to those of her husband. These fears were, as we have seen, present at both Mary's marriage and the beginning of the war in 1557 and clearly resurfaced in the aftermath of the defeat. The English council even told Philip's commissioners at the Treaty of Cateau-Cambresis that 'These wars wherein Calays was loste began at the request and for the sake of the Kyng'.[49] The loss of Calais made the dangers inherent in female monarchy tangible and provided ammunition for other polemicists who called for radical measures and argued that it was lawful for subjects to depose a tryannical and unjust monarch. Christopher Goodman's *How Superior Powers ought to be Obeyd of their Subject: And Wherein they may lawfully by Gods Word be disobeyed and resisted* was written in Geneva in

---

[46] Bartholemew Traheron, *A Warning to England to Repente, and to Turn to God from Idolatrie and Poperie by the Terrible Exemple of Calece* (1558), RSTC 24174. Traheron's description of the Calais council as not 'notoriously nawghtie men' is a reference to the tensions in the Pale over religion that had continued througout Mary's reign. Several among the garrison in the 1550s were evangelicals, most notably Wentworth and Lord Grey de Wilton. In 1555 the treasurer, Sir Thomas Cornewallis, had been ordered to round up Protestant dissidents in the town and garrison and the earl of Pembroke commissioned to inquire into Wentworth's administration and the effects of religious discontent within the Pale. Within the town prominent evangelicals like Thomas Broke continued to prove an embarrassment to the government if nothing else, while the intervention by the crown in the mayoral election of August 1557 may have had religious motives. Nevertheless, there is no evidence that religious divides compromised the town's defence in January 1558, nor that Protestants were in league with the French: Morgan, 'Government of Calais', 234–7.

[47] Pownall, *Admonition*, sig. A5v.

[48] Traheron, *Warning*, sig. A4.

[49] SP69/13/856.

January 1558, probably before news of the loss of Calais had reached the Marian exiles. Nevertheless, it was read in England with Calais fresh in the memory and the defeat provided a tangible justification for the deposition called for by Goodman.[50]

Nevertheless, it is clear that this narrative that identied the loss of Calais as being symptomatic of the weaknesses of Marian government and, by implication of female monarchy itself, was itself problematic in the opening months of Elizabeth's reign. On 28 November 1559, seven months after Wentworth's trial and almost two years after Calais's fall, Elizabeth established a special commission of *oyer et terminer* headed by the mayor of London, William Hewet, to try the other men cited in the indictments. Three days later Edward Grimstone, the former comptroller, was brought from the Tower to the Guildhall to answer the charges contained in the indictment of July 1558. Grimstone had been held in the Paris Bastille, unable to pay the ransom of ten thousand crowns demanded of him, but in October 1559 he had escaped, cutting through the bars of his prison with a saw blade passed to him by the English ambassador, Sir Nicholas Throckmorton. He was discharged by the jury of the charges laid against him, but he later claimed that he had the queen's promise of a pardon if found guilty.[51] On 22 December Ralph Chamberlain and John Harlestone were similarly brought from the Tower. They, however, were found guilty of the charges in the indictment and condemned to be hanged, drawn and quartered at Tyburn. It is difficult to believe that they were any more culpable than Wentworth or Grimstone for the loss of Calais (although Harlestone, of course, had abandoned Rysbank Tower as the indictment had alleged), but the diagnosis of defeat as stemming from faults of the captains rather than those of the monarchs may still have appealed to the Elizabethan regime.[52] Nevertheless, on 8 June 1560 Chamberlain was pardoned of his crimes, to be followed, some six weeks later, by Harlestone.[53]

---

[50] Christopher Goodman, *How Superior Powers ought to be Obeyd of their Subject: And Wherein they may lawfully by Gods Word be disobeyed and resisted* (Geneva, 1558) *RSTC* 12020. See also Herbert Grabes, 'England or the Queen? Public Conflict of Opinion and National Identity under Mary Tudor', in *Writing the Early Modern English Nation: The Transformation of National Identity in Sixteenth-Century England*, ed. Herbert Grabes (Amsterdam, 2001), 47–88, esp. pp. 1–3; Constance Jordan, 'Women's Rule in Sixteenth-Century British Political Thought', *Renaissance Quarterly*, xl (1987), 421–51, esp. pp. 28–9, 440.

[51] KB8/39/1; *Diary of Henry Machyn*, 218; C.S.L. Davies, 'Sir Edward Grimston', in *Oxford DNB*.

[52] KB8/39/2; *Diary of Henry Machyn*, 220. Like Wentworth's trial, those of the other captains appear to have elicited much debate. The reason for Chamberlain's guilt, it seems, was that Guise had entered the town by a breach in the castle and this was ordinarily considered to have been the strongest part of the defences: Sir John Hayward, *Annals of the First Four Years of the Reign of Queen Elizabeth*, ed. John Bruce (CS, old series, xl, 1840), 36.

[53] *CPR, 1558–60*, 331, 462. It is clear that Harlestone, at least, was not widely perceived as a traitor. In April 1559 the privy council had written to the sheriff of Essex expressing some surprise that Harlestone 'being indicted of Hiegh Treason' was being allowed to go at large in the county on his return from captivity. The council ordered his immediate arrest and transportation to the Tower: *APC*, vii. 83–4.

By the late 1560s many of the problems associated with female monarchy under Philip and Mary had been worked out in the new Elizabethan polity. While Calais remained an important topic in Elizabethan diplomacy and the prospect of its recovery was seriously considered by both the queen and her subjects, the discussion of the reasons behind its capture became less contested. It seems that by the late 1560s the general consensus was that the town had fallen to a combination of Marian inefficiency and Guise's brilliance. New discussion of the campaign and the defeat took two forms which reflected broader themes in the consideration of war and military service in Elizabethan England. First, a celebration of the individual prowess and feats of arms performed by the English defenders and, second, a more rational consideration of the reasons behind defeat that was part of a wider, technical military literature that began to appear in England in the second half of the sixteenth century.[54] Both these themes are apparent in the narratives of the campaign that appeared in the 1560s and which were incorporated into the accounts of the Elizabeth chroniclers, Grafton and Holinshed.

George Ferrers's account of the fall of Calais, probably written in 1568 and incorporated into Grafton's *Chronicle*, demonstrates how narratives of the event were changing in the first decade of Elizabeth's reign. Ferrers's narrative had a tone of incredulity; that 'a town of such strength, and so well furnished of all things as that was' should fall in only eight days was a 'great marvel'. His analysis identified the lack of prompt action as crucial, 'either by wilful negligence there [in Calais], or lack of credit by the Queen's council here'. This combined with 'conspiracy of traitors elsewhere' and the 'force and false practices of enemies' to lead to Calais's fall. In this, of course, Ferrers was repeating the commonplaces that had been offered since January 1558, but he also introduced another crucial factor, the storm of 11–12 January that had destroyed the English fleet anchored off Dover. These 'extreme storms and tempests' provided an explanation of defeat which (apart from the possibility that the storm itself was divinely sent) was not explicitly political. Other incidents, such as Alexander's surrender of Rysbank Tower, were reassessed in rational, military terms, as was Guise's own careful planning. Ferrers was also keen to draw attention to the feats of arms performed by the English defenders. The 'prowess and hardy courage' of the marshall, Sir Anthony Aucher, on 6 January, in defending the breach in the castle walls was praised, while particular credit was given to Lord Grey for his defence of Guînes.[55] Ferrers's account demonstrated that the narratives of the campaign were still contested, and that there were other stories, mainly from the soldiers of the garrison itself, that tried to portray the siege of Calais in a more positive light or at least challenge defamations of the defenders' own conduct.

The chivalric theme in English writing about the fall of Calais is most apparent in the prose eye-witness account of Arthur, Lord Grey de Wilton, son of William, Lord Grey, the defender of Guînes. Grey's narrative was part of a

54 David Eltis, *The Military Revolution in Sixteenth-Century Europe* (1998), 104–16.
55 *Tudor Tracts*, 290–301.

wider celebration of the deeds and feats of arms of his father, one of the leading English soldiers of the mid-Tudor period. William's own part in the campaign was recognised at the time: while the others languished in French prisons awaiting an uncertain fate on their return to England, he was elected to the Garter *in absentia*. Arthur's account was also, however, designed to recover his father's reputation from the disaster suffered at the siege of Leith in April 1560. Denied the chance to assault Edinburgh by the queen, William's force of some eight thousand had invested the well-defended town of Leith. When a breach appeared in the walls on 6 May it was decided that it was not suitable for assault; the following morning he, not having been informed of the results of the previous day's reconnaissance, assaulted the breach anyway. The English scaling ladders proved too short and the attackers suffered heavy casualties as a result. General opinion blamed Grey for the débâcle, although the lieutenant-general, Thomas Howard, duke of Norfolk, told the queen that he was in 'no waie to be blamed, except ... that he hath not his wytts and his memorie fayleth hym'. Before the assault Norfolk had complained that 'all is nott in hym that hath ben thought', and 'my Lord Graie's service doth consiste but upon a courage without ony conduct; every man that can leade a bande of horsemen is not for so greate an enterprise'. Sir William Cecil considered him 'a noble valiant careful gentleman', but in reality Grey's reputation was shattered. He died in 1562, broken financially by the ransom paid after his capture at Guînes and broken emotionally by his defeat at Leith.[56] His son's purpose in writing his *Commentarie of the Services and Charges of Lord Grey de Wilton* was to resurrect his father's reputation; by its incorporation into Holinshed's *Chronicle* it also served as a celebration of the deeds of a leading English soldier, providing inspiration for aspiring soldiers of the later sixteenth century.

Throughout the text Grey's role in the siege of Guînes is that of a chivalric hero, leading by example and exhorting his men to perform feats of arms in the service of their prince. On 19 January, as the French assault on the Mary Bulwark intensified, Grey 'gave woorde strayght too everie place to stande on theyr garde, encouraging everie man too continew in theyr well beegoon endevoures'. That night, after repelling the assault, he came to the bulwark 'where, after prayze fyrst to God, he guave thanckes and commendations to them all', arranging the burial of the dead and the treatment of the wounded.[57] When the bulwark finally fell Grey took this as a personal blow, leaping on top of the ramparts of Guînes castle 'wysshyng of God that soom shott would take hym' and saved only by one of his soldiers who dragged him down to safety.[58] Arthur's account of the surrender of Guînes stresses that Grey maintained his honour throughout, resisting the clamour of the garrison to come to terms with the duke of Guise. Grey's speech to his soldiers is a chivalric set-piece, a

---

[56] *A Collection of State Papers ... left by William Cecill, Lord Burghley*, ed. S. Haynes (1740), i. 298, 303, 311; *CSP, Scottish*, 435; Julian Lock, 'William Grey, Thirteenth Baron Grey de Wilton (1508/9–1562)', in *Oxford DNB*.
[57] *Lord Grey de Wilton*, 24, 28.
[58] Ibid., 30.

foreshadowing of words put into Henry V's mouth on the eve of Agincourt by the anonymous Elizabethan author of *The Famous Victories of Henry V* (1588) and Shakespeare:

> Wee have beegoon as beecoomed us; we have yet heald on as dutie dooth bynde us; lett us end then as honestie, dutie, and fame doothe wyll us. Neyther is there any sutche extremitie of dyspayre in owre case but that wee maye yet deerely ynowghe sell oure skynnes eare we looze them. Lett us then eyther martche owte under owre enseygnes displayed, or else heere within dye under them displayed.[59]

Unfortunately, the rest of the garrison did not share their commander's chivalric sensibilities and he was forced to make terms. The reader is left in no doubt of Lord Grey's credentials as a man of honour, but the author is also keen to show that he was also a man of reason, an intelligent and thoughtful soldier who employed 'conduct' as well as 'courage'. He also draws attention, but does not expand upon, the provisions that Grey made for the defence of Guînes when news arrived of Guise's approach and 'the advertisements that from tyme to tyme hee sent too queen Mary and king Phyllyp'.[60]

A stress on the chivalric and honourable conduct of the siege of Guînes is also apparent in Thomas Churchyard's account. Churchyard was first and foremost a soldier, serving in English armies in Scotland and on the continent from the 1540s until the 1560s and in the Protestant cause in France in the 1570s. His eye-witness account of the siege of Guînes appeared in his *A Generall Rehearsall of Warres ... called Churchyardes Choise*, a miscellaneous collection of tracts relating to war published in 1579.[61] Churchyard was explicit about why he had written his narrative, 'not because I had some charge there: but because sundry reports hath been raised thereof by those that never thoroughly knew or understood the matter'.[62] His account stresses the individual feats of arms performed by the various captains, particularly in the Mary Bulwark where he himself served, but also the 'lusty soldiers' of the garrison generally. Grey's conduct is vindicated, and, as in Arthur Grey's account, surrender comes only after he was over ruled by some of the garrison who threatened 'to fling my Lord Grey over the walls' if terms were not reached.[63] Significantly, however, Churchyard does not seek to vindicate himself and the other defenders through chivalric narrative alone. At the close of his account he lists sound military reasons why 'our peace was not so dishonourable, as some report'. The garrison had no chance of relief; the next French assault would surely have overthrown them; the castle keep was cut off from the other fortifications still in English hands and it was surrounded by the enemy's guns; the bulwark's capture made the medieval defences of the castle untenable; and the leading captains had been killed or

---

59 Ibid., 35–6. For similar sentiments expressed in Elizabethan accounts of Agincourt see Michael K. Jones, *Agincourt 1415* (Barnsley, 2005), 16.
60 *Lord Grey de Wilton*, 38.
61 Raphael Lyne, 'Thomas Churchyard (1523?–1604)', in *Oxford DNB*.
62 *Tudor Tracts*, 323.
63 Ibid., 327.

injured. Moreover, the defenders had acquitted themselves well, losing eight hundred of their number while inflicting four thousand casualties on the attackers.[64] Churchyard's account brought together the two strands of English military thinking in the second half of the sixteenth century. First, there was the revival in the idea of the chivalric hero, something apparent in renewed literary interest in Henry V and finding its political apogee in the figure of William Devereux, 2nd earl of Essex, in the 1590s. Second, there was the emerging interest in the practical, technical aspects of war.[65] Both Churchyard and Arthur Grey used contemporary technical language to describe the weaponry and tactics employed by both sides. Their accounts also thus functioned as military manuals, describing the practical employment of the arts of war described in such works of military theory as Sir Roger Williams's *A Briefe Discourse of Warre* (1590) or Thomas Styward's *The Pathwaie to Martiall Discipline*, published in three editions in the early 1580s.

* * *

The loss of Calais in January 1558 elicited much soul-searching among the English. There was nothing, despite the polemicists' claims, inevitable in its capture. The campaign was organised and conducted brilliantly by the duke of Guise, while the English response was sluggish, confused and inadequate. Despite a hopeless cause, the English defenders (and their Dutch and Spanish allies) fought courageously and, in Guînes at least, reasonably effectively. Certainly the English defeat was due to a disparity in the military technology or tactics employed by the two sides. This underlines the relative parity in the capabilities of the fighting men of the leading western European states in the mid-sixteenth century. The reaction to defeat in 1558 was more immediate and public than it had been a hundred or so years earlier when the English had lost Normandy and Gascony and suffered defeat in the Hundred Years War.[66] Many of the themes present in the diagnosis of defeat in 1449–50 (the role of supposed traitors leading to the trial of the duke of Suffolk, and allegations made against the duke of Somerset foreshadowing the proceedings against Wentworth and his colleagues) resurfaced in 1558. The latter discourse on defeat tapped into a much wider, contemporary discourse on the nature of the mid-Tudor polity, particularly in terms of religion and the problems of female monarchy, just as that a hundred years earlier had formed part of a wider critique of Lancastrian kingship. Significantly, it also attempted to rationalize defeat by analysing it in terms of military technology and the tactics and operations of the belligerents. Significantly, however, it was also conducted in

---

64 Ibid., 330.
65 Peter C. Herman, ' "O, 'tis a gallant king": Shakespeare's Henry V and the Crisis of the 1590s', in *Tudor Political Culture*, ed. Dale Hoak (Cambridge, 1995), 204–25; Jonathan Baldo, 'Wars of Memory in Henry V', *Shakespeare Quarterly*, xlvii (1996), 132–59, esp. pp. 34–7.
66 For the reaction to defeat in 1450 see C.R. Nall, 'The Production and Reception of Military Texts in the Aftermath of the Hundred Years War' (DPhil thesis, University of York, 2004).

language and terms that would have been familiar to readers of the mid-fifteenth century. Lord Wentworth's defence against treason was essentially a chivalric one, while the narratives of Lord Grey de Wilton and Thomas Church-yard underlined the essential continuities in war and military service throughout the fifteenth and sixteenth centuries.

9

Conclusion:
War and Military Service in England, *c.* 1437–1558

For over two hundred years the town and marches of Calais had been the most tangible symbol of the bellicose aspirations of the English kings and their subjects. Their military and symbolic importance were further heightened during the last century of English rule by the loss of Normandy and Gascony between 1450 and 1453. As well as its symbolic importance, Calais's economic significance, as the staple for the export of English wool, continued throughout this period. Calais, then, was for more than two centuries at the heart of the late medieval and Tudor polities. The dynamics of the relationship between the crown and the garrison of the town and marches reveal much about the wider importance of war in England, and the changing relationship between the crown and its subjects as negotiated through military service.

In 1436 Calais was just one theatre in a wider European war between the kings of England and France and their feudal vassals, the dukes of Burgundy and Brittany.[1] The failed Burgundian siege of that year revealed the importance attached to Calais by late medieval Englishmen. Calais was portrayed by the crown, and accepted in the popular imagination, as part of the realm of England; the siege generated a response in terms of money, men and patriotic fervour unrivalled in the fifteenth century. Significantly, when the English military position in Normandy collapsed in 1449–50 the domestic response was different. The threat to, and eventual loss of, Normandy and Gascony were perceived as symptomatic of deep-rooted problems within the Lancastrian polity itself. The popular response to the disaster in Normandy was not to organise and rally round the crown for its recovery, but to impeach the king's chief minister, William de la Pole, duke of Suffolk, call for fiscal and governmental reform at home, and, in the summer of 1450, to rise in rebellion against the king's corrupt counsellors.

War in general, and the defence of Calais in particular, continued to exercise the popular political imagination throughout the fifteenth and into the sixteenth centuries. Edward IV's failure to mount an effective campaign in France in the late 1460s was a factor in his temporary deposition in 1470; similarly, it was the crises occasioned by the call for extraordinary taxation to fund war in 1489 and

---

[1]   The kings of Scotland should also be added to this equation: Michael Brown, 'French Alliance or English Peace? Scotland and the Last Phase of the Hundred Years War, 1415–53', in *The Fifteenth Century VII*, ed. Linda Clark (Woodbridge, 2007), 81–100.

1497 that led to rebellions against Henry VII's authority. The ever greater demands for war taxation in Henry VIII's reign, particularly in 1511–13 and the 1540s, were achieved by an appeal to this popular enthusiasm for war. Printed propaganda, subsidy preambles and royal proclamations, as well as popular verse and polemic, reminded the king's subjects of the importance and Englishness of Calais, Henry's just title to the French throne, the perfidy of the king and his subjects' enemies, and how the health of the commonweal was maintained through successful war waged against foreign enemies.

If war continued to exercise the popular imagination throughout the period, then it also defined the identity, culture and actions of the political elite. The 1436 siege played an important role in shaping the political reputation of many nobles and gentlemen, most importantly the captain of Calais, Humphrey, duke of Gloucester. Gloucester used the popular regard in which the town was held to advance his own war policy, which favoured the defence of the Pale over the claims of Lancastrian France, against his enemies in the king's council. More widely, service in Calais was part of the *cursus honorum* of many important figures in the Lancastrian polity. This was often combined with service in Normandy, but long service in the garrison was not incompatible with a full career in local and national politics and government in England. While many men combined domestic responsibility with service in expeditionary armies during the fifteenth century, a significant minority demonstrated that service in garrison forces, whether in Calais, Normandy or Gascony, did not preclude playing a full part in affairs at home. Serving soldiers in the garrison attended their county courts, served as sheriff, on ad hoc commissions and as knights of the shire in parliament, as well as attending to their own estates and personal affairs. This has important consequences for the way in which we judge the English commitment to the Lancastrian possessions in France during the 1440s and beyond. Many historians have identified a reluctance to become actively involved in the French wars among the English elite, and a growing distance between those who fought and held lands in Lancastrian France and those whose landed and political concerns lay at home.[2] The continued willingness of important members of the political elite to spend large parts of their career in garrison service reveals their commitment to the English claims to the French throne and the way in which military service shaped the political community. Indeed, this commitment to foreign war persisted into the late fifteenth century and was manifested by the enthusiastic response to Edward IV's campaign of 1475 among those with connections to the Calais garrison. The sense of disappointment evident in the wake of Edward's bloodless settlement at Picquigny and the subsequent attraction of Burgundian service to the English military elite suggest that their notion of military involvement in France was, to some degree, self-defined and conceptualised by their own experience of war, reading of

---

2   See, for example, M.H. Keen, 'The End of the Hundred Years War: Lancastrian France and Lancastrian England', in *England and her Neighbours, 1066–1453: Esays in Honour of Pierre Chaplais*, ed. M. Jones and M.G.A. Vale (1989), 297–311; Christine Carpenter, *The Wars of the Roses: Politics and the Constitution in England, c. 1437–1509* (Cambridge, 1997), 99.

military texts and immersion in the chivalric culture of north-western Europe. The apparent reluctance among the aristocracy to take sides in the domestic rebellions and usurpations between 1483 and 1497 may reveal a conscious withdrawal from the somewhat sordid nature of late medieval English politics into a chivalric fantasy which looked back to the days of Edward III and Henry V.

It was the success of the early Tudors, particularly Henry VIII, to harness these chivalric longings in the service of the crown. The deputy of Calais, John, Lord Berners's translation of Froissart's *Chronicles* in 1523 was only the most tangible manifestation of this. War with France in 1513, 1522–3 and from 1543 until the end of the reign channelled the energies of the military and political elite into the service of the crown and strengthened the bond between the king and his aristocratic subjects.[3] Service in war, whether in the Calais Pale, the Boulonnais or Scotland, was part of the *cursus honorum* for the early Tudor political elite and the most successful royal servants of the reign combined regular service at court with long periods in garrison or employed as diplomats. Most significantly, while noblemen had always been, to quote K.B. MacFarlane, 'professional soldiers',[4] under Henry VIII soldiers became noble with the elevation of men like Thomas Poynings, Thomas Wharton and John Dudley to the peerage.[5] The importance of war in defining the political elite may have declined during the political and religious crises of Edward VI and Mary's reigns, but the ability of men like the earl of Pembroke and William, Lord Grey de Wilton to survive the mutable nature of mid-Tudor politics is testimony to the survival of military and chivalric factors in defining membership of the political elite.

From the late fifteenth century military ambition, networks and culture were

---

3   Steven Gunn, 'The French Wars of Henry VIII', in *The Origins of War in Early Modern Europe*, ed. J. Black (Edinburgh, 1987), 28–51; Craig Taylor, *Debating the Hundred Years War: Pour Ce Que Plusieurs (La Loy Salicque) and A Declaracion of the Trew and Dewe Title of Henry VIII* (CS, 5th series, xxix, Cambridge, 2006).

4   K.B. MacFarlane, *The Nobility of Later Medieval England* (Oxford, 1973), 162.

5   The elevation to the peerage of Dudley, Wharton and Poynings stands in contrast to the ennobling of prominent military men in the fifteenth century. Despite being accomplished soldiers, James Fiennes, created Lord Saye and Sele in 1447, Sir Richard Wydeville (the son of the lieutenant of Calais), created Lord Rivers in 1448, and William Hastings, created Lord Hastings in 1471, all owed their elevations not to their martial achievements but to their proximity to the king or other members of the royal family. It was this fact, rather than the question of their nobility per se, that created the political tensions that surrounded their creations, witnessed by the Yorkist earls' jibes directed at Rivers when he and his son were captured at Sandwich and brought to Calais in 1460: the earl of Warwick said 'his fader was but a squyer and broute vp wyth Kyng Herry the v^{te}, and sethen hym-self made by maryage and also made lord, and that it was not his parte to have swyche langage of lordys beyng of the Kyngys blood': *Paston Letters and Papers of the Fifteenth Century*, ed. N.B. Davis (EETS, special series, xx, 2004), i. 162. Rivers et al. had their sixteenth-century counterparts in men like Edward Seymour, earl of Hertford, Henry VIII's brother-in-law, one of the leading English generals of the 1540s and later lord protector of the young Edward VI. Hertford's rivalry with the Howards at the end of the Henry VIII's reign, like the opposition to Rivers in 1460 and 1469 (following his daughter's marriage to Edward IV four years earlier and his elevation to an earldom), revolved around his right to counsel the king and the displacement of the lords of the royal blood, not his suitability to join the ranks of the peerage.

tied ever more closely to the aims and aspiration of the crown. The organisation and nature of military service in Calais both reflected and helped to shape these developments. In the 1430s the defence of Calais was organised in the same way it had been when Edward III first garrisoned the town in 1347. The Calais garrison was comprised of a number of smaller sub-garrisons, the individual retinues of the various aristocratic captains with whom the crown had contracted for the defence of the Pale. The crown indented with the captains, but had very little involvement in the recruitment of the individual soldiers. What little evidence survives suggests that it was personal connections, of kinship or previous military service, or merely the opportunities for regular employment that determined the nature of service among the soldiery. While the crown guaranteed the wages of the captains and soldiers and demanded their allegiance, it wielded very little practical influence over the garrison's recruitment and their conduct. The potential dangers this presented to the crown in the form of a ready-made army for its opponents were forcibly demonstrated in the 1450s when control of the garrison became a defining part of the struggle between Lancaster and York.[6]

Edward IV's appointment of his close friend and chamberlain of his household, William, Lord Hastings, as lieutenant of Calais in 1471 marked the beginning of a significant shift in the balance of military power in the Pale. Hastings, although he ostensibly enjoyed all the privileges of previous captains, was the king's *locum tenens*; thereafter, it was royal authority, not the personal standing of the noble captain, that legitimated military service and war. From the 1470s onwards, captains in the garrison were increasingly tied to the crown through the payment of annuities and by membership of the royal household. Most importantly of all, the last years of the fifteenth century saw the gradual disappearance of the indenture for war, a contractual agreement marked by its reciprocity, for regulating service in the Pale. Thereafter, captains held their offices by royal patent, an intrinsic part of a wider range of responsibilities they carried out at the king's command. The fifteenth-century sense in which service in Calais was part of a military career which often involved service in the armies of other princes or knight-errantry was replaced with one very much focused on a career in the service of the English king. Among the soldiery as well, connections with the crown were strengthened and the captains' ability to recruit freely was limited. Indeed, captains were frequently royal servants with little landed resources of their own whose only means of filling the ranks was through the stewardship of royal lands they held or by the crown's direct appointment of soldiers. By the reign of Henry VIII the defence of Calais relied upon the public authority and resources of the crown, rather than on the private connections of noble captains. Developments in the garrison led and shaped the ways in which the kings of England sought to deploy the military potential of their subjects. It was this public authority, principally in the form of the commission of array, that

---

6 Michael Hicks, 'Bastard Feudalism, Overmighty Subjects and Idols of the Multitude during the Wars of the Roses', *History*, lxxxv (2000), 386–403.

allowed Henry VIII to field the vast armies deployed in and around the Pale in the mid-1540s.[7]

The changing dynamic of military service in the Pale in favour of the crown was also facilitated by solving one of the longest-standing problems of English Calais: that of finance. Intermittent crises and long arrears in the payment of the garrison's wages had characterised much of the period before 1466 when Edward IV and the merchants of the staple concluded the act of retainer. Before 1466 the successful financing of the garrison had relied on two factors. First, the willingness of the wool merchants to supply credit and cash to the crown and the soldiers, and, second, the ability of the garrison's noble captains to command sufficient credit to offset the crown's frequent failure to meet its commitments. The act of retainer formalised existing mechanisms for getting money to the soldiers, but also demonstrated the crown's ability to strengthen its hand *vis-à-vis* the merchants. The subordination of the mercantile community in Calais to the dictates of royal policy was amply demonstrated by their near-disastrous (for both parties) relationship with the first two Tudor kings. In guaranteeing the regular payment of the soldiers' wages the crown also lessened their dependence on their noble captains, and freed itself from the need to appoint commanders who could supplement shortfalls in royal provision from their own private resources.

The Tudors' success in financing and supplying the Pale, even in the face of an inexorable decline in the scale of English wool exports to the Low Countries, is also a measure of their ability to command ever greater amounts of their subjects' wealth for expenditure in war. While Henry VIII's war expenditure of the 1540s may not have exceeded, per capita, that of Edward I in the 1290s or even Edward III in the 1340s, it was a significant increase in the amounts that the Lancastrian or Yorkist kings could raise. Under Henry VIII and his children the costs of defending Calais were made part of a national defence budget, the treasurer of Calais being just one part of an integrated fiscal system designed to meet the burgeoning demands of defending the realm.[8]

The political dynamic of the military relationship between the king and his subjects was also affected by changes in the art of war itself. The fifteenth and sixteenth centuries saw important changes in the way in which war was waged in Europe. The proliferation of gunpowder weapons in the mid-fifteenth century, the development of effective artillery fortifications towards the end of the century which shifted the advantage in warfare decisively to the defender, and the resulting growth in the cost of war and size of armies in the sixteenth century

---

[7] David Grummitt, 'The Court, War and Noble Power in England, *c.* 1475–1558', in *The Court as a Stage*, ed. Steven Gunn and Antheun Janse (Woodbridge, 2006), 145–55.

[8] Mark Ormrod, 'The West European Monarchies in the Later Middle Ages', in *Economic Systems and State Finance*, ed. Richard Bonney (Oxford, 1995), 123–62; 'The English State and the Plantagenet Empire, 1259–1360: A Fiscal Perspective', in *The Medieval State: Essays Presented to James Campbell*, ed. J.R. Maddicott and D.M. Palliser (2000), 197–214; Peter Cunich, 'Revolution and Crisis in English State Finances, 1534–47', in *Crises, Revolutions and Self-Sustained Growth: Essays in European Fiscal History, 1130–1830*, ed. W.M. Ormrod, Margaret and Richard Bonney (Stamford, 1999), 110–37.

were all developments felt in Calais. The evidence shows that the Calais garrison were aware of and, at times, in the vanguard of these developments. Moreover, because of its role as a cultural and commercial entrepôt, the Pale was instrumental in introducing new military technology and tactics to a wider English audience. From the manufacture of gunpowder weaponry in the Pale in the late fifteenth century to the experience of the garrison's captains in the new pike-and-shot tactics of the 1540s, Calais served as a means of introducing the 'military revolution' to England.

By the end of our period, therefore, the English defence of Calais was part of a national military and fiscal system which shared common characteristics with those systems developing in contemporary France, Spain and the Habsburg Netherlands. The English polity experienced similar demands imposed upon it by war as its near neighbours and, within the constraints of its particular political, cultural and social systems, reacted to them in similar ways, developing institutions and strategies for waging war comparable with those in other western European countries. By the middle of the sixteenth century the French army was one characterised by effective royal control over armies and their noble commanders, a military bureaucracy and heavy state expenditure on dynastic war. Like England, however, the dominant culture of the military classes remained chivalry and both chivalric discourse and practice continued to exist side-by-side with the new Renaissance disciplines of logistics, tactics and technology.[9] Similarly, in the Habsburg Netherlands the centralised artillery arsenal established at Mechelen in 1520 had its contemporary English equivalents at Calais and the Tower of London. While England had no equivalent to the standing *bandes d'ordonnance*, Marian nobles probably enjoyed less freedom and flexibility in raising and commanding armed forces than their counterparts in the Low Countries. In the Habsburg Low Countries, just as in England, the demands of war led to the development of more complex fiscal systems disposing of vastly inflated revenues.[10] In Spain also, during the mid-sixteenth century, the government of Philip II made successful attempts to reassert royal control over its armed forces and deploy the resources of the Castilian crown for warfare in north-western Europe.[11]

Why, then, if Calais was the centre of a well-developed and, by contemporary European standards, effective national military–fiscal system, did over two hundred years of English occupation end in such miserable circumstances in the winter of 1558? The conclusion must be that the loss of Calais did not result from long-term structural weaknesses in the way in which the English went about the business of war. The Pale was not chronically underfunded, nor were its fortifications neglected or its soldiers ill-equipped. As we have seen in

[9]   David Potter, 'Chivalry and Professionalism in the French Armies of the Renaissance', in *The Chivalric Ethos and the Development of Military Professionalism*, ed. D.J.B. Trim (Leiden, 2003), 150–82; J.B. Wood, *The King's Army: Warfare, Soldiers and Society during the French Wars of Religion* (Cambridge, 1996).

[10] Steven Gunn, David Grummitt and Hans Cools, *War, State and Society in England and the Netherlands, c. 1477–1559* (Oxford, 2007), ch. 2.

[11] I.A.A. Thompson, *War and Government in Habsburg Spain, 1560–1620* (1976).

chapter eight, the campaign which ended in the loss of Calais was determined by luck, the generalship of the duke of Guise, and some startling incompetence on the part of most of the English commanders. Lord Grey de Wilton's defence of Guînes showed the ability of the English defenders of the Pale to wage war on equal terms with the armies of other European princes. The loss of Calais did not put an immediate end to English military ambitions in France (although they became increasingly impossible to realise), nor take away the importance of chivalry and military service in defining sixteenth-century English political culture. Nevertheless, the nature of war and military service in England had undergone a transformation of lasting significance in the years between 1436 and 1558. The Calais garrison provides the perfect mirror to allow the historian to chart these changes and place them in context.

Bibliography

Primary sources

Manuscripts
Canterbury, Cathedral Archives
CC/FA 1, 16 Canterbury chamberlains' accounts

Kew, The National Archives (Public Record Office)
C1 Chancery: Early Chancery Proceedings
C54 Chancery: Close Rolls
C56 Chancery: Charter Rolls
C66 Chancery: Patent Rolls
C76 Chancery: Treaty Rolls
C81 Chancery: Warrants for the Great Seal: Series, I
C82 Chancery: Warrants for the Great Seal: Series, II
C115 Chancery: Master Harvey's Exhibits: Duchess of Norfolk's Deeds
DL28 Duchy of Lancaster: Various Accounts
DL29 Duchy of Lancaster: Accounts of Auditors, Receivers, Feodaries and
      Ministers
E28 Exchequer: Treasury of the Receipt: Council and Privy Seal Records
E36 Exchequer: Treasury of the Receipt: Miscellaneous Books
E101 Exchequer: King's Remembrancer: Various Accounts
E122 Exchequer: King's Remembrancer: Customs Accounts
E159 Exchequer: King's Remembrancer: Memoranda Rolls
E314 Exchequer: Court of Augmentations and General Surveyors: Miscellanea
E315 Exchequer: Court of Augmentations and General Surveyors: Miscellaneous
      Books
E351 Exchequer: Pipe Office: Declared Accounts
E364 Exchequer: Pipe Office: Foreign Accounts Rolls
E401 Exchequer: Exchequer of Receipt: Receipt Rolls
E403 Exchequer: Exchequer of Receipt: Issue Rolls
E404 Exchequer: Exchequer of Receipt: Warrants for Issue
E405 Exchequer: Exchequer of Receipt: Tellers' Rolls and Books
KB8 Court of King's Bench: *Baga de Secretis*
SC1 Special Collections: Ancient Correspondence of the Chancery and the
      Exchequer
SP1 Secretaries of State: State Papers Henry VIII
SP3 Secretaries of State: Lisle Letters
SP10 Secretaries of State: State Papers Domestic, Edward VI
SP11 Secretaries of State: State Papers Domestic, Mary I
SP69 Secretaries of State: State Papers Foreign, Mary I
SP70 Secretaries of State: State Papers Foreign, Elizabeth I

Lewes, East Sussex Record Office
RYE60/3 Rye chamberlains' accounts

London, British Library
Additional charter 19808
Additional manuscripts 5948, 21481, 23971, 25114, 25459, 38092, 46454, 46455
 48988, 51020, 71009
Arundel manuscript 97
Cotton manuscripts Augustus I.II, Caligula E.II, Faustina E.VII, VIII, Faustina
 E.VIII, Galba E.IX
Egerton manuscript 2093
Harley charters 52 G.12, 76 E.39
Harley manuscripts 3880, 7547
Landsdowne manuscript 127
Royal manuscript 17 B.xlvii
Stowe manuscripts 146, 571

London, Society of Antiquaries
MS 129B Inventory of Henry VIII

Norwich, Norfolk Record Office
Norwich chamberlains' accounts 1551–67

San Marino, CA, Huntington Library
HA13886 Hastings letter book

Contemporary printed matter
Goodman, Christopher, *How Superior Powers ought to be Obeyd of their Subject: and Wherein they may lawfully by Gods Word be disobeyed and resisted* (Geneva, 1558).
Hall, Edward, *The Union of the Two Noble and Illustre Famelies of Lancastre & Yorke* (1548).
Markant, John, *The Purgacion of the Ryght Honourable Lord Wentworth, concerning the crime laid to his charge, made the x. of Januarie. Anno MDLviii.* (1559).
Pownall, Robert, *An Admonition to the Towne of Callays* (1557).
Traheron, Bartholemew, *A Warning to England to Repente, and to Turn to God from Idolatrie and Poperie by the Terrible Exemple of Calece* (1558).

Printed sources
Acts of the Privy Council of England, ed. J.R. Dasent (46 vols, 1890–1964).
The Anthony Roll of Henry VIII's Navy, ed. C.S. Knighton and D.M. Loades (Navy Records Society Occasional Publications, ii, 2000).
The Beauchamp Pageant, ed. Alexandra Sinclair (Donington, 2003).
British Library Harleian Manuscript 433, ed. R. Horrox and P. W. Hammond (4 vols, Gloucester, 1979–83).
The Brut, or the Chronicles of England, ed. F.W.D. Brie (2 vols, Early English Text Society, original series, xxi, xxvi, 1906–8).
Calendar of the Close Rolls, Edward IV–Henry VII (4 vols, 1949–63).
Calendar of Letter-Books Preserved among the Archives of the Corporation of London at the Guildhall, ed. R.R. Sharpe (11 vols, 1899–1912).
Calendar of Letters, Despatches, and State Papers, relating to the Negotiations between England and Spain, Preserved in the Archives at Simancas and Else-where (13 vols, 1862–1954).

Calendar of the Patent Rolls, Henry VI–Henry VII (10 vols, 1897–1916).

Calendar of the Patent Rolls, Philip and Mary (4 vols, 1937–9).

Calendar of State Papers, Domestic, Edward VI 1547–1553, ed. C.S. Knighton (revised edn, 1992).

Calendar of State Papers, Domestic Series, Mary I, 1553–1558, ed. C.S. Knighton (1998).

Calendar of State Papers and Manuscripts Existing in the Archives and Collections of Milan, ed. Allen B. Hinds, i. 1385–1616 (1912).

Calendar of State Papers Preserved in the Public Record Office, Foreign Series, Edward VI 1547–1553, ed. W.B. Turnbull (1861).

Calendar of State Papers Preserved in the Public Record Office, Foreign Series, Mary 1553–1558, ed. W.B. Turnbull (1861).

Calendar of the State Papers Relating to Scotland, ed. J. Bain et al. (13 vols, Edinburgh, 1898–1969).

Calendar of State Papers, Venetian, ed. R. Brown, C. Bentinck and H. Brown (9 vols, 1864–98).

The Cely Letters 1472–1488, ed. A. Hanham (Early English Text Society, cclxxiii, 1975).

A Chronicle of Calais in the Reigns of Henry VII and Henry VIII to the Year 1540, ed. J.G. Nichols (Camden Society, old series, xxxv, 1845).

A Chronicle of London from 1089 to 1483, ed. Edward Tyrell and N.H. Nicolas (1827).

The Chronicles of Enguerard de Monstrelet, ed. Thomas Johnes (1840).

A Collection of Political Poems and Songs Relating to English History, from the Accession of Edward III to the Reign of Henry VIII, ed. Thomas Wright (2 vols, Rolls Series, 1859–61).

Collection of State Papers ... left by William Cecill, Lord Burghley, ed. S. Haynes (1740).

A Commentary of the Services and Charges of Lord Grey de Wilton, K.G., ..., ed. Sir Philip de Malpas Grey Egerton (Camden Society, old series, xl, 1847–8).

Commynes, Philippe de, *Memoirs: The Reign of Louis XI, 1461–83*, trans. M. Jones (1972).

Debate between the Horse, Goose and Sheep: J. Lydgate, *Minor Poems*, ed. H.N. MacCracken (Early English Text Society, extra series, cxcii, 2 vols, 1910–34).

The Devon Muster Roll for 1569, ed. A.J. Howard and T.L. Stoate (Bristol, 1977).

The Diary of Henry Machyn, Citizen and Merchant-Taylor of London, from A.D. 1550 to A.D. 1563, ed. J.G. Nichols (Camden Society, 1st series, xlii, 1848).

An English Chronicle 1377–1461, ed. William Marx (Woodbridge, 2003).

An English Garner, ed. Edward Arber (1909).

English Historical Documents iv. 1327–1485, ed. A.R. Myers (Oxford, 1969).

Excerpta Historica, ed. Samuel Bentley (1833).

Extracts from the Register of the Stationers' Company from 1557–1587, ed. J. Payne Collier (1853).

Fabyan, Robert, *The New Chronicles of England and France*, ed. H. Ellis (1811).

'Financial Memoranda of the Reign of Edward V: Longleat Miscellaneous Manuscript Book II', ed. Rosemary Horrox, *Camden Miscellany* (Camden Society, 4th series, xxxiv, 1987).

Foedera, Conventiones etc, ed. T. Rymer (20 vols, 1704–35).

Fortescue, Sir John, *The Governance of England*, ed. C. Plummer (Oxford, 1885).

Gruffudd, Ellis, 'The Enterprise of Paris and Boulogne', ed. M.B. Davies, *Fouad I University Bulletin of Faculty of Arts*, xi (1949), 37–95.

——, 'Boulogne and Calais from 1545 to 1550', ed. M.B. Davies, *Fouad I University Bulletin of Faculty of Arts*, xii (1950), 1–90.

Hardyng, John, *Chronicle*, ed. H. Ellis (1812).

Hayward, Sir John, *Annals of the First Four Years of the Reign of Queen Elizabeth*, ed. John Bruce (Camden Society, old series, xl, 1840).

The Historical Collections of a Citizen of London in the Fifteenth Century, ed. James Gairdner (Camden Society, new series, xvii, 1876).

Historical Poems of the XIVth and XVth Centuries, ed. R.H. Robbins (New York, 1959).

Incerti Scriptoris Chronicon Angliae de Regnis Trium Regum Lancastrensium: Henrici IV, Henrici V, et Henrici VI, ed. J.A. Giles (1848).

The Inventory of King Henry VIII: The Transcript, ed. David Starkey (1998).

'John Benet's Chronicle', ed. G.L. and M.A. Harriss, *Camden Miscellany XXIV* (Camden Society, 4th series, ix, 1972).

Letters and Papers, Foreign and Domestic, of the Reign of Henry VIII, 1509–1547, ed. J. Brewer et al. (21 vols and addenda, 1862–1932).

Letters and Papers Illustrative of the Reigns of Richard III and Henry VII, ed. J. Gairdner (2 vols, Rolls Series, 1861–3).

Letters and Papers Illustrative of the Wars of the English in France during the Reign of Henry the Sixth, King of England, ed. J. Stevenson (Rolls Series, 2 vols in 3, 1861–4).

Letters of Queen Margaret of Anjou and Bishop Beckington and Others, ed. C. Munro (Camden Society, old series, lxxvi, 1863).

The Libelle of Englyshe Polycye, ed. Sir George Warner (Oxford, 1926).

The Lisle Letters, ed. Muriel St Clare Byrne (6 vols, Chicago and London, 1981).

Materials for a History of the Reign of Henry VII, ed. W. Campbell (2 vols, 1873).

Monstrelet, Eugerrand, *Chronique d'Euguerran de Monstrelet 1400–1444*, ed. L. Douet d'Arcq (6 vols, Paris, 1857–62).

The Ordinance Book of the Merchants of the Staple, ed. E.E. Rich (Cambridge, 1937).

The Parliament Rolls of Medieval England 1275–1504, ed. Chris Given-Wilson et al. (16 vols, Woodbridge, 2005).

Paston Letters and Papers of the Fifteenth Century, ed. N.B. Davis (Early English Text Society, special series, xx, 2004).

Proceedings and Ordinances of the Privy Council of England, 1386–1542, ed. Sir N.H. Nicholas (7 vols, 1834–7).

A Relation, or rather a True Account, of the Island of England, ed. C. Sneyd (Camden Society, old series, xxxvii, 1847).

Royal Commission on Historical Manuscripts, *Report on Manuscripts in Various Collections* (7 vols, 1901–14).

—— *Report on the Manuscripts of the late Reginald Rawdon Hastings, Esq., of the Manor House, Ashby de la Zouche* (4 vols, 1928–47).

—— *Calendar of the Shrewbury and Talbot Papers in Lambeth Palace Library and the College of Arms* (2 vols, 1966–71).

Royal and Historical Letters during the Reign of Henry IV, ed. F.C. Hingeston (2 vols, 1965 reprint).

Select Cases in the Council of Henry VII, ed. C.G. Bayne and William Huse Dunham (Seldon Society lxxv, 1956).

'A Short English Chronicle', in *Three Fifteenth-Century Chronicles*, ed. James Gairdner (Camden Society, new series, xxviii, 1880).

Six Town Chronicles of England, ed. R. Flenley (Oxford, 1911).

Statutes of the Realm, ed. A. Luders et al. (11 vols, 1810–28).

Taylor, Craig, *Debating the Hundred Years War: Pour Ce Que Plusieurs (La Loy Salicque) and* A Declaracion of the Trew and Dewe Title of Henry VIII (Camden Society, 5th series, xxix, Cambridge, 2006)

Three Books of Polydore Vergil's English History, ed. Sir Henry Ellis (Camden Society, old series, xxix, 1844).

Tudor Economic Documents, ed. R.H. Tawney and E.E. Power (3 vols, Oxford, 1924).

Tudor Royal Proclamations, ed. L. Hughes and J.F. Larkin (3 vols, New Haven, CT, 1964).

Tudor Tracts, ed. A.F. Pollard (1903).

Warkworth, John, *Chronicle of the First Thirteen Years of the Reign of King Edward IV*, ed. J.O. Halliwell (Camden Society, 1st series, vi, 1839).

Waurin, Jean de, *Recueil des croniques et anchiennes istories de la Grant Bretagne*, ed. W. and E.C.L. Hardy (5 vols, Rolls Series, 1864–91).

—— *Cronicques*, ed. L.M.E. Dupont (3 vols, Paris 1858–63).

York Civic Records, vols iv, v, ed. Angelo Raine (Yorkshire Archaeological Society Record Series, cviii, cx, 1943–6).

Secondary sources

Books and articles

Adams, Simon, 'The Dudley Clientele', in *The Tudor Nobility*, ed. G.W. Bernard (Manchester, 1992), 247–53.

Allmand, C.T., and M.H. Keen, 'The *Boke of Noblesse* of William of Worcester', in *War, Government and Power in Late Medieval France*, ed. C.T. Allmand (Liverpool, 2000), 291–302.

Anglo, S., 'An Early Tudor Programme for Plays and Other Demonstrations against the Pope', *Journal of the Warburg and Courtauld Institutes*, xx (1957), 176–9.

Anon., 'The Loss of Calais', *North British Review*, xlv (1866), 445.

Arnold, Thomas, *The Renaissance at War* (2001).

Baldo, Jonathan, 'Wars of Memory in *Henry V*', *Shakespeare Quarterly*, xlvii (1996), 132–59.

Baldwin, J.F., *The King's Council in England during the Middle Ages* (Oxford, 1913).

Ballard, Mark, 'An Expedition of English Archers to Liège in 1467 and the Anglo-Burgundian Marriage Alliance', *Nottingham Medieval Studies*, xxxiv (1990), 152–74.

Barber, Richard, *The Knight and Chivalry* (2nd edn, Woodbridge, 1994).

Bernard, George, *The King's Reformation: Henry VIII and the Remaking of the Church of England* (New Haven, CT, 2005).

Bindoff, S.T. (ed.), *The History of Parliament: The House of Commons 1509–1558* (3 vols, 1982).

Black, J.B., *The Reign of Elizabeth 1558–1603* (Oxford, 1959).

Blackmore, H.C., *The Armouries of the Tower of London*: I *The Ordnance* (1976).

Boardman, Andrew W., *The Medieval Soldier in the Wars of the Roses* (Stroud, 1998).

Boffey, Julia, 'Books and Readers in Calais: Some Notes', *The Ricardian*, xiii (2003), 67–74.

Boone, Marc, 'Jacqueline of Bavaria in September 1425: A Lonely Princess in Ghent?', *The Ricardian* xiii (2003), 75–85.

Boynton, Lindsay, *The Elizabethan Militia, 1558–1638* (1971).

Braddick, Michael J., *The Nerves of State: Taxation and the Financing of the English State, 1558–1714* (Manchester, 1996).

Braudel, Fernand, *Civilisation and Capitalism, 15th–18th Centuries*, trans. Siân Reynolds (3 vols, Berkeley, CA, 1992).

Brown, Michael, 'French Alliance or English Peace? Scotland and the Last Phase of the Hundred Years War, 1415–53', in *The Fifteenth Century VII*, ed. Linda Clark (Woodbridge, 2007), 81–100.

Bunbury, W. St P., 'A Treatise on the Art of War by Thomas Audley', *Journal of the Society for Army Historical Research*, vi (1927), 65–78, 129–33.

Burley, S.K., 'The Victualling of Calais', *Bulletin of the Institute of Historical Research*, xxxi (1958), 49–57.

Calton, Robert Bell, *Annals and Legends of Calais* (1852).

Carpenter, Christine, *The Wars of the Roses: Politics and the Constitution in England, c. 1437–1509* (Cambridge, 1997).

Cogswell, Tom, *Home Divisions* (Manchester, 1998).

Colvin, H.M. (ed.), *The History of the King's Works* (6 vols, 1963–82).

Contamine, Philippe, *War in the Middle Ages*, trans. Michael Jones (Oxford, 1984).

—— (ed.), *Histoire militaire de France*, i. *Des origines à 1715* (Paris, 1992).

Critchley, J.S., 'The Early History of the Writ of Judicial Protection', *Bulletin of the Institute of Historical Research*, lv (1972), 196–213.

Cruickshank, C.G., *Elizabeth's Army* (Oxford, 1966).

—— *The English Occupation of Tournai 1513–1519* (Oxford, 1971).

—— *Henry VIII and the Invasion of France* (Stroud, 1990).

Cunich, Peter, 'Revolution and Crisis in English State Finances, 1534–47', in *Crises, Revolutions and Self-Sustained Growth: Essays in European Fiscal History, 1130–1830*, ed. W.M. Ormrod, Margaret and Richard Bonney (Stamford, 1999), 110–37.

Currin, John M., ' "To Traffic with War"? Henry VII and the French Campaign of Henry VII', in *The English Experience in France, c. 1450–1558: War, Diplomacy and Culture Exchange*, ed. David Grummitt (Aldershot, 2002), 106–31.

Curry, Anne, 'English Armies in the Fifteenth Century' in *Arms, Armies and Fortifications in the Hundred Years War*, ed. Anne Curry and Michael Hughes (Woodbridge, 1994), 39–68.

—— 'The Loss of Lancastrian Normandy: An Administrative Nightmare?', in *The English Experience in France, c. 1450–1558: War, Diplomacy and Culture Exchange*, ed. David Grummitt (Aldershot, 2002), 25–45.

Davies, C.S.L., 'The English People and War in the Early Sixteenth Century', in *Britain and the Netherlands*, ed. A.C. Duke and C.A. Tamse, vi (The Hague, 1977), 1–18.

—— 'England and the French War, 1557–9', in *The Mid-Tudor Polity c. 1540–1560*, ed. Jennifer Loach and Robert Tittler (Basingstoke, 1980), 159–85.

—— 'Bishop John Morton, the Holy See and the Accession of Henry VII', *English Historical Review*, cii (1987), 2–30.

Davis, W.G., 'Whetehill of Calais', *The New England Historical and Genealogical Register*, cii (1948), 241–53; ciii (1949), 5–19.

Derville, Alain, 'Une Ville vers 1300: Calais', *Revue du Nord*, lxxii (1990), 737–56.

Dickinson, Joyceline Gledhill, *The Congress of Arras, 1435: A Study in Medieval Diplomacy* (Oxford, 1955).

Dillon, H.A., 'Calais and the Pale', *Archaeologia*, liii (1892), 289–388.

Dodd, Gwilym, 'The Calais Staple and the Parliament of May 1382', *English Historical Review*, cxvii (2002), 94–103.

Doig, James A., 'A New Source for the Siege of Calais in 1436', *English Historical Review*, cx (1995), 404–16.

—— 'Propaganda, Public Opinion and the Siege of Calais in 1436', in *Crown, Government and People in the Fifteenth Century*, ed. Rowena Archer (Stroud, 1995), 79–106.

Donnelly, J.A., 'A Study of the Coastal Forts built by Henry VIII', *Fort*, x (1982), 25–47.

Dunham, W.H., 'Lord Hastings' Indentured Retainers 1461–1483', *Transactions of the Connecticut Academy of Arts and Sciences*, xxxix (1955).

van Dyke, P., 'François de Guise and the Taking of Calais', *Annual Report of the American Historical Association, 1912–1913*, cxvi (1913), 99–109.

Eltis, David, *The Military Revolution in Sixteenth-Century Europe* (1998).

Elton, G.R., *England under the Tudors* (1955).

Ferguson, Arthur B., *The Indian Summer of English Chivalry* (Durham, NC, 1960).

Fissel, Mark Charles, *English Warfare 1511–1642* (2001).

Fleming, P.W., 'The Lovelace Dispute: Concepts of Property and Inheritance in Fifteenth-Century Kent', *Southern History*, xiii (1990), 1–18.

Fuller, Thomas, *The Church History of Britain: From the Birth of Jesus untill the Year 1648* (6 vols, 1655).

Gillingham, John, *The Wars of the Roses: Peace and Conflict in Fifteenth-Century England* (1981)

Given-Wilson, Chris, *The Royal Household and the King's Affinity: Service, Politics and Finance in England 1360–1413* (New Haven, CT, 1986).

Goodman, Anthony, *The Wars of the Roses: Military Activity and English Society 1452–1497* (1981).

—— *The Wars of the Roses: The Soldiers' Experience* (Stroud, 2005).

Goring, Jeremy, 'The General Proscription of 1522', *English Historical Review* lxxxvi (1971), 681–705.

—— 'Social Change and Military Decline in Mid-Tudor England', *History*, lx (1975), 185–97.

Grabes, Herbert, 'England or the Queen? Public Conflict of Opinion and National Identity under Mary Tudor', in *Writing the Early Modern English Nation: The Transformation of National Identity in Sixteenth-Century England*, ed. Herbert Grabes (Amsterdam, 2001), 47–88.

Gravett, Christopher, *Medieval Siege Warfare* (1990).

Gray, H.L., 'English Foreign Trade from 1446–1482', in *Studies in English Trade in the Fifteenth Century*, ed. E.E. Power and M.M. Postan (1933), 20–38.

Griffiths, Ralph A., *The Reign of Henry VI* (1981, 2nd edn, Stroud 1998).

Griffiths, Ralph A., and Roger S. Thomas, *The Making of the Tudor Dynasty* (Stroud, 1985).

Grummitt, David, 'The Financial Administration of Calais during the Reign of Henry IV, 1399–1413', *English Historical Review*, cxiii (1998), 277–99.

—— 'The Defence of Calais and the Development of Gunpowder Weaponry in England in the Late Fifteenth Century', *War in History*, vii (2000), 253–72.

—— ' "For the Surety of the Towne and Marches": Early Tudor Policy towards Calais 1485–1509', *Nottingham Medieval Studies*, xliv (2000), 184–203.

—— 'William, Lord Hastings and the Defence of Calais, 1471–1483', in *Social*

Attitudes and Political Structures in the Fifteenth Century, ed. T.J. Thornton (Stroud, 2000), 150–67.

—— 'Calais and Henry VIII: "un petit morceau d'Angleterre outremere" ', in *Le Detroit: Zone de recontres ou zone de conflits*, ed. Stéphane Curveiller et al., *Bulletin Historique et Artistique du Calaisis*, clxxiii (2001), 127–38.

—— 'William, Lord Hastings, the Calais Garrison and the Politics of Yorkist England', *The Ricardian*, xii (2001), 262–74.

—— ' "One of the Mooste Pryncipall Treasours Belongyng to his Realme of Englande": Calais and the Crown, *c.* 1450–1558', in *The English Experience in France, c. 1450–1558: War, Diplomacy and Cultural Exchange*, ed. David Grummitt (Aldershot, 2002), 46–62.

—— 'The Court, War and Noble Power in England, *c.* 1475–1558', in *The Court as a Stage*, ed. Steven Gunn and Antheun Janse (Woodbridge, 2006), 145–55.

—— 'Deconstructing Cade's Rebellion: Discourse and Politics in the Mid-Fifteenth Century', in *The Fifteenth Century* VI: *Identity and Insurgency in the Late Middle Ages*, ed. Linda Clark (Woodbridge, 2006), 107–22.

—— 'War and Society in the North of England, *c.* 1477–1559: The Cases of York, Hull and Beverley', *Northern History* (2008), 1–16.

Gunn, S.J., 'The Duke of Suffolk's March on Paris in 1523', *English Historical Review*, ci (1986), 596–634.

—— 'The French Wars of Henry VIII', in *The Origins of War in Early Modern Europe*, ed. J. Black (Edinburgh, 1987), 28–51.

—— 'Chivalry and Politics at the Early Tudor Court', in *Chivalry in the Renaissance*, ed. S. Anglo (Woodbridge, 1990), 107–28.

—— 'Wolsey's Foreign Policy and the Domestic Crisis of 1527–8', in *Cardinal Wolsey: State, Church and Art*, ed. S.J. Gunn and P. Lindley (Cambridge, 1991), 149–77.

—— *Early Tudor Government, 1485–1558* (Basingstoke, 1995).

—— 'Sir Thomas Lovell (*c.* 1449–1524): A New Man in a New Monarchy?', in *The End of the Middle Ages?*, ed. John L. Watts (Stroud, 1998), 117–54.

—— 'Sir Edward Poynings: An Anglo-Burgundian Hero', *Publications du Centre Européen des Etudes Bourguignonnes*, xli (2001), 157–69.

—— 'War, Dynasty and Public Opinion in Early Tudor England', in *Authority and Consent in Tudor England: Essays Presented to C.S.L. Davies*, ed. G.W. Bernard and S.J. Gunn (Aldershot, 2002), 131–49.

Gunn, S.J., David Grummitt and Hans Cools, *War, State and Society in England and the Netherlands, 1477–1559* (Oxford, 2007).

Haigh, Philip A., *The Military Campaigns of the Wars of the Roses* (Stroud, 1995).

Hale, J.R., *Renaissance War Studies* (1983).

Hall, Bert S., *Weapons and Warfare in Renaissance Europe: Gunpowder, Technology and Tactics* (Baltimore, MD, 2002).

Hammer, Paul, *Elizabeth's Wars* (2002).

Hanham, Alison, *The Celys and Their World: An English Merchant Family of the Fifteenth Century* (Cambridge, 1985).

Harriss, G.L., 'The Struggle for Calais: An Aspect of the Rivalry between Lancaster and York', *English Historical Review*, lxxv (1960), 30–53.

—— *Henry V: The Practice of Kingship* (Oxford, 1985).

—— 'Marmaduke Lumley and the Exchequer Crisis of 1446–9', in *Aspects of Late Medieval Government and Society: Essays Presented to J.R. Lander*, ed. J.G. Rowe (Toronto, 1986), 143–78.

—— *Cardinal Beaufort: A Study of Lancastrian Ascendancy and Decline* (Oxford, 1988).

Haward, A., 'The Relations between the Merchants of the Staple and the Lancastrian Government from 1449 to 1461', in *Studies in English Trade*, ed. E.E. Power and M.M. Postan (1933), 292–320.

Herman, Peter C., ' "O, 'tis a gallant king": Shakespeare's *Henry V* and the Crisis of the 1590s', in *Tudor Political Culture*, ed. Dale Hoak (Cambridge, 1995), 204–25.

Hicks, Michael, 'The Changing Role of the Wydevilles in Yorkist Politics to 1483', in *Patronage, Pedigree and Power in Late Medieval England*, ed. C.D. Ross (Gloucester, 1979), 60–86.

—— *Warwick the Kingmaker* (Oxford, 1998).

—— 'Bastard Feudalism, Overmighty Subjects and Idols of the Multitude during the Wars of the Roses', *History*, lxxxv (2000), 386–403.

Holmes, G.A., 'The "Libel of English Policy" ', *English Historical Review*, lxxvi (1961), 193–216.

Horrox, Rosemary, *Richard III: A Study in Service* (Cambridge, 1989).

—— 'Yorkist and Early Tudor England', in *The New Cambridge Medieval History*, VII c. *1415–1500*, ed. Christopher Allmand (Cambridge, 1998), 477–95.

Hoyle, Richard, 'War and Public Finance', in *The Reign of Henry VIII*, ed. Diarmaid MacCulloch (Basingstoke, 1995), 75–84.

Jack, Sybil, 'Henry VIII's Attitude towards Royal Finance: Penny Wise and Pound Foolish?', in *François Ier. Deux princes de la renaissance (1515–1547)*, ed. Charles Giry-Deloison (Arras, 1997), 145–64.

Johnson, P.A., *Duke Richard of York 1411–1460* (Oxford, 1988).

Jones, Michael K., 'John Beaufort, Duke of Somerset, and the French Expedition of 1443', in *Patronage, the Crown and the Provinces*, ed. R.A. Griffiths (Stroud, 1981), 79–102.

—— '1477 – the Expedition that Never Was: Chivalric Expectation in Late-Yorkist England', *The Ricardian*, xii (2001), 275–92.

—— 'The Battle of Verneuil (17 August 1424): Towards a History of Courage', *War in History*, ix (2002), 375–411.

—— *Bosworth 1485: Psychology of a Battle* (Stroud, 2002).

—— *Agincourt 1415* (Barnsley, 2005).

Jones, Michael K., and Malcolm G. Underwood, *The King's Mother: Lady Margaret Beaufort, Countess of Richmond and Derby* (Cambridge, 1992).

Jones, Thomas, 'A Welsh Chronicler in Tudor England', *Welsh Historical Review*, i (1960), 1–17.

Jordan, Constance, 'Women's Rule in Sixteenth-Century British Political Thought', *Renaissance Quarterly*, xl (1987), 421–51.

Keen, M.H., *Chivalry* (1984).

—— 'The End of the Hundred Years War: Lancastrian France and Lancastrian England', in *England and her Neighbours, 1066–1453: Essays in Honour of Pierre Chaplais*, ed. M. Jones and M.G.A. Vale (1989), 297–311.

Kenyon, John R., 'Coastal Artillery Fortifications in England in the Late Fourteenth and Early Fifteenth Centuries', in *Arms, Armies and Fortifications in the Hundred Years War*, ed. Anne Curry and Michael Hughes (Woodbridge, 1994), 145–51.

Kesselring, K.J., *Mercy and Authority in the Tudor State* (Cambridge, 2003).

Kingsford, C.L., *English Historical Literature in the Fifteenth Century* (Oxford, 1913).

Kirby, J.L. 'The Financing of Calais under Henry V', *Bulletin of the Institute of Historical Research*, xxiii (1950), 165–77.

—— 'The Issues of the Lancastrian Exchequer and Lord Cromwell's Estimates of 1433', *Bulletin of the Institute of Historical Research*, xxiv (1951), 121–51.

Kleineke, Hannes, 'The Commission *de Mutuo Faciendo* in the Reign of Henry VI', *English Historical Review,* ci (2001), 1–30.

Klinefelter, Ralph, ' "The Siege of Calais": A New Text', *Proceedings of the Modern Language Association of America*, lxvii (1952), 888–95.

—— 'A Newly-Discovered Fifteenth-Century English Manuscript', *Modern Language Quarterly*, xiv (1953), 3–6.

Lander, J.R. 'Council, Administration and Councillors', *Bulletin of the Institute of Historical Research*, xxxii (1959), 139–42.

—— 'The Hundred Years War and Edward IV's 1475 Campaign in France', in *Tudor Men and Institutions: Studies in English Law and Government*, ed. A.J. Slavin (Baton Rouge, LA, 1972), 70–100.

Lefebrve, G., *Histoire générale et particulière de Calais et du Calaisis* (2 vols, Paris, 1766).

Lennel, F., *Histoire de Calais* (3 vols, Calais, 1908–13).

Lloyd, T.H., *The English Wool Trade in the Middle Ages* (Cambridge, 1977).

Loach, Jennifer, *Edward VI* (New Haven, CT, 2000).

Loades, David, *The Reign of Mary Tudor: Politics, Government and Religion in England, 1553–1558* (Harlow, 1991).

—— *The Tudor Navy: Administrative, Political and Military History* (Aldershot, 1992).

Luckett, Dominic, 'Crown Office and Licensed Retinues in the Reign of Henry VII', in *Rulers and Ruled in Late Medieval England*, ed. Rowena E. Archer and Simon Walker (London 1995), 223–38.

MacCraken, H.N., 'A New Poem by Lydgate', *Anglia*, xxxiii (1910), 283–6.

MacFarlane, K.B., *The Nobility of Later Medieval England* (Oxford, 1973).

Mackie, J.D., *The Earlier Tudors, 1485–1558* (Oxford, 1952).

MacMahon, Luke, 'Chivalry, Professionalism and the Early Tudor Army in Renaissance Europe: A Reassement', in *The Chivalric Ethos and the Development of Military Professionalism*, ed. D.J.B. Trim (Leiden, 2003), 184–210.

Mayhew, G., *Tudor Rye* (Falmer, 1987).

Meek, Edward L., 'The Career of Sir Thomas Everingham, "Knight of the North" in the Service of Maximilian, Duke of Austria 1477–1481', *Historical Research*, lxxiv (2001), 238–48.

—— 'The Practice of English Diplomacy in France 1461–1471', in *The English Experience in France, c. 1450 1558: War, Diplomacy and Cultural Exchange*, ed. David Grummitt (Aldershot, 2002), 63–84.

Millar, Gilbert John, *Tudor Mercenaries and Auxiliaries, 1485–1547* (Charlottesville, VA, 1980).

Millard, Frank D., 'An Analysis of the *Epitaphium Eiusdem Ducis Gloucestrie*', in *The Fifteenth Century III: Authority and Subversion*, ed. Linda Clark (Woodbridge, 2003), 117–36.

Munro, John H.A., *Wool, Cloth and Gold: The Struggle for Bullion in Anglo-Burgundian Trade* (Toronto, 1972).

Myers, A.R., 'The Outbreak of War between England and Burgundy in February 1471', *Bulletin of the Institute of Historical Research*, xxxiii (1960), 114–15.

Newhall, R.A., *Muster and Review* (Cambridge, MA, 1940).

Nightingale, P., 'England and the European Depression of the Mid-Fifteenth Century', *Journal of European Economic History*, xxvi (1997), 631–56.

Nolan, J.S., 'The Militarisation of the Elizabethan State', *Journal of Military History*, lviii (1994), 381–420.

Oman, C.W.C., *The Art of War in the Sixteenth Century* (1937).

Ormrod, Mark, 'The West European Monarchies in the Later Middle Ages', in *Economic Systems and State Finance*, ed. Richard Bonney (Oxford, 1995), 123–62.

—— 'The English State and the Plantagenet Empire, 1259–1360: A Fiscal Perspective', in *The Medieval State: Essays Presented to James Campbell*, ed. J.R. Maddicott and D.M. Palliser (2000), 197–214.

Oxford Dictionary of National Biography: From the Earliest Times to the Year 2000, ed. H.C.G. Matthew and B.H. Harrison (61 vols, Oxford, 2004).

Parker, Geoffrey, 'The Military Revolution, 1560–1660 – a Myth', *Journal of Modern History*, xlviii (1986), 241–78.

—— *The Military Revolution: Military Innovation and the Rise of the West, 1500–1800* (Cambridge, 1988).

Pepper, Simon, 'Artisans, Architects and Aristocrats: Professionalism and Renaissance Military Engineering', in *The Chivalric Ethos and the Development of Military Professionalism*, ed. D.J.B. Trim (Leiden, 2003), 000–00.

Perroy, Edouard, 'L'Administration de Calais en 1371–2', *Revue du Nord*, xxxiii (1951), 218–27.

Petrina, Alessandro, *Cultural Politics in Fifteenth-Century England: The Case of Humphrey, Duke of Gloucester* (Leiden, 2004).

Phillips, Gervase, *The Anglo-Scots Wars 1513–1550* (Woodbridge, 1999).

—— 'Longbow and Hackbutt: Weapons Technology and Technology Transfer in Early Modern England', *Technology and Culture*, xl (1999), 576–93.

Pollard, A.J., *John Talbot and the War in France, 1427–1453* (1983).

Potter, D.L., 'The Duc de Guise and the Fall of Calais, 1557–8', *English Historical Review*, xcviii (1983), 481–512.

—— 'The International Mercenary Market in the Sixteenth Century: Anglo-French Competition in Germany, 1543–50', *English Historical Review*, cxi (1996), 24–58.

—— 'Cross Cultural Friendship in the Sixteenth Century: The Lisles and their French Friends', in *The English in France, c. 1450 1558: War, Diplomacy and Cultural Exchange,* ed. David Grummitt (Aldershot, 2002), 200–22.

—— 'Chivalry and Professionalism in the French Armies of the Renaissance', in *The Chivalric Ethos and the Development of Military Professionalism*, ed. D.J.B. Trim (Leiden, 2003), 150–82.

Power, Eileen, *The Wool Trade in English Medieval History: Being the Ford Lectures* (Oxford, 1941).

—— 'The Wool Trade in the Fifteenth Century', in *Studies in English Trade in the Fifteenth Century*, ed. E.E. Power and M.M. Postan (1933), 000–00.

Powicke, M., 'Lancastrian Captains', in *Essays in Medieval History Presented to Bertie Wilkinson*, ed. T.A. Sandquist and M. Powicke (Toronto, 1969), 371–82.

Prescott, W.H., and A.J. McJoynt (eds.), *The Art of War in Spain: The Conquest of Granada, 1481–1492* (1995).

Prestwich, Michael, *Armies and Warfare in the Middle Ages: The English Experience* (New Haven, CT, 1996).

Ramsey, P., 'Overseas Trade in the Reign of Henry VII: The Evidence of the Customs Accounts', *Economic History Review*, 2nd series, vi (1953–4), 173–82.

Raymond, James, *Henry VIII's Military Revolution: The Armies of Sixteenth-Century Britain and Europe* (2007).

Redworth, Glyn, ' "Matters Impertinant to Women": Male and Female Monarchy under Philip and Mary', *English Historical Research*, cxii (1997), 597–613.

Reynolds, David, 'At Calais Gate', in *Premodern Places* (Oxford, 2004), 22–90.

Richmond, C.F., 'The Keeping of the Seas during the Hundred Years War: 1422–1440', *History*, xlix (1964), 283–98.

—— 'English Naval Power in the Fifteenth Century', *History*, lii (1967), 1–15.

—— 'Fauconberg's Rising of 1471', *English Historical Review*, xxxv (1970), 673–92.

Roberts, Michael, 'The Military Revolution, 1560–1660', in *Essays in Swedish History*, ed. Michael Roberts (Minneapolis, 1967), 195–225.

Rogers, Clifford J., 'The Military Revolutions of the Hundred Years War', in *The Military Revolution Debate*, ed. Clifford J. Rogers (Boulder, CO, 1995), 55–93.

Roskell, J.S., Linda Clark and Carole Rawcliffe (eds), *The House of Commons 1386–1421* (4 vols, Stroud, 1992).

Ross, Charles, *Richard III* (1981).

—— *Edward IV* (2nd edn, New Haven, CT, 1998).

Rowney, Ian, 'The Hastings Affinity in Staffordshire and the Honour of Tutbury', *Bulletin of the Institute of Historical Research*, lvii (1984), 35–45.

—— 'Resources and Retaining in Yorkist England: William, Lord Hastings and the Honour of Tutbury', in *Property and Politics: Essays in Later Medieval English History*, ed. A.J. Pollard (Gloucester, 1984), 139–55.

Sandeman, G.A.C., *Calais under English Rule* (Oxford, 1908).

Saygin, Susanne, *Humphrey, Duke of Gloucester (1390–1447) and the Italian Humanists* (Leiden, 2002).

Scarisbrick, J.J., *Henry VIII* (1969)

Scattergood, V.J., *Politics and Poetry in the Fifteenth Century* (1971).

Scofield, C.L., 'The Capture of Lord Rivers and Sir Anthony Woodville on 19 January 1460', *English Historical Research*, xxxviii (1908), 253–5.

—— *The Life and Reign of Edward the Fourth* (2 vols, 1923).

Shelby, L.R., *John Rogers, Tudor Military Engineer* (1967).

Slavin, A.J., 'Cromwell, Cranmer and Lord Lisle: A Study in the Politics of Reform', *Albion*, ix (1977), 316–36.

Smith, Bill, 'The Financial Priorities of Lancastrian Government, 1450–55', in *Social Attitudes and Political Structures in the Fifteenth Century*, ed. T.J. Thornton (Stroud, 2001), 168–83.

Smith, Robert Douglas, and Kelly de Vries, *The Artillery of the Dukes of Burgundy 1363–1477* (Woodbridge, 2006).

Somerville, R., *History of the Duchy of Lancaster*, i. *1265–1603* (1953).

Sommé, Monique, 'L'Armée bourguignonne au siége de Calais de 1436', in *Guerre et société en France, en Angleterre et en Bourgogne XIVe–Xve siècle*, ed. P. Contamine et al. (Lille, 1991), 197–219.

Spufford, Peter, and Peter Woodhead, 'Calais and its Mint', in *Coinage in the Low Countries*, ed. N.J. Mayhew (Oxford, 1979), 171–202.

Starkey, David, 'Intimacy and Innovation: The Rise of the Privy Chamber 1485–1547', in D. Starkey et al., *The English Court from the Wars of the Roses to the English Civil War* (1990), 71–118.

—— 'Representation through Intimacy: A Study in the Symbolism of Monarchy and Court Office in Early Modern England', in *The Tudor Monarchy*, ed. John Guy (1997), 42–77.

Storey, R.L., *The End of the House of Lancaster* (2nd edn Stroud, 1999).

Sutton, Anne F., *The Mercery of London: Trade, Goods and People, 1130–1578* (Aldershot, 2005).

Sutton, Anne F. and L. Visser-Fuchs, *Richard III's Books: Ideals and Reality in the Life and Library of a Medieval Prince* (Stroud, 1997).

Thielmans, M., *Bourgogne et Angleterre: Relations politiques et économiques entre les Pays-Bas Bourguignons et l'Angleterre, 1435–1467* (Brussels, 1966).

Thompson, I.A.A., *War and Government in Habsburg Spain, 1560–1620* (1976).

Tittler, Robert, *The Reformation and the Towns in England: Politics and Political Culture, c. 1540–1640* (Oxford, 1998).

Tout, F., 'Firearms in England in the Fourteenth Century', *English Historical Review*, xxvi (1911), 606–702.

Trim, David J.B. (ed.), *The Chivalric Ethos and the Development of Military Professionalism* (Leiden, 2006).

Vale, Malcolm, *War and Chivalry: Warfare and Aristocratic Culture in England, France and Burgundy at the End of the Middle Ages* (1981).

Vaughan, Richard, *Philip the Bold: The Formation of the Burgundian State* (1962).

—— *Charles the Bold: The Last Valois Duke of Burgundy* (1973).

de Vertot, R.A., *Ambassades de Messieurs de Noailles* (5 vols, Leiden, 1763).

Vickers, Kenneth H., *Humphrey, Duke of Gloucester* (1907).

de Vries, Kelly, 'Gunpowder Weaponry and the Rise of the Early Modern State', *War in History*, v (1998), 127–45.

—— 'The Use of Gunpowder Weaponry in the Wars of the Roses', in *Traditions and Transformations in Late Medieval England*, ed. Douglas Biggs, Sharon D. Michalove and Albert Compton Reeves (Leiden, 2002), 21–38.

Wakelin, D.L., 'The Occasion, Author and Readers of *Knyghthode and Bataile*', *Medium Aevum*, lxxiii (2004), 260–72.

Walker, Greg, 'The "Expulsion of the Minions" of 1519 Reconsidered', *Historical Journal*, xxxii (1989), 1–16.

Walker, Simon, *The Lancastrian Affinity 1361–1399* (Oxford, 1990).

Walker, Stanley, 'The Calais Mint 1347–1470', *British Numismatic Journal*, 2nd series, vi (1922), 77–90.

Ward, Philip, 'The Politics of Religion: Thomas Cromwell and the Reformation in Calais 1534–1540', *Journal of Ecclesiastical History*, xvii (1992), 152–71.

Warner, M., 'Chivalry in Action: Thomas Montague and the War in France, 1417–1428', *Nottingham Medieval Studies*, xliii (1998), 146–73.

Watts, John, *Henry VI and the Politics of Kingship* (Cambridge, 1996).

Wedgwood, J.C., and A.D. Holt, *Register and Biographies of the Members of the House of Commons, 1439–1509* (2 vols, London, 1936–8).

Weiss, R., 'Humphrey Duke of Gloucester and Tito Livio Frulovisi', in *Fritz Saxl 1890–1948: A Volume of Memorial Essays*, ed. D.J. Gordon (Oxford, 1957), 218–27.

Wheeler, James Scott, *The Making of a World Power: War and the Military Revolution in Seventeenth Century England* (Stroud, 1999).

Willen, Diane, *John Russell, First Earl of Bedford: One of the King's Men* (1981).

Wolffe, B.P., *The Royal Demesne in English History: The Crown Estate in the Governance of the Realm from the Conquest to 1509* (1971).

—— *Henry VI* (1981).

Wood, J.B., *The King's Army: Warfare, Soldiers and Society during the French Wars of Religion* (Cambridge, 1996).

Unpublished theses

Davies, C.S.L., 'Supply Services of the English Armed Forces, 1509–1550' (DPhil thesis, University of Oxford, 1963).

Goring, Jeremy, 'The Military Obligations of the English People, 1509–1558' (PhD thesis, University of London, 1955).

Grummitt, David, 'Calais 1485–1547: A Study in Early Tudor Politics and Government' (PhD thesis, University of London, 1997).

Jones, Michael K., 'The Beaufort Family and the War in France, 1421–1450' (PhD thesis, University of Bristol PhD).

Morgan, P.T.J., 'The Government of Calais, 1485–1558' (DPhil thesis, University of Oxford, 1966).

Nall, C.R., 'The Production and Reception of Military Texts in the Aftermath of the Hundred Years War' (DPhil thesis, University of York, 2004).

Rainey Jr., John Riley, 'The Defence of Calais, 1436–1477' (PhD thesis, Rutgers University, 1987).

Waas, D.A., 'Arthur Plantagenet, Viscount Lisle and the Administration of Calais 1533–1540' (PhD thesis, University of Illinois, 1958).

Woodger, L.S., 'Henry Bourgchier, Earl of Essex and his Family (1408–83)' (DPhil thesis, University of Oxford, 1974).

Wright, T.E.F., 'Royal Finance in the Latter Half of the Reign of Henry IV of England' (DPhil thesis, University of Oxford, 1984).

Index

Warfare in History

The Battle of Hastings: Sources and Interpretations, *edited and introduced by Stephen Morillo*

Infantry Warfare in the Early Fourteenth Century: Discipline, Tactics, and Technology, *Kelly DeVries*

The Art of Warfare in Western Europe during the Middle Ages, from the Eighth Century to 1340 (second edition), *J.F. Verbruggen*

Knights and Peasants: The Hundred Years War in the French Countryside, *Nicholas Wright*

Society at War: The Experience of England and France during the Hundred Years War, *edited by Christopher Allmand*

The Circle of War in the Middle Ages: Essays on Medieval Military and Naval History, *edited by Donald J. Kagay and L.J. Andrew Villalon*

The Anglo-Scots Wars, 1513–1550: A Military History, *Gervase Phillips*

The Norwegian Invasion of England in 1066, *Kelly DeVries*

The Wars of Edward III: Sources and Interpretations, *edited by Clifford J. Rogers*

The Battle of Agincourt: Sources and Interpretations, *Anne Curry*

War Cruel and Sharp: English Strategy under Edward III, 1327–1360, *Clifford J. Rogers*

The Normans and their Adversaries at War: Essays in Memory of C. Warren Hollister, *edited by Richard P. Abels and Bernard S. Bachrach*

The Battle of the Golden Spurs (Courtrai, 11 July 1302): A Contribution to the History of Flanders' War of Liberation, 1297–1305, *J.F. Verbruggen*

War at Sea in the Middle Ages and the Renaissance, *edited by John B. Hattendorf and Richard W. Unger*

Swein Forkbeard's Invasions and the Danish Conquest of England, 991–1017, *Ian Howard*

Religion and the conduct of war, c.300–1215, *David S. Bachrach*

Warfare in Medieval Brabant, 1356–1406, *Sergio Boffa*

Renaissance Military Memoirs: War, History and Identity, 1450–1600, *Yuval Harari*

The Place of War in English History, 1066–1214, *J.O. Prestwich, edited by Michael Prestwich*

War and the Soldier in the Fourteenth Century, *Adrian R. Bell*

German War Planning, 1891–1914: Sources and Interpretations, *Terence Zuber*

The Battle of Crécy, 1346, *Andrew Ayton and Sir Philip Preston*

The Battle of Yorktown, 1781: A Reassessment, *John D. Grainger*

Special Operations in the Age of Chivalry, 1100–1550, *Yuval Noah Harari*

Women, Crusading and the Holy Land in Historical Narrative, *Natasha R. Hodgson*

The English Aristocracy at War: From the Welsh Wars of Edward I to the Battle of Bannockburn, *David Simpkin*